SUSTAINASPEAK

Architecture 2030; BUG; Biophilic Design; BIPV; Circular Economy; LEED; Passive Design; Solar Chimney; Systems Thinking; WELL; Xeriscaping.
  What does it all mean?
  The complex and evolving language used in the sustainable design community can be very challenging, particularly to those new to environmentally friendly and resource-efficient design strategies that are needed today.

- Definitions of over two hundred terms with further sources.
- Clearly cross-referenced with *Sustainaspeak*, *Theoryspeak*, and *Archispeak* terms.
- Illustrated throughout with sustainable award-winning buildings by e.g. Behnisch, Brooks + Scarpa, EHDD, KieranTimberlake, HOK, Lake|Flato, Leddy Mahtum Stacy, SmithGroup, Perkins+Will, ZGF, VMDO, and McDonough + Partners.

Sustainaspeak: A Guide to Sustainable Design Terms provides a current guide to the sustainable design strategies, terms, and practices needed for the next generation of designers, architects, students, and community leaders to design a carbon-neutral world for future generations.

Elizabeth Lewis, AIA, LEED AP, Associate Professor at Florida A&M University School of Architecture, USA, has over twenty-five years of design teaching experience with a research focus on high-performing and net-zero buildings. A graduate of Washington University in St. Louis, she is active in the profession and AIA leadership, a founder of USGBC Florida Capital Region Chapter, and a contributor to *Decoding Theoryspeak*.

SUSTAINASPEAK
A Guide to Sustainable Design Terms

ELIZABETH LEWIS

With contributions by:

Olivier Chamel
Mahsan Mohsenin
Enn Ots
Edward T. White

Routledge
Taylor & Francis Group

NEW YORK AND LONDON

First published 2018
by Routledge
711 Third Avenue, New York, NY 10017

and by Routledge
2 Park Square, Milton Park, Abingdon, Oxon, OX14 4RN

Routledge is an imprint of the Taylor & Francis Group, an informa business

© 2018 Taylor & Francis

Library of Congress Cataloging-in-Publication Data
Names: Lewis, Beth, 1952– author.
Title: Sustainaspeak : a guide to sustainable design terms / Beth Lewis ;
  with contributions by: Olivier Chamel, Mahsan Mohsenin, Enn Ots, Edward T. White.
Description: New York : Routledge, 2018. | Includes bibliographical references and index.
Identifiers: LCCN 2017034792 | ISBN 9781138283329 (hb : alk. paper) | ISBN 9781138283336
  (pb : alk. paper) | ISBN 9781315270326 (ebook)
Subjects: LCSH: Sustainable design—Terminology. | Sustainable buildings—Terminology.
Classification: LCC NK1520 .L45 2018 | DDC 720/.47014—dc23
LC record available at https://lccn.loc.gov/2017034792

ISBN: 978-1-138-28332-9 (hbk)
ISBN: 978-1-138-28333-6 (pbk)
ISBN: 978-1-315-27032-6 (ebk)

Typeset in Din
by Apex CoVantage, LLC

This book is dedicated to my parents, George and Carol Lewis, who instilled in me the importance of hard work, life-long learning, love and joy, and my loving children who inspire me every day, Jason, Ashley, KC and John.

And to all those making this a better world for our grand-children and their grandchildren . . .

To live in the hearts we leave behind is to live forever.
Carl Sagan (1997)

Contents

Illustrations

Contributors

Olivier Chamel is an Assistant Professor at the School of Architecture and Engineering Technology at Florida A&M University with a focus in design/build projects, furniture design, and sustainable architecture. Olivier is also a LEED Accredited Professional and a registered architect with twenty years of experience in the U.S., Europe and Asia.

Mahsan Mohsenin joined Florida A&M University as Assistant Professor in 2015, teaching environmental systems, design studios, and fabrication. Mahsan completed her Ph.D. at North Carolina State University, and contributed as Research Assistant at the Building Systems Integration Lab. Her research includes daylight modeling and simulation, environmental technology, and healthy built environments.

Enn Ots is a practicing architect and professor at the Florida A&M University School of Architecture. In addition to design studio, he teaches facilities management and graduate level architectural systems courses. He is the author of *Decoding Theoryspeak* and a contributor to *Archispeak*.

Edward T. White is an architect and professor of architecture at Florida A&M University. His prior teaching experience includes the University of Arizona, Oxford Polytechnic University in England, and the Drury University Program in Volos, Greece. He teaches in Florence, Italy for Florida State University during the summers. Tim has authored twenty-six books that are used at numerous architecture schools in the U.S. and abroad.

Acknowledgments

I want to acknowledge how fortunate I have been with the support and encouragement of my family and friends in completing this book, and this includes many of the people I work with, who I have been fortunate to call friends first. This includes the generous contributions of Olivier, Tim, Mahsan, Ashley, and especially Enn Ots, who inspired me with his *Theoryspeak*, the second book in this "*Speak*" series. This book would not have been possible without the sabbatical award from Florida A&M University, and the illustrations assistance and reassurance of my graduate assistant Robert Peck.

I also want to thank all the many "green" pioneers of sustainable thinking and making who inspired me with their designs, words, and knowledge. I am grateful for the words of E.O. Wilson, Aldo Leopold, Rachel Carson, Buckminster Fuller, Carl Sagan, Ray Anderson, and Ban Ki-moon, among so many others. I want to thank the many architects that generously provided the amazing images included in this book, bringing the concepts and strategies to life.

Contributors

Olivier Chamel, Mahsan Mohsenin, Enn Ots, Edward T. White

Illustrations

Architerra Inc., Architects
Behnisch Architekten
BNIM Architects
Brooks + Scarpa Architects
Centerbrook Architects and Planners
Croxton Collaborative Architects
EHDD Architects
Elliot Marshall Innes, P.A., Architects
HOK Architects
Holst Architecture
KieranTimberlake, Architects
Lake|Flato Architects
Leddy Maytum Stacy Architects
Perkins+Will Architects
SmithGroupJJR Architects
SMP Architects
The Kubala Washatko Architects, Inc.
VMDO Architects
William McDonough+Partners, Architects
ZGF Architects LLP
Thank you all—Beth

Preface

Follow the sun. Observe the wind. Watch the flow of water. Use simple materials. Touch the earth lightly.

—Glenn Murcutt

Whatever you can do or dream you can do, begin it.
Boldness has genius, power, and magic in it.

—Goethe

Sustainaspeak: A Guide to Sustainable Design Terms looks to contribute and expand upon the green building terms introduced in *Theoryspeak* and *Archispeak*, the first two books in the "Speak" series. Together the three books provide an introduction to over 750 architectural design and green building terms.

Understanding the terminology and interrelationships of green building strategies can seem daunting. I challenge my students to take a philosophical approach and to critically respond to the environment through sustainable design. This book explains the "need to know" terms of passive and active design strategies, performance tools, and the conceptual frameworks required by the many related design disciplines. These strategies and tools can be used to improve the performance, health, and ecosystem impacts of both our built and natural environments. Interrelated terminology and further sources are provided after each term, along with relevant illustrations and sustainable diagrams of top award-winning buildings from many of the world's best architecture firms.

The intention of this book is to explain, in a straightforward manner, the terminology, strategies and compelling reasons needed to incorporate a sustainable approach to design and in our daily lives. This book is offered to students or anyone with a newfound interest in sustainability with a spirit of hope for a brighter future.

The earth, the air, the land and the water are not an inheritance from our fore fathers but on loan from our children. So we have to hand over to them at least as it was handed over to us.—Mahatma Gandhi

Introduction

The place to improve the world is first in one's own heart and head and hands and then work outward from there.
—Robert M. Pirsig, *Zen and the Art of Motorcycle Maintenance: An Inquiry Into Values*

In many ways, the environmental crisis is a design crisis. It is a consequence of how things are made, buildings are constructed, and landscapes are used. Design manifests culture, and culture rests firmly on the foundation of what we believe to be true about the world.
—Sim Van Der Ryn, *Ecological Design*

It has long been recognized that the world we inhabit is in a state of rapid change. The last century saw tremendous changes in technology, industrialization, population, urbanization, and materialization, driven primarily by the availability and combustion of fossil fuels. We are now a far cry from Carl Sagan's words of a "lovely blue planet, . . . a heaven for humans" (Sagan 1980) with its unlimited resources, close sense of community, and connections with nature. Today we have polluted the Earth's atmosphere, separated ourselves from nature, filled it with waste, and have become a global economy with very limited resources. As the world's population continues to expand, our consumption of energy, water, land, and other natural resources has increased faster than the environment can replenish them. The result has been environmental degradation and loss of biodiversity.

The good news is that the world is waking up, and understanding that the forecast for our future quality life on Earth will be grim if we continue on our current path. We recognize that the emissions of carbon dioxide and other greenhouse gases have increased global temperatures and climate change extremes. In December 2015, at the COP21 Paris Climate Agreement, with global unity and hope, 195 countries supported keeping global warming under 2°C above pre-industrial levels and even established a stretch target of 1.5°C.

Unfortunately, we are still on an upward trend with atmospheric concentrations continuing to rise. In Tony Blair's 2004 climate speech before the G8 Summit, he referred to climate change as a "challenge so far-reaching in its impact, and irreversible in its destructive power, that it alters radically human existence" (Blair 2004). We have quickly realized that being "less bad" isn't good enough and must look beyond just incremental change, to adopt an inspiring carbon-neutral vision for the future prosperity of our planet.

We can do, and we've got to do better than this. —Dr. Seuss, the message he wanted to leave the world before he died in 1991.

It will be a tremendous challenge to build a "sustainable world" with net-zero emissions, particularly since it is predicted that by even mid-century over nine billion people will live in cities. We will have to reinvent the way we live our lives and what we take for granted. In the U.S. alone, buildings account for about 40% of the national CO_2 emissions and energy consumption, and out-consumes both the industrial and transportation sectors, while also consuming about 14% of all potable water. We are producing massive amounts of carbon dioxide with current conventional design practices, construction, and operations. Our solutions in building, infrastructure, and community design need to be as big and monumental as the challenges themselves.

The Brundtland Report of 1987 called for the importance of "meeting the needs of the present without compromising the ability of future generations to meet their own needs," and has become the most accepted definition of sustainability (Brundtland Commission 1987). To achieve this, low- and zero-carbon solutions must be developed for building resilient communities that use renewable energy resources and strive for zero waste to meet our future goals.

New innovative green buildings that reduce energy needs, improve occupant health, reduce air, water, and land pollution, conserve natural resources, and protect ecosystem biodiversity are illustrated in *Sustainaspeak*. It is important also to remember that sustainability goes beyond just ecological issues and addresses the concerns of social justice, equity, cultural richness, mental and physical well-being, economic growth, community connectivity, and preserving life's diversity. Stepping up to these critical challenges have been the visionary designers of net-zero energy, net-zero wastes, and net-zero water buildings, many of which are illustrated with sustainable strategies in *Sustainaspeak*. These designers understand that the notion of sustainability is simply just good design.

These high-performing buildings employ crucial passive design strategies, such as daylighting, natural ventilation, and passive heating/cooling, to reduce any energy loads before utilizing energy-intensive active systems. Many interrelated design strategies are used to achieve net-zero energy, water, and carbon goals in building design. *Sustainaspeak* highlights these strategies such as passive solar heating and cooling, high-efficient equipment, super insulation, intelligent building controls, rainwater harvesting, smart skins, and many others.

Guiding these green building practices are different philosophical principles, conceptual frameworks, and green certification systems that recognize the exemplary performances of communities, buildings, infrastructure, sites, products, and organizations. The disciplines involved in designing and constructing green high-performing buildings, work together in integrated design to blend their knowledge and expertise. These integrated practices use the latest building performance tools, parametric design, and building information modeling to improve the building performance and health of the environment. As we strive toward a resilient and carbon-neutral future, our built environment must be a healthy, ecologically responsible investment that makes our world a better place to live for all.

I cannot teach anybody anything, I can only make them think.
—Socrates

As for the future, your task is not to foresee it, but to enable it.
—Antoine de Saint-Exupéry, *The Wisdom of the Sands*, 1948

Terms

Designing is not a profession but an attitude . . . thinking in relationships. The designer must see the periphery as well as the core, the immediate and the ultimate. . . . He must anchor his special job in the complex whole.

—Lazlo Moholy-Nagy, *Vision in Motion*, 1947

Adaptation
Adaptive Reuse
Affordable Housing
Agenda 21
Albedo
Alternative Construction
Alternative Fuels
Anthropogenic
Architectural Programming
Architecture 2030
ASHRAE Standards
Athena Impact Estimator
Backlight-Uplight-Glare (BUG) Rating
BEES Method
Biodiversity
Biomass Power
Biomimicry
Biophilic Design
BREEAM Building Certification
Brise-Soleil
Building Automation Control Systems
Building Information Modeling
Building Orientation
Building Science
Building-Integrated Photovoltaics
Built Environment
Carbon Footprint
Carbon Price
Carbon-Neutral
Carrying Capacity
Certified Wood
Charrette
Chilled Beams
Chlorofluorocarbons
Circular Economy
Climate Change

Climate Responsive Design
Closed-Loop Supply Chain
Cogeneration
Commissioning
Community Connectivity
Constructed Wetland
Construction Waste Management
Cool Roofs
Cradle-to-Cradle
Daylighting
Declare Label
Deconstruction
Deforestation
Demand Response
Dematerialization
Desertification
Design for Disassembly
Design for the Environment
Design Quality Assessment
DGNB Certification
Downcycling
Durability
Ecological Design
Ecological Footprint
Ecological Rucksack
Ecotechnology
EDGE Certification
Embodied Carbon
Embodied Energy
Energy Efficiency
Energy Modeling
Energy Recovery
Energy Star Certification
Energy Use Intensity
Envelope Driven Design
Environmental Product Declaration
Estidama Pearl Rating System
Eutrophication
Facilities Management
Facility Performance Evaluation
Factor 4 and Factor 10
Forest Stewardship Council
Forest Sustainable Management
Formaldehyde
Fossil Fuels
Geothermal Energy
Global Warming
Globalization
Green Building
Green Building Certification Systems
Green Chemistry
Green Economy

Green Globes Certification
Green Roofs
Green Star Certification
Greenhouse Gases
GreenScreen
GRESB Initiative
Greywater
Ground Sourced Heat Pump
Hannover Principles
Health Product Declaration
High-Performing Buildings
Hydrofluorocarbons
Hydrogen Fuel Cell
Hydropower
Indoor Environmental Quality
Industrial Ecology
Integrated Design
Intergovernmental Panel on Climate Change
International Green Construction Code
International Organization for Standardization
JUST Program
Kyoto Protocol
Land Ethic
Laudato Si': On Care for Our Common Home
LEED Building Certification
Life-Cycle Assessment
Life-Cycle Cost Analysis
Lifeboat Ethics
Light Pollution
Lighting
Livable Streets
Living Building Challenge
Location and Transportation
Materials and Resources
Methane
Mitigation
Montreal Protocol
Nanotechnology
Natural Capital
Natural Step
Natural Ventilation
Naturescaping
Neighborhood Development
Net-Zero Energy Building Certification
New Urbanism
Ocean Energy
Off-Site Prefabricated Construction
Operations and Maintenance
Our Common Future
Ozone Depletion
Paris Climate Agreement
Parksmart Certification

Passive Cooling
Passive Design
Passive House Building Standard
Passive Solar Heating
Passive Survivability
PEER Certification Standard
Permeable Pavement
Photovoltaics
Population Growth
Precautionary Principle
Prescriptive Versus Performance-Based Design
Rainwater Harvesting
REACH Regulation
Reclaimed Water
Regenerative Design
Renewable Energy
Renewable Energy Certificates
Resilient Design
Reveal Label
SBTool Assessment
Sense of Place
Seventh Generation Principle
Shading Coefficient
Sick Building Syndrome
Site Analysis
Site Remediation
SITES Initiative
Smart Growth
Social Equity
Solar Chimney
Solar Energy
Solar Heat Gain Coefficient
Solar Reflectance Index
Spaceship Earth
Stack Ventilation
Stormwater Management
Structural Insulated Panels
Sustainability
Sustainable Design
Sustainable Development
Sustainable Preservation
Sustainable Site Design
Systems Thinking
Thermal Comfort
Thermal Insulation
Tragedy of the Commons
Triple Bottom Line
Trombe Wall
Underfloor Air Distribution
Universal and Inclusive Design
Upcycling
Urban Design

Urban Heat Island
Urban Tree Canopy
Value Engineering
Vegetated Walls
Vernacular
Volatile Organic Compounds
Waste Reduction
Water Efficiency
Water Sourced Heat Pump
Water-Energy Nexus
WaterSense
WELL Building Standard
Whole Building Design
Wind Energy
Wind Towers
Windows and Glazing
Xeriscaping
Zero Waste
Zero-Energy Building

Acronyms for Further Sources

AIA	American Institute of Architects
ANSI	American National Standards Institute
ASHRAE	American Society of Heating, Refrigerating, Air Conditioning Engineers
ASLA	American Society of Landscape Architects
ASTM	American Society for Testing and Materials
BREEAM	Building Research Establishment Environmental Assessment Method
BSI	British Standards Institute
CABE	Commission for Architecture and the Built Environment
CBE	Center for the Built Environment
COTE	AIA Committee on the Environment
CRS	Center for Resource Solutions
DOE	U.S. Department of Energy
EBN	Environmental Building News
EEA	European Environment Agency
EERE	U.S. Office of Energy Efficiency and Renewable Energy
EIA	U.S. Energy Information Administration
EPA	U.S. Environmental Protection Agency
EU	European Union
FSC	Forest Stewardship Council
GBCI	Green Building Certification Institute
GBI	Green Building Initiative
ICC	International Code Council
IDeA	Center for Inclusive Design & Environmental Access
IEA	International Energy Agency
IECC	International Energy Conservation Code
IESNA	Illuminating Engineering Society of North America
IgCC	International Green Construction Code
iiSBE	International Initiative for a Sustainable Built Environment
IISD	International Institute for Sustainable Development
ILFI	International Living Future Institute
IPCC	Intergovernmental Panel on Climate Change
IPMVP	International Performance Measurement and Verification Protocol
ISO	International Organization for Standardization
LBC	Living Building Challenge
LEED	Leadership in Energy and Environmental Design
MA	United Nations Millennium Ecosystem Assessment
NCI	National Charrette Institute
NGBS	National Green Building Standard

NIBS	National Institute for Building Sciences
NOAA	National Oceanic and Atmospheric Administration
NREL	National Renewable Energy Laboratory
PHIUS	Passive House Institute U.S.
RMI	Rocky Mountain Institute
SEEA	United Nations System of Economic and Environmental Accounting
SFI	Sustainable Forestry Initiative
SITES	Sustainable Sites Initiative
UCS	Union of Concerned Scientists
UNEP	United Nations Environment Programme
USGBC	US Green Building Council
WBCSD	World Business Council on Sustainable Development
WBDG	Whole Building Design Guide
WEO	World Energy Outlook
WMO	World Meteorological Organization
WWF	World Wildlife Fund

Adaptation   ▮

**Scientists have been warning about global warming for decades.
It's too late to stop it now, but we can lessen its severity
and impacts.** —David Suzuki

Anthropogenic greenhouse gases have been increasing, driven primarily by carbon-intensive economic development and population growth. In the atmosphere, the concentrations of carbon dioxide, methane, and nitrous oxide are currently higher than the last eight hundred thousand years and are the primary "drivers" of the observed warming in our climate system in the past fifty years. Climate events linked to human activities are increased warm temperature extremes, decreased cold temperature extremes, shrinking ice caps, increased extremely high sea levels, and increased heavy rainfalls in particular regions.

Adaptation is adapting to life in a changing climate by reducing our vulnerability to these changes, such as sea level rise, extreme weather events, and the related food and water insecurity. Climate change has been partially responsible for the rise and fall of past civilizations, particularly from droughts. Climate change is a global concern, but its impacts are felt locally, and cities are at the forefront of *adaptation*. Flood defenses are being built, zoning and building codes are changing, stormwater management infrastructure is improving, water capture and storage planned, and heat wave contingencies are underway. An example is Architerra's Regenerative Design International Exposition BOSTON 2100 vision plan which images an energy-positive future city that can withstand increased storm events and seawater by raising the ground plane over large thermal storage tanks (Figure 1). This creates a vibrant urban experience that can leverage climate *adaptation* and

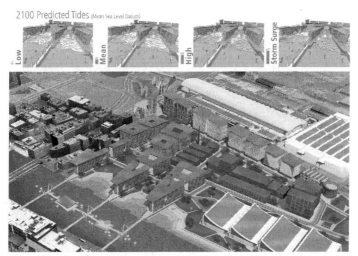

Figure 1 Architerra's ReDe Boston 2100 vision plan
Courtesy ©Architerra Inc., Architects

low-carbon transit investments, and lessen the impacts of warming as David Suzuki states at the beginning of this chapter.

Since the Industrial Revolution began, about half of the CO_2 emitted is still in the atmosphere, and if the world immediately stopped emitting CO_2, it would still take hundreds of years to get back to pre-industrial levels. With the accumulated CO_2 existing in our atmosphere, and with the "committed warming" due to the ocean's thermal capacity and delay in catching up to the atmosphere's temperature, future climate impacts will be even more severe. The complementary strategies of both *adaptation* and mitigation will be needed to diminish the long-term and short-term impact risks simultaneously.

See also: **Anthropogenic • Carbon Footprint • Carbon Price • Circular Economy • Climate Change • Fossil Fuels • Global Warming • Intergovernmental Panel on Climate Change • Mitigation • Paris Climate Agreement**

Further sources: Climate Wiki; Designing Building Wiki; educate-sustainability.eu; EPA Climate Change Indicators; Atmospheric Concentrations of Greenhouse Gases, https://www.epa.gov/climate-indicators/climate-change-indicators-atmospheric-concentrations-greenhouse-gases; IPCC; NASA; Suzuki and Hanington (2012); UN IEA; UNEP; WBDGC

▌Adaptive Reuse

Existing buildings represent the most significant opportunity for energy efficiency. As we upgrade our current building stock, deep energy retrofits can save energy and money. —New Buildings Institute

Many of us still live innocently in a static three-dimensional world of Newtonian conception, which has long since collapsed. In today's design terminology the profound change has been acknowledged by what we call "space-time" relations. There is no such thing as finality or final truth . . . transformation is the essence of life. —Walter Gropius, *The Scope of Total Architecture*, 1956

A looming challenge for cities is the disposition of their growing inventory of obsolete 20th-century buildings. As these buildings are often not nimble enough to respond to a rapidly changing world, they are becoming cost-prohibitive to operate and maintain. They are also becoming economically and functionally obsolete. They must be abandoned, demolished, or undergo extensive retooling. As developed countries continue to transition from industrial/ manufacturing economies into service/ post-industrial economies, factories and warehouses are becoming obsolete. These buildings often have an attractive potential for conversion to urban lofts and "hip" retail. Since a warehouse is typically a large shell, with little in the way of mechanical services, it is suited to being fitted out with energy-efficient technology. Since the building is not demolished, it avoids the environmental costs associated with demolition and transportation to a landfill.

The Kubala Washatko Architects' sustainable award-winning Madison Children's Museum is a great example of *adaptive reuse* that converted a former department store into a dynamic museum-based learning environment. Several floor plates were opened to create multi-story spaces, and a green roof playscape showcases rainwater collection and photovoltaic panels (Figure 2).

Figure 2 Madison Children's Museum, Madison, WI
Courtesy ©The Kubala Washatko Architects, Inc.

As building uses disappear, and new ones emerge, *adaptive reuse* can also be found in the countless gas stations converted to corner bistros and Goodwill collection centers. Churches have become residences, banks have become taverns, video stores have become discount outlets, and decommissioned schools have become community centers. A related growing problem in America is the large number of large retail stores and malls that have been vacated due to loss of customers to online shopping. An economical reuse for these large suburban developments has yet to be found. There have been some instances of churches moving into malls with empty movie theaters and large parking lots. Perhaps some retail malls could also become community education centers, with preschool, elementary, high school, and senior learning academies.

Solutions in the past to this problem have included the 1960s notion of "Kleenex" architecture, meant to be temporary from the start, Archigram's megastructures that differentiate between temporary and permanent elements, and Mies Van der Rohe's "universal or general space" designed to accommodate a range of uses. None of these were strategies seriously considered—until perhaps now. Contemporary examples such as the basketball venue at the 2012 London Olympics that was disassembled and reconfigured in a different location are perhaps a harbinger of things to come. Buildings may one day become transformers (Gropius)—able to adapt to new uses and energy demands largely on their own. Until then, architects should consider designing buildings with built-in mechanisms for seamlessly accommodating future *adaptive reuse*. That might include designing for the differential obsolescence of individual and integrated building systems. EO

See also: **Embodied Carbon • Embodied Energy • Materials and Resources • Sustainable Design**

Further sources: Brand (1994); Gropius (1956); Herron and Crompton (1980)

▌Affordable Housing

Affordable housing brings stability, economic diversity and improves the physical quality of the neighborhood. —John Woods

Affordable housing can be defined as reasonably priced housing for lower and middle-income households so that they can meet their other basic needs. *Affordable housing* is also described as being of reasonable quality and located conveniently for people to be able to carry on the various activities of everyday life without significant hindrance. Typically, *affordable housing* includes specific apartments or housing units subsidized by government agencies to provide housing options for households whose needs are not being met by the market. This social responsibility is shown in the Colorado Court Affordable Housing by Brooks + Scarpa Architects (Figure 3), the first 100% energy neutral *affordable housing* project in the U.S., using climate responsive and passive solar design in an urban environmental 44-unit and five-story environmental project.

Figure 3 Colorado Court Affordable Housing, Santa Monica, CA
Photo: Marvin Rand ©Brooks + Scarpa Architects

Housing is typically considered to be the biggest expenditure for low- and middle-income families, and affordability is usually measured by evaluating the percentage of income that a household spends on housing expenditures. Since the beginning of the 21st century, the world experienced a sustained and unprecedented rise in housing prices, which led to a deep economic recession in 2008. Over the course of fewer than ten years, housing prices doubled in some countries and almost tripled in others. In contrast with that, household incomes have not kept up with rising housing prices. Globally the rise of housing prices can be attributed to a number of factors among which are strong population growth, global urbanization, smaller family units and financial deregulation.

A lack of *affordable housing* options can place a burden on local communities in economic terms but also when it comes to health, social well-being and overall sustainability. For example, the inability for low-income workers to live close to their jobs affects their health and social life, as they have to spend more time commuting to work. The lack of housing options for these workers further impacts transportation needs and creates an additional burden on cities in terms of transportation infrastructure. In countries with heavy reliance on automobile transportation like the U.S., increased commuting trends usually translate to increased pollution levels and other related health issues. The lack of *affordable housing* options in cities can lead to a shortage in professions such as teachers, police officers, firefighters and other important public servants. More broadly the availability of *affordable housing*, as John Woods states at the beginning of this chapter, is essential to maintaining a well-balanced social fabric in growing urban centers and is an important factor to the sustainable development of cities. OC

See also: **Community Connectivity • JUST Program • Location and Transportation • Social Equity • Sustainability**

Further sources: Queensland Affordable Housing Consortium (2012); Yates and Wulff (1999)

Agenda 21   I

Current lifestyles and consumption patterns of the affluent middle class—involving high meat intake, use of fossil fuels, appliances, air-conditioning, and suburban housing—are not sustainable.
—Maurice Strong, 1992 Rio Earth Summit

At the UN Conference on Environment and Development (Earth Summit), held in Rio de Janeiro, Brazil in June 1992, *Agenda 21* was implemented as a voluntary, non-binding action plan for addressing 21st century sustainable development on international, national, regional, and local levels.

The *Agenda 21* program addressed four major global sustainable development concerns and was adopted by 178 countries. Section I, Social and Economic Dimensions, targets health, population issues, sustainable developments, poverty in developing countries and consumption patterns. Section II, Conservation and Management of Resources for Development, was directed at combating deforestation,

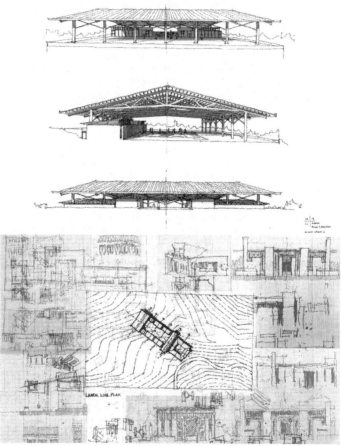

Figure 4 Aumazo School for Girls, Cameroon
Courtesy ©HOK

atmospheric protection, fragile environments, biological diversity, controlling pollution, management of radioactive wastes and biotechnology. Section III, Strengthening the Role of Major Groups, encompasses children and youth, women, NGOs, local authorities, workers, business and industry, and support of indigenous peoples, their communities and farmers. Section IV, Means of Implementation, includes education, technology transfer, science, international institutions and financial mechanisms. It has been affirmed but modified at subsequent UN conferences such as Rio+5 (1997), Rio+10 (2002), *Agenda 21* for Culture (2002) and Rio+20 (2012).

The HOK Architects' design for the Aumazo School in rural Cameroon exemplifies the development goals of strengthening the role of girls with education to achieve higher levels of success in life (Figure 4). The facility embodies the Aumazo School Foundation's guiding principles of innovation, excellence, integrity, and community by forming an allegiance with the land with rainwater capture, natural ventilation, daylighting, community gardens, and using regional and cultural construction practices of timber and Zoma block walls.

Many countries and localities have implemented versions of *Agenda 21* with the legislation of national and state governments, understanding that our current lifestyles are not sustainable. The UN Department of Economic and Social Affairs' Division of Sustainable Development assesses the *Agenda 21* progress nation by nation, but support and implementation are often closely tied to the particular challenges of each country such as extreme climate conditions, lack of infrastructure, pervasive poverty, and challenging political environments. Opposition to *Agenda 21* has increased in some U.S. local, state, and federal areas, with property rights movements saying the program is erosive of individual sovereignty.

ICLEI, Local Governments for Sustainability, is a global network organization that promotes the development goals of *Agenda 21* globally. ICLEI has the membership of over 1,500 cities, towns and regions in over eighty-six countries with the highest numbers in the Unites States and Australia. They support cities striving for a sustainable future with leadership, tools, methodologies and technology in promoting sustainable, low-carbon, resilient, bio-diverse, resource-efficient, productive, and healthy communities.

See also: **Paris Climate Agreement • Population Growth • Resilient Design • Sustainable Development**

Further sources: ICLEI.org

Albedo   ▌

Global surface albedo (surface whiteness) and greenhouse gas changes account for practically the entire global climate change.
—James Hansen, Climate Scientist

The *albedo* of a material or surface is synonymous with its solar reflectance. It is the ratio of the reflected solar energy to the incoming solar energy. *Albedo*, Latin for white, is measured on a scale of 0–1 reflectance, where white surfaces have the highest *albedo*, and dark surfaces have the lowest. A 100% reflectance, or a score of 1, means that all of the solar energy striking a reflective surface is reflected, and none of the energy is absorbed by the surface, whereas an *albedo* of 0 means no reflection from the surface occurs. Solar radiation is all of the light and energy from the sun. Sunlight is the visible spectrum of electromagnetic radiation that is seen by humans, whereas infrared radiation is the longer, invisible wavelength part of this range that we encounter most in our everyday lives, which we feel as heat.

The surface temperature of a material is a result of the amount of solar radiation it rejects, and its ability to emit infrared radiation back into the environment. The Solar Reflectance Index (SRI) calculation is used to determine the effect of the albedo and emittance on the surface temperature of material.

For much of history, builders have used this property of building materials to make indoor environments more comfortable, for example as in parts of Greece where the buildings are painted white each year to reflect radiation and keep the interiors cool. Light-colored interior walls are used to reflect and bounce light deep into rooms.

The existing dark hard surfaces of our developed urban areas with low *albedo* rates absorb more heat than are reflected. Black asphalt roads and dark roofs contribute to what is known as the urban heat island effect, where the average urban temperature is higher than the surrounding rural areas, and this has contributed to our climate change. Hot cities require more energy needed to cool the buildings in order to maintain the inhabitant's thermal comfort. The term "cool roof" is a roof designed with an outer surface that has a very high solar reflectivity of sunlight, and a high emittance to reduce the interior heat gain. On hot sunny days, the roof stays cooler than a standard roof and therefore reduces the energy needed to cool the interior with air conditioning.

The *albedo* of the Earth is approximately .33, which maintains the equilibrium of the global temperature, as nearly a third of incoming radiation is reflected back into space from the Earth. The amount of the reflected energy changes with surface changes, such as with forests' *albedo* of .08– .15, and deserts' about .30. Bright snow and ice have an *albedo* of .6–.9, but when snow and ice melt, less energy is reflected, and more heat is absorbed by the melted water and the ground. This lowers the *albedo* of the Earth, traps infrared radiation, and contributes to global warming.

See also: **Solar Reflectance Index • Sustainable Site Design • Urban Heat Island • Urban Tree Canopy**

Further sources: NASA; WBDG

Alternative Construction

To make the continuity between the natural and the human, we have only two sources of instruction: nature itself and our cultural tradition. —Wendell Berry, *Getting Along with Nature*

As Earth's population continues to increase, more and more people are abandoning the lower impact materials and traditional construction methods of native cultures for the resource and energy-intensive practices of the industrialized world. *Alternative construction*, or natural building, is a return to learning the lessons of nature and cultural traditions of building materials and low-impact construction systems, such as earth and straw-based systems. These lessen the environmental impact of construction by using durability, renewable resources, and minimally processed materials. *Alternative construction* often has the intangible quality of the soul and spirit of natural materials, the softness, the imperfect, and the appreciation for handcrafted quality.

The materials selected in alternative construction are based on local ecological resources, geology of the soils, and microclimate of the particular site to provide a comfortable healthy living environment. Natural construction uses primarily locally available, abundant, rapidly renewable, reused, or safe recycled materials, which are rooted in place and community. Using materials that are generally considered waste, such as straw and low-grade soils, have significant environmental benefits. The traditional American building material of wood is being used faster than it can be replaced and most all of the old growth forests in the U.S. have already been harvested for lumber.

Natural building systems often integrate industrial materials and modern engineering to reduce maintenance, enhance safety, and increase performance. Passive design strategies, such as proper site orientation, utilizing the local climate and site conditions, thermal insulation or mass, and emphasizing natural ventilation can reduce environmental resource and energy costs. *Alternative construction* practices also often use on-site power generation, and on-site water harvesting and reuse.

Alternative materials to conventional wood frame and steel frame construction are often clay, sand, or straw. Adobe, rammed earth, cob, and strawbale are the dominant natural building systems, followed by earth-bag, light-clay, and hybrid systems.

Inspired by organic forms and natural systems, the Van Dusen Botanical Garden Visitor Centre in Vancouver by Perkins+Will creates a harmonious balance between architecture and landscape by using *alternative construction* methods. The prefabricated roof floats over the curved rammed earth and concrete walls that flow seamlessly into the surrounding landscape (Figures 5, 23, 38).

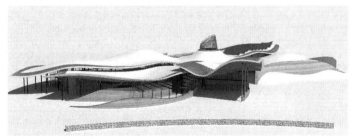

Figure 5 Van Dusen Botanical Garden Visitor Centre, Vancouver
©Nic Lehoux. Courtesy Perkins+Will

Adobe, one of the oldest construction methods, is clay and sand mixed with water, usually with suitable soil as a brick method of wall construction. The resulting thick walls have a high thermal mass allowing for the thermal heat lag effect, which offsets a low insulating R-value. Exterior adobe walls often need moisture protection with large overhangs and exterior finishes.

Rammed earth is made of suitable soil compacted into molds, resulting in a durable thicker wall than most other earthen techniques. Rammed earth is seeing a significant resurgence with the benefits of less maintenance required, greater strength than other earthen techniques, and the beauty of the strata as compressed into the form is visible.

Cob construction is an earthen wall construction made of labor-intensive hand packed balls of mud and straw. The walls can be sculpted in soft organic forms, but the structural limitations may require a frame for larger buildings.

Strawbale construction is essentially stacked straw bales having a plaster, earth, or stucco finish for protection. Straw has a small thermal mass and a low R-value as well, but the thickness of the walls make up for those factors. Strawbale has limited structural strength, so usually strawbale is used as infill between structural framed supports.

Hybrids of these systems can be used together and combined with conventional construction. Other new inventive systems are emerging, such as corrugated cardboard construction, stacked carpet tiles, and 3-D printed buildings acting similar to earth-bag construction. *Alternative construction* can be a significant step in co-evolving with nature rather than destroying the living systems on which life depends.

See also: **Deforestation • Ecological Design • Ecological Footprint • Embodied Carbon • Materials and Resources**

Further sources: Designing Buildings Wiki; EBN; Elizabeth and Adams (2005); WBDG

Alternative Fuels

Alternative fuels are used to supplement and replace petroleum-based gasoline, since burning fossil fuels releases carbon dioxide (CO_2), damaging the environment and increasing global warming. Acid rain, smog, and air pollution are other environmental costs. The World Health Organization estimates over 5.5 million premature deaths worldwide are due to air pollution every year. *Alternative fuels* come from sources other than petroleum and can originate from natural gas, such as propane, methanol, or compressed natural gas, or from biomass materials, such as ethanol, soy diesel, or methanol. In some countries, gasohol—a mixture of gasoline and alcohol—and liquefied petroleum gas are also considered *alternative fuels*.

Alternative fuels can have both advantages and disadvantages with production, supply, emissions, and environmental impacts. Ethanol is an alcohol-based fuel fermented and distilled from the renewable crops of corn, barley, or wheat, but ethanol subsidies can have negative price and availability impacts on food. Natural gas is widely available and used in specially designed engines to burn cleaner than gaso-line or diesel. That said, natural gas production emits methane, with 21 times the impact of CO_2 on global warming. Electricity is used as a highly efficient *alternative fuel* in transportation for battery-powered electric and fuel cell vehicles. Fuel cells as an *alternative fuel* produce electricity without combustion or pollution, but much of today's elec-tricity is generated from natural gas or coal-fired plants, with high car-bon emissions. Hydrogen as an *alternative fuel* is mixed with natural gas in certain types of internal combustion vehicles and is used in fuel cell vehicles, which have no emissions other than water. Hydrogen is costly, and there is currently a lack of fueling infrastructure. Propane as an *alternative fuel* is a widely used byproduct of processing natural gas and refining crude oil and has a highly developed transportation and distribution infrastructure with fewer emissions. Though again, the production of natural gas creates the potent greenhouse gas methane. The *alternative fuel* biodiesel uses vegetable oils or animal fats, often recycled from restaurants, and is safe, biodegradable, and has few vehicle emissions, but has limited infrastructure for distribution and production. The *alternative fuel* methanol, or wood alcohol, can be used in flexible fuel vehicles designed to use M85, a blend of 85% methanol and 15% gasoline, but automakers are no longer producing methanol-powered vehicles. The alternative P-Series fuels blend natural gas liquids, ethanol, and a c-solvent from biomass, and are a high-octane *alternative fuel* for flex-fuel vehicles, but again, manufacturers are not making those vehicles.

Gasoline and diesel are still currently the rulers of the fuel supply chain, with known established technology and infrastructure. Though the production method of *alternative fuels* can be affected by weather and droughts, they are from renewable resources, have lower vehicle emissions, and can enhance the energy security of countries.

See also: **Fossil Fuels • Greenhouse Gases • Hydrogen Fuel Cells • Methane**

Further sources: Institute for Health Metrics and Evaluation; Interna-tional Resource Panel; RMI; WHO

Anthropogenic   ∎

Of, relating to, or resulting from the influence of human beings on nature. —Merriam-Webster Dictionary

There can be no Plan B, because there is no Planet B. —Ban Ki-Moon, former UN Secretary-General

Humans inherited 3.8 billion years of precious and vital environmen-tal resources, but have contributed to their degradation since they first learned how to control fire, and later to smelt metals. The Industrial Revolution, starting around 1760 in England, created densely populated cities, manufactured goods, fossil fuel burning factories, and sew-age dumped in rivers, which all caused air and water pollution. These *anthropogenic*—from the Greek root word "anthrop" meaning human—impacts on the environment caused disease, health problems, fish loss, damage to wildlife, and loss of biodiversity. In recent history, as new compounds have developed, the nature and distribution of contaminant toxins in the environment have changed.

The reduction in the rate of toxins has occurred through improved wastewater legislation, clean air acts, and ozone protecting agreements. Though paralleling these efforts, we are developing new chemical substances in manufacturing processes, such as endocrine disrupting compounds (EDCs), nanotechnology, and increasing fossil fuel use in energy generation and transportation.

With our disproportionate global wealth of natural resources, the reckless use and consumption of these resources, along with the incumbent waste and pollution, causes social unrest, harm, and fails to address the ecosystem health and sustainability needed for our future life on this planet. As human activity has been the dominant influence on Earth's geological processes of climate and environment, there are proposals to distinguish this new human-dominated time period from the preceding Holocene geological epoch, as the Anthropocene, starting mid-20th century.

Responsible nations and the global civil society came together in September 2015 to back the 17 aspirational United Nations Sustainable Development Goals (SDGs), in Resolution A/RES/701. These global community goals include ending poverty and hunger, improving health and education, making cities more sustainable, combating climate change, and protecting our oceans and forests.

See also: **Biodiversity • Ecological Footprint • Greenhouse Gases • Renewable Energy • Sustainable Development**

Further sources: IPCC; Iyengar (2015: 4)

Architecture 2030

We tend to rush toward the complex when trying to solve a daunting problem, but in this case, simplicity wins. Better buildings, responsible energy use, and renewable energy choices are all we need to tackle both energy independence and climate change.
—Edward Mazria

The 2030 Challenge is an initiative set up by *Architecture 2030* and architect Ed Mazria, to reduce carbon dioxide (CO_2) and greenhouse gas (GHG) emissions from the built environment. *Architecture 2030* states that in developed countries, the construction and use of buildings are the leading consumers of energy and contributor of global greenhouse gases emissions associated with extensive climate change. Energy consumption from the building sector comes from not only the energy used for building construction and operation, but also must take into account the embodied energy of resources and the energy needed for commuting.

In future years, the majority of our global built environment will either be redesigned or rebuilt. If these buildings are designed and constructed using outdated, inefficient methods and are powered by our current fossil fuel burning electricity plants, then we can't avoid reaching a tipping point and irreparably damaging our Earth's climate. *Architecture 2030* states, however, that if these buildings use energy-efficient strategies and use both on-site and off-site renewable power generation, then the building sector can keep global warming to approximately 1°C (1.8°F) above today's level and be a solution to the climate crisis.

The *Architecture 2030* Challenge proposes that the global architecture and construction community adopt a series of greenhouse gas reduction targets for all renovated and new buildings—that all new buildings, developments, and renovations be built to meet a performance standard of a 70% reduction for fossil fuel consumption, GHG emissions, and energy consumption, relative to the regional or national average for that type of building. This increases to 80% in 2020, then 90% in 2025, and by 2030 all new buildings are to be carbon-neutral (using zero fossil fuel to operate).

In 2009, The Wall Street Journal asked William McDonough + Partners to envision a home of the future. The team used nature as inspiration to design a home that functions like a tree: using sunlight to generate energy and food on site, cleans its water, captures carbon and produces oxygen while regenerating the habitat. As with a tree, the house grows with positive benefits and at the end of its life can be disassembled and used in the cradle-to-cradle cycle (Figure 6).

Figure 6 House Like a Tree
Courtesy ©William McDonough+Partners

The emerging market of net-zero energy (NZE) buildings supports the targets of the *Architecture 2030* Challenge in striving to generate as much energy from renewable sources as they consume on a net-year basis. Achieving these targets will require both innovative high-performing design strategies and state of the art renewable technologies.

The road to energy independence, economic recovery, and greenhouse gas reductions runs through the building sector. —Edward Mazria

See also: **Cradle-to-Cradle • Greenhouse Gases • Net-Zero Energy Building Certification • Renewable Energy • Solar Energy**

Further sources: Iyengar (2015: 15); Kibert (2016: 8); Yudelson (2007: 29)

▌Architectural Programming

Good buildings don't just happen. They are planned to look good and perform well, and come about when good architects and good clients join in thoughtful, cooperative effort. Programming the requirements of a proposed building is the architect's first task, often the most important. —William M. Peña

If I were given one hour to save the planet, I would spend 59 minutes defining the problem and one minute resolving it. —Albert Einstein

Architectural programming is a phase of the building delivery process when information about the project is collected, organized, and studied for its possible influences on the design of the new facility. This information is then brought to bear on the planning and design decisions that will shape the building scheme. This is the architect's first task in the design process and often the most important as emphasized by William Peña. There is a correlation between the kinds of information pursued in programming, the kinds of decisions to be made to create the design, and the kinds of ways the building must serve and perform after it is constructed and in use.

The main purpose of *architectural programming* is to thoroughly understand all the information about the project that might affect the building's long-term success. As Einstein states above, gathering all this information is crucial to solving the problem. Programming also aims to communicate this understanding to others participating in the building delivery process and to identify those project factors that might inspire creative ideas.

Information typically found in a program might include the client's project goals, organizational structure, and operation; client's operational departments, spaces, and staffing; required adjacencies between departments and spaces; parking requirements; square footage areas of rooms, departments and total building; furniture and equipment; project budget and schedule; codes and regulations; project site information and climate data. The kinds, breadth, and depth of information vary with the unique situation, concerns, issues, and goals of the project.

Types of information in the program affect corresponding types of design decisions that shape the building scheme. Example decision areas are building placement and orientation on the site, parking location and layout, landscaping, roads and sidewalks, department and space layout in the building, circulation, building form, materials, windows, façade design, structural system, heating and cooling, lighting, and furniture.

Data collection in programming requires the architect to pursue various kinds of sources who can provide the needed information. The client, client's staff, code officials, contractors, bankers, real estate agents, engineers and furniture and equipment consultants are examples. The project architect will also sometimes study built facilities that are similar to the one about to be planned to learn lessons from the existing building's design and performance. These lessons can then be applied to the new project.

Sustainability goals and guidelines are frequently addressed in *architectural programming* when those design issues and concerns are a project focus. Sustainability concerns are interlaced and integrated into many kinds of program information from site and climate data to materials, windows, and heating/cooling equipment. Where sustainability is of particular interest in the project, program information can be specifically oriented toward those intentions. Some examples are:

- Built facilities are chosen for precedent studies that employ sustainability elements and strategies.
- Project goals address sustainability issues.
- Project requirements include sustainability guidelines.
- Opportunities to simplify and streamline the client's operation and utility needs are investigated.
- Ecofriendly materials, equipment, and technical systems are specified.
- Site and climate are analyzed for applications of passive ventilation, heating/cooling strategies, and water capture/storage/recycling.
- Larger ecological texts are included in the site analysis to ensure positive/neutral project impacts on natural systems.
- Economics of scale are investigated for possible shared use with other facilities of land, parking, and utilities. EW

See also: **Charrette • Design (*Archispeak*) • Integrated Design • Passive Design • Sustainable Site Design**

Further sources: Peña and Parshall (2001)

ASHRAE Standards   ∎

ASHRAE is an organization devoted to the advancement of indoor-environment-control technology in the heating, ventilation, and air conditioning industry. —ASHRAE website

The *American Society of Heating, Refrigerating and Air-Conditioning Engineers (ASHRAE)*, founded in 1894, is an influential international organization with an emphasis on building systems, energy efficiency, indoor air quality, refrigeration, and sustainability. The 2012 slogan, "Shaping Tomorrow's Built Environment Today" conveys the sustainable mission of advancing technology to increase human well-being in the built environment. *ASHRAE* develops building standards and guidelines about the indoor environment's mechanical system performances of heating, ventilation, and air conditioning (HVAC), energy use, and commissioning. Accredited by the American Standards Institute (ANSI), and extensively used worldwide by architects and engineers, *ASHRAE* standards define the minimum acceptable value levels of building performance. These minimum *ASHRAE* levels must usually be exceeded when striving for high performance to comply with certain green building codes and rating systems, such as the International Green Construction Code (IgCC) and USGBC's LEED.

ASHRAE Standard 90.1: Energy Standard for Buildings has been a benchmark for energy codes worldwide for over forty years. It provides the minimum requirements for the energy efficiency of the building envelope, HVAC, service water heating, electric power distribution, and lighting systems.

ASHRAE Standard 62.1: Ventilation for Acceptable Indoor Air Quality addresses the building occupants' human health considerations by specifying acceptable minimum ventilation rates (fresh air) and indoor air quality conditions. This air quality standard considers the chemical, physical, and biological contaminants in a facility, such as CO_2 levels and number of occupants.

ASHRAE Standard 55: Thermal Environmental Conditions for Human Occupancy specifies the thermal comfort conditions acceptable to 80% or more of the occupants within a space. The indoor comfort factors addressed are temperature, thermal radiation, air speed, and humidity.

ASHRAE Standard 189.1: Design of High-Performance Green Buildings addresses the siting, construction, and operation of high-performance buildings. It addresses site sustainability, efficient water use, efficient energy use, indoor environmental quality, and the building's overall environmental impact on the atmosphere, materials, and resources.

Other *ASHRAE* standards also play an important part in creating value in the built environment, such as Standard 52.2, which focuses on air quality and filtration, and Standard 34, which monitors refrigerants for toxicity and flammability. In partnership with AIA, IES, and USGBC, *ASHRAE* has embarked on a new series of Advance Energy Guides: Achieving Zero Energy to promote a global sustainable built environment by focusing on achieving zero energy buildings.

See also: **Commissioning • Energy Efficiency • High-Performing Buildings • Indoor Environment Quality • Zero-Energy Building**

Further sources: ASHRAE; DOE; WBDG

Athena Impact Estimator

Life cycle assessment is the science behind environmental footprinting. —Athena Sustainable Material Institute website

Buildings have an enormous environmental footprint even before the building is occupied. These embodied impacts can include the resources and emissions to manufacture, transport, install, maintain, and recycle the building products and materials. This part of a building's short-term embodied impact is often put aside for the building's long-term operating energy. Though in the urgency of reducing global carbon emissions, and as buildings become more energy-efficient, the life-cycle assessment of building materials becomes vital.

The Athena Sustainable Materials Institute created the first *Athena Impact Estimator* in 2002, to calculate the life-cycle assessment of buildings or assemblies, such as roofs, walls, floors, and structural parts. After numerous updates, the current *Impact Estimator for Buildings (IE4B)* provides a cradle-to-grave life-cycle profile for all North American building types, such as new construction, renovations, and additions.

The architects, engineers, or consultants input the primary building elements with dimensions and choose specific building materials, and the *Impact Estimator* creates a bill of materials and associated environmental impacts. These impacts are the environmental flows to and from nature: such as energy and raw material flows with emissions to air, land, and water. The *Impact Estimator* reports the environmental impact measures for the building that are consistent with U.S. EPA TRACI (Tool for Reduction and Assessment of Chemicals and other Environmental Impacts) methods. These six TRACI impacts are: global warming potential, acidification potential, human health particulates, ozone depletion potential, smog potential, and eutrophication potential.

The *Impact Estimator for Buildings* calculations can be customized for regional location, electricity grids, transportation means and distances, and building type, and can also report fossil fuel consumption and operating energy use. The tool is useful early in the design process, as when in the conceptual stage addressing the environmental footprint can affect decisions about size and building mass. With the *Impact Estimator*, designers can conduct whole building life-cycle assessments to understand trade-offs, look for improvements, and assess individual components, as well as to meet the LCA requirements of green building rating systems, codes, and standards.

See also: **BEES Method • Indoor Environment Quality • Life-Cycle Assessment • Materials and Resources • Sustainable Design**

Further sources: Athena Sustainable Materials Institute; US EPA; BuildingGreen

Backlight-Uplight-Glare (BUG) Rating

Every night come out these envoys of beauty, and light the universe with their admonishing smile. —Ralph Waldo Emerson, *Nature and Selected Essays*

The sun, the moon, and the stars would have disappeared long ago . . . had they happened to be within the reach of predatory human hands. —Havelock Ellis, *The Dance of Life*, 1923

A building's exterior lighting should provide safety, building identity, wayfinding, and security; however inadequate, inefficient lighting design can cause light pollution and light trespass. The "beauty" of the night sky as referenced by Emerson above has indeed been altered by our "human hands"—as Havelock Ellis warned in 1923—by the rampant light pollution from our cities and industries. For responsible outdoor lighting that is efficient in meeting its intended purpose, it is important to select the minimum appropriate lighting needed, locate fixtures in the appropriate locations, and select the appropriate luminaires for aim and mounting height. Luminaires are the complete lighting unit parts that protect, position, distribute the light, and the power connection.

Good exterior lighting design requires reducing three forms of light pollution: light trespass, uplight, and glare. A light pollution reduction classification, TM-15–11 *BUG*, is a prescriptive standard for outdoor lighting fixtures developed by the Illuminating Engineering Society of North America (IES). The *BUG* rating is an acronym for *Backlight, Uplight, and Glare*, and is intended to shield these three forms of light pollution as well as limit lamp lumens to appropriate lighting zone levels. *Backlight* creates light trespass, which is unwanted light from a neighboring property and can cause visibility loss, distraction, and aggravation. *Uplight* creates artificial skyglow and is mostly wasted energy. For the most sensitive lighting zones where the protection of a dark environment is critical, such as wilderness preserves and near astronomical observatories, zero *uplight* is allowed. *Glare* is an intense blinding light that can be annoying and reduce visibility, as it is brighter than to what the eye can adapt. Lighting designers can use this standard in exterior light fixture specifications to match the project's particular lighting zone to stipulate well-directed and well-shielded luminaires.

See also: **Light Pollution • Sustainable Site Design • SITES Initiative**

Further sources: Emerson (2003); Illuminating Engineering Society of North America; International Dark Sky Association

BEES Method

Building construction and renovation can have significant negative impacts on the environment. Raw material extraction can lead to resource scarcity and alter ecosystem diversity. The manufacture and transportation of building materials consumes energy and generates pollution and carbon emissions, which lead to smog, acid rain, and climate change. Material waste leads to landfill burdens, while toxic emissions from indoor materials can result in adverse health and productivity effects. The National Institute of Standards and Technology (NIST) along with support from the U.S. EPA developed the *BEES (Building for Environmental and Economic Sustainability)* method in 1994. The intended goal was to identify cost-effective and environmentally friendly building products for use in construction.

Designers, product manufacturers, and builders can use the science-based economic and environmental data provided by *BEES*, for comparison in selecting a preferable low-impact building product.

The environmental performance of building products is measured with *BEES* by using the life-cycle assessment (LCA) approach, following guidance in the International Standards Organization (ISO) 14040 series of standards for LCA. The LCA approach is based on the "cradle-to-grave" systems approach. All life-cycle stages of a product generate environmental impacts, so all stages are analyzed: raw material acquisition, manufacture, transport, installation, operation, recycling, and waste management. Environmental impacts also can have very real economic implications such as global warming, water pollution, and resource depletion.

The economic performance is separately measured using the American Society for Testing and Materials (ASTM) standard life-cycle cost (LCC) method. This covers the initial investment costs, replacement, operation, maintenance and repair, and then disposal. These two performance measures are then combined into an overall environmental and economic performance measure. The building products throughout the *BEES* analysis are defined and classified according to the ASTM standard classification for building element, UNIFORMAT II.

See also: **Athena Impact Estimator • International Organization for Standardization • Life-Cycle Assessment • Materials and Resources**

Further sources: ASTM; NIST; WBDG, BuildingGreen

Biodiversity   **I**

If we pollute the air, water and soil that keep us alive and well, and destroy the biodiversity that allows natural systems to function, no amount of money will save us. —David Suzuki

A thing is right when it begins to preserve the integrity, stability, and beauty of the biotic community. It is wrong when it tends otherwise. —Aldo Leopold, *A Sand County Almanac*

Biological diversity, or *biodiversity*, describes the abundant variety of all aspects of life on Earth. Species richness, ecosystem complexity, and genetic population variation are all studied as organized parts of biological diversity. *Biodiversity* studies the many different ecosystems in which species form unique communities, interacting with each other and the air, water, and soil. Tropical rainforests have by far the most diverse species in their ecosystems, as opposed to fewer found in arctic plains or desert ecosystems.

For over 3.5 billion years, evolution has provided a remarkable number and diversity of species, from whales to trees, to humans, and to microscopic bacteria. So far we have identified only about 1.9 million species, out of estimates of 11 million yet to be discovered (O'Loughlin 2009). *Biodiversity* is critical for the health and stability of ecosystems, including human health and cultural diversity. It provides us with a variety of ecosystem services such as nutrients, materials, pollinators, plants, medical discoveries, clean water, and oxygen, without which we could not exist.

In the history of our planet, species have survived, evolved, and gone extinct due to natural shifts in the environment over extended periods of time. Today, many species are going extinct at an accelerated and alarming rate, due to the loss of *biodiversity* and ecosystem quality, caused by non-natural environmental changes triggered by human activities, as warned by Suzuki and Leopold above. When one species disappears, other species are affected, starting a negative chain reaction of unprecedented ecological pressures. The International Union for Conservation of Nature (IUCN) estimates on its website, iucn.org, that we are losing species at least 1,000–10,000 times the expected natural extinction rate. Globally, about one-third of all known species are threatened with extinction, including 29% of all amphibians, 21% of all mammals and 12% of all birds. Unlike the five known mass extinction events in geological history, the current extinction crisis is often referred to as the "sixth extinction" and caused by the human species.

Human impacts on *biodiversity* and loss of ecosystem functions are primarily habitat destruction and degradation, such as deforestation; followed by over-exploitation, such as harvesting and overfishing; land, air and water pollution; disease; alien species invasions; and global climate change; resulting in migratory changes and coral bleaching. Habitat destruction can be caused by population stress such as sprawling development, poverty, social inequality, and trade agreements that work against poorer countries.

The notable Chesapeake Bay Foundation Brock Environmental Center designed by SmithGroupJJR Architects achieved LEED Platinum and Living Building Challenge certifications by being net-positive water, waste, and energy while using *biodiversity* to address education, health, materials, and equity. The existing site *biodiversity* provided the positive, regenerative, and resilient design approach of raising the building above the ground plane to respond to future storm surges (Figures 7, 56, 71).

Combinations of various conservation measures are needed in protecting native and wildlife habitats and ecosystems to prevent continued *biodiversity* loss. It is more effective to protect ecosystem habitats first, than it is try to restore after they have been damaged or destroyed. Examples of conservation measures used are the establishment of protected areas for migratory species, wildlife and plants; restoration of habitats and ecosystems; limiting chemical pollutants and pesticides; prohibition of trade in endangered species; and enforcing global agreements to protect biological diversity.

If I keep a green bough in my heart, the singing bird will come.
—Chinese proverb

Figure 7 Chesapeake Bay Brock Environmental Center
©Prakash Patel. Courtesy of SmithGroupJJR

See also: **Carrying Capacity • Deforestation • Ecological Design • Eutrophication • Natural Capital • Tragedy of the Commons**

Further sources: Hawken (1993: 27–29); IUCN.org; Kibert (1999: 208); Leopold (1949); Massoleni (2013: 37); World Wildlife Fund

Biomass Power   ∎

We have used biomass energy, or "bioenergy" —the energy from plants and plant-derived materials —since people began burning wood to cook food and keep warm. Wood is still the largest biomass energy resource today, but other sources of biomass can also be used. These include food crops, grassy and woody plants, residues from agriculture or forestry, oil-rich algae, and the organic component of municipal and industrial wastes. Even the fumes from landfills can be used as biomass energy sources. —National Resources Defense Council website

Biomass power is electricity generated from renewable organic waste that would otherwise be burned, dumped in landfills, or left to feed forest fires. Materials that serve no other purpose, such as dead timber, scrap lumber, agricultural residues, industry byproducts, and animal and human wastes, can be used to generate renewable electricity.

There are over a hundred million dead trees on just California public and private lands, many killed by recent droughts and bark beetle infestations, which increase the risk of forest fires (USFS 2016). Every year, the biomass industry removes over sixty-eight million tons of forest rubble, reducing this risk, while improving forest health, and growth.

As organic wastes decompose, methane and carbon dioxide are slowly emitted to the atmosphere as greenhouse gases. Power plants that use biomass take advantage of this process by turning waste into fuel to generate electricity, and in the process, the methane is eliminated, and CO_2 is reduced.

There are both positive and negative impacts of using biomass for energy. Biomass energy also relies on growing plants for burning. Burning biomass, just as burning fossil fuels, releases CO_2, but also the biomass plants sequester nearly the same CO_2 equivalent through photosynthesis. Burning municipal solid wastes (MSW), or garbage, in waste-to-energy plants results in less waste to bury at landfills, but chemicals in the waste can be released, creating air pollution that is hazardous to human health and the environment.

Biogas contains methane and CO_2, potent greenhouse gases, primarily as a result of the organic anaerobic processes in waste landfills, livestock manure collection, and sewage treatment plants. Biogas can be burned for heat or electric generation and is considered renewable, as it replaces the burning of fossil fuels. Ethanol and biodiesel are biofuels created primarily for transportation fuel from biomasses, such as corn, sugarcane, soybeans and palm oil trees. Biofuels are considered to be carbon-neutral, as growing the plants also sequesters CO_2. Growing plants for biofuels is controversial though, as food crops could be grown with the same energy, fertilizer, land, and water used.

See also: **Energy Recovery • Greenhouse Gases • Methane • Renewable Energy**

Further sources: NREL; USEIA; Union of Concerned Scientists

▌Biomimicry

The more our world functions like the natural world, the more likely we are to endure on this home that is ours, but not ours alone.
—Janine Benyus

For a long time we thought we were better than the living world, and now some of us tend to think we are worse . . . but neither perspective is healthy. We have to remember how it is to have equal standing in the world, to be "between the mountain and the ant . . . part and parcel of creation." —Janine Benyus

Understanding that our lifestyles, technologies, and increasing populations are creating massive sustainability problems, and believing that we have a responsibility for the continued survival of future generations, we must look to sustainable principles and philosophies to guide us on this path. One such principle is respecting and learning from our natural systems.

Scientist Janine Benyus, in her 1997 book *Biomimicry: Innovation Inspired by Nature*, states that for 3.8 billion years nature has been evolving and solving most of the problems that have ever existed. The term *biomimicry* comes from the Greek words bios (life) and mimesis (imitate), so *biomimicry* or *biomimetic design* is an innovating approach seeking sustainable solutions to human challenges by learning from nature's best biological processes and strategies. Benyus (1997) states that the innovations of nature have similarities, such as relying on sunlight, using only needed energy, fitting form to function, recycling everything, working cooperatively, and building on diversity.

Many major discoveries in engineering, technology, and science have been inspired by nature's genius. Leonardo da Vinci studied birds in hopes of enabling human flight, while later the Wright brothers learned to reduce airplane turbulence at low-speeds from turkey vulture feathers. The cockpit of the supersonic Concorde lowers its head on approach as does the head of a swan, while fighter and commercial planes have learned from the vortexes off the wings of geese in V-formation. Velcro is a direct interpretation of the way seeds stick to animal hair, spider silk can be stronger and tougher ounce per ounce than steel, underwater blue mussels have inspired non-toxic and formaldehyde-free glues, and abalone shells inspired the non-stick Teflon.

Nature builds shelter structures with an efficient functionality that can be applied to building design. Perkins+Will Architects used *biomimetic design* in the Shanghai Natural History Museum in China by using the form of the nautilus shell to inspire the shape and internal organization of the building. A spiraling grass-covered plane rises up and wraps around an oval pond, which is the central focus of the exhibition route spiraling down through the building. The building focuses our awareness on the fundamental elements of plants, Earth and water (Figures 8, 39, 67).

Figure 8 Shanghai Natural History Museum, China
©James and Connor Steinkamp Photography. Courtesy Perkins+Will

Biometric research is influencing building products, systems, and whole building design. Photovoltaic systems harvest solar energy, mimicking the way a leaf harvests energy. The bumpy surface of the lotus leaf, which acts as a self-cleaning mechanism, has inspired new self-cleaning building products, such as tiles, glass, paints, concrete, and textiles, that reduce detergent use and maintenance. The strength of *biomimicry* is that it teaches how to achieve sustainable design as nature does, with systems that conserve energy and materials, work in closed loops, use renewable energy, and work as integrated ecosystems.

The answers to our questions are everywhere; we just need to change the lens with which we see the world. —Janine Benyus

See also: **Biomimicry (***Theoryspeak***)** • **Biophilic Design** • **Ecological Design** • **Nature (***Theoryspeak***)** • **Naturescaping**

Further sources: Benyus (1997)

▌Biophilic Design

They travel long distances to stroll along the seashore, for reasons they can't put into words. —Edward O. Wilson

Always in the big woods when you leave familiar ground and step off alone into a new place, there will be, along with the feelings of curiosity and excitement, a little nagging of dread. It is the ancient fear of the Unknown, and it is your first bond with the wilderness you are going into. —Wendell Berry

The German psychologist Erich Fromm coined the term *biophilia* in 1964 to describe our human attraction to all things alive and vital. Edward O. Wilson, the noted Harvard entomologist, later popularized the term in his 1986 book, *Biophilia*. Wilson theorized that humans possess an innate biological tendency to affiliate with natural systems, such as walking along the seashore, and other life form processes to maintain their health and productivity. Wilson elegantly explained, "To explore and affiliate with life is a deep and complicated process in mental development. To an extent still undervalued . . . our existence depends on the propensity our spirit is woven from it; hope rises on its currents."

Biophilic design is an innovative approach that expresses this special human need to partner with nature by enhancing and restoring this beneficial experience of nature in the built environment. The typical modern urban built environment has encouraged an increasing alienation of people from nature and outdoors.

For much of human history, our built environment integrated with nature by using local materials, patterns of nature and culture, indigenous heritages, and the context of the natural environment. *Biophilic design* strives for mutuality, respect and enriching relationships between human society and the natural world. Our minds and bodies have adapted over time by being connected to both a sensory and fertile natural world with sunlight, water, weather, plants, landscapes, and animals. This constant natural connection is essential to our functional development, intellectual maturation, spiritual being, health and emotional happiness, as expressed above by Wendell Berry.

The Manassas Park Elementary School in Manassas, Virginia by VMDO Architects is an excellent example of *biophilic design*. The design pushes the school up against the existing historic forest to preserve open space and create a suburban "school in the woods" by maximizing the connection between indoors and out (Figures 9, 28). The project is organized around three wings themed around different seasons with courtyards to provide daylight and fresh air. Native grasses and wildflowers were planted echoing the eastern woodlands of the Native Americans.

Figure 9 Manassas Park Elementary School, VA
Courtesy ©VMDO Architects/Prakash Patel

In fostering the human-nature connection at the building, neighborhood, community, and urban levels, *biophilic design* seeks to become a restorative environmental design process. Stephen Kellert puts forth two important basic dimensions of *biophilic design* in his 2008 book, *Biophilic Design*. First, an organic or naturalistic aspect that directly, indirectly, or symbolically represents shapes and forms of nature such as daylight, water, plants, natural habitats, or ecosystems. Second, a place-based or vernacular dimension, where landscapes or buildings connect to the collective identity of local culture or ecology and strive to embody the experience and spirit of the place.

Incorporating ecological features, daylight, open space, natural patterns and shapes, and linkages to place can reinforce the human connection to nature with *biophilic design*. Multi-sensory experiences that can stimulate connections to nature are colorful and aromatic gardens, glazing to enhance wayfinding, exterior views for orientation and context, and the changing color temperatures of daylighting to reinforce circadian rhythms. Plants and trees give human scale and seasonal comfort, and moving water gives natural sound complexity; and all these stimulate feelings of safety, environmental support, and harmony with nature that contributes to a sense of well-being.

See also: **Behavior and Environment (*Theoryspeak*) • Biomimicry • Ecological Design • Kinesthesia (*Archispeak*) • Nature (*Theoryspeak*) • Natural Capital • Naturescaping • Organic (*Archispeak*) • Sense of Place**

Further sources: Wilson (1986: 1, 35); Kellert, Heerwagen, and Mador (2008: 5–6)

BREEAM Certification

BREEAM was created as a cost-effective means of bringing sustainable value to development. —BREEAM website

The world's first sustainability assessment system for buildings, *BREEAM*, was started in the United Kingdom and is used by many of the world's Green Building Councils as a template for their sustainable building rubrics, including USGBC's LEED. Short for Building Research Establishment (BRE) Environmental Assessment Method for buildings, *BREEAM* focuses on cost-effective, sustainable value and efficiency. Used in seventy-eight countries according to the website BREEAM.org, there are more than 550,000 certified developments and over two million buildings registered for assessment since the method was launched in 1990. The acquisition of CEEQUAL (Civil Engineering Environmental Quality Assessment) enabled civil engineering and infrastructure projects to have a new sustainability rating system to achieve more sustainable and resilient infrastructure. In June 2016, *BREEAM* USA was launched in the U.S. by BuildingWise with *BREEAM* In-Use for Existing Buildings.

The assessment system sets best-practice standards for the building's environmental performance through all the phases of design, specifications, construction, and operation. There are two stages of assessment and certification in the process: the design stage assessment and the final post-construction assessment. *BREEAM* measures holistic performance against nine issues: building/construction management, health and well-being, energy, transportation, water, materials, waste, land use and ecology, and pollution. Each concern tackles a particular building-linked issue and has credits allocated to it. Credits are earned when a building shows that it meets the best-practice performance levels for that particular issue. Assessment credits are measured and delivered by trained third-party certified assessors, who determine the ratings. The final benchmark scores determine if a building meets the criteria of unclassified, pass, good, very good, excellent, or outstanding. *BREEAM* training and consultants are used to help facilitate the successful design and construction of an environmentally sustainable building. *BREEAM* also aligns with the WELL Building Institute for projects pursuing both standards.

See also: **Green Building Certification Systems • Green Globes Certification • LEED Building Certification • Sustainable Design • Sustainable Development**

Further sources: Sustainable Dev. Dictionary; BREEAM.org; Kibert (2016: 136); Iyengar (2015: 238)

Brise-Soleil   ∎

The clock and the solar calendar brought to architecture the "brise-soleil" to be installed in front of the windows of modern buildings.
—Le Corbusier, *Le Poeme de L'Angle Droit* 1953

A screen, usually louvered, placed on the outside of a building to shield the windows from direct sunlight. —Dictionary.com

Designing a building flooded with daylight can be a challenge if appropriately responding to the needs of the owner and the occupants, especially with issues of glare and heat gain. Designing for daylighting must balance and integrate concerns for aesthetics, design benefit, human comfort, cost-effectiveness, and energy efficiency. In current buildings, a range of sun-shading structures can combine both unique architectural expressions with the practical functions of solar control.

Architects often use *brise-soleil* as a solution for overheating in many hot climates with long exposures to direct sunlight. *Brise-soleil* typically are horizontal projections that deflect direct sunlight to shade façades with large amounts of glass facing the sun. The French term means sun breaker—*brise* is to break, and *soleil* is the sun—and is used in many of French architect Le Corbusier's buildings. Louvers can be incorporated into the *brise-soleil* shades to mitigate the high-angle hot summer rays from hitting the façade, but can also permit the winter's low-angle sunlight to provide solar heating passively. The shades, or sun baffles, can be outside the windows or extend over the entire building façade with a variety of patterns to act as light filtering screens. For the louver to provide the optimum protection from the sun, the overhang depth must be calculated to match the building situation, such as latitude, orientation, and height of the glazing to be shaded.

The NASA Sustainability Base designed by William McDonough + Partners is an Earth-based space-aged facility intended to merge NASA's space exploration expertise with the built environment. The building uses the concepts of "native to place" and biophilia (life-loving) by using building-integrated photovoltaics and vegetation on the *brise-soleil* to shade the façade while also generating energy (Figures 10, 19, 45, 52, 61).

Traditional methods of reducing the sun's glare and heat gain have existed for thousands of years. The lattices (mushrabíyah) of the Middle East, or the pierced screens (qamariyah) as used at the Taj Mahal, and split bamboo blinds (sudare) used outside windows in Japan all provide solar shade and screening.

Brise-soleil sunshades can range from simple patterns of concrete fins, as in many of Le Corbusier's buildings, to more elaborate wing-like mechanisms like Santiago Calatrava's Milwaukee Art Museum that are adjusted for the changing solar angles during the day and across the seasons. Incorporating the use of *brise-soleil* can enable maximizing high levels of natural lighting and reduce the energy needed for artificial lighting, while solar control can be provided for indoor environmental quality promoting views, comfort, and well-being.

Figure 10 NASA Sustainability Base, Moffett Field, CA
Photo: Cesar Rubio. Courtesy ©William McDonough+Partners

To introduce the sun is the new and most imperative duty of the architect. —Le Corbusier, *The Athens Charter*, 1933–41

See also: **Biophilic Design • Daylighting • Indoor Environmental Quality • Passive Design • Shading Coefficient • Solar Heat Gain Coefficient • Thermal Comfort**

Further sources: Arcadia Inc.; Architizer; Le Corbusier (1953, 1933); Renson Sun Protection; WBDG

▋Building Automated Control Systems

Building management systems and intelligent buildings are in the control technologies, which allow integration, automation, and optimization of all the services and equipment that provide services and manages the environment of the building. —www.business balls.com

Building services and systems are usually a necessity for environments to be comfortable, functional, secure, and efficient. High-performing buildings today use *building automation control systems (BACS)* to manage these building services for their efficient operation. Smart building controls use a computerized network of electronic devices to monitor and control the functionality of building services, such as mechanical, electrical, lighting, HVAC, and security systems. Advanced technology with smart and customizable building management platforms allows for the automation, integration, and optimization of today's increasingly complex operations and building performance.

Building automation control systems (BACS) refers to the centralized systems that can monitor, control, record, and learn from data on building services. These smart systems tend to maintain the building environment more efficiently while reducing its energy costs and environmental impact. The primary functions of *BACS* are to maintain control of the building's environment, operate systems according to energy and occupancy demands, and monitor and adjust the performance of the system. A part of *BACS* is Building Energy Management Systems (BEMS), which deals only with power distribution, energy consumption, metering, and power supply.

Currently, Direct Digital Controls (DDC) process data digitally and can control the building service devices using microprocessors, software, and electronic control devices. The control system monitors the service devices with sensors, using the data input to compare with the control system's rules and settings. If the input data is outside of an acceptable range, the control system will trigger commands to change the operation of the controlled device.

An automated building has a reduced environmental impact due to its reduced energy consumption, therefore reducing greenhouse gas emissions. *BACS* can also improve the building's indoor air quality, i.e. thermal comfort and lighting controls, which have been shown to increase occupant productivity and the owner's bottom line. With advancing technology, buildings are not only automatically managing the built environment, but also learning from the data collected; therefore, these logically automated high-performing buildings are referred to as intelligent or smart buildings.

See also: **Building Information Modeling • Energy Efficiency • High-Performing Buildings • Indoor Environment Quality • Intelligent Buildings (*Archispeak*) • Thermal Comfort**

Further sources: Designing Buildings Wiki; WBDG

Building Information Modeling   ▌

If you want to survive, you're going to change; if you don't, you're going to perish. —Thom Mayne, FAIA

However beautiful the strategy, you should occasionally look at the results. —Winston Churchill

Since the evolution of two-dimensional computer-aided design (CAD) in the last century, the design and construction process has now evolved to using three-dimensional modeling technology to design, communicate and review building information with *Building Information Modeling (BIM)*. Innovative 3-D modeling, virtual reality technology, and data management have improved communication among the disciplines to achieve better environmental, financial, and resource efficiency.

The visual expression of *BIM* allows all integrated design partners from key building development disciplines, including design, financial, fabrication, manufacturing, and construction installation to freely exchange simulated design information to detect incompatible and conflicting design strategies by looking at the results, as Churchill warns above. This can eliminate costly errors, reduce requests for information (RFIs), speed time to project completion, reduce litigation, and enhance the efficiency of the project.

Firms use *BIM* to optimize solutions by testing applications and simulations, such as daylight, glare, thermal, and computational fluid dynamics, which studies the efficient flows of heating, ventilating, and air conditioning. As stated by Thom Mayne above, using *BIM* has been a necessity for architecture firms to analyze and coordinate their designs, if they are going to be successful. Building Performance Analysis (BPA) is used for issues such as climate, energy loads, sun and shadow studies, solar loads, wind loads, and lighting. These *BIM* visualized design iterations can manipulate the building volume, orientation, shape, openings, structure, façade materials, and innovative technologies for maximum operational, resource, and environmental efficiency, as well as occupant comfort and owner profitability throughout the design. Modeling early and often is key to streamlining efficiencies.

The handling of complex high-performing green building projects requires the use of *Building Information Modeling* along with plug-ins for additional modeling, complex specifications, and tracking during the construction process. *BIM* can provide the documentation needed for green building certifications, codes, and standards, such as data on construction waste management, indoor air quality during and after construction, erosion control, recycled materials, material emissions, daylight simulations, energy modeling and life-cycle assessment of building systems.

Building Information Modeling allows faster collaborative decision-making; 3-D visualization allows rapid simulations within an integrated system; compliance with global environmental, engineering, architectural, and material standards; and delivers high-performing projects more quickly, profitably, and sustainably.

See also: **BIM (*Theoryspeak*) • Energy Modeling • Feedback (*Archispeak*) • Integrated Design • Life-Cycle Assessment • Parametric Design (*Theoryspeak*)**

Further sources: AIA.org; Autodesk; Kibert (2016: 567)

▌Building Orientation

Now in houses with a south aspect, the sun's rays penetrate into the porticos in winter, but in the summer the path of the sun is right over our heads and above the roof so that there is shade. If then, this is the best arrangement, we should build the south side loftier to get the winter sun and the north side lower to keep out the winter winds.
—Socrates, 470–399 BC

The historic precedents of how living things have adapted to the specifics of climate, place, and nature, can provide valuable information for energy-efficient building design. Ancient civilizations developed in tune with nature to heat, cool and light buildings, as noted by Socrates twenty-four hundred years ago. Buildings are again taking advantage of free sunlight and wind for daylighting, passive solar heating, passive cooling, and ventilation. The use of energy conservation, along with passive design in tandem with active building systems, is critical to the goal of achieving net zero-carbon buildings.

High-performing buildings use whole systems thinking early in the design process to integrate the building programmatic elements with the site, context, and microclimate opportunities and constraints. *Building orientation* is situating the building on the site in a manner sensitive to its context while maximizing all free benefits of nature: solar heat, daylighting, wind, topography, thermal mass, rain, views, and vegetation. The Yin-Yang House in California by Brooks + Scarpa Architects is a net-zero live/work home and office that uses *building orientation* to maximize passive design strategies. Designed to be only a single room deep to provide natural light and ample ventilation to all rooms, the house takes advantage of the mild climate to use passive cooling strategies with cross-ventilation and a thermal chimney (Figures 11, 44).

In the Northern Hemisphere, most passive building designs orient the major axis running east-west to take advantage of the daily and seasonal solar path. Deep horizontal overhangs or porticos on the south elevation can block the high-angle summer sun from hitting the building envelope. South-facing glazing allows low-angle winter sun in for solar gain, and with a material of high thermal mass, such as concrete, can store this heat until distributed with natural heat flow. In this orientation, east-west elevations have less heat exposure, but require both horizontal and vertical shading devices to reduce heat gain from the rising and setting sun. North-facing windows should be smaller or highly insulated in northern latitudes to minimize heat loss and cold north wind infiltration. In southern latitudes, larger north-facing glazing can be used if shielded from summer western and high overhead solar radiation.

Proper *building orientation* can enhance passive solar heating opportunities to maximize solar gain while minimizing conductance, and passive cooling to remove or reject heat to maintain cool temperatures. Passive cooling can also be achieved by orienting for natural ventilation with natural heat flows and using prevailing winds to reduce mechanical cooling, as with solar chimneys and wind towers.

Proper *building orientation* is also important for integrating active systems, such as wind turbines, and south-facing photovoltaics (PV), whether they are building-integrated or stand-alone arrays, and solar thermal. The climatic, site and orientation opportunities and constraints must all be evaluated as to how they relate to energy use and energy flow through the site. The sustainable goal should be to incorporate any free energy available by proper *building orientation* and massing on the site.

See also: **Envelope Driven Design • Climate-Responsive Design • Building-Integrated Photovoltaics • Natural Ventilation • Passive Cooling • Passive Design • Passive Solar Heating • Photovoltaics • Stack Ventilation**

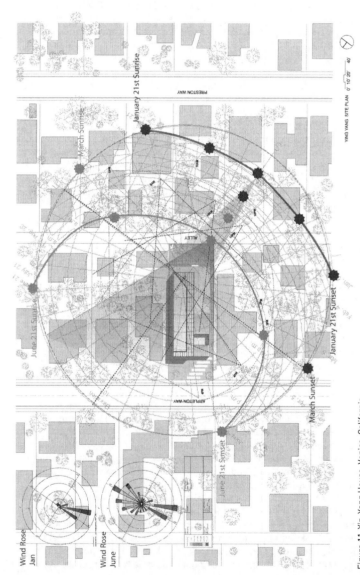

Figure 11 Yin-Yang House, Venice, California
Courtesy ©Brooks + Scarpa Architects

Further sources: EBN; Hootman (2012: 217); Iyengar (2015); Olgyay (1963); WBDG

Building Science   **I**

Our science is a drop, our ignorance a sea. —William James 1895

We live at a time when emotions and feelings count more than truth, and there is a vast ignorance of science. —James Lovelock

Contemporary *building science* is an integrated collection of architectural and engineering technical knowledge, including physics, chemistry, and the life sciences, and even as William James and James Lovelock implied above, there is so much more we have to learn. Essential to the success of high-performing buildings, *building science* technology uses the physical behavior of the buildings interrelated systems to increase energy efficiency, human comfort and health, indoor air quality, safety, durability, and the performance of the entire building. Building performance is the level of service provided, relative to the predetermined quality of service expected. This systems-thinking approach is concerned with the full life-cycle of the building in modeling, analyzing, and modifying these systems through the phases of planning, design, construction, commissioning, and facilities management.

Science is part of the reality of living; it is the what, the how, and the why of everything in our experience. —Rachel Carson, acceptance speech National Book Award, *The Sea Around Us* 1950

As innovative technological strategies increasingly became a part of architectural expression, building science evolved as a whole-systems thinking concept. As Rachel Carson notes that science is everything in our experience, this is particularly relevant to how we design our built environments for efficiency and health. Advanced building practices today rely on applying scientific methods and modeling for analysis and enhancement. Past inappropriate traditional building methods relied on generations-old precedents, which did not advance high-performing buildings.

With the highly specific character of current building science, it is important to properly integrate the many innovative materials and component assemblies to achieve a well-performing building. Most performance issues involve the skin of the building or enclosure, which most importantly comprises the control of the passive environmental system. In moderating outside climate and weather for the indoor environment atmosphere, the building enclosure system must resolve the major forces affecting the building atmosphere. These primary forces are the conductive, convective and radiative flow of heat; the airflow due to air leakage and ventilation; the flow of water and vapor; and the insulation impact of enclosure components on solar radiation.

Building science focuses primarily on the design, selection, and arrangement of materials and component assemblies of the building enclosure, or skin, which are vital to long-term performance. Other *building science* elements considered are the occupant's comfort; the building services, such as mechanical/electrical systems; the site and services; and the outside environment's weather and microclimate. Coordinating all these elements is essential to achieving high-performing buildings.

See also: **Envelope Driven Design • High-Performing Buildings • Passive Design • Systems Thinking • Whole Building Design**

Further sources: Carson (1950); EBN; Inhabit; National Institute of Building Sciences; WBDG

Building-Integrated Photovoltaics

We need to bring sustainable energy to every corner of the globe with technologies like solar energy mini-grids, solar powered lights, and wind turbines. —Ban Ki-moon, former UN Secretary-General

Photovoltaic (PV) systems are one of the best ways to harness clean and abundant solar power. PV systems use semiconductor materials to make electricity out of sunlight, with no pollution, no depletion of resources, and minimal maintenance, and need to be available everywhere along with wind energy, as stressed by Ban Ki-moon above. *Building-integrated photovoltaic (BIPV)* systems integrate photovoltaics into the building envelope, serving the dual function of replacing conventional building materials, and generating electricity. By avoiding the costs of conventional materials, the life-cycle costs of the photovoltaic system can be improved.

Integrating photovoltaic modules into the building envelope is growing worldwide with creative design methods of generating solar electricity, some referred to as "Solar Electric Architecture." Typically *building-integrated photovoltaic* systems are planned during the architectural design phase and are incorporated during initial construction, whereas systems designed for retrofits are called building-added PV (BAPV).

Rigid photovoltaic cells, made of silicon, usually combine in a series in a photovoltaic panel that combines with other panels to form a PV array. Thin-film solar cells use micro-thin layers of solid-state materials that form a semi-flexible PV application. These thin-film solar cells are printed on materials using solar dyes integrated with conductive plastics, which can be for *building-integrated PV* on brise-soleil, glass panels, or PV peel-and-stick membranes for metal roofing. Thin-film solar cells currently have low efficiencies and need almost twice the area required, but typically cost less.

Design consideration must be given to the building occupants' needs, such as views and daylighting, along with the energy efficiency of *BIPV*. *Building-integrated PV* systems are incorporated into façades, rooftops, and glazing applications. The Bosch Siemens Centre at Park 20|20 in the Netherlands by William McDonough+Partners uses a *building-integrated PV* glass atrium roof along with living green walls to maximize energy, daylighting, and fresh air for the occupants' well-being (Figures 12, 48, 69).

Figure 12 BIPV atrium and vegetated walls, Bosch Siemens Centre, Netherlands
Photo: Van der Torren Fotografie. Courtesy ©William McDonough+Partners

For the façade, PV can replace glass windows with crystalline or semi-transparent thin-film solar panels. Vertical building surfaces have less access to direct sunlight but often offer a larger surface area. For the roof, PV material can replace roofing material with solar shingles, laminated solar rooftop skylights, or thin-film membranes. Ultra-thin solar cells may be used to produce semi-transparent surfaces, such as skylights, roof monitors, greenhouses, or glazing, allowing daylighting and views for the occupants, while generating electricity.

See also: **Carbon Footprint • Energy Efficiency • Green Building • High-Performing Buildings • Life-Cycle Cost Analysis • Net- Zero Energy Building Certification • Photovoltaics • Renewable Energy • Solar Energy • Zero-Energy Building**

Further sources: ASES; Autodesk; EBN; RMI; SEIA; US DOE; US EPA; WBDG

Built Environment   ▮

It is clear that transforming our world for the better means transforming our towns and cities. That means better urban governance, planning, and design. —Ban Ki-Moon, former UN Secretary-General, UN-Habitat III

We create our buildings and then they create us. Likewise, we construct our circle of friends and our communities and then they construct us. —Frank Lloyd Wright

The *built environment* is considered the human-made surroundings where people gather to live, work, and play. It includes the physical structures where human activities take place, and the supporting infra- structures needed to support these activities, such as transportation, utility, and communication networks. The *built environment* is a spatial, material, and cultural result of human will and creative imagination that shapes and defines our lives as reiterated by both Ban Ki-moon and Frank Lloyd Wright. Over time, people modify these spaces to fit their physical needs, cultural heritage, spiritual desires, or sense of place.

The *built environment* has a tremendous impact on the health and well-being of people. The suitability of an individual's built surround- ings is determined by the quality of the settings' structures, forms, and intended functions, as well as available natural environmental assets. The *built environment*, no matter how big or small, puts pressure on limited natural resources, through the consumption of land, water, and energy, as well as the build-up of wastes and pollution.

The *built environment* should be understood as an interrelated whole, where synergies create improvements in community well-being. Many collaborative fields, such as public policy, health, design, engineering, planning, and environmental expertise address the critical relation- ships needed for the design, construction, management, and use of these built surroundings.

The major challenge facing most *built environments* is population growth, which can lead to higher densities, lack of open space, conges- tion, mental stress, poor access to healthy food, and stresses on the cit- ies' natural assets, as well as increased demand for water, energy, and waste disposal. The natural assets of cities can be open spaces, public parks, green spaces, water flows, and fresh air. Cities now contain over half of the world's population, and with the population to increase by at least two billion by 2050, this is expected to increase to over 70% urban dwellers (UN 2014). China is projected to construct the equivalent of the current built environment of all Central and South America by 2030, according to the World Bank.

However, an increasing population need not result in a less efficient or less livable environment. Sound policies, sustainable development vision, inspirational urban planning, context appreciation, smart sys- tems, and innovative leadership for change can mitigate the effects of population pressures, and result in more resilient cities that promote well-being, health, and continuing prosperity.

See also: **Embodied Carbon • Embodied Energy • Materials and Resources • Smart Growth • Sustainable Development • Urban Design • WELL Building Standard**

Further sources: UN New Urban Agenda; UN World Urbanization Pros- pects; World Bank

Carbon Footprint   ∎

Carbon footprint: the amount of carbon dioxide or other carbon compounds emitted into the atmosphere by the activities of an individual, company, country, etc. —Free Dictionary

Human activity is putting such a strain on the natural function of the Earth that the ability of the planet's ecosystems to sustain future generations can no longer be taken for granted. —UN 2000 Millennium Ecosystem Assessment

Since ancient times, carbon has been known as coal, charcoal, and peat, and derives from Latin for charcoal, "carbo." Carbon forms very strong bonds to itself and is resistant to chemical harm, and all living cells contain carbon atoms. Most food is comprised of carbon compounds, and 23% of the human body is carbon. Huge amounts of carbon are extracted from Earth and burned as fossil fuels for energy generation. These increase carbon dioxide (CO_2) levels in the atmosphere, contributing to the greenhouse effect, which results in disastrous global warming and adverse health and environmental impacts. CO_2 lingers in the air for about 100 years before breaking down, so the global heating this year is accountable to the last century of emissions.

Carbon footprint is a measure of carbon dioxide (CO_2) emissions from fossil fuel use for a particular period, by individual daily activities, or a product's manufacture and transportation. *Carbon footprint* is converted into the naturally productive land areas needed to sequester the CO_2 emissions and is expressed in metric tons of CO_2 released per year. The *carbon footprint* is usually added to ecological footprint calculations, as it is a competing use of biologically productive space or land. Americans generate about 150 pounds of CO_2 per day, which is more than twice the European average, and approximately five times the global average. Our primary CO_2 emission sources are solid fuels, such as coal (35%), liquid fuels as oil or petroleum (36%), and gaseous fuels as natural gas (20%). Heating, cooling, lighting, water treatment, and transportation account for most of these emissions, along with 5% from deforestation, which increases CO_2 emissions by decreasing the CO_2 sequestration achieved by forests. As stated by the UN Millennium Ecosystem Assessment, these practices are unsustainable for our planet's ecosystems.

Carbon footprint measuring and accountability are critical to attaining the goals of economic, social and environmentally sustainable development, as it is projected we need to reduce our carbon footprint by at least 80% to reverse global warming (Biello 2009).

See also: **Climate Change • Ecological Footprint • Embodied Carbon • Embodied Energy • Energy Efficiency • Fossil Fuels • Greenhouse Gases**

Further sources: Biello (2009); Encyclopedia of Human Thermodynamics, www.eoht.info/page/Element; Kibert et al. (2012: 63); NASA; IPCC; UCSI

Carbon Price

Some solutions are relatively simple and would provide economic benefits; implementing measures to conserve energy, putting a price on carbon through taxes and cap-and-trade and shifting from fossil fuels to clean and renewable energy sources. —David Suzuki

Economists consider climate change to be a market failure, as it imposes risks and enormous costs on those in the future that will suffer the consequences, and these future risks and expenses are not reflected in today's market prices. As David Suzuki proposes above, the world needs to assume the costs of the future harm to the planet by putting a price on the particular cause of this future damage, namely carbon emissions. A *carbon price* is a price that must be paid to emit one ton of CO_2 into the atmosphere and is thought by many to be the most effective way for countries to reduce their carbon emissions.

In placing a price on carbon, the costs of stopping climate change would be distributed currently and through generations rather than being an overwhelming burden for future generations only. It would also encourage lower-carbon behavior while increasing finances for carbon-free technology research and the cleanup of current polluting activities.

Carbon pricing can be established by either a carbon tax or emissions trading system (ETS), sometimes called cap-and-trade, both with the goal of greenhouse gas reductions. A government can charge a carbon tax on the distribution, sale, or use of the carbon content of fossil fuels, which raises the price of the fuels and the services dependent on them, encouraging greener production and less carbon-intensive activities. The government revenues from a carbon tax can be reinvested or distributed back to the people, as in the fee-and-dividend model. The second method is an emissions trading system (ETS), or cap-and-trade, which sets in advance a quota, or cap, on the total allowable emissions for a country. Each country within its emissions budget has eligible "permits to pollute" that can be auctioned or traded within companies. This creates a "market for pollution" that should keep carbon emissions down due to the added financial burden. The key is setting a high enough *carbon price* for either the carbon tax or ETS to encourage polluters to cut greenhouse gas emissions.

Many countries have targets to reduce carbon emissions; the U.K. aims to reduce carbon emissions from 1990 levels by 80% by 2050. Many EU companies pay a small *carbon price* through the EU's emission trading scheme. Legislators in the U.S. recently proposed a carbon tax with a fee-and-dividend system, but also propose doing away with federal regulations limiting CO_2 emissions. The imperative of a uniform *carbon price* worldwide makes good sense, since a ton of carbon dioxide emitted does the same amount of climate change damage over time and globally, regardless of where on Earth it is emitted.

See also: **Carbon Footprint • Climate Change • Embodied Carbon • Global Warming • Greenhouse Gases**

Further sources: BuildingGreen; Energy and Climate Intelligence Unit, eciu.net/briefings/uk-energy-policies-and-prices/how-is-the-uk-tackling-climate-change; World Bank; US EPA

Carbon-Neutral   ∎

We are all part of the solution. Whether you are an individual, a business, an organization, or a government, there are many steps you can take to reduce your climate footprint. It is a message we all must take to heart. —Ban Ki-moon, former UN Secretary-General, *Kick the Habit*

The world needs to make tremendous reductions this century in our greenhouse gas emissions in order to minimize the dangerous and irreversible impacts to our climate system. Individuals, organizations, and governments can voluntarily reduce their demand for energy and can purchase carbon offsets to balance out their emissions. Ban Ki-moon in *Kick the Habit* calls for us all to be a part of the solution in reducing our climate footprint, which is the same as reducing our carbon footprint to prevent increasing climate change dangers.

To be *carbon-neutral* is to first calculate the total amount of climate-damaging carbon dioxide or other carbon compounds released into the atmosphere by one's activities and lifestyle, such as driving, flying or eating out; then try to reduce these emissions if possible, and then balance out these remaining emissions with equal sequestration or carbon offsets purchased from a third party. An individual or group must have a balanced zero-carbon footprint to be entirely *carbon-neutral*. An excellent example of *carbon-neutrality* is the Kubala Washatko Architects' Aldo Leopold Foundation's Legacy Center in Baraboo, Wisconsin. The Center is a LEED Platinum, net-zero energy, and carbon-neutral building by producing over 110% of its annual energy needs. This design honors Leopold's *Land Ethic* philosophy that conservation measures should include soils, water, plants, as well as animals (Figure 13).

The term "climate-neutral" has become more relevant in some ways than *carbon-neutral*, as the focus has shifted to the broader impacts of global climate change as opposed to just global warming. Carbon dioxide (CO_2) makes up 65% of the world's greenhouse gases, but nitrous oxide, hydrofluorocarbons, perfluorocarbons, sulfur hexafluoride, and methane are the five other major gases. All six greenhouse gases were to be limited by the international Kyoto Protocol climate treaty.

The initial step in attempting to live a *climate-neutral* lifestyle is to calculate one's energy usage and then make improvements over time. Climate footprint and carbon footprint calculators can help track information and suggest improvements, such as energy and water use, driving habits, public transit use, diet, recycling, composting, reuse, waste, and other lifestyle habits. For carbon emissions that cannot be eliminated, carbon offsets can be purchased or measures can be taken to sequester carbon, such as planting trees. Carbon offsets are emission reduction credits purchased from a third-party organization to make up for an emission made elsewhere, such as purchasing credits from a renewable energy utility.

Figure 13 Carbon-neutral Aldo Leopold Legacy Center, Wisconsin
Courtesy ©The Kubala Washatko Architects, Inc.

According to the UN Environment Programme's publication, *Kick the Habit: A U.N. Guide to Climate Neutrality*, for individuals emissions less than 50% are "direct emissions" such as from driving or flying, and about 20% are from the production, use, and disposal of things we use. About 25% is to power workplaces; and 10% come from maintaining public foundational frameworks, such as roads, bridges, water supplies, treatment, and electric distribution (Kirby and UN Environment Programme 2008).

See also: **Carbon Footprint • Carbon Price • Climate Change • Ecological Footprint • Factor 4 and Factor 10 • Greenhouse Gases • Kyoto Protocol • Land Ethic • Methane • Montreal Protocol**

Further sources: IPCC (2014), www.ipcc.ch/report/ar5/wg3/; Earth Lab; UC Berkeley Consumer Footprint Calculator; Kirby and UN Environment Programme

Carrying Capacity

It would take 1.5 Earths to sustain our present level of consumption. Environmentally, the Earth is in an overshoot mode. —Lester Brown (2011), *World on the Edge*

Earth exceeded its carrying capacity of one billion at the time of the civil war. You can temporarily exceed the carrying capacity, but not indefinitely. —William R. Catton Jr., environmental sociologist

Carrying capacity is defined as the largest number of individuals or living things that can be supported indefinitely in a given area with the available food, land, water, and other necessities within natural resource limits. This includes not damaging the current natural social, cultural and economic environment for those living in the present or for future generations. As the world population continues to grow, and increasing pressures are put on an area, its environment becomes degraded, the *carrying capacity* shrinks, allowing fewer and fewer species to live sustainably and as has William Catton stated above, we already exceeded the Earth's capacity over 150 years ago.

Our ecological footprint, the demands an individual or community places on our environment, is tied to the *carrying capacity* of an area. As our ecological footprint increases and with growing population, the carrying capacity of the land shrinks. As Lester Brown indicates above, we are already in overshoot and it would take one and a half Earths to satisfy our current level of consumption. According to the World Wildlife Fund 2016 Living Planet Report, the worldwide average of productive land area per person is approximately 1.8 global hectares (gha). The average American's footprint (including land, water, food, energy, and wastes) is about 9 gha, while China's is only 1.8 gha.

With the negative consequences of population growth, resource degradation, and societal and technological changes, the *carrying capacity* of an area usually declines, as in overfishing by industrialized fleets, chainsaws accelerating rapid deforestation, and earth movers clearcutting land for suburban sprawl. An example was the 1845 potato fungus in Ireland, which resulted in over a million deaths, and over three million people emigrating to other countries. On the other hand, the *carrying capacity* of an area can increase with a favorable climate, improved energy and agricultural management, advanced medical control of diseases, and technology enhancements such as fertilizers, fish farming, and land reclamation.

See also: **Ecological Footprint • Population Growth**

Further sources: Brown (2011: 7);Hardin (1968); Carrying Capacity Network; WWF: 2016 Living Planet Report, www.worldwildlife.org/pages/living-planet-report-2016

Certified Wood

When one tugs at a single thing in nature, he finds it attached to the rest of the world. —John Muir

Certified wood is grown in and harvested from sustainably managed forests, which show both environmental and socially responsible practices in forest operations. Third-party forest auditors certify compliance with the accepted practices and standards of good responsible forest management. As John Muir states above, all these practices—such as protection of biodiversity and wildlife habitat, protection of watersheds and water quality, sustainable harvesting levels, and prompt reforestation—are interrelated.

After a forest is certified as complying with accepted sustainable management practices, then when the forest is timbered, the chain of custody documentation or paper trail of the wood, tracks the lumber. Chain of custody (CoC) certifications track the timber products from the certified forest, through the processing and manufacturing of the wood product, to the final point of purchase. The largest international *certified wood* programs are Forest Stewardship Council (FSC) and Programme for the Endorsement of Forest Certification (PEFC). In the U.S., the primary certifications are FSC, Sustainable Forestry Initiative (SFI), and the American Tree Farm System (ATFS). The first ban in the world on trading illegally sourced wood products was the U.S. Lacey Act of 1990, which banned trafficking in illegal wildlife and was amended in 2008 to include plants and plant products such as timber and paper.

The SUNY College of Environmental Science and Forestry's Gateway Center by Architerra Architects, is an energy-positive LEED Platinum bioclimatic design that uses eight species of FSC-*certified wood* serving as a teaching tool for research and public education (Figures 14, 30).

Figure 14 FSC-certified wood in SUNY ESF Gateway Center
©David Lamb Photography. Courtesy Architerra Inc., Architects

The forest certification movement started in Germany in 1993 and since has grown rapidly with collaboration between concerned consumers and timber production corporations wanting socially responsible branding. While recognizing the importance of legal wood and chain of custody sources, *certified wood* and forest certification have long been lightning rods between ASHRAE Standard 189.1, ASTM-07612-10, and International Green Construction Code (IgCC), as well as green building rating systems, such as LEED, Living Building Challenge, and Green Globes. The USGBC now takes *certified wood* from SFI and ATFS now, whereas for years the only certified wood allowed was FSC.

See also: **Deforestation • Forest Stewardship Council • Forest Sustainable Management • Materials and Resources**

Further sources: EBN; Diamond (2005: 469–478); FAO; WBDG

▌Charrette

An intensive workshop in which various stakeholders and experts are brought together to address a particular design issue, from a

single building to an entire campus, installation, or park. —Whole Building Design Guide

In all of my travels around the world, the important decisions were made where people sat in a circle, facing each other as equals. —Dan West, Heifer International founder

The French word *charrette* refers to the "cart" that would be circulated at the project deadline to pick up the final frantically finished drawings by architecture students at the École des Beaux-Arts in Paris during the 19th century. Over time, the term has come to refer to short, creative, concentrated work sessions, usually by design students or firms. It draws on the method that artists and architects have used for centuries, that to become totally immersed in a problem for an uninterrupted period, usually a few days, is the best way to break through to a creative solution.

Even though short, intense work sessions have been used by planning and design teams for years, in the 1990s the use of *charrettes* became an essential part of the integrated design process, bringing all interested parties together, usually with a focus on sustainability, and as Dan West indicates above that is where the most important decisions are made. Now sustainable and green strategies are entirely integrated into the entire whole building design process, so as not to be a separate topic, marginalized or value-engineered out.

Bringing together a team with different roles and interests to collaborate creatively helps break down barriers and move toward innovative solutions. These charrettes usually include a facilitator, the owner, architect, consultants, contractors, landscape architects, commissioning agents, etc., as well as collaborative community involvement. A productive team-oriented *charrette* is usually able to distinguish and integrate green strategies in a built project, saving time and money, and that also minimizes life-cycle costs, reduces resource consumption, and increases environmental performance and health.

See also: **Charette (*Archispeak*) • Integrated Design • Whole Building Design**

Further sources: EBN; WBDG

Chilled Beams ∎

Chilled beams are energy efficient systems that combine radiant cooling and ventilation. —www.treehugger.com

A *chilled beam* is a unique air distribution system with an integral water-cooled heat exchanger coil installed typically in ceiling-mounted fixtures, to provide sensible cooling and heating. Primarily used in commercial environments, and more often used in Europe, *chilled beams* eliminate excess fan energy and dependence on reheated air by acting as a radiator chilled by recirculating water. Warm air naturally rises in the space, is cooled by the *chilled beam* coil at the ceiling, the cooled air then drops

NEW MEZZANINE
MECHANICAL DISTRIBUTION
CIRCULATION
DISPLAY
MEETING SPACE

REPLACE EXISTING SKYLIGHT
WITH HIGH-PERFORMANCE
GLAZING

OCCUPANCY CONTROLLED
SUN-SHADE

NEW SIPS ROOF PANELS (R-30)

NEW VISION GLAZING

RE-OPEN ORIGINAL
WINDOWS FOR DAYLIGHT

NEW WALL INSULATION (R-20)

WORKROOMS / PERIMETER RADIANT HEATING
ACTIVE CHILLED BEAMS / DIRECT OUTDOOR AIR SYSTEM
LED LIGHTING

ATRIUM
PASSIVE CHILLED BEAMS / DEDICATED OUTDOOR AIR SYSTEM
LED LIGHTING

Figure 15 Center for Building Energy Science & Engineering chilled beams, Philadelphia
Courtesy ©KieranTimberlake

back to the floor, creating a pressure drop behind it that draws more warm air through the chilled coil, and the convective cycle begins again. Effectively taking advantage of water's thermal ability to store and transport energy more efficiently than air, *chilled beams* also minimize fan use, as it is more efficient to pump water than it is to blow air.

Chilled beams come in variations of passive, active, and integrated/ multi-service beams. Passive and active beams primarily differ by the way airflow and fresh air is brought into the occupied space. Multi-service beams are less common and might include lighting, sprinklers, and speakers, etc. Active *chilled beams*, used for cooling, heating, and ventilation, have ventilation air supplied to the pressurized plenum by ductwork from a central air-handling system. Passive *chilled beams* used for cooling, are not ducted, do not provide primary air, and do not use fans to move the air across the coil. Passive systems depend on inducted air being pulled across the cooling coil by natural gravitational forces and the buoyancy of warm air. Sensors and smart controls might be considered in very moist environments, primarily when using natural ventilation, due to possible condensation issues.

The Consortium for Building Energy Innovation (CBEI) in Philadelphia works to develop means to reduce the energy usage of commercial buildings by 20% by 2020. As a retrofit headquarters, the Center for Building Energy Science & Engineering by KieranTimberlake Architects achieves a high level of sustainability as a living laboratory to demonstrate advanced retrofit technology. It showcases a decentralized mechanical strategy using groundwater-sourced heat pumps with energy recovery wheels, along with *chilled beams* (Figures 15, 31, 32).

Benefits of using *chilled beams* are potential reductions in initial equipment and construction material costs, space and retrofit adaptability, increased occupant comfort, quiet operation, simple maintenance, and—most significantly—energy efficiency.

See also: **Energy Efficiency • Natural Ventilation • Stack Ventilation • Thermal Comfort**

Further sources: EBN; Buildings.com; WBDG

Chlorofluorocarbons   **I**

Any of several simple gaseous compounds that contain carbon, chlorine, fluorine, and sometimes hydrogen that are used as refrigerants, cleaning solvents, and aerosol propellants and in the manufacture of plastic foams, and that are believed to be a major cause of stratospheric ozone depletion. —Merriam-Webster Dictionary

Chlorofluorocarbons (*CFCs*) are a group of manufactured, colorless, odorless, and non-toxic chemical compounds, including Freon, that are classified as halocarbons, compounds that contain carbon and halogen atoms. Freon became the preferred coolant in refrigerant and air conditioning systems in the mid-1930s, and after World

War II *chlorofluorocarbons* were also used as propellants for aerosol bug sprays, cosmetic products, and paints. *CFCs* can last more than 100 years and are safe and inert in our lower atmosphere, but when they reach the upper atmosphere or the stratosphere, they break apart and release chlorine atoms. When a chlorofluorocarbon molecule reaches our 21-mile deep stratosphere above our lower troposphere, it can hang around for a hundred years, and the chlorine within the molecule can destroy tens of thousands of ozone molecules.

In 1974 a group of scientists raised the alarm, showing that chlorofluorocarbons could be the primary source of the chlorine in our stratosphere that was destroying the protective ozone layer. Ozone absorbs harmful ultraviolet radiation, so a loss of stratospheric ozone results in more harmful ultraviolet-B (UV-B) radiation reaching the Earth's surface. UV-B radiation damages plants and animals, especially humans, causing cancers, cataracts, and weakened immune systems.

In response to this research, governments signed the 1987 Montreal Protocol phasing out almost 100 ozone-depleting substances (ODSs) and achieved one of the most effective global environmental agreements ever reached. *Chlorofluorocarbons* are also potent greenhouse gases, so the Montreal Protocol has been credited with being five times more effective than the Kyoto Protocol, the main climate treaty until the Paris Agreement, in reducing climate change. The 1995 Nobel Prize in Chemistry was awarded to the scientists F. Sherwood Rowland, Mario J. Molina and Paul J. Crutzen, for their work in atmospheric chemistry, in particular, the decomposition of ozone by *chlorofluorocarbons*.

The alternatives that replaced *CFCs* are the less harmful hydrochlorofluorocarbons (HCFCs), but they are not entirely ozone-friendly, and hydrofluorocarbons (HFCs) that contain no chlorine and are safer, but both chemicals are potent greenhouse gases contributing to climate change. In 2007, the Protocol's signing parties agreed to phase out HCFCs, and in November 2015, all 197 signing parties to the Montreal Protocol on Substances That Deplete the Ozone Layer also agreed on a Dubai Pathway for controlling the climate change inducing hydrofluorocarbons (HFCs).

See also: **Climate Change • Global Warming • Kyoto Protocol • Montreal Protocol • Ozone Depletion**

Further sources: Earth Journalism; NASA; NOAA

▌Circular Economy

Using less of the Earth's resources more efficiently and productively in a circular economy and making the transition from carbon-based fuels to renewable energies are defining features of the emerging economic paradigm. In the new era, we can each become a node in the nervous system of the biosphere. —Jeremy Rifkin, economist

The economy can be defined as the careful management of the wealth and resources of a community. The traditional linear economy of "take, make, waste" is reaching its limits by relying on enormous quantities of easily accessible cheap energy and materials. The current supply chain follows the reduce, reuse, recycle concept, but this is still a waste hierarchy relying on finite resources and the ecosystem's limited ability to break down wastes.

The idea of a *circular economy* aims for the sustainable use and protection of material resource efficiencies by engineering everything to be continuously reused or recycled. Every aspect of design, manufacturing, retail, reusing and recycling would require rethinking to be restorative and regenerative by design. With the massive amounts of waste from irresponsible manufacturing, disposable lifestyles, volatile prices, and increasing geopolitical tensions with the scarcity of resources, a *circular economy* can help stabilize these problems by decoupling economic growth from natural resource consumption. There would be tremendous economic advantages for businesses adopting the *circular economy* concept, as well as transitioning to renewable energies as indicated by economist Jeremy Rifkin above.

The Ellen MacArthur Foundation (2013), in *Towards the Circular Economy*, lists three driving principles of a *circular economy*: the preservation and enhancement of natural capital, the optimization of resource yields, and the fostering of system effectiveness. In enhancing natural capital, finite sources and renewable resource flows need to be controlled by dematerializing what we use. Extending product life can optimize resource yields, and improve reuse by always keeping the highest quality of product usefulness.

Recycling is a limited solution, as remanufacturing is energy intensive and results in products that are downgraded from their original quality, leading to the continuing demand for virgin resources. In an ideal *circular economy*, wastes and toxins would be "designed out," allowing materials to be used over and over with high quality.

The European Union adopted a Circular Economy Package in December 2015 setting challenging waste targets of bans on sending wood, plastics, textiles, and food to landfills. The goal is to generate the maximum value and use from all the raw materials, products, and waste, creating energy savings and thereby reducing greenhouse gas emissions. The German Resource Efficiency Program (ProgRess) and Toronto's Tool Library, as well as the progressive material assessment standards, such as Cradle-to-Cradle and the Living Product Challenge, are all examples of innovative resource rethinking.

The *circular economy* comes down to matching existing material waste streams with new applications. Sharing information, optimizing resources use, closed-looping, and exchanging both materials and information will be needed for industries to reduce the environmental damage from natural resource extractions.

See also: **Closed-Loop Supply Chain • Cradle-to-Cradle • Green Economy • Materials and Resources**

Further sources: Ellen MacArthur Foundation; European Union Law; Greenbiz; Rifkin (2011); Zbicinski, et al. (2006)

Climate Change

The rising world of waters dark and deep. —John Milton (1898), *Paradise Lost*

The emission of greenhouse gases . . . is causing global warming at a rate that began as significant, has become alarming and is simply unsustainable in the long term. And by long-term, I do not mean centuries ahead. I mean within the lifetime of my children certainly; and possibly within my own. And by unsustainable, I do not mean a phenomenon causing problems of adjustment. I mean a challenge so far-reaching in its impact and irreversible in its destructive power that it alters radically human existence. —Tony Blair (Sept. 15, 2004), *G8 Summit Climate Speech*

Due to the deterioration of our Earth's atmosphere, we face a global ecological crisis threatening all species and human civilization. *Climate change* will touch every aspect of our lives and economy, from work, transportation, manufacturing, farming, forests, and how we power our homes, schools, and factories, as so powerfully stated above by Tony Blair in his speech to the G8 Summit in 2004.

The National Oceanic and Atmospheric Administration (NOAA) describes *climate change* as "long-term (decades to centuries) changes in some environmental conditions for a given place and time—such as in temperature, rainfall, humidity, cloudiness, wind and air circulation patterns." As opposed to climate change, global warming is described only as an increase in the annually averaged air temperature near the Earth's surface.

The latest UN Intergovernmental Panel on Climate Change (IPCC) Report states that the increase in greenhouse gas emissions has been caused by human activities. Greenhouse gases, primarily emitted from burning fossil fuels, absorb the long-wave radiation that is reflected off the Earth's surface, and then re-emit this radiation back down to Earth, causing the atmosphere to warm as in the greenhouse effect.

Changes in climate are causing adverse impacts on sensitive human and natural systems on all continents and oceans, and vary considerably in both nature and severity depending on the location, altitude, latitude, and other regional factors. These changes have been linked to threatening weather and climate events, such as decreasing extremes in cold and warm temperatures, warming and acidification of the oceans, progressing extremely high sea levels, and an increasing frequency of heavy precipitation. As in John Milton's words from *Paradise Lost*, "the rising world of waters dark and deep" (Book 3, Line 11), so too will be the impact of rising sea levels on many population centers, especially those located near or surrounded by ocean water.

The 1997 Kyoto Protocol to the UN Framework Convention on Climate Change (UNFCCC) legally bound the agreeing countries to reduce anthropogenic greenhouse gas emissions by at least 5% below the 1990 levels, for a commitment period from 2008–2012. The defining greenhouse gas emissions were carbon dioxide, methane, nitrous oxide, hydrofluorocarbons, perfluorocarbons, and sulfur hexafluoride. In 2005, without the support of U.S. or Canada, the Kyoto Protocol was entered into force, and later in 2012 with the Doha Amendment, new commitments were established for the years 2013–2030.

The 2008 U.K. Climate Change Act was the first legally binding climate change framework by a country and aimed to cut emissions by at least 34% by 2020, and 80% by 2050, compared with 1990 levels. The later 2016 U.K. 5th carbon budget proposed a 57% emission cut by 2028–2032, which might cost 0.5% of their GDP, but many think this is still not enough to meet the Paris Climate targets.

The IPCC has stated the continuous emissions of greenhouse gases will continue to cause further warming and long-lasting changes in our climate system, increasing the chance of severe, persistent and most importantly, irreversible permanent impacts for civilization and our ecosystems.

In the COP21 Paris Agreement, a significant diplomatic effort signed on December 12, 2015, 196 countries agreed to reduce the risks of global temperature rise to below 2°C, even aiming for 1.4°C. Later at COP22 Marrakech in November 2016 working to implement the Paris agreements, the parties proclaimed the "extraordinary momentum on climate change worldwide is irreversible," and called for advancing full decarbonization of energy by 2040.

See also: **Greenhouse Gases • Global Warming • Intergovernmental Panel on Climate Change • Kyoto Protocol • Methane • Paris Climate Agreement**

Further sources: Blair (2004); CarbonBrief; Designing Buildings Wiki; IPCC; Milton (1898); https://www.climate.gov

Climate Responsive Design   **I**

Climate responsive architecture takes into consideration seasonality, the direction of the sun (sun path and solar position), natural shade provided by the surrounding topography, environmental factors (such as wind, rainfall, humidity) and climate data (temperature, historical weather patterns, etc.) to design comfortable and energy efficient homes. —Marni Evans, *Sustainable Businesses*

Climate responsive design was the norm throughout the early history of human habitation. The habitation of caves was in response to climate as well as the dangers posed by wild animals. The primitive hut was a product of a pragmatic design process that embraced the use of found materials fashioned together to respond to climate. However, as the primitive hut evolved into the iconic temple or classical architecture, it became tradition-based design. Eventually, classical architecture spread to regions with climates unsuited to the form. The Northern England climate has little in common with the climates of Athens or Rome. The design of buildings not suited to their climate was taken to another level with the emergence of the "International Style" in the first half of the 20th century. In the 1970s, the energy crisis briefly caused climate to reemerge as an important design consideration. However, it never became mainstream and largely died away in the postmodern architectural era of the 1980s. Since then, awareness of accelerating climate change is refueling the growth of *climate responsive design.*

Although early *climate responsive design* was largely passive, current climate responsive design is a combination of passive and active strategies, as indicated above by Marni Evans from her article *Steps to Climate Responsive Architecture.* Basic passive strategies include careful building orientation, proper window location and design, and the incorporation of the beneficial effects of landscape.

An excellent example of passive *climate responsive design* is the HOK-designed King Abdullah University of Science and Technology (KAUST) in Saudi Arabia, which is the world's largest LEED Platinum project at over 5.3 million square feet (496,000 sq. meters). Located in an extremely hot, humid climate, the design is rooted in the local Saudi culture by using compressed building layouts for shading, solar-powered wind towers, stack ventilation, shading screens (mashrabiya) creating dappled light, and—similarly to Arabic Bedouin tents—a monumental roof blocking the sun from the façades and courtyards (Figures 16, 43, 58, 75).

Figure 16 KAUST University, Saudi Arabia
Courtesy ©HOK

Active *climate responsive design* involves the use of building envelopes that are designed and finely tuned to the climate. Increasingly active climate responsive buildings employ integrated computer-based systems that are capable of sensing—and actively responding to—changing environmental conditions. Solar shading devices can now follow the sun and adjust to maintain desirable energy utilization levels and optimum glare avoidance.

The future of *climate responsive design* is very bright. High-performance building skins and real-time monitoring and control of whole building performance, combined with the ability to incorporate artificial intelligence capability to the response to changing microclimates, bodes well for the energy efficiency and sustainability of buildings. EO

See also: **Skin (*Archispeak*) • Smart Materials (*Archispeak*) • Passive Cooling • Passive Design • Passive Solar Heating • Responsive Design (*Theoryspeak*) • Wind Towers**

Further sources: Evans (2016); Olgyay (1963); Rudofsky, B. (1964)

Closed-Loop Supply Chain   ❚

Ideally, a zero-waste supply chain that completely reuses, recycles, or composts all materials. —Dictionary of Sustainable Management

Closed-loop supply is a resource-planning model that incorporates returned products as part of the supply chain. This maximizes the value created over the entire life-cycle of a product. There are several types of *closed-loop systems* related to sustainable design, such as closed-loop biomass, closed-loop cooling, closed-loop recycling, the circular economy, and closed-loop ecological systems.

In closed-loop manufacturing resource planning, the original manufacturer takes responsibility for the return loop process. Product returns can come from customers, as in take-back programs or from production and manufacturing byproducts or components. Closed-loop biomass refers to any organic material from a plant which is planted exclusively for use at a qualified biomass facility to create electricity.

In a closed-loop ecological system, the waste products produced by one species must be utilized by at least one other species and does not rely on matter exchange with any part outside the system. So if the goal is to maintain a life form such as a human, all the waste products (carbon dioxide, urine, and feces) must be eventually converted into oxygen, water, and food. This would be the goal of small human-made ecospheres, which would be self-contained, self-sustaining ecosystems, and could potentially be used as systems for life support during space flights and colonization.

See also: **Circular Economy • Cradle-to-Cradle • Life-Cycle Cost Analysis • Materials and Resources • Upcycling**

Further sources: Ellen MacArthur Foundation; EPA

Cogeneration   ❚

Just because something doesn't do what you planned it to do doesn't mean it's useless. —Thomas A. Edison

In the conventional generation of electricity, nearly two-thirds of the energy is wasted in the form of heat released to the atmosphere, while additional energy is then wasted in the distribution of electricity to the end users. *Cogeneration, or combined heat and power (CHP)*, is the simultaneous on-site generation of electricity and thermal energy in a single integrated system using the same fuel source. With cogeneration, an electric generating plant can capture the potentially wasteful heat to provide thermal energy that is useful, such as steam or hot water, for space heating, domestic water heating, or industrial processes. As implied by Thomas Edison earlier, if the energy generation were so efficient with no waste, there would be no need to capture what is released. *Cogeneration* can increase production efficiency, decrease fuel consumption, and with on-site generation preventing the losses from transmission and distribution, *cogeneration* can achieve efficiencies of over 80% rather than the 33% efficiency of a conventional fossil-fueled power plant.

Combined heat and power can be configured in two typical *cogeneration* systems, a topping or bottoming cycle. In a topping system, fuel can be combusted in a gas or steam turbine, reciprocating engine, microturbine, or fuel cell, which drives the overall system to generate electricity. A bottoming cycle system also called waste heat to power, fuel is combusted for thermal heat to a furnace or process, and the heat that is rejected is used for generating electricity. *Cogeneration* is used for commercial, municipal, and manufacturing processes, and is a valuable investment for reliable district energy use for multi-building sites, such as hospitals, airports, universities, and government complexes.

The advantage of *cogeneration* systems is they are not vulnerable to central power plant outages or transmission disruptions, as they are located on-site, independently fueled and operated, so can provide reliable critical power as needed, such as to hospitals. By using the fuel's energy twice, *combined heat and power or cogeneration systems* can reduce the emissions associated with conventional power plants by almost half. These harmful emissions of carbon dioxide and the air pollutants of nitrogen oxide, sulfur dioxide, and volatile organic particles can add to the environmental problems of acid rain, haze, water acidification, eutrophication, and climate change.

See also: **Energy Efficiency • Energy Recovery**

Further sources: US EPA; BuildingGreen; Whole Building Design

Commissioning

You cannot manage that which you do not measure. —Jack Welch, former CEO General Electric

The devil is in the details. —Idiom

Energy efficiency in green building design starts with strategies to reduce the overall energy needs, such as passive design measures, climate-appropriate materials, renewable energy, and high-efficiency systems. In high-performing buildings, *commissioning (Cx)* is an important systematic process by a third-party *commissioning* authority (CxA) to verify that the project meets the owner's requirements and functions as intended. The CxA, an independent agent representing only the owner's interests, tests all energy-related equipment and life-safety systems before occupancy to make sure everything works as intended. The involvement of a qualified *commissioning* authority early in the design process can help enhance the planning, coordination, and quality of construction; reduce change orders; reduce long-term energy costs; and long-term maintenance problems. During the construction phase, the *commissioning* team verifies the contractors correctly installed and programmed all the systems according to the owner's requirements and design intent. After occupancy, another benefit of *commissioning* is occupant comfort, health and well-being due to appropriate lighting, ventilation, and temperature controls. As Jack Welch implies above, you can't manage the efficiency of the systems or comfort of the occupants if you don't measure them.

Many sustainable and performance-based programs, standards, certifications, and codes require *commissioning*s, such as LEED, ASHRAE 90.1, and IgCC. *Commissioning* authorities can integrate *Cx* into the design process, view design drawings, inspect construction progress, test mechanical equipment performance, and train building staff by creating an Operations and Maintenance Plan (OMP) for the proper functioning of the equipment after the building is turned over.

A second step in the process is enhanced *commissioning*, which allows the commissioning authority to further verify the building's operation beyond occupancy, and to act as the owner's advocate in conducting in-depth reviews of any documents to verify equipment and materials were installed and operate as requested. Monitoring-based *commissioning* (MBCx) gives a continual stream of data and information to help identify any operational inconsistencies at the time of occurrence, allowing the owner and operators to quickly remedy any problems, saving time and money, and reducing energy waste.

Building envelope *commissioning* (BECx) is yet an even further step in validating a building's efficiency by testing and verifying its thermal envelope. Building envelope *commissioning* early in the design process can verify envelope performance through documents and submittals that can prevent later problems that would be expensive or impossible to correct after construction is complete. When the building is occupied, building enclosure *commissioning* can verify any active energy systems, and any passive load-defining enclosure systems that might affect comfort due to glare, infiltration, and solar heat gain.

See also: **ASHRAE Standards • Energy Efficiency • International Green Construction Code • LEED Building Certification • Prescriptive Versus Performance-Based Design • Whole Building Design**

Further sources: ASHRAE; EBN; LEED; USGBC; WBDG

Community Connectivity   ❙

Cities need to be generous, as generous as life itself. —Janine Benyus

We create our buildings, and then they create us. Likewise, we construct our circle of friends and our communities, and then they construct us. —Frank Lloyd Wright

Community connectivity can be defined as the ability of a residential neighborhood to provide pedestrian access to a range of basic amenities within a relatively short distance.

This urban planning concept poses itself as an alternative to the traditionally isolated residential neighborhood and proposes to create healthier and more socially vibrant communities. Some of the stated goals of *community connectivity* include limiting automobile dependence and improving the physical environment of a neighborhood by designing amenities conducive to a walkable community, such as enlarged sidewalks, dedicated pedestrian walkways, urban furniture, landscape features, and lighting fixtures. Some of the positive outcomes associated with this type of urban planning approach include lower energy consumption (associated with transit), health benefits from walking, safer neighborhood due to increased social interaction, and an overall increased sense of identity and of belonging to a community. Frank Lloyd Wright refers to this as creating communities that "construct us."

Within the USGBC Leadership in Energy and Environmental Design (LEED) certification system, Building Design + Construction, a building meeting the *community connectivity* criteria is described as a structure located within a half-mile of a residential area and within a half-mile of at least ten basic services. The specific uses of such services can be retail, hospitality, social, or religious gathering, cultural, or educational. As Janine Benyus indicates, a city needs to be generous, and this can be accomplished by providing open vegetated spaces, available public transit, libraries, fresh food markets, and many other amenities that enhance everyone's lives. OC

See also: **Context (*Archispeak*)** • **Location and Transportation**
• **Neighborhood Development** • **New Urbanism** • **Scale (*Archispeak*)**
• **Townscape (*Archispeak*)** • **Urban Design** • **Walkability (*Archispeak*)**

Further sources: Charter of the New Urbanism; LEED-ND

▌Constructed Wetland

Natural wetland systems have often been described as the "earth's kidneys" because they filter pollutants from water that flows through on its way to receiving lakes, streams, and oceans. —U.S. EPA, *Constructed Treatment Wetlands*

Natural wetlands are swamp, bog, and marsh areas that are inundated or saturated by water frequently and for long enough to support vegetation adapted for life in saturated soil conditions. Wetlands are one of the most productive natural ecosystems on the planet, contributing needed services for the well-being of humans, such as fish, fiber, water filtration, climate regulation, flood regulation, coastal protection, and recreation. As water flows through a vegetated wetland, it slows down and many of the suspended solid pollutants and trace metals in the water become trapped by vegetation and settle out, thereby improving the water quality. The wetland plants foster the needed conditions to nurture living microorganisms, which then take up many of the other pollutants. Plant roots keep the soil and rocks loose, allowing water to flow through easily.

Constructed wetlands are artificial wastewater treatment systems that duplicate the operations of natural wetlands. These *constructed wetlands* are treatment systems built to improve water quality and support wildlife habitat by using the natural wetland processes, including wetland vegetation, appropriate soils, and their related gatherings of living microorganisms. Stormwater runoff deposits nutrients such as nitrogen and phosphorous from areas where manure or fertilizers are used, and from leaking septic tanks. Wetland plants and soils can absorb and take up these surplus nutrients, and the microorganisms can convert organic nitrogen into usable forms necessary for plant growth.

Wastewater treatment and water reuse can be conducted in a cost-effective and aesthetically pleasing manner with a *constructed wetland*. Constructed treatment wetlands can have lower operating and maintenance costs, can handle changing water levels, and be less expensive to build than conventional wastewater treatment systems.

Built on uplands and outside of floodplains, *constructed wetlands* are located to avoid damaging natural wetlands and other water-related resources. Most *constructed wetlands* require large land areas of 4–25 acres per million gallons of flow per day, so are best suited for small communities. They are constructed to establish the desired hydraulic patterns by excavating, backfilling, grading, diking, and installing engineered frameworks to control the flow direction, liquid retention time, and water level. The vegetation for the wetland can be planted, or allowed

Figure 17 Kroon Hall School of Forestry and Environmental Studies, Yale University
©Derek Hayn. Courtesy Centerbrook

to generate naturally. A great small urban example is the rainwater collecting and cleansing *constructed wetland* designed by Centerbrook Architects for the AIA COTE award-winning Kroon Hall at Yale University. The LEED Platinum building for the School of Forestry and Environment also features solar PV panels, ground sourced heat pumps, high thermal retention, daylight harvesting, energy recovery ventilation, a green roof, and recycled, local, and sustainable building materials (Figure 17).

See also: **Biodiversity • Ecological Design • Eutrophication • Reclaimed Water • Water Efficiency**

Further sources: Greywater Action; National Small Flows Clearinghouse; UNC Finance Center; US EPA Constructed Treatment Wetlands; WBDG

▌Construction Waste Management

We are not to throw away those things which can benefit our neighbor. Goods are called goods because they can be used for good; they are instruments for good, in the hands of those who use them properly. —Clement of Alexandria (c.150–215)

The foundation of the economy and the environment is formed by material use, and how these materials are used influences economic growth, climate change, and energy use. With new technology advances, growing populations, and increased standards of living, this translates directly into the increased consumption of water, energy, and materials, such as for infrastructure and construction.

Materials used for the construction of buildings have huge environmental and energy impacts spanning from the extraction, transport, processing, and maintenance to the eventual disposal of the construction materials. Building and demolition waste totals account for about about 40% of the total U.S. solid waste stream, and about 25% of the European Union's waste stream. The U.S. Environmental Protection Agency (EPA) promotes source reduction, reuse, recycling, and waste to energy recovery as the four prime strategies to reduce waste.

Source reduction strategies to avoid and reduce the ecological impacts of materials can be using prefabricated components, off-site construction, circular economy methods, and designing to conventional construction dimensions. Reusing existing materials avoids the environmental impacts of replacing existing materials with new ones, such as the greenhouse gas emissions due to extraction, transport, and manufacture. Recycling prevents materials from ending up in landfills, which are reaching capacity, and land for new ones is hard to find and distant. Waste-to-energy recovers the energy of the materials by burning for electricity or heat, therefore reducing the landfill burdens while minimizing the further extraction of fossil fuels for energy.

Construction waste management (CWM) should start early in the sustainable design process, with responsible material selection and procurement practices, such as using durable materials, recycled or salvaged materials, off-site components, and locally sourced materials. Material selection should take into account the entire life-cycle of the material from initial extraction to eventual disposal or reuse, while also considering occupant health and environmental consequences. Several green building rating systems acknowledge waste reduction strategies, such as USGBC's LEED gives credit for: Storage and Collection of Recyclables, a Construction and Demolition Waste Management, and taking into account the Life-Cycle Impacts and Sourcing of Raw Materials, among others.

By carefully selecting building materials and keeping construction waste to a minimum, the impacts of development can be significantly reduced or eliminated. Getting the maximum benefit of materials, as Clement of Alexandria refers to almost two thousand years ago, as "goods" while generating minimum waste, can substantially reduce the extraction of natural resources, reduce pollution and greenhouse gas emissions, and reduce both energy and water use.

See also: **Deconstruction • Design for Disassembly • Downcycling • Energy Recovery • Sustainable Design • Upcycling • Waste Reduction • Zero Waste**

Further sources: Iyengar (2015: 144); USGBC; US EPA

Cool Roofs

A cool roof reflects and emits the sun's solar energy back to the sky instead of absorbing and transferring heat to the building below. — Cool Roof Rating Council

Worldwide power consumption for air conditioning is surging as urbanization increases and economies rise. This rising demand for air conditioning threatens to undermine global greenhouse gas emission targets, as cooling the indoor environment is primarily achieved by burning fossil fuels. Heat transmission can occur throughout the building enclosure, but primarily happens through the roof due to the large area with full exposure to the sun. Energy-efficient roofing systems, or *cool roofs*, can drastically decrease a building's energy costs for air conditioning, by reflecting more of the sun's radiant energy, absorbing less heat, and efficiently emitting radiation. *Cool roofs* stay cooler and reduce the amount of heat conducted to the building below while also reducing the heat island effect which causes developed urban areas to become warmer than the surrounding undeveloped areas.

A *cool roof* refers to a roof with an outer exterior layer or surface that has high solar reflectivity and high emittance, and reduces the heat penetrating the building, also called thermal load. Light-colored, reflective roofing surfaces can stay more than 50°F cooler in the summer and use 40% less energy in the building than standard dark roofing surfaces, which absorb the sun's energy and can reach temperatures of more than 150°F. High emitting roof surfaces are preferable as heat escapes by radiating out to the sky, while low-emitting surfaces absorb heat into the roof system. *Cool roofs* save energy, reduce carbon emissions, reduce air pollution, reduce heat island effect, and save on air conditioning costs. A good example is the reflective TPO (thermoplastic polyolefin—a single-ply reflecting roofing membrane) *cool roof* on the Lake|Flato Architects-designed LEED Platinum renovation of the Arizona State University Health Services Building. The *cool roof*, planted

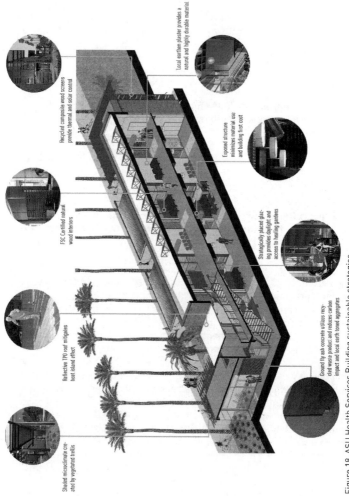

Local earthen plaster provides a natural and highly durable material

Recycled composite wood screens provide thermal and solar control

Exposed structure minimizes material use and building first cost

FSC Certified natural wood interiors

Strategically placed glazing provides daylight and access to healing gardens

Reflective TPO roof mitigates heat island effect

Ground fly ash concrete utilizes recycled waste product and reduces carbon impact and local earth toned aggregates

Shaded microclimate created by vegetated trellis

Figure 18 ASU Health Services Building sustainable strategies
Courtesy ©Lake|Flato Architects

trees and vegetative trellises all reduce energy costs and mitigate the urban heat island effect (Figures 18, 64).

Solar reflectance and thermal emittance are used to measure the effects of cool roofing. Solar reflectance, or albedo, is the ability to reflect sunlight and is expressed as a 0 value when all the solar radiation is absorbed by the surface, and a 1 value when all is reflected. Thermal emittance is the ability of a material to emit absorbed heat. The solar reflectance index (SRI) incorporates both solar reflectance and emittance measures into a single value, calculating the *cool roof's* ability to reject solar heat. Self-washing roofing systems help maintain the white color and reflectivity of cool roofs to improve energy performance and reduce maintenance.

There are several types of *cool roofs*: roofs made from cool roofing materials such as white thermoplastic membranes; roofs painted with a white reflective coating; and green or vegetated roofs, which cool by evaporative cooling. A perfect roof would absorb no solar heat in the hot summer and lose no heat in the cold winter.

See also: **Albedo • Green Roofs • Solar Reflectance Index • Urban Heat Island**

Further sources: Cool Roof Rating Council; EBN; EPA; Kibert (2016: 290); WBDG

CRADLE TO CRADLE CERTIFIED^CM PRODUCTS

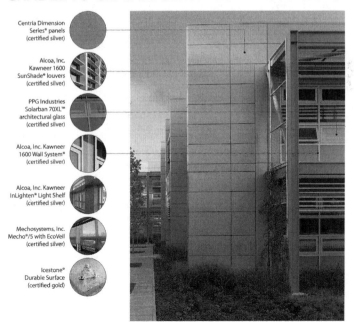

Centria Dimension Series® panels (certified silver)

Alcoa, Inc. Kawneer 1600 SunShade® louvers (certified silver)

PPG Industries Solarban 70XL™ architectural glass (certified silver)

Alcoa, Inc. Kawneer 1600 Wall System® (certified silver)

Alcoa, Inc. Kawneer InLighten® Light Shelf (certified silver)

Mechosystems, Inc. Mecho®/5 with EcoVeil (certified silver)

Icestone® Durable Surface (certified gold)

Cradle to Cradle Certified^CM is a certification mark licensed to Cradle to Cradle Products Innovation Institute

©William McDonough + Partners. All rights reserved.

Figure 19 NASA Sustainability Base cradle-to-cradle products
Courtesy ©William McDonough+Partners

Cradle-to-Cradle   ❚

Pollution is nothing but resources we're not harvesting. We allow them to disperse because we've been ignorant of their value.
—Buckminster Fuller, *I Seem to Be a Verb*

Waste equals food, whether it's food for the earth, or for a closed industrial cycle. We manufacture products that go from cradle to grave. We want to manufacture them from cradle to cradle.
—William McDonough

We live in a throwaway economy in which finite resources are being wasted. More and more resources are being extracted from the Earth's crust, while requiring more energy in the production, processing, manufacturing, transportation, and disposing of these materials. Buckminster referred to not harvesting our valuable and wasted resources as a type of pollution. Our products purchased are just the tip of a vast pile of extracted resources, carbon-emitting fuels, and toxic wastes, and are often the products of unfair labor practices.

The potential for reducing material use in modern industrial economies by using only one-fourth of the virgin raw materials and still functioning very efficiently was recognized in Germany in the 1990s by Schmidt-Bleek and von Weizsäcker, who called this potential resource reduction strategy Factor 4.

Material use reduction begins with recycling, which also generates tremendous energy savings, reduces carbon emissions, reduces air and water pollution, and slashes the size of our growing landfills. The steel discarded each year is enough to meet the needs of the U.S. auto industry. Steel made from recycled scrap metal takes only 26% as much energy as that from iron ore. A recycled aluminum can saves 95% of the energy of manufacturing a new can. Steel and aluminum can be recycled indefinitely. Recycled plastic uses only 20% of the energy, and recycled paper uses only 64% as much energy and far fewer chemicals for processing (Brown 2009, p. 98).

Conventional product designs have limited reusability, and are called "cradle-to-grave" products. Product systems need to be designed as nature-mimicking to support reuse in regenerative products and services, much like nature's larger system where all materials are nutrients in nature's processes. William McDonough and Michael Braungart, in *Cradle to Cradle: Remaking the Way We Make Things* (McDonough & Partners and Braungart, 1992) conclude that waste and pollution need to be avoided entirely and everything we own should be recycled, remade or buried in the ground to compost. They call for waste-free closed-loop life-cycles that recycle outputs and byproducts of one process as inputs for another, such that "waste equals food" in efficient manufacturing practices. The *Cradle-to-Cradle* (C2C) Protocol is a voluntary sustainable product certification that guarantees products are high-performing, efficient and harmless to nature and human body balances. An example is the William McDonough+Partners-designed NASA Sustainability Base that uses *cradle-to-cradle* certified products (Figures 19, 10, 45, 52, 61).

Pollution is a symbol of design failure. —William McDonough and Michael Braungart, *Cradle to Cradle*

See also: **Biomimicry • Closed-Loop Supply Chain • Deconstruction • Design for Disassembly • Downcycling • Factor 4 and Factor 10**

• **Green Economy** • **Industrial Ecology** • **Regenerative Design** •
Upcycling • **Zero Waste**

Further sources: Benyus (1997); Brown (2009); C2C; McDonough + Partners and Braungart (2002); Zbicinski et al. (2006)

Daylighting   **I**

A room is not a room without natural light. —Louis Kahn

**Daylighting requires an integrated design approach to be successful
because it can involve decisions about the building form, siting,
climate, building components (windows and skylights), lighting
controls, and lighting design criteria.** —Gregg Ander (2003),
Daylighting Performance And Design

Daylighting is the controlled use of natural light in the building often
used to reduce energy consumption. *Daylighting* has a direct impact on
people's productivity and health, which requires the best use of the sun
based on the sky condition. While designing for daylighting, it is important to consider the angle of the sun entering a space and create a balance
between natural lighting and energy consumption, and consideration
should be given to shading devices to control excessive light or glare.

Daylighting strategies include a series of qualitative and quanti-
tative measurement techniques such as rules of thumb, simulation,
and high dynamic range photography. For instance, based on a rule
of thumb, the depth of light entering a space is two times the window head height. Does following this rule of thumb provide us with
"good" *daylighting*? It will provide a reasonable light, while further
studies based on the performance of the building will answer more
detailed questions, such as the integrated design strategies described
by Gregg Ander earlier.

There are different methods to measure light in a space. The Daylight Factor is a static *daylight* metric that quantifies the amount of diffuse daylight, using a ratio of the interior illuminance and the outside
illuminance under an overcast sky. Climate-Based Daylight Modeling
is a daylight prediction model using the sun angle and sky condition,
which can vary based on the location.

The LEED Platinum Genzyme Center in Cambridge, MA, by Behnisch
Architekten, is a superb example of natural daylighting and transparency, exemplifying Louis Kahn's notion of the importance of natural
light. The atrium roof is topped with a series of roof-mounted heliostats
(mirrors) that track the sun's movement to reflect sunlight to fixed mirrors. These then reflect to prismatic louvers allowing diffuse light into
the twelve-story atrium where it is further reflected by hanging prismatic mobiles, reflective panels and walls in the atrium. Blinds in the
exterior envelope reflect light up to reflective ceiling panels to reflect
the light deep into the floor plates (Figures 20, 76).

USGBC's LEED *daylighting* credits require a minimum percentage of
space receiving 300 lux for 50% of the occupied time while setting an
upper threshold for the percentage of space with excessive light. MM

Figure 20 Genzyme Center atrium daylighting, Cambridge, MA
Photo: Anton Grassl ©Behnisch Architekten

See also: **Biophilic Design • Energy and Atmosphere • Filter (*Archispeak*) • Glazing • LEED Building Certification • Passive Design • Shading Coefficient • WELL Building Standard**

Further sources: Ander (2003); Leslie, Radestsky, and Smith (2011: 277–290); WBDG

▌Declare Label

Why should we tolerate a diet of weak poisons, a home in insipid surroundings, a circle of acquaintances who are not quite our enemies, the noise of motors with just enough relief to prevent insanity? Who would want to live in a world which is just not quite fatal? —Rachel Carson, *Silent Spring*

The *Declare Label* is a material health initiative for manufacturers to list their products and building materials in a transparent database for selection by consumers. *Declare* uses the data and information on the product, starting from the raw material sourcing acquisition to the complex chemical analysis looking for toxic substances, and discloses this in an easy-to-use format for the consumer, similar to a nutrition label. The International Living Future Institute created the *Declare Label*, as well as the Living Building Challenge and The Red List of toxic substances. The *Declare* database includes a variety of building products, such as greywater treatment equipment, green roof systems, and cellulose insulation, as well as furnishings. Rachel Carson asks in *Silent Spring*, why should we tolerate "weak poisons" and "insipid surroundings"? Interior furnishings can often have many toxic, cancer-causing ingredients, such as cushions containing halogenated flame retardants, the formaldehyde in particleboard, and perfluorinated uses in fabrics.

The *Declare Label* product database can be used to select products that meet several green building rating systems' stringent material requirements. This simplifies both the materials specifications and certification process. *Declare* products with an ingredient disclosure of 99%, will meet the LEED v4 Building Product Optimization and Disclosure under the Material Ingredients credit, as well as Living Building Challenge's Materials Petal. The WELL Building Standard and New Zealand's Green Star program have also adopted *Declare*.

At least 99% of the material's ingredients must be disclosed to increase transparency. Manufacturers must declare if the product is compliant with the list of chemicals on ILFI's Living Building Challenge's Red List of toxic chemicals. The *Declare* levels of compliance are Red List free, LBC compliant in containing some chemicals with exceptions, and lastly Declared, which means the product is not compliant with the Red List or exceptions. A product can be listed in *Declare* regardless of how toxic the components might be, but only if there are no undisclosed ingredients. The ILFI checks the ingredients against two other chemical lists: the chemical action plan of the U.S. Environmental Protection Agency, and the list of very highly concerning ingredients in the European Union's REACH program.

See also: **Green Building Certification Systems • GreenScreen • Indoor Environmental Quality • REACH Regulation • Sick Building Syndrome**

Further sources: EBN; Carson (1962: 12); ILFI; LBC; USGBC; WBDG

Deconstruction

Building art is a synthesis of life in materialized form. We should try to bring it under the same hat, not a splintered way of thinking, but all in harmony together. —Alvar Aalto

The careful dismantling of a building or components, giving the materials a new life as reused or recycled, is referred to as *deconstruction*, or "construction in reverse." Designing for *deconstruction* is an important sustainable building practice by taking into account the complete life-cycle of a structure. This addresses what Alvar Aalto refers to as "not in a splintered way of thinking" but to bring it "all in harmony together." Buildings demolished at the end of their useful life are often sent to landfills, accounting for up to 20% of solid waste stream. This enormous waste of materials and resources can be harvested and reclaimed into useful building materials on the same or other sites.

Reusing building materials reduces the greenhouse gas emissions required for the extraction, transportation, and manufacture of new virgin materials. Just as the positive impacts of using locally sourced building materials, *deconstruction* can also reduce transportation costs, pollutant emissions, and carbon impacts, as well as supporting the local community with jobs and renovated buildings.

As *deconstruction* can sometimes take more time and incur higher labor costs than conventional demolition, this can often be offset by the added revenues from selling reusable materials, avoiding landfill tipping fees, and community engagement. Some building systems are easily disassembled, and others can yield higher returns of salvaged materials, such as large timber-framed buildings, modular or panelized systems. While there are hundreds of thousands of buildings coming down each year, mostly abandoned buildings, there are challenges to reusing rather than demolishing small scale run-of-the-mill buildings, primarily residential. Cost-effective impediments are the manual labor costs, low tipping fees, worker safety requirements, and hazardous material regulations.

To reduce the challenges of future *deconstruction*, buildings must be designed for this intended future disassembly in the early planning stages, by using Design for Disassembly (DfD) or Design for Deconstruction (DfD) principles. Simplifying disassembly efforts require allowance for simple, standardized connections, minimizing parts and materials, reducing building complexity, and careful selection of fasteners and adhesives. Using prefabrication, modular construction, and off-site construction methods can all increase the potential of *deconstruction* to maximize resource efficiency.

See also: **Circular Economy • Deconstruction (*Archispeak*) • Design for Disassembly • Materials and Resources • Off-Site Prefabricated Construction**

Further sources: Designing Buildings Wiki; EBN; WBDG

▌Deforestation

What we are doing to the forests of the world is but a mirror reflection of what we are doing to ourselves and to one another. — Mahatma Gandhi

The world's forests have been cut for thousands of years, primarily for food crops and livestock grazing. Tropical forests are spread over both sides of the equator, flourishing with direct solar rays in warm, wet climates, and include dense rainforests, seasonal forests, and open woodlands. Although tropical forests are only about 7% of Earth's dry land, they nourish about half of all species on Earth. Forests are quickly disappearing as the natural landscape is being cleared for roads, urban development, farms, pastures, fuel, and timber for construction in what Mahatma Gandhi states is but a mirror reflection of what we are doing to ourselves. *Deforestation* is the clear cutting of forests and converting to a non-forest use, such as grazing land, farming, or development. The negative consequences can be soil erosion, social conflict, loss of biodiversity, desertification, plant and animal extinctions, and climate change. Our increasing global meat-based diet requires more and more grazing land, whereas each vegetarian's plant-based diet can save over an acre of trees each year.

The timber industry and agricultural conversion accounts for approximately 80% of global deforestation, especially in tropical rainforests of South America, Africa, and South and Southeast Asia. As forests decline, carbon is released, biodiversity declines, water and soil quality declines, and livelihoods suffer.

The organic nutrients and materials in tropical rainforests are mostly in the plant life, not in the soil. When forest trees are cut, the soil erodes with rainfall, and farmers or ranchers move on to cut more forests. The aerial "fishbone" pattern of deforestation begins with construction of one major "spine" access road that leads to "rib" roads of degradation. Indigenous communities are displaced, and cultures gradually disintegrate with a lack of land and resources.

Deforestation changes local weather patterns as rainfall increases over cleared land more than over intact forests. Carbon that is usually stored in the forest biomass is released into the atmosphere, with slash-and-burn agriculture practices contributing to global warming. Tropical forests store more than 210 gigatons of carbon, and deforestation accounts for over 15% of global greenhouse gas emissions. The unsustainable practices of logging, farming, and mining decreases the prospects of rainforest products that depend on sustainable harvestings, such as fruits, cork, nuts, timber, latex, spices, oils, resins, and medicines. Tropical rainforests have the richest genetic diversity in the planet's gene pool, and may yet provide discoveries both in medical cures, such as cancer, and improving the nutritional value and yield of food needed for the growing population.

We abuse land because we see it as a commodity belonging to us. When we see land as a community to which we belong, we may begin to use it with love and respect. —Aldo Leopold, *A Sand County Almanac* foreword

Although *deforestation* is widespread, global efforts to mitigate future disaster are increasing by maintaining natural resources with low-impact agricultural activities, such as shade farming, parks and protected areas, and engaging native indigenous communities to use sustainable harvesting practices.

On the international scale, the COP21 2015 Paris Agreement recognized the essential role of intact forests in providing carbon sinks to offset human actions, by absorbing tremendous amounts of carbon dioxide. The UN Environmental Protection: REDD+ (Reducing Emissions from Deforestation and Forest Degradation) program was endorsed to offer financial incentives to developing countries. The goal is reducing greenhouse gas emissions from forested lands; value the carbon storing services of intact forests; invest in low-carbon sustainable developments and enhance conservation. As Aldo Leopold so prophetically states, if we view "land as a community to which we belong" and use it "with love and respect", we will further the sustainable management of forests.

See also: **Albedo • Carbon Footprint • Certified Wood • Forest Stewardship Council • Forest Sustainable Management • Materials and Resources • Paris Climate Agreement**

Further sources: Leopold (1949); NASA; UNEP; Worldwildlife.org, www. worldwildlife.org/threats/deforestation

Demand Response

We should learn to live more with our climate and rely less on electricity to alter our climate. —James Dyson, industrial inventor

The electrical grid must respond quickly to surges in power needs, such as when outdoor temperatures rise or fall dramatically, increasing the demand for indoor air conditioning or heating. Utilities must meet customers' power needs equally, consistently, and with reasonable costs, especially in dense urban, commercial, or industrial areas where loss has significant impacts. To improve energy generation and distribution to customers, *demand response* systems urge commercial customers to reduce their use of electricity amid peak demand times, requesting as James Dyson states "to live more with our climate" and "rely less on electricity to alter our climate." Peak demand is the maximum electricity demand at a particular time, or over a given period of time, such as during business hours and extreme temperatures.

Electric utilities promote *demand response* programs by offering tiered demand prices or incentive programs to encourage customers to change their energy use patterns, from high market price times or when system reliability might be at risk. Customers can transfer energy consumption to off-peak hours in permanent load shifting when both demand and costs are lower or in emergency situations; load shedding reduces the load on the system by the utility. An incentive program might reward commercial customers for changing their typical usage when the utility company sends a warning declaring a *demand response* event. This alert can be directed to a building operator to manually lower usage demands with adjustable components, or to a building automation system that automatically reduces the electricity demand with pre-programmed measures.

Commercial renewable wind and solar power generation systems benefit from *demand response* systems by urging customers to lower their demands when renewable sources are unavailable at night or on windless days. Implementing smart energy monitoring systems can save over 10% of energy, and *demand response* systems can average 15–30% energy savings. Green building rating systems, such as LEED and BREEAM, offer credits to encourage *demand response* participation. *Demand response* programs help to make energy generation and distribution networks more efficient, improve grid reliability, and reduce the environmental impacts and emissions of building additional power generation plants, transmission lines, and distribution stations.

See also: **Energy Efficiency • Renewable Energy • Resilient Design**

Further sources: GreenBiz; Institute of National Building Sciences; US DOE

Dematerialization   **I**

Aesthetics of Wabi-Sabi: Limit everything to the essential. But do not remove the poetry. —Dieter Rams

Dematerialization in design means a fundamental change from viewing material and energy resources, not as plentiful and boundless, but as limited assets with potential negative impacts tied to the possibility of sustaining future life on the planet.

The last few generations, particularly in Western nations, have had dominant economic systems that have been branded as "cowboy economics" or "extraction economies" where once the current place or location resources have been depleted or destroyed, one just up and "goes west" for the next place to deplete. After the oil shocks in the 1970s, Western economies gradually became more efficient with energy, but energy use and carbon dioxide emissions rose with the economic growth that followed, overshadowing any efficiency gains.

Reducing the total material or energy intensity that goes into providing building products can be achieved by: great efficiency in design, editing and manufacturing, such as with rematerialization or upcycling; the use of higher quality, durable and appropriate materials for reusability, such as when using life-cycle analysis and intelligent materials pooling; or by inventing another service or product that provides the same or greater benefit than the original, in "limiting everything to the essential" as urged by Dieter Rams, the German industrial designer. In the 1970s, Amory Lovins, along with the *Factor 4* concept, argued that energy and resource efficiency could be increased fourfold with the widespread adoption of existing technologies.

The Factor 10 House is an affordable Chicago Housing Competition won by EHDD Architects that uses modular units to reduce construction material waste and uses passive design measures to reduce energy loads, such as a solar chimney incorporated into the stairwell with water bottles for thermal mass (Figure 21).

If *dematerialization* is thought of as a process of editing, then what buildings are still relevant or obsolete? Can the built space needs be combined? And in what innovative ways can the number of materials be efficiently engineered out, while quality is engineered in?

The most sustainable way is not to make things. The second most sustainable way is to make something very useful, to solve a problem that hasn't been solved. —Thomas Sigsgaard

The fitting *dematerialization* aphorism, "less is more," is attributed to architect Mies van der Rohe in his 1947 modernist ethics, but was used earlier by his mentor, Peter Behrens, who was considered the

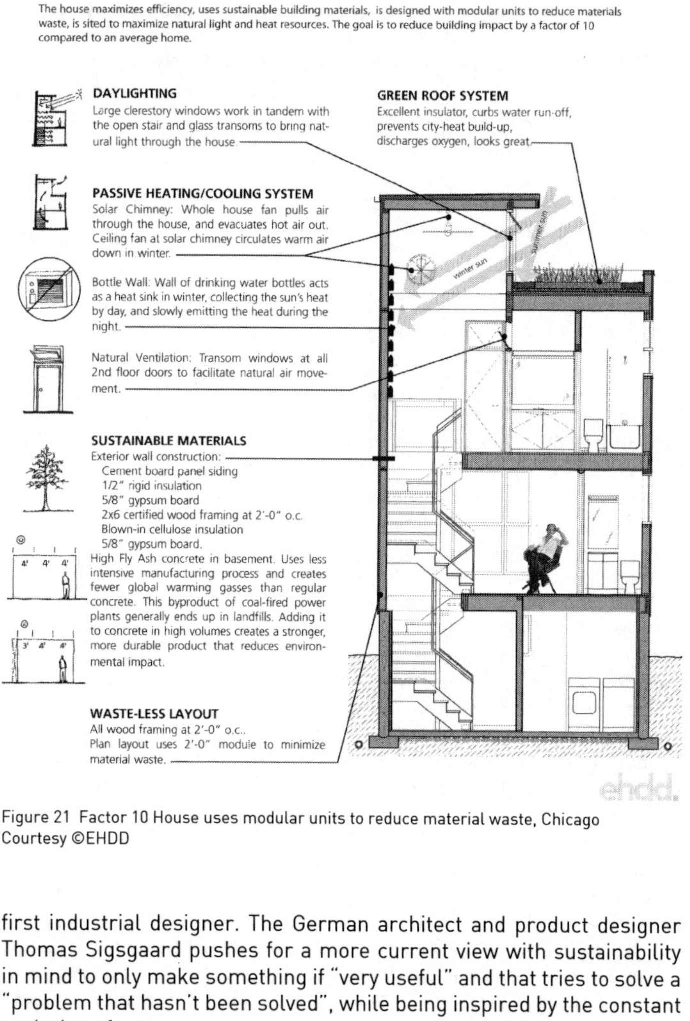

The house maximizes efficiency, uses sustainable building materials, is designed with modular units to reduce materials waste, is sited to maximize natural light and heat resources. The goal is to reduce building impact by a factor of 10 compared to an average home.

DAYLIGHTING
Large clerestory windows work in tandem with the open stair and glass transoms to bring natural light through the house.

PASSIVE HEATING/COOLING SYSTEM
Solar Chimney: Whole house fan pulls air through the house, and evacuates hot air out. Ceiling fan at solar chimney circulates warm air down in winter.

Bottle Wall: Wall of drinking water bottles acts as a heat sink in winter, collecting the sun's heat by day, and slowly emitting the heat during the night.

Natural Ventilation: Transom windows at all 2nd floor doors to facilitate natural air movement.

SUSTAINABLE MATERIALS
Exterior wall construction:
  Cement board panel siding
  1/2" rigid insulation
  5/8" gypsum board
  2x6 certified wood framing at 2'-0" o.c.
  Blown-in cellulose insulation
  5/8" gypsum board.
High Fly Ash concrete in basement. Uses less intensive manufacturing process and creates fewer global warming gasses than regular concrete. This byproduct of coal-fired power plants generally ends up in landfills. Adding it to concrete in high volumes creates a stronger, more durable product that reduces environmental impact.

WASTE-LESS LAYOUT
All wood framing at 2'-0" o.c..
Plan layout uses 2'-0" module to minimize material waste.

GREEN ROOF SYSTEM
Excellent insulator, curbs water run-off, prevents city-heat build-up, discharges oxygen, looks great.

Figure 21 Factor 10 House uses modular units to reduce material waste, Chicago
Courtesy ©EHDD

first industrial designer. The German architect and product designer Thomas Sigsgaard pushes for a more current view with sustainability in mind to only make something if "very useful" and that tries to solve a "problem that hasn't been solved", while being inspired by the constant evolution of nature.

In anything at all, perfection is finally attained, not when there is no longer anything to add, but when there is no longer anything to take away. —Antoine De Saint-Exupery, author of *The Little Prince*

In our shifting world, *dematerializing* the built environment necessitates reexamining our design approaches. In the words of Antoine De Saint-Exupery, "when there is no longer anything to take away" perfection is attained. This applies to resources used not only for manufacture but also in the operation of our buildings. Deconstructability, durability, flexibility, ecodesign, upcycling, and prefabrication are all valued *dematerialization* approaches to living more sustainably.

See also: **Circular Economy • Closed-Loop Supply Chain • Deconstruction • Design for Disassembly • Factor 4 and Factor 10 • Green Economy • Materials and Resources • Off-site Prefabricated Construction • Upcycling**

Further sources: Hawken, Lovins and Lovins (1999)

Desertification   I

In the desert, an old monk had once advised a traveler; the voices of God and the Devil are scarcely distinguishable. —Loren Eiseley, American anthropologist, philosopher, educator

Without a long-term solution, desertification and land degradation will not only affect food supply but lead to increased migration and threaten the stability of many nations and regions. —Ban Ki-moon, former UN Secretary-General

Desertification is a global issue of land and soil degradation, in which a previously biologically productive land area becomes increasingly drier and drier until ultimately becoming a desert wasteland. This *desertification* occurs in arid, semi-arid, and dry sub-humid areas, resulting from both climate change and human activities. *Desertification* happens when trees and plants are stripped away, often in combination; for firewood, timber, mining, unsustainable farming practices, overgrazing of pasturelands, and deforestation. The topsoil is exposed, depleted, eaten away, degraded, and eventually carried away by water or the wind, leaving an infertile mix of sand and dust.

Over two billion people, mostly in developing countries, depend on agricultural ecosystems in dry land areas to live. In these overpopulated areas, poor farming practices, overgrazed, exhausted dry lands, and the groundwater becomes depleted. This now harsh, degraded environment becomes what Loren Eiseley calls the indistinguishable "voices of God and the Devil." When rural areas are unable to support human populations with food, health, and the inherent social stability, then people, communities, and cultures tend to uproot and move. This movement can lead to ethnic conflict, cultural upheaval, and—as we are witnessing—mass migrations to urban areas, which as Ban Ki-moon states, "threatens the stability of many nations and regions." With climate change projections of the increased severity and frequency of droughts, *desertification* will continue to grow, with projections of possibly over fifty million people displaced within the next ten years.

Historically, *desertification* has contributed to the displacements of large populations, leading to the collapse of civilizations such as Carthage, Ancient Greece, and the Roman Empire. Today the global estimates of land degradation areas are already occurring at rates of 30–35 times the historical rate, leading to a loss of biodiversity, increased hunger, and socioeconomic unrest.

The UN Convention to Combat Desertification has (CCD) identified the interlinked forces of *desertification*, climate change, and loss of

biodiversity as the greatest challenges to future sustainable development. Parties to the Convention work to maintain and restore the productivity of land and soil, and to mitigate drought effects in dry areas.
The UN goals of rehabilitating over twelve million hectares a year, are
seen in efforts such as reforestation and tree regeneration; water management, by saving, reusing, rainwater harvesting, soil water retention,
and desalination; soil stabilization, by shelterbelts, fences, and windbreaks; and enrichment of the soil by innovative planting methods.

See also: **Adaptation • Biodiversity • Climate Change • Deforestation**

Further sources: GreenFacts.org; UN CCD: UN Food and Agriculture
Organization, www.fao.org/docrep/017/i1688e/i1688e.pdf

Design for Disassembly

**If you want a lovable building, a strategic decision needs to be made
right at the beginning. The design and construction can fruitfully take
either the High Road or the Low Road, toward beloved permanence
or toward beloved disposability.** —Stewart Brand, *How Buildings
Learn*

Efforts to reduce resource exploitation by closing material loops are an
integral part of sustainable design and construction. Deconstruction,
the dismantling of buildings for new life as reused or recycled materials, is an important first step in minimizing these resource flows.

Design for Disassembly (DfD) or Design for Deconstruction is more
of an upstream approach to deconstruction by incorporating the
potential for future change or disassembly into the design process of
a building or product. This method maximizes material conservation
by creating adaptable buildings and components to avoid the end-of-
life issues.

With increasing population, prosperity and technology, society
has a growing disposal problem with massive amounts of consumer
goods and products, such as vehicles, cell phones, TVs, furniture,
food wastes, and building materials. Disposing of these products
rather than designing them to be reused results in the loss of finite
material resources, embodied energy in products, and increasing
pollution impacts to the environment. The U.S. EPA estimates the
construction industry uses over 50% of material flows, and over 90%
of construction waste is due to demolition and renovation and will
increase with existing aging building renovations and demolition.
William McDonough in *Cradle to Cradle* advocates that all products
should be planned with the end in mind. The E.U. End of Life Direc-
tive has prevented pollution by making dismantling and recycling
products more environmentally friendly but also is an incentive to
manufacturers to reduce hazardous substances, and label parts for
recovery and reuse. So why not also with buildings?

William McDonough+Partners designed the ICEhouse (Innovation for
the Circular Economy house) for the 2016 World Economic Forum in

Davos, Switzerland to demonstrate the Cradle-to-Cradle framework, the UN Sustainable Development goals, and the circular economy's reuse of resources. The ICEhouse structure is what Stewart Brand calls a "lovable building" where a strategic decision was made "right at the beginning" but in this case it is not between permanence and disposability but in reusable portability. The ICEhouse is a *design for disassembly* and reconstruction, and is made of four "technical nutrient" materials: aluminum, polymer, aerogel, and Nylon 6. It was assembled in nine days by four workers, used for a week in the Alps, and then disassembled to be used elsewhere (Figure 22).

Figure 22 ICEhouse, Davos, Switzerland
Courtesy ©William McDonough+Partners

Design for Disassembly calls for redefining the way things are designed, made and used, using early collaboration between the designing disciplines of the collective, but different parts, components, or skins. Stewart Brand describes in his book, *How Buildings Learn*, the six S's system of site, structure, skin, service, space plan, and stuff of a building. Explaining how these parts suggest buildings as "shearing layers of change," this approach can inform the design of separate but interconnected layers in the *DfD* design process.

Design principles of *DfD* include: use prefabrication, preassembly, and modular construction; simplifying and standardizing connections; simplify and separate systems; reduce building complexity; and design for flexibility and adaptability. *Design for Disassembly* planning calls for a collective intelligence in developing the different components, assemblies, and construction techniques, so all parts work together in assembly, disassembly, and re-assembly of the building.

See also: **Circular Economy • Closed-Loop Supply Chain • Cradle-to-Cradle • Deconstruction • Dematerialization • Off-site Prefabricated Construction**

Further sources: Brand (1994:193); Guy (2008: 1–8); McDonough (2002)

Design for the Environment

The sea was wet as wet could be,
The sands were dry as dry.
You could not see a cloud, because
No cloud was in the sky:
No birds were flying overhead —
There were no birds to fly. —Lewis Carroll, *Through the Looking Glass*

When people fail to design with ecological competence, unwanted side effects and disasters multiply. —David Orr

Design plays a crucial role in the product planning, problem definition, and innovation of environmentally responsible goods and services. *Design for the Environment (DfE)* is a process to help industries improve the environmental and human health impacts of their processes, products, and services throughout design development. *DfE* seeks to improve the product's design methods, the engineering process, and the technological procedures used, by using innovative eco-efficient practices in minimizing resource use, waste, and pollution throughout the entire life-cycle. And as David Orr states above, when designing without ecology in mind, the multiplying of negative side effects can result.

This process requires significant effort in front-loading *Design for the Environment* policies early in the design development phase to minimize the environmental and economic costs to consumers and producers. *DfD*, also referred to as ecological or green design, seeks to ensure the maximum material efficiency, therefore eliminating wastes, by "designing in" the processes of recovery, reuse, recycling, or remanufacturing of all product parts or assemblies.

Strategies for using the *Design for the Environment* methods can be: designing products with the reduction of energy consumption throughout a product's life, dematerialization measures, the use of design for disassembly and reuse methods, and using the latest innovative analysis tools for life-cycle assessment. *DfE* in processing and manufacturing services should ensure that raw material extractions minimize wastes, hazardous byproducts, air pollution, and energy impacts. *DfE* in environmental packaging processes should ensure environmentally friendly materials use, reuse, recyclability, and efficient material use and space. *Design for the Environment* in the disposal or reuse of materials should ensure products are refurbished, disassembled for reuse, and emit no toxic chemicals into the air, land, or water at the end of life.

The life-cycle analysis of products can be used as a tool to forecast the impacts of different product or service alternatives, so as to choose the healthiest and most environmentally responsible product. Life-cycle assessments in *Design for the Environment* can help designers compare products by looking at energy use, toxicity, acidification, CO_2 emissions, ozone depletion, resource depletion, and other negative impacts on humans and our planet.

See also: **Circular Economy • Dematerialization • Design for Disassembly • Ecological Design • Life-Cycle Assessment**

Further sources: Birkeland (2002: 26); Kibert (2016: 58); Orr (2008)

Design Quality Assessment   █

Even though quality cannot be defined, you know what quality is. —
Robert Pirsig, *Zen and the Art of Motorcycle Maintenance: An Inquiry into Values*

A great building must begin with the unmeasurable, must go through measurable means when it is being designed, and in the end must be unmeasurable. —Louis Kahn, architect

The Roman architect Vitruvius described building design in terms of "utilitas, firmitas, and venustas," being translated today as commodity, firmness, and delight. These design qualities today are interpreted as the functionality, built quality, and impact of buildings. Currently in buildings, the functional issues of size, use, and access can take into account the quality, layout, interrelationships of spaces, and how well it is integrated into the social and urban surroundings. The built quality of construction and performance looks at how well the building is put together by taking into account structure stability, envelope, and finishes, as well as mechanical, safety, and environmental systems. A building's impact can be a positive or regenerative effect on the local community, and its occupants' well-being, by creating a valued sense of place and this quality is what Robert Pirsig refers to in the quote beginning this chapter as not being definable but known.

The design qualities required in a building should be clearly defined by the client early in the process to be prioritized, measurable, and testable as the architect Louis Kahn states and later should move beyond the measurable. This standard of quality should have a strong vision, clearly understood objectives, and be able to be monitored and evaluated. Benchmarking and assessing existing similar buildings can help in setting requirements needed by the business, users, and local or national environmental policies. Time and costs can conflict with a project's design objectives, but life-cycle cost assessments can encourage long-term, cost-effective investments, and responsible design.

There are existing systems for assessing the design quality of projects, mostly used in the U.K., where Common Minimum Standards and the National Planning Policy Framework mandates the consideration of design quality. One such system is the 1999 Construction Industry Council's standard, the Design Quality Indicator (DQI), which as a web-based assessment tool has since expanded to the U.S. as DQI USA. New York City's Design and Construction Excellence program (D+CE) adopted the Design Quality Indicator as a required design strategy to create outstanding public works.

See also: **Commodity Firmness Delight (*Archispeak*) • Design (*Theoryspeak*) • Design Integrity (*Archispeak*) • Whole Building Design**

Further sources: Design Quality Indicator; Designing Buildings Wiki; Kahn (1957); Vinoly.com

DGNB Certification

We understand sustainability as the obligation of the whole of society to shoulder responsibility for current problems, such as climate change and resource depletion, instead of merely leaving them for future generations to deal with. —DGNB website

The German Sustainable Building Council *(DGNB)*, or *Deutsche Gesellschaft für Nachhaltiges Bauen*, is a German and international green building platform, founded in 2007 by construction and real estate members to promote sustainable and economically efficient buildings and urban districts. The German Ministry for the Environment website (www.bmub. bund.de/en/) states that buildings account for roughly one-third of the resources consumed, one-third of the carbon emissions, and one-third of the wastes generated in Germany, and these can all be reduced through sustainable building practices. The *DGNB* system provides a holistic approach to defining the sustainability goals in the planning phases and continues to assess throughout the entire life-cycle of the projects.

The system ensures quality and transparency by going beyond just the three-pillar model of sustainability by addressing other critical areas as well. The system uses up to fifty sustainability criteria in the *DGNB* assessment system from ecology, economy, socio-cultural, functional aspects, technology, process workflows, and site. The first four quality sections have equal weight in the assessment, which is unusual in giving as much importance to economics as it does to environmental criteria. If the project meets the performance standards, a certificate is awarded in platinum, gold or silver. The system is tailored to be flexible in various building use types and meets country-specific requirements, and encourages outperforming the overall sustainable concepts that are commonly used today.

See also: **Green Building Certification Systems • Sustainability • Sustainable Design**

Further sources: German Sustainable Building Council (DGNB); Sustainable Building Alliance

Downcycling

Recycling . . . I call it downcycling. They smash bricks. They smash everything. What we need is "upcycling" where old products are given more value not less. —Reiner Pilz, automation technology

The world's landfills contain billions of tons of wastes, including valuable metals, minerals, plastics, glass and much more. Nature rarely wastes anything, and our human world, with innovative design, can be a similar closed-loop resource system. In 2002, Michael Braungart and William McDonough wrote *Cradle to Cradle: Remaking the Way We Make Things*, making a case for constructing all things with a designed-in plan for the product's end of life, where all parts circulate back with a useful new life.

Metal, glass, plastic, and minerals do not disappear when discarded; they just get mixed and moved around. Many durable "wastes" are reused over and over again, but less durable materials are destroyed gradually, and lose value with repeated recycling. This slow loss of quality and mixing of different materials in the recycling process results in the subsequent *downcycling* into products of lesser quality with fewer applications. The basic idea of recycling is to break down finished goods into their essential parts, and then to use those physical parts to make new products, regardless if melting glass, paper pulp, or plastic polymers. For some durable products, this recycling can be repeated indefinitely without any loss of quality, such as pure glass and some metals, such as aluminum. Manufacturers can save up to 95% of the energy when using recycled aluminum, and 30% when using reclaimed glass.

Paper and plastic materials can only be recycled a finite number of times, as they are much less durable. Paper fibers are shortened each time they are processed, and after several times the fibers become too weak to be reused. Clean white paper can never be recycled back into premium white paper but is *downcycled* into degraded forms such as cardboard, paper towels or newspaper, and then eventually composted. However, plastic, an environmental hazard, never biodegrades, and its polymers can only be reused a few times. Fleece, building siding, car parts, and park benches are *made from downcycled* plastic bags and drink bottles, but they usually require extra treatment, and then are not recyclable again.

Downcycling keeps materials in use for a while, reduces raw material consumption, and reduces processing energy, but as we move through the waste hierarchy of "Reduce, Reuse, and Recycle," the better material reduction goal should be to keep all materials in the closed-loop reuse process and move toward "upcycling" more materials. Reiner Pilz, a German automation technology manufacturer, first used the "upcycling" term in a 1994 interview referring to the potential creative reuse of waste materials into products of higher quality or value. Later in 2013, William McDonough and Michael Braungart wrote another book, *The Upcycle: Beyond Sustainability—Designing for Abundance*.

See also: **Cradle-to-Cradle • Materials and Resources • Upcycling • Waste Reduction**

Further sources: EBN; McDonough + Partners and Braungart (2002, 2013); WBDG; Wastemanagement.com

Durability   ■

Architecture is the very mirror of life. You only have to cast your eyes on buildings to feel the presence of the past, the spirit of a place; they are the reflection of society. —I. M. Pei

Buildings keep being pushed around by three irresistible forces —technology, money, and fashion. —Stewart Brand, *How Buildings Learn*

The construction of buildings invests a significant amount of material resources and embodied energy. Designing for *durability* and long life are essential principles of sustainable design in seeking to increase the ecological, social, and economic values of buildings over time. *Durability* is more than just selecting long-lasting materials; it is achieved by long-term flexibility to change, adaptability to other uses, resilience to disaster, and as I.M. Pei states above, designing to be valued by the users for positive aesthetical reflections of past, place, and society.

Designing for "long life and loose fit" in buildings is a top measure of sustainable design promoted by the American Institute of Architects (AIA) Committee on the Environment (COTE). Strategies to support the long service life of buildings are: planning early in the process for disassembly or deconstruction; designing materials and systems to improve versatility, *durability*, and adaptive reuse; enhancing long-term flexibility and adaptability; and determining how the project anticipates and celebrates weathering over time.

In *How Buildings Learn*, Stewart Brand describes how buildings are a shearing series of six layers, from the outside site to the inside "stuff". The skin and structure have the greatest impact on the longevity of the building. The inside three layers of services, space plan, and stuff depend on the skin and structure for their *durability*. Designing to allow the inside less durable layers to be changed or updated easily, without interfering with the durable outside layers, is critical. Using modular design or "kit of parts" components that can be easily disconnected, reorganized, replaced, or updated with new technologies allows for easier maintenance, repair, and renewal for environmental efficiency.

Building longevity is tied to the function, related technologies, environmental conditions, local culture, economic, and political issues over the life of the building. Moisture intrusion is one of the most damaging environmental problems in construction. Warm, moist air can condense in steel frame buildings, causing rust and corrosion. Condensation on cold concrete surfaces can cause mold on adjacent drywall, while exterior concrete can spall or scale due to water seepage, and steel reinforcing can rust. Moisture can lead to mold, decay, and insects in wood buildings. Regular maintenance, upkeep, and updates, such as moisture sensors, are essential to a long service life.

Other environmental conditions can threaten the life of buildings, such as material movement due to thermal stress, materials degraded by ultraviolet light, acid rain and ozone damage, and flooding or wind damage. From a life-cycle approach, durability planning involves choosing a reasonable service life target for the building and addressing issues in the early design stages.

Building rating certifications, as well as codes and standards, address the *durability* of construction, in concern for resource conservation and embodied energy. For example, LEED v4 BD+C: Homes has a Durability Management credit; British Standard BS 7543:2015 guides the Durability of Building Elements, Products, and Components; and the International Green Construction Code (IgCC) addresses a building's service life plan to permit future reconfigurations, modifications, and disassembly within the interior spaces.

See also: **Deconstruction • Design for Disassembly • International Green Construction Code • Sustainable Design**

Further sources: AIA COTE; Blakemore (2017); Brand (1994: 193); Rocky Mountain Institute

Ecological Design █

Any form of design that minimizes environmentally destructive impacts by integrating itself with living processes. —Sim Van der Ryn and Stuart Cowan, *Ecological Design*

We but mirror the world. All tendencies present in the outer world are to be found in the world of our body. If we could change ourselves, the tendencies in the world would also change. —Mahatma Gandhi

In many ways, the environmental crisis is a design crisis. It is a consequence of how things are made, buildings are constructed, and landscapes are used. —Sim Van der Ryn and Stuart Cowan, *Ecological Design*

The term ecology was first coined in 1866 by Ernst Haeckel as "okologie," from the Greek word "oikos," meaning home of all humankind, as the study of the interactions between organisms and their environments. Mahatma Gandhi references these interactions in stating, "we but mirror the world." Design is the shaping of matter, energy, and method into form and structure to meet an apparent need or want. *Ecological design*, or ecodesign, can be defined as an integrative design that attempts to improve natural conditions or reverse environmentally destructive impacts by assimilating itself with living systems for a higher quality design.

Ecological design is an environmentally responsible design discipline that connects sustainable construction and green building design, transportation, urban design, agriculture, ecological engineering, product design, forestry, and sustainable development, along with other allied design and planning disciplines that shape our daily experiences. The green design of a building is a multilevel relationship to issues of cultural and social sustainability, urban development and form, the environmental impacts of the building, and its occupants. Ken Yeang writes in *Ecodesign* that placing ecological thinking at the forefront of design addresses issues of minimizing pollution; energy, water, and material efficiency; healthfulness of materials; restoring ecosystems and biodiversity; preserving natural habitats; and fostering the cultural health and beauty of the community.

In *Ecological Design* (1996), Sim Van der Ryn and Stuart Cowan explore the integration of sustainable design with nature and the importance of making natural processes visible in creating a sense of place. The interdependence of design, nature and function are clearly expressed in their Five Principles of Ecological Design:

1. Solutions Grow from Place.
2. Ecological Accounting Informs Design.
3. Design with Nature.
4. Everyone Is a Designer.
5. Make Nature Visible.

Using the *ecological design* principle of fully integrating with nature, our buildings and cities can become more like organisms, producing their energy, while consuming and recycling their wastes. An excellent building example of integrating with nature is the Per-kins+Will-designed Van Dusen Botanical Garden Visitor Centre in Vancouver, which was inspired by organic forms and natural systems. Using a prefabricated roof form that as a green roof appears to float above the rammed earth walls creating a harmonious balance between the building and landscape. The building form flows from the surrounding landscape into a central oculus that acts as a solar chimney (Figures 23, 5, 38). This shows how *ecological design* can create awareness of how our human built environments can become an integral, restorative and caring part of life on the planet.

Figure 23 Van Dusen Botanical Garden Visitor Centre, Vancouver
Photo: ©Nic Lehoux. Courtesy Perkins+Will Architects

While the human animal is the most polluting one in nature, it is also the only species that has the capability to plan and manage its own future. —Ken Yeang, *Ecodesign*

See also: **Arcology (*Archispeak*) • Biodiversity • Biomimicry • Ecological Footprint • Forest Sustainable Management • High-Performing Buildings • Integrated Design • Natural Capital • Regenerative Design • Sense of Place • Site Remediation • Sustainable Design • Sustainable Development**

Further sources: Edwards (2005: 102–104); Kibert (1999: 331); Van Der Ryn and Cowan (1996: 9, 24); Yeang (2006: 18); Zbicinski et al. (2006)

▌Ecological Footprint

On a finite planet, at human carrying capacity, a society driven mainly by selfish individualism has all the potential for sustainability of a collection of angry scorpions in a bottle. —William Rees, *Our Ecological Footprint*

We as a nation must undergo a radical revolution of values. We must rapidly begin the shift from a thing-oriented society to a person-oriented society. —Martin Luther King Jr., *Beyond Vietnam* 1967

Ecology is derived from the Greek words oikos and logos, meaning "study of home," and explores Earth's interrelationships between all living things and their environmental context. Mathis Wackernagel and William Rees (1996) created the term *ecological footprint* in their book, *Our Ecological Footprint: Reducing Human Impact on the Earth*, describing the total ecological impact of individual people, community groups, and organizations on the Earth's environment. This impact includes natural resources, such as water, land, food, timber, transport, housing, and energy sources, and is expressed in the amount (acres or hectares) of productive land needed, such as crop and grazing land, forests, and fishing grounds.

Civilization has become a global culture increasingly driven by excessive consumption, competitive expansion, and the exploiting of our finite planet's limited resources, and as Martin Luther King Jr. states above we need to "undergo a radical revolution of values." As the population increases and consumption grows, there is an essential need to measure and calculate these daily impacts of supply and demand, along with nature's capacity to provide the renewable resources necessary and absorb the resultant wastes.

The Living Planet Report of 2014 reports humanity's footprint has more than doubled since 1961 and using *ecological footprint* accounting; we would need five planets if everyone lived the average American lifestyle. It states the amount of time it takes the planet to regenerate humanity's footprint is over 1.5 years, showing that our demand on the planet is 50% larger than what nature can renew. This jeopardizes not only the well-being of humanity, but also mammal, bird, reptile, amphibian, and fish populations. Vertebrate wildlife populations have declined by more than half in only four decades. This global overshoot of our carrying capacity means that we are harvesting timber faster than trees can regrow and emitting CO_2 faster than nature can sequester it. As Buckminster Fuller states below, we need to "make the world work for 100% of humanity . . . without ecological offense."

Strategies for reducing our individual *ecological footprint* can be as simple as living the mantra of reduce, reuse, recycle and following the old depression-era wise saying, "use it up, wear it out, make it do, or do without." In our constructed environment, using high-performing building standards, designing for zero-energy and zero-water, reducing building footprints, incorporating passive design strategies, reusing existing buildings and construction materials, and incorporating methods such as The Natural Step, Cradle-to-Cradle and Factor 10, will all help achieve a smaller built and *ecological footprint*.

We are called to be architects of the future, not its victims. [The challenge is] to make the world work for 100% of humanity in the shortest possible time, with spontaneous cooperation and without ecological damage or disadvantage of anyone. —Buckminster Fuller

See also: **Carbon Footprint • Carrying Capacity • Ecological Design • Ecological Footprint (*Archispeak*) • Natural Capital • Sustainability**

Further sources: Buckminster Fuller Institute; Global Footprint Network; Living Planet Report 2014; Wackernagel and Rees (1996: xi); WWF Living Planet Report 2014

▮ Ecological Rucksack

Earth provides enough to satisfy every man's need, but not every man's greed. —Mahatma Gandhi

Human development and economic growth are linked with people's control and production of materials. Archaeological eras, the Stone, Iron, and Bronze Ages, were named for the materials and tools responsible for expanding civilizations, altering labor, enhancing food and nutrition, and controlling with warfare. The Industrial Revolution led to intensified resource extractions and outputs of coal, steel, aluminum, and crude oil. The environmental problems facing the planet today are directly related to material extraction, production, and use.

As the population grows and developing countries' economies expand, the "technosphere" will grow with consumerism: causing pollution, resource extraction, and depletion. The technosphere is all the human-made "things" constructed on Earth, such as buildings, roads, computers, phones, cars, equipment, and all the wastes in landfills. Each year the global consumption of natural resources amounts to more than seventy billion tons, and currently, the technosphere is calculated to weigh thirty trillion tons.

The *ecological rucksack* attempts to measure the mass amount of materials that must be moved or displaced to extract a particular resource. The notion is a measure of prosperity, in that with each product or service we use or consume, we are carrying a "rucksack" full of all the materials that have been destroyed or moved from nature to make that particular product or service. Mining, drilling, and excavating all displace massive amounts of earth materials, only to gain small amounts of diluted resources. For example, to get one ton of copper, five hundred tons of non-renewable natural resources have to be moved from the environment, so the *ecological rucksack* of copper is 500:1. The *ecological rucksack* of products is the entire material amounts, including energy, needed to manufacture that product from the cradle (birth or extraction) to the sale, minus its weight. This *ecological rucksack* is also related to the material concepts of embodied energy, material intensity, and embodied carbon. For services, the *ecological rucksack* is the sum of the material and energy, or *rucksacks*, needed to provide and deliver that service.

Reduce, re-use, and recycle! And reconsider what really makes us happy. —David Suzuki

Material consumption must be dramatically reduced to avoid exceeding our "planetary boundaries," the number of natural resources humankind can extract or displace without irreversible damage to global ecosystems. Along with David Suzuki's eloquent preceding quote, strategies for reducing material consumption can be: dematerializing the production process, recycling all material back into the material stream in a circular economy, engineering durable and reusable or recycled products within closed loops, and always extracting raw materials' maximum value.

See also: **Circular Economy • Cradle-to-Cradle • Dematerialization • Ecological Footprint • Ecological Footprint (*Archispeak*) • Materials and Resources**

Further sources: UN Sustainable Development; Zbicinski et al. (2006: 46)

Ecotechnology

I

Ecotechnics: the ecology of technics, and the technics of ecology.
—Institute of Ecotechnics

Most people are more comfortable with old problems than with new solutions. —Charles Brown

Innovations in design or technology occur when a need, problem, or opportunity arises, hence the adage that "necessity is the mother of invention." The "high tech" school of architecture in the 1970s, personified by such influential buildings such as Renzo Piano and Richard Rogers's 1977 Pompidou Centre in Paris and Rogers's 1984 Lloyds Building in London was briefly challenged in the 1980s by the emergence of Postmodernism. The following rejection of the objectivity and mechanical instrumentality that had informed the practice of modern architecture through much of the 20th century gave way to picturesque and historical interpretation, along with old solutions as Charles Brown refers to earlier. The tectonics and systematic organization of services then received little attention. Later, the growing awareness of the limited resources of fossil fuels and their irreversible destruction of the Earth's climate created a new perspective on the methods of environmental controls in buildings. In his influential book *Design with Climate*, Victor Olgyay (1963) constructs a framework for the interconnected balance between the ecological functions of architecture and technology and explains working with nature rather than against it.

  Currently, new generations of buildings and architects have begun to expand again the vocabulary of architectonic language articulated in buildings but with different objectives, the most significant of which is the importance of sustainability in architecture. *Ecotechnology* integrates the ecology of technology and the technology of ecology while emphasizing tackling a problem with a holistic approach. The expression of clear functional relationships between space, construction and environmental systems is expressed again. Brise-soleil, glass façades, independent framework, roof gardens, and other elements of the external envelope—as well as rain gardens, treatment wetlands, and vegetation used for erosion control—are again becoming more intricate in the service of environmental control. The increasing and rapid technological advances we are seeing must also be balanced with thoughtful wisdom, as so eloquently stated by Apple's founder Steve Jobs, yearning for an afternoon with Socrates.

I would trade all of my technology for an afternoon with Socrates.
—Steve Jobs

Sustainable development requires environmentally friendly technologies that are efficient and adapted to the local conditions of place to improve economic performance, cleaner processes, and products while minimizing impacts to our ecosystems, but also must keep the elegance and beauty of art as stated by Fazlur Rahman Kahn, the father of tubular designs for skyscrapers. The term *ecotechnology* is used for designs that are organizationally efficient, energy and material conscious and technologically appropriate in addressing the broad spectrum of ecological and cultural issues while increasing awareness of ways to protect and enhance life on this planet.

The technical man must not be lost in his own technology. He must be able to appreciate life, and life is art, drama, music and, most importantly, people. —Fazlur Rahman Kahn, architect and structural engineer

See also: **Cradle-to-Cradle • Ecological Design • Ecological Footprint • Green Building • Sustainability • Technology and Architecture (***Theoryspeak***) • Techtonics (***Archispeak***)**

Further sources: Institute of Ecotechnics; Kellert (2008: 12); Olgyay (1963); Yeang (2006)

▌EDGE Certification

In today's competitive world, property developers are trying their best to build sustainably. Resource-efficient buildings clearly have impact, from the corporate bottom line to a homeowner's pocket. — EDGEbuildings.com

By 2050, it is expected that two and a half billion more people will live in cities, a 50% increase from today. These new urban residents will need housing, services, and affordable energy, while at the same time the world attempts to lower levels of greenhouse gas emissions to a level for a sustainable future.

EDGE (Excellence in Design for Greater Efficiencies) is a green building standard and certification system for new commercial and residential buildings in emerging markets in developing countries. The program engages financial investors in showing the return on investment (ROI) in constructing affordable resource-efficient buildings. *EDGE* includes a simple online software application that allows the client to readily see and understand the cost analysis of sustainable strategies—such as energy, water, and material savings—before they can be value-engineered out.

EDGE can show that first costs of energy-saving strategies can be lower than those of conventional choices, or at least the early paybacks and ROI.

The World Green Building Council (WorldGBC) with the International Finance Corporation (IFC), a World Bank Group member, created *EDGE*. The WorldGBC uses its network of green building to certify the buildings if they realize a minimum 20% energy reduction, 20% water reduction, and 20% embodied energy reduction compared to a local base building.

The *EDGE* software allows project teams to determine early in the design process if the green building project is financially viable by using credible and readily available data. *EDGE* incorporates local climate data, cost data from local developers, local building regulations, and local utility costs, to give an accurate estimate of costs, benefits, and payback projections. The *EDGE* system and certification has great potential in the next few years for reducing the energy, water, and embodied energy in rapidly urbanizing economies, and putting their development on a low-carbon path.

See also: **Affordable Housing • Climate Responsive Design • Embodied Energy • Energy Efficiency • Sustainable Development • Water Efficiency**

Further sources: EBN; EDGEbuildings; GBCI; WorldGBC; World Bank; UN World Urbanization Prospects (2014), www.un.org/en/develop ment/desa/news/population/world-urbanization-prospects-2014.html

Embodied Carbon   **I**

We're running the most dangerous experiment in history right now, which is to see how much carbon dioxide the atmosphere . . . can handle before there is an environmental catastrophe. —Elon Musk, investor, engineer, inventor

Embodied carbon (eCO₂) is the carbon footprint of material, which is the measure of the amount of carbon emissions released into the atmosphere to produce the material. A carbon footprint can be used to measure the greenhouse gases of a building or activity, such as air travel, whereas embodied carbon can only be associated with materials or products. The term carbon is used to represent carbon dioxide (CO_2) or carbon dioxide equivalents, greenhouse gases with global warming potential (GWP). These emissions are measured throughout the manufacture supply chain needed to produce a material and are usually measured from cradle (Earth)-to-gate (factory), or from cradle-to-site (use). This supply chain or life-cycle accounting includes the extraction of materials from the ground, transport, refining, processing, assembly, use of the product, and its end of life. Not only are the emissions from sourcing and processing evaluated, but also any mechanical or chemical operations, byproducts created and sequestering of carbon within materials, such as timber, and any chemical reactions, such as concrete carbonation which sequesters CO_2

As Elon Musk indicates above "we are running the most dangerous experiment in history." With the interconnected urgency of climate change and negative impacts on our ecosystems, global industries and governments are beginning to mandate *embodied carbon* accounting. The *embodied carbon* measure of buildings in the construction sector is often 20–50% of the whole-life energy and carbon, including operational emissions. During the lifetime of a building, operational carbon emissions can be reduced by new technologies and efficiency measures, but *embodied carbon* and energy can never be reversed once released.

It is possible to create a low-carbon building and reduce *embodied carbon* by using natural materials that sequester carbon, such as stabilized earth or straw bales; use recycled existing materials; use material simple to manufacture; use local materials with fewer transport emissions; use durable materials; and best of all, reuse an existing building.

As regulations and progress in the operations efficiency of buildings continue to improve, the assessment of the *embodied carbon* in building materials becomes even more imperative to the goal of a zero-carbon future.

See also: **Adaptive Reuse • Circular Economy • Climate Change • Deconstruction • Dematerialization • Embodied Energy • Global Warming • Green Economy • Greenhouse Gases • Materials and Resources**

Further sources: Building UK; Circular Ecology; Designing Buildings Wiki; EBN; WBDG

▌Embodied Energy

Embodied energy is the amount of energy consumed to extract, refine, process, transport and fabricate a material or product (including buildings). —Circularecology.com

Embodied energy is the total amount of energy that goes into making a product, material, or building. It is an accounting method to find the energy required for the entire life-cycle of the product, from extraction to deconstruction, and also measures the environmental impact of a product, usually due to emissions and greenhouse gases associated with power consumption. Energy processes involved from extraction to demolition are called cradle-to-grave, whereas the embodied energy of products is often specified to when the product leaves the manufacturer or factory gate, therefore called cradle-to-gate.

Evaluating the *embodied energy* of buildings took hold when the industry began using detailed life-cycle assessments to calculate the whole-life environmental load of buildings and looking at circular ecology issues. Building design primarily focuses on energy efficiency and reducing the related operational emissions, but a significant portion of a building's lifetime energy consumption can be attributed to its *embodied energy*. A higher *embodied energy* product may be justified if it significantly reduces the operational energy requirements of the building, but as improvements in the operating energy efficiencies increase, especially with net-zero energy buildings, *embodied energy* becomes even more necessary.

The high-embodied energy in aluminum and plastics mandates these must be recycled; recycling saves 95% of the energy in aluminum and most of the energy in plastics and lowers their *embodied energy* when recycled, according to lessismore.org. Durable longer-lasting products can have a lower *embodied energy* if considering the time the product was in use. Recycled steel has an *embodied energy* of about 20% of virgin steel made from ores. The manufacturing of cement, the binding agent in concrete, is a major source of greenhouse gases, accounting for over 8% of worldwide human carbon dioxide emissions. Fly ash, a waste product from coal-fired power plants, can replace up to 70% of the cement in traditional concrete, making it stronger, and reduces the energy consumption, wastes, air and water pollution, and the *embodied energy* of the concrete used.

See also: **Adaptive Reuse • Circular Economy • Deconstruction • Dematerialization • Embodied Carbon • Global Warming • Green Economy • Life-Cycle Assessment • Materials and Resources • Upcycling**

Further sources: Circular Ecology; Designing Buildings Wiki; EBN; WBDG

Energy Efficiency

We tend to rush toward the complex when trying to solve a daunting problem, but in this case, simplicity wins. Better buildings, responsible energy use, and renewable energy choices are all we need to tackle both energy independence and climate change.
—Edward Mazria, Architecture 2030

The current worldwide demand for building energy is dominated by the fossil fuel use of oil, gas, and coal, whose greenhouse gas emissions are the primary contributors to climate change. These non-renewable and limited resources are being consumed faster than they are being replaced; involve destructive extraction methods, uncertain supplies and prices, national security vulnerability; and pollute the air, water, and soil. In the U.S., the building operations of heating, cooling, lighting, ventilation, and equipment are responsible for over 40% of the greenhouse gas emissions, and three-fourths of the electricity. These facts demand better *energy efficiency* and conservation, as well as urgent advances in renewable energy technologies and development, such as biomass, solar and wind, as called for by Edward Mazria in his Architecture 2030 Challenge.

High-performing buildings practice first use passive strategies of building orientation, natural ventilation, passive heating and cooling, natural ventilation, and maximizing daylighting to reduce the need for energy early in the design phase. High-efficiency equipment and HVAC choices, building automation and controls, and climate-appropriate building materials and glazing can all reduce the energy use of a building. Renewable energy generation on site, or purchasing green power, can lower the demand for traditional fossil fuel energy sources even more. In high-performing buildings, the commissioning process is critical to verifying the design functions as intended, prevents wasted energy, and optimizes the effective and efficient performance of the building.

The Wade Science Center by SMP Architects integrates the Germantown Friends School's science curriculum with the sustainable building strategies to create a building that teaches by showcasing the photovoltaic array, green roofs, natural stack ventilation, geo-exchange wells, and distributed mechanical systems. An electronic monitoring system that measures cistern water collection/use and the photovoltaic and ground coupled heat pump system's *energy-efficiency* performance/consumption is displayed in "real time" in the lobby and throughout the school's website (Figures 24, 59).

The USGBC LEED certification system uses the Energy and Atmosphere (EA) credit category to reduce energy consumption by rewarding designs promoting *energy efficiency* and using renewable energy sources. The Energy and Atmosphere category addresses commissioning and verification, optimizing energy performance, energy metering, refrigerant management, demand response, renewable energy production, green power, and carbon offsets. Green Globes also addresses optimizing building energy performance, though as a self-assessment certification.

The Living Building Challenge certification defines the most advanced measure of sustainability by requiring that buildings be net-positive energy. The Challenge aims to positively impact the world by asking why every design decision shouldn't make the world a better place with greater biodiversity, beauty, and a deeper understanding of place, culture, and climate.

Tools such as EPA's Target Finder, AIA's 2030 Commitment Reporting Tool and the Architecture 2030 Challenge reference materials can provide comparison baselines for energy use and convert energy consumed into equivalent carbon-emission impacts.

If new and innovative cost-effective and *energy-efficient* strategies are used in renovating all existing buildings and all new construction projects, the building sector's energy demand would drop tremendously and be a giant step toward the goal of a zero-carbon future.

The greenest power is the power you don't have to produce.
—Unknown

See also: **Architecture 2030 • Building Automated Control Systems• Commissioning • Energy Efficiency (*Archispeak*) • High-Performing Buildings • LEED Building Certification • Net-Zero Energy Building Certification • Passive Design • Renewable Energy • Sustainable Design • Vital Signs (*Archispeak*)**

Further sources: AIA 2030 Commitment Reporting Tool; IEA; UNEP; WBDG; USGBC; LEED; ILFI; Franta (2010); US EPA Target Finder

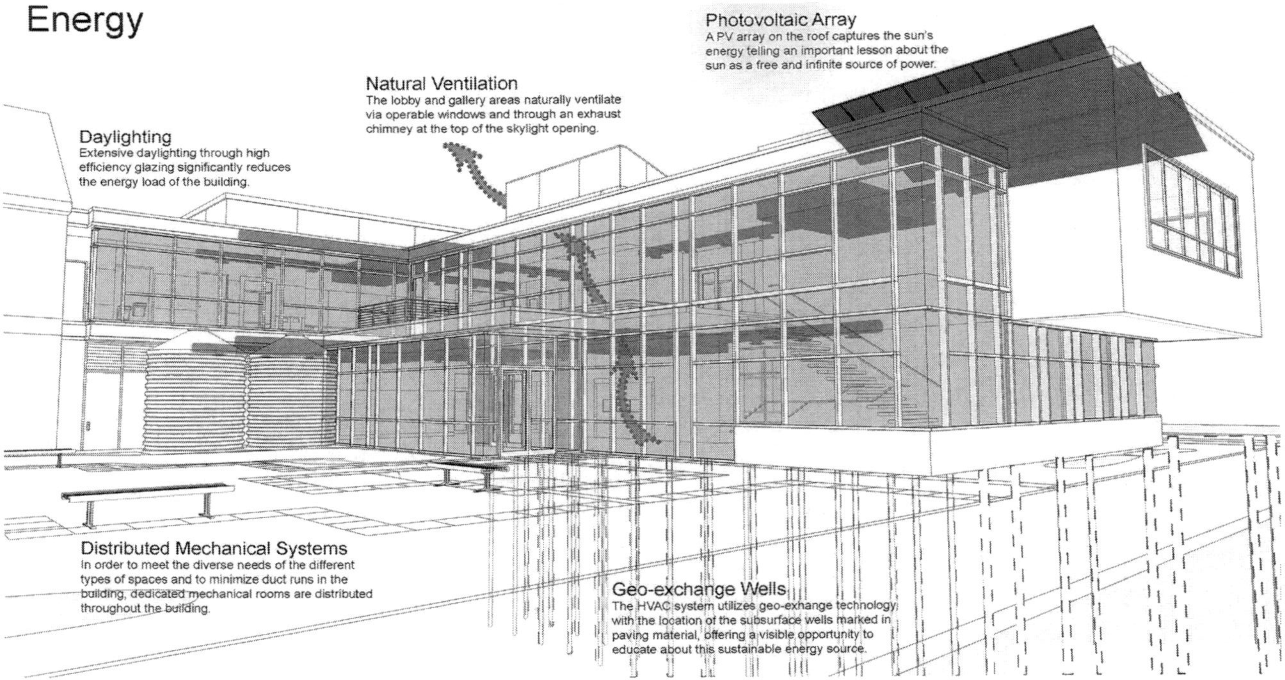

Energy

Photovoltaic Array
A PV array on the roof captures the sun's energy telling an important lesson about the sun as a free and infinite source of power.

Natural Ventilation
The lobby and gallery areas naturally ventilate via operable windows and through an exhaust chimney at the top of the skylight opening.

Daylighting
Extensive daylighting through high efficiency glazing significantly reduces the energy load of the building.

Geo-exchange Wells
The HVAC system utilizes geo-exchange technology with the location of the subsurface wells marked in paving material, offering a visible opportunity to educate about this sustainable energy source.

Distributed Mechanical Systems
In order to meet the diverse needs of the different types of spaces and to minimize duct runs in the building, dedicated mechanical rooms are distributed throughout the building.

Figure 24 Wade Science Center, Philadelphia
Courtesy ©SMP Architects

Energy Modeling

To take advantage of the full capability of these modeling tools, the design approach must transform from a sequential process to a collaborative process, with all the disciplines involved in the building design and construction working as a team from the beginning. — Lynn G. Bellenger, ASHRAE

Building *energy modeling* is the energy analysis of a building using computer simulation. The integration of energy modeling is encouraged in the early stages of design to optimize the energy efficiency beyond minimum code ratings. The purpose of *energy modeling* is to evaluate buildings' energy consumption during the design phase, and well before construction to modify the design, materials, insulation, and use of natural energy resources to have a more efficient design. By beginning *energy modeling* early and in a collaborative effort as ASHRAE's Lynn Bellenger states in the quote beginning this chapter, an average 10% increase can be seen in energy performance as compared to projects that do not implement early energy modeling. And compared to non-modeled buildings, modeled buildings can have a 20% better energy performance.

There are two types of building *energy modeling*: mass mode and building component mode. The mass mode is beneficial for building envelope design, especially during conceptualization, while the building component mode is used for detailed calculations and HVAC sizing. *Energy modeling* requires critical inputs such as weather data, geometry and material properties of a building, building type, interior loads, HVAC types, etc. The modeling software then calculates building heating/cooling loads and provides a myriad of information on the details of building loads, carbon emission, life-cycle analysis, costs and recommendations on decreasing the energy consumption, if needed. The primary *energy modeling* calculation engines are EnergyPlus and DOE2, in addition to Radiance for daylighting. MM

See also: **Building Information Modeling • Energy Efficiency • Feedback (*Archispeak*) • High-Performing Buildings • LEED Building Certification • Net-Zero Energy Building Certification • Prescriptive Versus Performance-Based Design • Vital Signs (*Archispeak*)**

Further sources: AIA Energy Modeling Working Group (2016: 7); ASHRAE; Santos (2017)

Energy Recovery

Energy saving technologies keep improving faster than they're applied, so efficiency is an ever larger and cheaper resource. — Amory Lovins

The cheapest energy is the energy you don't use. —Anonymous

Energy consumption is usually a necessary part of daily living, and this usually involves converting mechanical energy to electric energy. *Energy recovery* systems gather this output of power and provide this as an input of power to the same or another activity. Most *energy recovery* systems transfer heat from outgoing air to incoming air in the winter, and from incoming air to outgoing air in the summer. This lowers energy heating and cooling costs, and saves energy.

For *energy recovery* to be feasible even with increases in technology, the ability to store the energy is critical. This can be either daily thermal energy storage or seasonal thermal energy storage (STES), when heat or cold storage happens between seasonal needs. Waste heat from factories or solar thermal collectors can be stored in buffer tanks, or even in large masses of bedrock equipped with heat-exchanging boreholes for inter-seasonal storage. This stored heat can be used months later when the seasonal changes demand heat. Seasonal thermal energy storage can also store the cold of winter in an aquifer or borehole cluster to be used later for summer air conditioning.

The principle of *energy recovery* is often used in systems with a waste or exhaust stream that can be transferred to supplement or replace the input flow of energy. With the exhaust flow usually higher in temperate areas, the temperature differential allows heat transfer or heat recovery. The goal is to close the loop of external energy needed by preventing the input power from being wasted.

The Stanford Central Energy Facility in Palo Alto, California designed by ZGF Architects LLP showcases a new innovative heat recovery system along with an expansive solar panel trellis that provides shade and cover while generating electricity (Figure 25). The new *energy recovery* system reduces greenhouse gas emissions by 68%, the equivalent of removing thirty-two thousand cars from the road. Incoming air had to be cooled to remove the humidity and then reheated to comfortable temperatures. The excess heat discharged from the evaporative cooling is now captured by a new extensive heat recovery loop, reducing the campus's total energy use by a third and capturing nearly two-thirds of waste heat. This is an excellent example of Amory Lovins' statement above, that as energy-saving technologies continue to improve, energy efficiency becomes an "ever larger and cheaper resource."

Figure 25 Stanford University Central Energy Facility, Palo Alto, CA
Photo: ©Matthew Anderson. Courtesy ZGF Architects LLP

Energy recovery in the form of heat can be captured from the manufacturing and industry sectors and used to heat buildings in the surrounding area. Electric cars and trains use regenerative braking to return the elevating power back to the supplier when released. Pressurized fluid flows, energy, heat recovery ventilation systems, and water heat recycling are other means of *energy recovery* that can save on inputs of energy by capturing waste energy streams.

Another type of *energy recovery* is from transforming solid waste, such as non-recycled plastics, into alternative fuels or new manufactured materials. This kind of *energy recovery* uses emerging technologies of waste-to-energy, gasification, plastics-to-fuels, and solid recovery fuels. Plastics can have a "captured energy" that is significantly more than wood or paper, enabling *energy recovery* facilities to potentially divert up to 80% of waste that would normally go to the landfill.

See also: **Energy Efficiency • Renewable Energy • Waste Reduction • Zero Waste**

Further sources: American Chemistry Council; Energy Recovery Council; Stanford University, news.stanford.edu/features/2015/sesi/; WBDG; US DOE

Energy Star Certification

Conserving energy and thus saving money, reducing consumption of unnecessary products and packaging and shifting to a clean-energy economy would likely hurt the bottom line of polluting industries, but would undoubtedly have positive effects for most of us. —David Suzuki

The U.S. Environmental Protection Agency (EPA) introduced *Energy Star* in 1992 to help identify ways for consumers to save energy. *Energy Star* started as a voluntary labeling program to promote energy-efficient products to reduce greenhouse gas emissions. Partnering with public and private organizations, *Energy Star* provides the technical information that consumers need to make informed choices in best-management practices and energy-efficient solutions.

The EPA expanded *Energy Star* in 1995, from labeling office equipment, HVAC equipment, appliances, and lighting to a partnership with the Department of Energy to broaden just the labeling of products to certifying the environmental performance of new homes, commercial and industrial buildings, and plants. Since 1999, tens of thousands of *Energy Star* certified buildings, from skyscrapers to local small businesses, have met the strict EPA energy performance standards to use less energy, operate at lower cost, reduce carbon footprints, and emit fewer greenhouse gases, benefiting us all. Being recognized as an energy efficiency leader, *Energy Star* is incorporated into the top green certification systems, such as USGBC's LEED, GBI's Green Globes, and the US High Performance and Sustainable Buildings Principles.

To use *Energy Star*, commercial buildings enter their building information and utility bill data into EPA's free online tool, Portfolio Manager, to measure and track energy use, water consumption, and greenhouse gas emissions. Industrial plants enter data into a separate tool, called Energy Performance Indicators. Both online tools calculate an *Energy Star* score between 1–100. Buildings or facilities scoring 75 or more can apply to be verified for *Energy Star* certification, indicating that the building performs better than at least 75% of similar buildings in the U.S. A building must maintain its certification on an annual basis by maintaining its high performance year to year.

Energy Star has developed a comprehensive resource website for energy efficiency advice and climate change information at energystar. gov along with its report, *Climate Change Indicators*. The website states that the *Energy Star* label has saved more than $362 billion on utility bills and reduced greenhouse gas emissions by more than 2.4 billion metric tons.

As the climate is changing, the temperatures are rising, and weather patterns are shifting and becoming more extreme. These observed changes are linked to the rising levels of greenhouse gases in the atmosphere, primarily caused by fossil fuel-driven human activities. The EPA's *Energy Star* program plays a critical role in how buildings and communities are designed, built and operated, fostering an environmentally and socially responsible quality of life.

See also: **Ecological Footprint • Energy Efficiency • Green Building • Green Building Certification Systems • Greenhouse Gases • Water Efficiency • Water-Energy Nexus**

Further sources: EBN; Energystar.gov; US EPA; US DOE; WBDG

Energy Use Intensity   ▌

I have been struck again and again by how important measurement is to improving the human condition. —Bill Gates, Microsoft co-founder

There are two possible outcomes: If the result confirms the hypothesis, then you've made a measurement. If the result is contrary to the hypothesis, then you've made a discovery. —Enrico Fermi, nuclear reactor inventor

Energy Use Intensity (*EUI*) is the total energy used in a building per square foot per year, measured in $kBtu/ft.^2$-yr. *Energy Use Intensity* is one of the key metrics to evaluate the energy performance of a building, and move forward with energy efficiency improvements. The value of measurement is key to making new discoveries and improving our human condition, as stated by both Bill Gates and Enrico Fermi above. Depending on its type and size, some buildings are more energy intensive than others; for instance, the median source EUI for K-12 schools is 144-$kBtu/ft.^2$ per year with a median site EUI of 58-$kBtu/ft.^2$ per year. Architecture 2030 sets *EUI* targets to reduce energy and emissions for new buildings and retrofits, and architects are encouraged to evaluate and measure the *EUI* of their buildings. The standard definition of Building *Energy Use Intensity* is:

$$\frac{\text{Annual Building Energy Use (kBtus or MJ)}}{\text{Building Area (ft.}^2 \text{ or m}^2\text{)}} = \text{EUI}$$

Site *Energy Use Intensity* (predicted *EUI* = site *EUI*) reflects the amount of heat and electricity shown on the bill. Site Energy can be generated on-site or purchased from the grid. EPA *Energy Star* has determined that Source Energy is the most equitable unit of evaluation. Source Energy (*EUI* proposed = source *EUI*) shows the total amount of raw fuel that is needed to operate the building. It incorporates all the transmission, distribution, and production losses. By taking all energy use into account, the score provides a complete assessment of energy efficiency in a building. According to Architecture 2030, Source Energy values are figured using a conversion for electricity of 1 kBtu Site Energy = 3.34 kBtu Source Energy. To convert Site Energy to Source Energy, we need a multiplier that includes the mix of electricity generation types such as natural gas or fuel. According to Architecture 2030, Source Energy values are measured using a conversion for:

- Electricity of 1 kBtu Site Energy = 3.34 kBtu Source Energy
- Natural gas of 1 kBtu Site Energy = 1.047 kBtu Source Energy
- District heat of 1 kBtu Site Energy = 1.40 kBtu Source Energy
- Fuel oil of 1 kBtu Site Energy = 1.01 kBtu Source Energy

Energy Use Intensity designations are used as targets for codes, standards, incentives, and as benchmarks for building operation throughout the industry. As *EUIs* are measurable, they are usually applied to existing buildings, whereas with proposed new construction, computer energy modeling can compare with a bare minimum code-compliant building with comparable parameters. Building owners and operators need to know how their buildings are performing and continually improve the performance metrics, not only because of mandated regulations but because it makes good business sense. MM

See also: **Architecture 2030 • Commissioning • Energy Efficiency (*Archispeak*) • Energy Star Certification • High-Performing Buildings • LEED Building Certification •Net-Zero Energy Building Certification • Sustainable Design • Vital Signs (*Archispeak*)**

Further sources: Architecture 2030; Energy Star; EPA; HPB Summer 2010

▌Envelope Driven Design

The building envelope serves as a filter between the exterior environment and the interior of the building. . . . The specific requirements of the building envelope depend on both the climate and the expectations of the occupants. . . . The façade also plays a major role in the aesthetics of a building. —Peter Smith, *Building Design and Human Performance*

Buildings are shelter and thus have always been concerned with providing protection from the elements. Architecture, as distinct from building, began to emerge when the building assumed additional responsibilities to culturally and aesthetically enhance the experience of sheltering. Classical Palladian villa design was façade driven, and thus could be regarded as the precursor to today's *envelope driven design*. Façade driven design was briefly interrupted in the first half of the 20th century as modern architecture shifted to form driven. In the latter part of the 20th century, the postmodern design movement rediscovered the façade as the primary concern of the architect. Façade driven design has even persisted into the 21st century, but the focus has increasingly shifted from aesthetics and "meaning" to function and performance. The primary determinant of building performance has become the building envelope as the arbitrator of climate and comfort (Figure 26). "Form follows function" has become "envelope follows performance requirements." As Peter Smith has stated in previous and following quotes in this chapter, building envelopes have become sophisticated, active building skins modeled on biological skins.

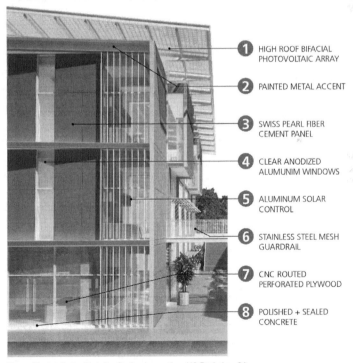

1. HIGH ROOF BIFACIAL PHOTOVOLTAIC ARRAY

2. PAINTED METAL ACCENT

3. SWISS PEARL FIBER CEMENT PANEL

4. CLEAR ANODIZED ALUMUNIM WINDOWS

5. ALUMINUM SOLAR CONTROL

6. STAINLESS STEEL MESH GUARDRAIL

7. CNC ROUTED PERFORATED PLYWOOD

8. POLISHED + SEALED CONCRETE

Figure 26 Jacobs Institute for Design Innovation, UC Berkeley, CA
Courtesy ©Leddy Maytum Stacy Architects

With a climate-adapted building and an "active" building envelope, together with devices in the envelope itself to control heat and light admission, energy consumption can be reduced and heating, ventilating, and air-conditioning equipment can be used for interior fine tuning only. —Peter Smith

A secondary envelope design responsibility has increasingly become that of entertaining and impressing, as evidenced by the parametric shape contortions and digital screening of many of the world's 21st century museum and gallery buildings. New York's Times Square is serving as the model for building envelope driven digital messaging and entertainment design.

Thus, with the emergence of building envelopes that are asked to perform a range of environmental and entertainment tasks, the outer layers of the building have taken on a more significant role in the shaping of architectural design.

An unrelated example of *envelope driven design* is the Scarborough Civic Center by Raymond Moriyama. The design was conceived on a flight to Helsinki in 1969. The back flap of a hotel envelope drove his design concept. EO

See also: **Building Science • Climate Responsive Design • Energy Efficiency (*Archispeak*) • Envelope Driven Design (*Theoryspeak*) • High-Performing Buildings • Integrated Design • Passive House Building Standard • Solar Heat Gain Coefficient • Thermal Insulation • Windows and Glazing**

Further sources: EBN; Smith (1989: 131, 265); Canadian Architect Nov. 1973

▌Environmental Product Declaration

The most alarming of all man's assaults upon the environment is the contamination of air, earth, rivers, and sea with dangerous and even lethal materials. —Rachel Carson, *Silent Spring*

The Earth is becoming increasingly crowded, and with growth comes resource consumption, then waste disposal. Before the late 20th century environmental awareness, little thought was given to resource extraction for construction materials, and the resultant ecological damage. The built environment's products increasingly come from petrochemicals, often with added synthetic chemicals, and whose waste byproducts can contain persistent, bioaccumulative, and toxic (PBT) chemicals.

Rachel Carson initiated the modern environmental movement with her book, *Silent Spring*, which warned of the dangers to all natural systems from the misuse of chemicals. When thrown away, many of these chemicals never actually go "away," as the Earth has a limited ability to absorb all wastes. Commercial markets introduce thousands of new chemicals every year, and while most developed countries have strict chemical and waste regulations, many building products come from developing countries that do not.

As crude a weapon as the cave man's club, the chemical barrage has been hurled against the fabric of life. —Rachel Carson

The *Environmental Product Declaration (EPD)* was developed by American Society of Testing and Materials (ASTM) International to provide transparent, scientifically based information that discloses the full environmental impact of a product or product family, much like a nutrition label. Primarily used in Europe and expanding to the U.S., *EPDs* conform to ISO standard 14025—Type III Environmental Labels and Declarations. An *Environmental Product Declaration* is based on a detailed Life-Cycle Assessment (LCA), which tells the life story of a product from its raw material extraction to end of life. An *EPD's* purpose is for disclosure only and not to certify the product meets any environmental performance standards.

An *Environmental Product Declaration* summarizes how the product affects the environment, in specific impact categories including global warming, ozone depletion and creation, water consumption and pollution, greenhouse gas emissions, eutrophication, acidification, primary energy, and fossil fuel consumption. *EPDs* only cover the impacts up to product delivery to the job site, so they do not disclose the product's potential health hazards to the future occupants. A Health Product Declaration (HPD), which reports the product ingredients and health related concerns, can be used to supplement the *Environmental Product Declaration* or LCA. Usually produced by manufacturers with third-party consultants, all products are classified into categories with established Product Category Rules (PCRs), to make product comparisons possible. Architects, designers, and consumers can use the Life-Cycle Assessment and resulting *Environmental Product Declarations* in the responsible selection of products with fewer damaging environmental impacts.

See also: **Athena Impact Estimator • Declare Label • Design for Environment • Green Chemistry • GreenScreen • Health Product Declaration • Life-Cycle Assessment • Natural Step • WELL Building Standard**

Further sources: AIA; Carson (1962); EBN; Popular Network; Sustainable Products; WBDG

Estidama Pearl Rating System   I

On land and in the sea, our forefathers lived and survived in this environment. They were able to do so because they recognized the need to conserve it. To take from it only what they needed to live and to preserve it for future generations. —Sheik Zayed Bin Sultan Al Nahyan, United Arab Emirates founder

Estidama is Arabic for "sustainability" and is the guiding principle for the sustainable design, construction, and operation of buildings and communities in the United Arab Emirates and its capital city of Abu Dhabi. *Estidama* was developed by the Abu Dhabi Urban Planning Council to create a model of sustainable urbanization in community development, cities, governance, and global initiatives. Endeavoring to follow the guiding words of Sheik Zayed Bin Sultan Al Nahyan, the Urban Planning Council seeks to balance the four pillars of *Estidama*: environmental, economic, social, and cultural.

Estidama started from the need to think differently in approaching the design, construction, and operation of developments by respecting both the historic cultural traditions and the tough climatic nature of the region. *Estidama* is the first program customized to the Middle East by making the system more responsive to the cultural, climatic, and resource issues of the region.

The program is central to the Abu Dhabi Vision 2030 drive to build with innovative green standards. *Estidama* is not a green building rating system, but within the principle is the *Estidama Pearl Building Rating System (PBRS)*, used to promote the development of sustainable communities and improve the quality of life. The system aligns with many of the same criteria and standards of the LEED and BREEAM programs, such as minimizing building water, energy, and wastes, using local materials, and improving closed-loop supply chains for recycled materials and products. In Abu Dhabi, all buildings must at least achieve a minimum 1 Pearl Rating, with government buildings meeting a minimum of 2 Pearl Rating. To date, the *Estidama Pearl Rating System* has made significant improvements in the planning, design, and construction industries in the sustainable development of the Emirates.

See also: **Climate Responsive Design • Green Building Certification Systems • High-Performing Buildings • Passive Cooling • Passive Design • Solar Heat Gain Coefficient**

Further sources: Abu Dhabi Urban Planning Council; PBRS; WBDG

▌Eutrophication

When we go down to the low-tide line, we enter a world that is as old as the Earth itself—the primeval meeting place of the elements of earth and water, a place of compromise and conflict and eternal change. —Rachel Carson, *Edge of the Sea*

Aquatic plants, like all other plants, require two essential nutrients for growth: nitrates and phosphorous. In ecological systems, they are valuable in small amounts, but when supplied at high levels, they cause *eutrophication*, a type of water pollution. *Eutrophication* promotes the rapid and excessive growth of algae (blooms), blocking sunlight and causing underwater plants to die. Bacteria eat the decomposed plants, which results in the depletion of oxygen in the water. Estuarine waters and bays, usually found where rivers meet the sea, can become oxygen-poor (hypoxic) or completely depleted of oxygen (anoxic) from algal blooms, even with their tidal mixture of changing fresh and salt waters. This is what Rachel Carson refers to in her quote at the beginning of this chapter as "a place of compromise and conflict and eternal change."

Animals, fish, and shellfish can be stressed by low levels of oxygen in estuaries, but will die with anoxic levels of no oxygen. *Eutrophication* can be devastating to ecosystems, but also to the aesthetic and economic viability of communities, with unsightly views, foul odors, and disruption of recreational and commercial fishing. *Eutrophication* can produce toxic blooms of red and brown tides, toxic hydrogen sulfide, and single-celled organisms, such as Pfiesteria, that release potent toxins into the water causing serious health problems in birds, fish, and mammals, especially humans.

The nutrient oversupply of water bodies is usually the result of agricultural and landscape fertilizer, sewage discharge, urban runoff, and erosion. In the U.S., conventional power plant emissions are responsible for two-thirds of annual sulfur dioxide emissions and one-quarter of the nitrogen oxide emissions impacting water pollution. As well as the agricultural fertilizers used currently, historically, two other trends around the world have contributed significantly to *eutrophication*: river channelization for navigation and flood control, and landscape alteration by humans, such as deforestation and agricultural drainage.

Internationally, nutrient pollution has led to the degradation of many water bodies such as the dead zones in the Gulf of Mexico at the mouth of the Mississippi River and in the Baltic Sea. The Baltic Sea, due to over-nutrients, is one of the most polluted seas in the world, with extensive anoxic areas and widespread algal blooms in the summers. Land-based activities cause most of the *eutrophication* inputs, such as from sewage, industrial and municipal waste, agricultural runoff, and the burning of fossil fuels.

Improvements in reducing point sources of pollution have made substantial gains, such as improving wastewater treatment facilities and addressing industrial runoff, but the impacts of agricultural runoff and the burning of fossil fuels continue in many parts of the world. Unfortunately, the phosphorus already released can be stored in the sediments of the deeper parts of the water bodies, to be released by oxygen-free zones in "internal loading" for then future algal blooms.

See also: **Constructed Wetland • Naturescaping • SITES Initiative • Smart Growth • Stormwater Management • Forest Sustainable Management• Sustainable Site Design • Water-Energy Nexus • Xeriscaping**

Further sources: Carson (1955, 1962); Lenntech; NOA; USEPA; WBDG

Facilities Management

Facilities management **refers to the integrated management of multiple and interdisciplinary technologies, personnel, systems, and processes. The goal behind facility management is to promote an efficient and collaborative environment to meet and fulfill the key objectives and mission of an organization.** —Technopedia

The field of professional *facilities management* is a relatively new development in the history of buildings. For most of their history, buildings have managed themselves with no need for a "manager." When feeling hot or cold, building occupants have managed the facility by stoking the fire or opening and closing windows. Security was a matter of locking the front door. However, with the rapid increase in the reliance on building technology that emerged in the 19th century (Banham 1969), it became necessary to manage facilities with custodial staff. As building technology continued to become more multifaceted and complex in the 20th century, *facilities management* evolved from a custodial duty to professional management. It now became necessary for the facilities manager to operate computer systems that control the HVAC plant and integrated lighting, security, and communications systems. To support this new profession, the Institute for Facility Management (IFMA) was formed in 1980. It has become the world's largest and most widely recognized international association for *facilities management* professionals, supporting twenty-four thousand members in 104 countries with educational programs and networking.

In the 21st century, the role of the building manager is approaching that of the captain of a high-tech submarine. Mobile communications technology, combined with the possibilities presented by augmented reality space planning, means that the facilities manager is now able to operate and reconfigure all building systems remotely from any location. We are all doing it. Most of us can already operate our home thermostats, security, and home electronics from our smartphones, even if we are thousands of miles from the house.

In the near future, there will be artificial intelligent (AI)-enabled *facilities management* digital assistants. These assistants will assume the routine tasks of monitoring and independently react to conditions affecting the performance of facilities. The role of the facilities manager will become that of the spokesperson for the actions of the assistant. She/he may also be the one who sets the performance criteria and limits for the systems involved. Thus, the facilities manager becomes the navigator setting the course for the facility and not the captain or even the crew stoking the fire in the boilers. This may lead to the facilities manager becoming less familiar with the detailed inner working of the systems they are navigating. Paul Newman, as architect Doug Roberts in the 1974 movie *The Towering Inferno*, may be one of the last professional facilities managers to know which unmarked electrical breaker to throw in case of a fire on the penthouse floor. EO

See also: **Building Automated Control Systems • Commissioning • Facility Performance Evaluation • Feedback (***Archispeak***) • Intelligent Buildings (***Archispeak***) • Operations and Maintenance**

Further sources: Giedeon (1950); Banham (1969); IFMA.org, www.ifma.org/about/about-ifma

Facility Performance Evaluation

Evaluation is creation: hear it, you creators! Evaluating is itself the most valuable treasure of all that we value. It is only through evaluation that value exists: and without evaluation the nut of existence would be hollow. Hear it, you creators! —Friedrich Nietzsche

With the increasing emphasis in constructing high-performing buildings, many building owners are using third-party green building rating systems, such as LEED, BREEAM, Green Globes, and the Living Building Challenge. These owners are using cutting-edge construction materials and methods to optimize the building's performance and reduce the environmental impacts. Consistent and proper operation and maintenance are required for these investment measures to be as efficient as possible. These cutting-edge strategies may be unfamiliar to the facility staff, so a *Facility Performance Evaluation (FPE)* provides useful feedback to adjust the procedures needed to operate and maintain the equipment and systems. A *Facility Performance Evaluation* is also referred to as a Post-Occupancy Evaluation (POE) or a Building Performance Evaluation (BPE).

The *Facility Performance Evaluation* is a tool to evaluate the quality of the building's performance, provide design process feedback, and identify ways to improve the building's performance to meet the needs of the owner and occupants. As Friedrich Nietzsche states in the quote above, it is "only through evaluation that value exists." *Facility Performance Evaluations* use site visits, data performance collection, analysis, surveys, interviews, and photography to document facility conditions as constructed, building operations, and occupant feedback. The *FPE* data collected demonstrates the operational efficiency, durability, maintenance required, sustainability, occupant comfort, and cost-effectiveness of the owner's investment. *FPEs* can be performed at any time but are usually done every 1–5 years.

Performance measures based on the specifications, goals, and objectives must be developed to evaluate the systems and materials properly. Energy modeling and life-cycle costing analysis from the decision-making and design process is used as a comparison baseline against the as-built conditions. Building strategies and features that are evaluated in a *Facility Performance Evaluation* may include water conservation measures, renewable energy systems, sustainable materials, energy efficiency systems, indoor environmental controls, building site features, and building operation standards.

See also: **Building Automated Control Systems • Commissioning • Energy Efficiency • Indoor Environmental Quality • LEED Building Certification • Post-Occupancy Evaluation (*Archispeak*) • Sustainable Site Design • Vital Signs (*Archispeak*) • Water Efficiency**

Further sources: AIA FPE Guidance Document; EBN; NASFA; WBDG

Factor 4 and Factor 10

A society in which consumption has to be artificially stimulated in order to keep production going is a society founded on trash and waste, and such a society is a house built upon sand. —Dorothy L. Sayers

Today humanity is already exceeding our planet's carrying capacity. We now use the equivalent of 1.6 planets to provide the resources we use and absorb our wastes and emissions. Developed countries account for 20% of the global population but consume over 80% of the world's resources (energy and materials). In some areas of the world, ecological shortages are leading to devastating effects, such as resource loss, poverty, famine, debt, ecosystem collapse, and war. Dorothy Sayers refers above to this kind of society as "a house built upon sand." If our global population and consumption trends continue into 2030, the UN estimates we will then need the equivalent of two planets to live on.

The consumption society has made us feel that happiness lies in having things, and has failed to teach us the happiness of not having things. —Elise M. Boulding

The *Factor 4* concept imagines being twice as productive—or happy, as Elise Boulding states in the preceding quote—with half the materials and energy needed, leading to a Factor of 4 improvement in efficiency. Ernst von Weizsäcker, Amory Lovins, and Hunter Lovins introduced the idea in their 1998 book, *Factor 4: Doubling Wealth—Halving Resource Use*. The idea is that society can last twice as long while using half the resources and reducing pressure on the environment by half. In aiming for resource efficiency and sustainable practices using contemporary technologies, innovative engineering, and cutting-edge methods of production, more products and services can be produced with less money, less pollution, less waste and fewer resources (Von Weizsäcker, A. Lovins, and H. Lovins 1997).

The concept of *Factor 10* is even a greater challenge, in being ten times as productive with half the resources, resulting in a Factor of 10 improvement in efficiency. *Factor 10* states that to attain the required sustainable and environmental protection the Earth needs for our survival, we need to reduce our resource consumption by 90% globally within the next fifty years. *Factor 10* focuses on the input side of the economy and material use, primarily with requiring innovative technologies and advanced manufacturing processes. *Factor 10* reductions have been achieved in some manufacturing and building areas, such as the carpet industry, mechanical engineering systems, and more.

Doing more for longer periods of time with less energy and fewer resources also requires significant social and cultural change to not exceed the capacities or tolerable limits of our nature or society.

See also: **Carrying Capacity • Circular Economy • Cradle-to-Cradle • Dematerialization • Ecological Footprint • Embodied Carbon • Materials and Resources • Upcycling • Waste Reduction**

Further sources: EBN; Factor 10 Institute; IISD Business Sustainable Development; WBDG; Worldwatch Institute, www.worldwatch.org/node/810

▌Forest Stewardship Council

God has cared for these trees, saved them from drought, disease, avalanches, and a thousand tempests and floods. But he cannot save them from fools. —John Muir

The clearest way into the Universe is through a forest wilderness.
—John Muir

John Muir, a Scottish-American naturalist, was the father of the U.S. conservation movement and a founder of the Sierra Club. His poetic and cautionary words in 1890 helped create Yosemite National Forest and the preservation of many areas of wilderness. Muir's work in protecting the wilderness for future generations became some of the guiding principles of sustainable forest management.

The *Forest Stewardship Council (FSC)* certifies forests, companies and wood products all over the world to make sure they meet the environmental and social standards of sustainably harvested forests. *FSC* is a third-party certification program established in 1993 by a group of loggers, foresters, activists, and environmental NGOs to help prevent the loss of the world's forests.

To promote environmentally appropriate, socially beneficial and economically viable management of the world's forests. —Forest Stewardship Council mission

The *Forest Stewardship Council* accredits third-party auditors, such as the Rainforest Alliance, to assess the management and harvesting practices of forests. These management practices include maintaining old growth forests ecosystems, chemical use, clearcutting, and wetland and water management. The management must also meet the equitable social justice, cultural, and economic needs of the workers in a fair manner.

In 2008, The Kubala Washatko Architects completed a sustainable award-winning addition to the National Historic Landmark First Unitarian Society Meeting House designed by Frank Lloyd Wright in 1951. The addition creates a coherent whole by reflecting a contemporary approach to Wright's idea of Organic Architecture, by using wood as a structural system, along with using certified wood throughout the project. Red pine columns prominently featured were locally salvaged from windstorm-felled trees on tribal lands in northern Wisconsin and provided an outstanding acoustic environment in the auditorium (Figure 27).

The *Forest Stewardship Council* also certifies the "chain of custody" monitoring of timber through the supply chain from forest, truck, mill, and market by following the invoicing process for Chain Of Custody Certification. The wood product is labeled with the *FSC* logo only after it is certified as sustainably managed and harvested, and has been chain of custody certified. The *Forest Stewardship Council* practices rules for ecosystem management, stream and wetland restoration, as well as social equity criteria. *FSC* also offers certifications for Project Certification, Controlled Wood Certification, and Multiple Site Chain of Custody Certification. There are three types of *Forest Stewardship Council* labels: FSC 100%; FSC Mix; and FSC Recycled.

The American Forest & Paper Association formed a forest certification in the 1990s, the Sustainable Forestry Initiative (SFI). The SFI has been aligned primarily with landowners and the forestry industry. A number of different forest certification systems have developed worldwide, such as the Programme for the Endorsement of Forest Certification (PEFC) that certifies forests in North America, Europe, and Asia.

Figure 27 First Unitarian Society Meeting House Addition, Madison, WI
Courtesy ©The Kubala Washatko Architects, Inc.

See also: **Conservation (*Theoryspeak*) • Deforestation •
Desertification • Forest Sustainable Management • Global Warming
• Natural Capital • Tragedy of the Commons**

Further sources: EBN; Designing Buildings Wiki; Iyengar (2015: 146);
Kibert (2016: 387); USGBC; WBCSD; WBDG

Forest Sustainable Management

I took a walk in the woods and came out taller than the trees. —Henry
David Thoreau

**Land health is the capacity for self-renewal in the soils, waters,
plants, and animals that collectively comprise the land.** —Aldo
Leopold, *Conservation: In Whole or Part?*

Wood is a renewable, natural material, and timber has been a popular
building material for centuries as it is strong, light to handle, workable,
durable, and beautiful. Forests are not only our principal source of timber products, but they also absorb carbon dioxide from the atmosphere,
producing oxygen as they sequester carbon, clean our air and water,
and provide habitats for wildlife. Forests also provide us with a biophilic
connection to our innermost selves, as Thoreau so eloquently states in
the quote opening this chapter. The UN Food and Agriculture Organization (FAO) estimates that forests sequester 290 gigatons (Gt) in their
biomass. About half the dry weight of a tree is stored carbon, released
when the tree is burned or rots. If the forests are harvested at a rate
no higher than the reproduction rate, the yield can be sustained indefinitely. But we are harvesting faster than can be sustained.

Investing in forests is an insurance policy for the planet. —Ban Ki-moon, former UN Secretary-General

Many areas, especially in North America, are now being managed so the forests recover from timbering within a relatively short period, by either reforestation (replanting) or natural regeneration. A forest plantation is a forest established by seeding or planting species, often indigenous, in the process of afforestation or reforestation. A natural forest with a continuum of species native to a site should be preserved and not converted to a forest plantation, and as Ban Ki-moon states, these forests become an "insurance policy for the planet."

Forest certification systems are independent organizations that develop standards for *forest sustainable management* and issue certificates to those forest operatives that meet the requirements. Such requirements for forest certification might address protection of biodiversity and wildlife habitat, sparing forests of unique conservation value, sustainable harvest levels, water quality protection, nutrient recycling; soil integrity, protection of watersheds, rights and well-being of forest workers and indigenous communities, and reforestation rapid enough to replace felled trees. This needed capacity for renewal is what the wildlife ecologist Aldo Leopold referred to as "land health" in his writings on a "land ethic" seeking to foster a caring relationship between people and nature.

The largest international forest certification programs around the world are the Forest Stewardship Council (FSC) and the Programme for the Endorsement of Forest Certification (PEFC), both of which are recognized by the major green building rating systems. The goal of these forest certifications is positive on-the-ground impacts on forest health and the related socioeconomic impacts. Ultimately, as development increases with future population growth, sustainably managed natural forests alone will not be able to meet the growing demand for wood products, so more intensive production systems will be required, such as sustainably managed forest plantations.

See also: **Biophilic Design • Certified Wood • Deforestation • Embodied Carbon • Forest Stewardship Council • Land Ethic • Materials and Resources • Natural Capital**

Further sources: Diamond (2005: 469–478); UN Food and Agriculture Organization: Global Forests Assessment 2015, www.fao.org/3/a-i480 8e.pdf; FSC; PEFC

Formaldehyde   ▌

If we are going to live so intimately with these chemicals, eating and drinking them, taking them into the very marrow of our bones —we had better know something about their nature and their power.
—Rachel Carson

Formaldehyde (CH$_2$O) is a colorless, flammable, pungent smelling gas or liquid chemical often used in building materials and many household products. It occurs naturally in the outdoor air and is produced in small amounts by the metabolic processes of most living organisms, including humans. *Formaldehyde* is a volatile organic compound (VOC) that can quickly become a gas or vapor and is the most common VOC in construction. *Formaldehyde* is used as a disinfectant, preservative, and adhesive binder in pressed materials such as molded plastic items, paints, paper coatings, cosmetics, permanent press coatings on fabrics, textiles, and in building insulation. In her prolific book *Silent Spring*, Rachel Carson (1962) urgently warned us about the chemicals surrounding us and that we need to know more about "their nature and their power."

The International Agency for Research on Cancer (IARC) has classified *formaldehyde* as a human carcinogen. It is highly soluble in water, therefore can irritate body parts that contain moisture, such as the upper respiratory tract and eyes. Low levels of exposure include health effects such as allergic reaction, irritation, and an asthma trigger, while long-term exposure is linked to leukemia and cancers of the nose and throat, where these moist areas are exposed by inhalation.

In building environments, the levels are affected by the potency of the *formaldehyde*-emitting products present, the surface area of the emitting materials to the volume of space, product age, environmental factors, and ventilation rates. *Formaldehyde* is emitted from many construction materials, but the highest concentrations are from particleboard, hardwood plywood, and medium density fiberboard. Relative humidity and temperature can elevate levels, as *formaldehyde* has a high vapor pressure, which enables it to emit fumes rapidly at room temperature. All volatile organic compound levels, including *formaldehyde*, are greatest when a building first opens as the emitting materials would have had less time to off-gas. Many products will off-gas significant amounts of *formaldehyde* for five or more years after manufacture, and these fumes tend to be absorbed by interior finishes and rereleased over time.

Urea formaldehyde (UF) resins are higher emitting than products made with *phenol formaldehyde* (PF), and better still methylene diphenyl diisocyanate (MDI) is increasingly used as a melamine resin, as an alternative to urea formaldehyde, in laminate countertops, glues, and fabrics. Alternative products for substrates in countertop and woodworking applications have come on the market, comparable in performance and costs, as substitutes to *formaldehyde*-loaded conventional plywood and particleboard, such as wheat board. Wheat board is manufactured from wheat straw agricultural waste and is bound together with MDI binder resins, which are formaldehyde-free. MDI is a substitute for *formaldehyde* in producing rigid polyurethane foams, which are good thermal insulators and used in freezers, refrigerators, and buildings worldwide.

See also: **Environmental Product Declaration • Health Product Declaration • Indoor Environmental Quality • Sick Building Syndrome • Volatile Organic Compounds**

Further sources: Carson (1962); EPA; IARC; National Cancer Institute; NIH

Fossil Fuels

Coal, oil, and gas are called fossil fuels because they are mostly made of the fossil remains of beings from long ago. The chemical energy within them is a kind of stored sunlight originally accumulated by ancient plants. Our civilization runs by burning the remains of humble creatures who inhabited the Earth hundreds of millions of years before the first humans came on the scene. Like some ghastly cannibal cult, we subsist on the dead bodies of our ancestors and distant relatives. —Carl Sagan

Human development has progressed due to energy, primarily from *fossil fuels*, that have given people the power to survive, thrive, and raise our standards of living. *Fossil fuels* are highly concentrated types of ancient solar energy trapped in carbon-based cells. Over millions of years, ancient organic remains (fossils) in sediment layers became energy sources of solid, liquid, and gas fuels. Vegetable matter transformed by pressure becomes coal, while both animal and plant matter changed by pressure and heat become oil and natural gas, as eloquently stated by Carl Sagan in his quote opening this chapter. Since the mid-19th century with the combustion engine bringing the Industrial age, *fossil fuels* have become the primary energy source for human civilization.

Fossil fuels are extracted from the ground using both drilling and mining methods. Drilling forces liquid or gaseous fossil fuels, such as oil and natural gas, to the surface. Mining digs and scrapes to expose buried solid fossil fuels, such as coal. Both processes have serious health and environmental consequences, such as mountaintop removal and strip mining for coal, and hydraulic fracturing (fracking) for natural gas, and all can result in contaminated drinking water.

Anything else you're interested in is not going to happen if you can't breathe the air and drink the water. Don't sit this one out. Do something. You are by accident of fate alive at an absolutely critical moment in the history of our planet. —Carl Sagan

Fossil fuels are used for electricity generation, heat, and transportation. Combustion for electricity generation in conventional power plants releases into the atmosphere carbon dioxide (CO_2), methane, mercury, and nitrous oxide, which all contribute to severe environmental and health problems. Environmental damages can be acid rain, haze, acidification of waterways, eutrophication of important estuaries, and global climate change. And as Carl Sagan states, the air we breathe is vital to our health as airborne pollutants can cause severe animal and human health problems, such as asthma and lung, kidney, and heart disease. These emissions are the largest source of pollutants and greenhouse gases over the last 150 years, contributing to warming the atmosphere and climate change.

If we put all our energy and resources into continued fossil fuel extraction, we will have lost an opportunity to have invested in renewable energy. —David Suzuki

The fact that fossil fuels are a limited or exhaustible resource implies they could run out in the future, or their extraction will get progressively costlier and more difficult, to the point that it takes more energy for extraction than would be delivered by their use, and we may miss the opportunity for renewables. But far before this happens, the use of fossil fuels will have damaged our planet beyond repair. Fossil fuels are clearly not sustainable, and civilization must move immediately to carbon-free renewable energy sources if we are to stay under the global 2°C climate targets set for long-term survival.

See also: **Climate Change • Carbon Footprint • Carbon Price • Energy Efficiency • Global Warming • Greenhouse Gases • Methane • Paris Climate Agreement •Renewable Energy**

Further sources: UCSUSA; WBDG; UNEP; Naam (2013: 199–221); Sagan (1997); Suzuki (2004)

Geothermal Energy

The transition from coal, oil, and gas to wind, solar, and geothermal energy is well under way. In the old economy, energy was produced by burning something —oil, coal, or natural gas —leading to the carbon emissions that have come to define our economy. The energy economy harnesses the energy in wind, the energy coming from the sun, and heat from within the earth itself. —Lester R. Brown

The center of the Earth, about 4,000 miles (6437.4 km) deep, hovers around the same temperature as the surface of the sun. *Geothermal energy* captures this heat through drilled well holes, circulating hot water or steam to generate electricity at the surface. The Greek words, gé, meaning Earth, and thérm, meaning heat, combine as the term geothermal. This renewable "heat from within the Earth," as Lester Brown states, is part of the energy economy and can be harnessed as electric power generation or for direct use, such as heating and cooling. Geothermal hot springs have been used since ancient times, but productive geothermal use for industrial purposes began in Italy in 1904.

The mid-2016 global *geothermal energy* operating capacity was 12.6 GW, with planned development capacity to reach 21.5 GW by 2020. As part of the COP21 Paris Climate Agreement, The Global Geothermal Alliance was formed and pledged a five-fold growth in geothermal capacity to reach 32GW by early 2030. Kenya generates half of its electric needs from geothermal, and several "hot spots" with active or young volcanoes have prospects for growth, such as the Caribbean and Chile. Worldwide governments and communities have only tapped into 6–7% of the total global *geothermal energy* potential.

Geothermal energy, as a sustainable renewable resource, is not without some environmental impacts. The fluids drawn from deep earth carry gases—notably carbon dioxide, but also hydrogen sulfide, methane, ammonia, and radon—which contribute to acid rain, radiation, and global warming if released. Most contemporary geothermal plants are closed-loop systems that do not allow gases to be released, injecting them back into the ground. In open-loop systems, these emissions can escape and hydrogen sulfide can change into sulfur dioxide, causing acid rain which can cause heart and lung disease. However, these emissions from geothermal plants are about thirty times lower than coal plants, which are the largest source of U.S. sulfur dioxide emissions. The greenhouse gas emissions of *geothermal energy* plants are, on average, less than 5% of conventional coal-fired power plants.

See also: **Climate Change • Greenhouse Gases • Paris Climate Agreement • Renewable Energy**

Further sources: Brown (2009, 2011); Global Geothermal Alliance; IPCC; UNEP

Global Warming

Scientists have been warning about global warming for decades. It's too late to stop it now, but we can lessen its severity and impacts. —David Suzuki

Can there be any question that the human is the least harmonious beast in the forest and the creature most toxic to the nest? —Randy Thornhorn

The Earth's atmosphere traps solar energy and heat, and life could not exist on our planet without this natural process. Human (anthropogenic) activity—in particular the emission of greenhouse gases (GHG)—has been escalating this process, resulting in a gradual warming of the atmosphere, oceans, and surface of the Earth. Anthropogenic greenhouse gas emissions have increased since the pre-industrial era, driven primarily by increasing populations and fossil fuel-based economic growth. Increasing GHG emissions have led to atmospheric concentrations of carbon dioxide (CO_2), methane, and nitrous oxide that are at unprecedented levels during at least the last 800,000 years and have resulted in significant climate change. We have become what Randy Thornhorn calls "the creature most toxic to the nest." The UN Intergovernmental Panel on Climate Change (IPCC) concludes a rise of over 2°C from pre-industrial levels would have disastrous increases in severe climate events.

The National Oceanic and Atmospheric Administration (NOAA) describes *global warming* as an increase in the annual average air temperature near the Earth's surface. As opposed to this, climate change is described as "long-term (decades to centuries) changes in many environmental conditions for a given place and time—such as in temperature, rainfall, humidity, cloudiness, wind and air circulation patterns."

Carbon dioxide, the most prevalent anthropogenic GHG, is a naturally occurring gas. CO_2 is also a byproduct of burning fossil fuel deposits of fossil carbon deposits, such as coal; oil; gas; biomass; and industrial processes and land use changes. Coal is burned for heat and electricity, oil-based products such as gasoline, diesel, and jet fuel are used for transportation, and industrial processes use natural gas, coal, and oil. Burning these fossil fuels accounts for the single largest amount of the air pollution responsible for global warming. Carbon dioxide is the principal greenhouse gas impacting the Earth's radiative balance and is the reference gas against which other greenhouse gases are measured, so CO_2 is measured with Global Warming Potential (GWP) of 1.

Global warming will alter the Earth's albedo, the reflectance of light from the sun, by melting snow and the polar ice caps. Bright polar ice and snow have a high albedo and reflect sunlight back into space; and when melted, the remaining snow and ice reflect less energy. As more and more sunlight is absorbed by the ground and dark ocean water, the Earth's temperature rises, causing more and more snow and ice to melt, contributing to increasing global warming and sea level rise. We cannot stop global warming now, but as David Suzuki so aptly states, we can "lessen its severity and impacts."

The UN Framework Convention on Climate Change established the Kyoto Protocol in 1997. Legally bound countries agreed to reduce anthropogenic greenhouse gas emissions by at least 5% below the 1990 level, from 2008–2012, which was later updated by the Doha Amendment to cover 2013–2030. In 2005, the Protocol was entered into force lacking the support of the U.S. and Canada.

In a significant diplomatic effort signed on December 12, 2015, 196 countries agreed in the Paris Climate Agreement (COP21) to reduce the risks of global temperature rise to below 2° Celsius, even aiming for 1.4°C.

See also: **Carbon Footprint • Climate Change • Fossil Fuels • Greenhouse Gases • International Panel on Climate Change • Kyoto Protocol • Methane • Paris Climate Agreement • Renewable Energy**

Further sources: Earth Science; IPCC; National Geographic; NOAAclimate.gov; NRDC

Globalization   **I**

In the final analysis, our most basic common link is that we all inhabit this small planet. We all breathe the same air. We all cherish our children's future, and we are all mortal. —President John F. Kennedy, 1963

Globalization is the notion of a worldwide movement toward economic, financial, trade, and communications integration. It implies opening local or national perspectives to a broader global outlook of an interdependent and interconnected world, allowing the free movement of people, products, resources, banking, and markets, as well as ideas and knowledge, and builds on our common links which President Kennedy refers to in his words, "we all inhabit this small planet. We all breathe the same air."

Motivated by international trade and investment, *globalization* is promoted by the increase in information technology and communication. It can affect culture, well-being, political systems, economic development, prosperity, and the environment. *Globalization* is an intensely controversial topic, as one person's freedom to travel, work, or migrate may be another person's threat to job security, health, or culture. Those for *globalization* argue it allows poorer countries to raise their standard of living with economic development, while those against argue an unrestrained international free market will benefit the wealthy and multinational corporations to the detriment of local cultures and ordinary people. As Kofi Anan states below, globalization is a powerful movement that is hard to argue against.

It has been said that arguing against globalization is like arguing against the laws of gravity. —Kofi Anan, former UN Secretary-General

World trade, communication, and information technology—all key aspects of *globalization*—have dramatically increased education, incomes, literacy, and life expectancy for the 40% of the world's population living in India and China. Despite enhanced growth in some developing countries, the gap between the rich and the poor continues to grow. The World Health Organization (WHO) highlighted this with the term "globesity," addressing the problem of over three hundred million overweight and wealthy people, while many times that number are poor and undernourished.

A global environmental consciousness has been elevated when tied to an awareness of global development issues, such as the Paris Agreement, Rio Earth Summit, Montreal Protocol, and international agreements on species protection, emissions, and over-exploiting resources, such as whaling and overfishing. If anything, the environmental regulations lag behind the realities, but with technology, education, and awareness, responsible change is possible. For it is all about the environment, because a global world economy cannot be separated from the environment and the resources needed to sustain it.

See also: **Globalization (*Archispeak*) (*Theoryspeak*) • Green Economy • Population Growth • Sustainable Development**

Further sources: Business Dictionary; World Health Organization International, Body Mass Index, http://www.who.int/nutrition/topics/obesi ty/en/, http://www.who.int/kobe_centre/publications/hiddencities_me dia/ch1_who_un_habitat_hidden_cities.pdf

▌Green Building

How long can men thrive between walls of brick, walking on asphalt pavement, breathing the fumes of coal and of oil, growing, working, dying, with hardly a thought of wind, sky, and fields of grain, seeing only machine-made beauty, the mineral-like quality of life? —
Charles A. Lindbergh

Buildings take an enormous amount of natural resources to construct and operate. The extraction, manufacture, and transportation of construction materials and the lifetime operational needs of powering heating, cooling, and lighting are just a few of the consumptive energy and resource requirements of the built environment. These demanding impacts release enormous amounts of greenhouse gases, which increase climate change effects, and are harmful to humans by "breathing the fumes of coal and of oil," as Charles Lindberg states above. The construction of buildings not only damages the environment but can also be harmful to human health as most people spend 90% of their time indoors, where pollutants may be 2–5 times higher than outdoors.
What makes a building "green" has different interpretations, but it generally is accepted that *green buildings* are efficient in using energy, water, and materials, and reduce negative impacts on human health and environment through proper siting, design, construction, operation, maintenance, and waste removal. These strategies need to be incorporated throughout a building's life-cycle from site selection, design, and to the end of a building life, whether demolished or recycled.
Green buildings should be designed, constructed, and operated to consume far fewer resources and address the major environmental problems we have today. Current construction practices deplete valuable natural resources; consume enormous amounts of limited fossil fuels; emit harmful greenhouse emissions, and create dangerous indoor environments for occupant health. A *green building* should

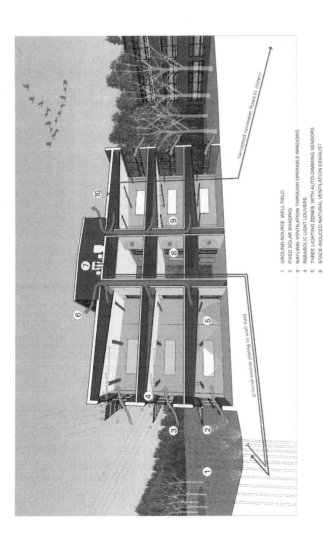

1   GROUND-SOURCE WELL FIELD
2   FIXED SOLAR SHADING
3   NATURAL VENTILATION THROUGH OPERABLE WINDOWS
4   PARABOLIC LIGHT LOUVERS
5   THREE LIGHTING ZONES WITH AUTO-DIMMING SENSORS
6   STACK-INDUCED NATURAL VENTILATION EXHAUST
7   GROUND SOURCE HEAT PUMP PER CLASSROOM
8   GREEN LIGHT INDICATOR FOR NATURAL VENTILATION MODE
9   GLARE-FREE TEACHING WALL
10 RAINWATER COLLECTION

Figure 28 Manassas Park Elementary School sustainable diagram
Courtesy ©VMDO Architects

preserve our valuable natural resources and improve everyone's quality of life and well-being. According to the U.S. General Service Administration (GSA), *green buildings* use 26% less energy and release 33% fewer carbon dioxide emissions. Green practices try to reuse existing buildings, salvage materials, use recycled and local materials, and have on-site recycling strategies to use less construction material and generate less waste.

Green buildings should improve the health and thermal comfort of occupants by improving indoor air quality, views, daylighting, comfort controls, natural ventilation, and a connection to the natural environment. Studies have shown that student test scores improve, work productivity increases, and retail spaces sell more goods with incorporating green building strategies into building design.

The Manassas Park Elementary School in Virginia is a sustainable award-winning green project designed to meet the 2030 Challenge and uses 50% less energy than a code-compliant school. A spray-foam insulated envelope significantly surpasses the most stringent codes for airtightness and insulation, while ground-sourced heat pumps provide conditioned air to classrooms only when needed. Operable windows with green light mode indicators let students know when the conditions are right to open the windows for natural ventilation and red for when to close. Sloped classroom ceilings and light louvers funnel daylight deep into the classrooms. Rainwater is harvested from every roof surface and used for toilet flushing and irrigation, saving about 1.3 million gallons of water each year (Figures 28, 9).

Green building is not the same as sustainable design, and is only a part of sustainable design, which is designing and developing for the long term, with development that "meets the needs of the present without compromising the ability of future generations to meet their own needs" (Brundtland Commission 1987: 1). Sustainable construction takes into account the three pillars of sustainability: the right of all people to live in a socially, economically, and environmentally friendly healthy building or community.

See also: **Architecture (*Archispeak*) • Architecture 2030 • Ecological Design • Green Building Certification Systems • High-Performing Buildings • LEED Building Certification • Living Building Challenge • Sustainability • Sustainable Design**

Further sources: AIA COTE Top Ten; Bruntland Commission (1987:1); Iyengar (2015); ILFI; Kibert (2016); US EPA; USGBC (2011), www.usgbc.org/resources/roadmap-green-government-buildings; US GSA; USGBC; WBDG; Wikipedia; WGBC

▌Green Building Certification Systems

The best way to predict the future is to design it. —Buckminster Fuller

Moving from built environments that produce a sea of unintended externalized impacts to knowing and taking responsibility for those impacts is how green cities can take root. —Rick Fedrizzi, U.S. Green Building Council

Buildings are the largest natural resource consumers of energy, water, and raw materials, as well as emitting potentially hazardous pollutants into the air, and generating huge amounts of waste. According to the U.S. Department of Energy, in the U.S buildings account for 41% of energy consumption, 40% of carbon dioxide emissions, and 14% of all potable water. These environmental impacts have driven the formation of green building standards, rating systems, and certifications to mitigate these negative impacts of construction on the natural environment. *Green building certification systems* rate the different levels of performance or compliance of specific environmental or human health requirements, and then reward with points to achieve escalating levels of certification. Certified green buildings acknowledge and take "responsibility for those impacts" as stated by the head of the U.S. Green Building Council, Rick Fedrizzi.

The first *green building certification system* for improving the environmental performance of buildings started in the U.K. in 1990 with the Building Research Establishment's Environmental Assessment Method (BREEAM) and was the core structure for many green building rating systems to follow. In 2000, the U.S. Green Building Council (USGBC) developed Leadership in Energy and Environmental Design (LEED), which is now the most widely used rating system in the world. In 2005, the Green Building Initiative (GBI) helped develop the Green Globes rating system for the U.S., and since then many national and regional green building rating systems have evolved.

The award-winning Discovery Elementary School in Arlington, Virginia designed by VMDO Architects is the largest net-zero energy school in the U.S. The school integrates design, sustainability, and learning, offering positive examples to students of solutions that they can participate in to solve climate change. The net-zero energy building is designed with on-site rooftop photovoltaics to produce as much energy as the amount of energy used annually. Passive design strategies include a high thermal mass with insulated concrete form (ICF) construction, terraced building sections to bring light deep into the building, and a stringent focus on airtightness (Figure 29).

Figure 29 Discovery Elementary School, Arlington, VA
Courtesy ©VMDO Architects

Several *green building certification systems* go beyond mainstream sustainable practices by focusing on more stringent requirements or concentrating on specific areas of sustainability. The best way to influence the future, as Buckminster Fuller states, is "to design it." Examples of this are the rigorous International Living Futures (ILFI) Living Building Challenge, which requires net-zero energy, net-zero water, and zero pollutants; ILFI's Net-Zero Energy Building (NZEB); the WELL Building Standard, which looks at occupant health; and the SITES Initiative for sustainable site design. The Energy Star rating system administered by the U.S. EPA and DOE focuses on building energy and water use, while the Passive House Institute focuses on airtightness, source energy limits, and space conditioning.

Globally, other *green building certification systems* tailor to their particular climates, policies, standards, and practices, or to specific goals. Examples are the EDGE for developing countries, Green Star of South Africa, BCA Green Mark in Singapore, Beam in Hong Kong, CASBEE of Japan, and the United Arab Emirates' Pearl Rating System for Estidama.

Green building certification systems continue to evolve, improve, and expand. Green product certifications also continue to increase, with nearly six hundred around the world. A *green building certification* verifies the green or sustainable performance of the project and can be an educational and marketing tool while incentivizing further sustainable and high-performing building practices.

See also: **BREEAM Certification • EDGE Certification • Energy Star Certification • Estidama Pearl Rating System • Green Globes Certification • Green Star Certification • LEED Building Certification • Living Building Challenge • Net-Zero Energy Building Certification • Passive House Building Standard • Sustainable Design**

Further sources: EBN; ILFI; Sustainable Buildings Wiki; US DOE (2011), http://www.pnl.gov/main/publications/external/technical_reports/PNNL-19369.pdf; US EPA; USGBC.org; WBDG

Green Chemistry

If it should turn out that we have mishandled our own lives as several civilizations before us have done, it seems a pity that we should involve the violet and the tree frog in our departure. —Loren Eiseley

The saddest aspect of life right now is that science gathers knowledge faster than society gathers wisdom. —Isaac Asimov

In our building products, there are tens of thousands of unregulated hazardous chemicals that have the potential to do harm either by themselves or through interaction with other factors. As Loren Eiseley implies above, the harm we are doing is not only to ourselves, but to other species as well. With the increasing insights into the science of chemical manufacture and the releases into our environment, Isaac Asimov acknowledges above, that society has just been turning our heads.

Green chemistry is a design approach focused on reducing or eliminating the use and generation of polluting and hazardous substances from building products or processes. *Green chemistry*, also called sustainable chemistry, develops new methods to reduce waste and chemical risk in the entire life-cycle of a product, from intent to extraction, manufacturing, and use, and finally to disposal. Chemical and product manufacturers should at the beginning of design first reduce any negative impacts, such as toxicity and wastes, and then manage the human health and environmental risks of exposure to any remaining hazards.

Green chemistry applies innovative scientific solutions to the world's environmental problems, even at the molecular level of pollution and source reduction. In the 1990s in the U.S., Europe, and the U.K., there was increasing awareness to the depletion of resources and chemical pollution. The U.K.'s Green Chemistry Network and the U.S. Environmental Protection Agency (EPA) moved to actively avoid pollution by using innovative production technologies. The 1990 U.S. Pollution Prevention Act defines source reduction as "reducing the amount of hazardous substance, pollutant, or contaminant entering any waste stream or otherwise released into the environment prior to recycling, treatment, or disposal."

The 2007 EU Registration, Evaluation, Authorization and Restriction of Chemicals (REACH) program requires companies to provide hazard assessments, exposure assessments, and data that their products are safe. Unlike remediation, which involves treating and removing hazardous materials from our environment, *green chemistry* focuses on designing hazardous materials out of the environment from the beginning. It is more ecologically efficient and more economical to prevent polluting wastes than to clean up wastes after they are started.

The U.S. EPA lists several important principles in the *green chemistry* approach: preventing waste, maximizing atom economy, designing safer products and chemicals, using safer solvents, increasing energy efficiency, using renewable starting materials (feedstock), avoiding chemical derivatives, and developing products and chemicals to degrade after use.

Tools for chemical transparency—such as Health Product Declarations, Declare, Cradle-to-Cradle Certification, and GreenScreen—tell us which product groups contain chemicals and compounds such as formaldehyde, polyvinyl chloride, bisphenol-A, flame retardants, and perfluorinated compounds, along with the amounts and hazards. Most green building certification systems contain a material human hazard and exposure assessment credit. In defining the risks and hazards of chemicals, one must take into account that one's risk is relative to the amount of one's exposure to a hazard. Reducing the danger level or exposure reduces your risk. Eliminating the hazard eliminates the risk.

See also: **Athena Impact Estimator • Cradle-to-Cradle • Declare Label • Design for the Environment • Environmental Product Declaration • Formaldehyde • GreenScreen • Health Product Declaration • Natural Step • REACH Regulation • WELL Building Standard**

Further sources: ECHA; EPA; European Commission; Green Chemistry Institute; U.S. Pollution Prevention Act

Green Economy

Show me a healthy community with a healthy economy and I will show you a community that has its green infrastructure in order and understands the relationship between the built and the un-built environment. —Will Rogers, Trust for Public Land

The UN General Assembly held the 2012 Rio+20 summit to promote the global priorities of poverty reduction, job empowerment, clean energy, and the sustainable and equitable use of resources, resulting in Agenda 21. The aim was to transition to a *green economy*, defined by the UNEP in their 2011 *Towards a Green Economy: Pathways to Sustainable Development and Poverty Eradication*, as an economy that results in "improved human well-being and social equity, while significantly reducing environmental risks and ecological scarcities"—essentially, an economy in which public and private partnership investments grow global socioeconomic development while being resource-efficient, low-carbon, and socially just. As the Trust for Public Land's Will Rogers states, a healthy economy values the "relationship between the built and the un-built environment." A *green economy* might use intelligent tax systems, pricing policies, incentives, or regulatory changes to translate environmental assets into market incentives, and with surpluses continually reinvested into an active cycle of further research and development.

Developed countries have created a global crisis based on a flawed system of values. There is no reason we should be forced to accept a solution informed by that same system. —Marlene Moses, Ambassador to the UN for Nauru, 2009

In a world facing increasing energy and resource uncertainty, environmental degradation, and rising climate change, a major challenge is integrating the competing economic hopes of wealthy nations and emerging countries alike with good growth investment and socially equal resource protection. The principle of "common, but differentiated, responsibilities" disputes as to whether developed countries assume expected responsibility, or transfer the burden of a green economy to developing countries, as referred to by Marlene Moses from the sea-level threatened small island of Nauru.

A *green economy* can promote the 2030 UN Sustainable Development Goals—the first three are to end poverty, end hunger, and ensure health and well-being for all—only if growth is distributed equally and does not bypass the poorer communities most in need of developmental aid. Economic growth must be measured in the rising standard of living for the clear majority of citizens, and not only gross domestic product.

It's perilous and foolhardy for the average citizen to remain ignorant about global warming, say, or ozone depletion, air pollution, toxic and radioactive wastes, acid rain, topsoil erosion, tropical deforestation, and exponential population growth. Jobs and wages depend on science and technology. —Carl Sagan

Existing for years in a world where wealth and growth were created by fossil fuel consumption, our "brown economies" have not responsibly addressed the resulting social injustice, environmental degradation, and resource depletion. Our world has changed, along with higher risks, and a *green economy* supports the economic progress of growth, income, and jobs that Carl Sagan states "depend on science and technology." Investments in new technologies promote energy, resource, and material efficiency while providing growth opportunities in sectors such as such as sustainable forestry, green buildings, agriculture, less food chain waste, better waste management, and public transportation for short-, medium- and long-term jobs. Where natural capital is already severely depleted in some sectors, such as fisheries, workers need protection from loss of income for short to medium term, but the depleted sectors would then be able to replenish stocks as long-term assets for future generations.

See also: **Circular Economy • Ecological Footprint • Globalization (*Archispeak*) (*Theoryspeak*) • Social Equity • Sustainable Development**

Further sources: Green Economy Coalition; UNEP (2011), www.unep.org/greeneconomy; Wikipedia; World Resources Institute

Green Globes Certification   ∎

Life solves its problems with well-adapted designs, life-friendly chemistry and smart material and energy use. —Janine Benyus, The Biomimicry Institute

Green Globes is an online green building assessment and certification used in Canada and the U.S. Calling itself the "practical" and affordable rating system, *Green Globes* is flexible for users and provides interactive evaluation and guidance through the phases of design, operation, and management of commercial buildings. The rating system was developed by ECD Energy and Environment Canada in 2000, and is administered by the Building Owners and Managers Association. In 2004 the Green Building Initiative (GBI), through the American National Standards Institute (ANSI), acquired *Green Globes* for the American market, as an alternative to the U.S. Green Building Council's LEED rating system. The mission of GBI is to accelerate the adoption of building practices that result in resource-efficient, healthier and environmentally sustainable buildings.

The U.K.'s 1980s BREEAM rating system was the origin of both *Green Globes* and LEED, and each has undergone significant updates to include more efficient modules and building types. *Green Globes* recently prioritized items that reduce health impacts, such as reducing carbon emissions and increasing indoor air quality, along with a risk-based assessment of materials. These priorities follow Janine Benyus's quote statement on the importance of "life-friendly chemistry and smart material and energy use." *Green Globes* also increased weighting for water efficiency and building longevity and works with the ANSI/GBI 01–2016: Green Building Assessment Protocol for Commercial Buildings.

Green Globes has three assessment modules—new construction/ significant renovations, commercial interiors, and existing buildings— which are used for a wide variety of commercial, institutional, and multi-residential building types. There are seven green building credit categories: project and environmental management, site, energy, water, materials and resources, emissions, and the indoor environment. *Green Globes* provides a final certification level of one to four *Green Globes*, depending on the percentage of points achieved compared to the maximum available. A minimum of 35% points is required for the base certification of one *Green Globe*.

See also: **BREEAM Certification • Energy Star Certification • Green Building Certification Systems • LEED Building Certification • Living Building Challenge • Sustainable Design**

Further sources: ANSI; EBN; GBI; Greenglobes.com; Kibert (2016: 189–211)

Green Roofs

We should preserve every scrap of biodiversity as priceless while we learn to use it and come to understand what it means to humanity.
—E.O. Wilson

Green roofs are layers of living vegetation located on the roof of a habitable structure or dwelling, called "green" roofs because of the color of vegetation when viewed from above. Historically, sod would be used to cover rooftops for the purpose of insulation, keeping buildings cool in summer and warm in winter. *Green roofs* originated thousands of years ago; the Hanging Gardens of Babylon were a series of green roofs constructed over arched stone beams and waterproofed with layers of reeds and thick tar.

Contemporary *green roof* systems involve the successful design and implementation of a multilayer system comprising a structural support, waterproof membrane, drainage layers, specialized soil medium, soil stabilizer and a selection of appropriate plant species. *Green roofs* may or may not be irrigated.

There are two general categories of *green roofs*: intensive and extensive. Intensive green roofs typically have deep soil layers, are much heavier in weight, and can support a larger and more diverse range of vegetation. Extensive *green roofs* have shallow soil depth, are much lighter in weight, and typically support smaller vegetation types, such as grasses and sedums. Extensive systems can be comprised of modular soil and vegetation systems, or in-situ. Intensive *green roofs* are custom in-situ designs typically requiring significant structural support.

Green roofs have a range of ecological and aesthetic benefits, in addition to potentially increasing the longevity of the rooftop. Advantages include stormwater management, air pollution reduction, reduction of urban heat island effect, water quality improvement, providing green space, and preservation of habitat and biodiversity. As E.O. Wilson says, we should "preserve every scrap of biodiversity" which may be priceless to humanity. A good example is the Architerra design for the State University of New York's College of Environmental Science and Forestry green roof, which provides ecological and aesthetic benefits as well as informal and bleacher-style class gathering spaces on the angled wood roof monitors (Figures 30, 14).

Roofs can represent up to 32% of the horizontal surface of built-up areas and are important determinants of a building's energy flux and water issues. The addition of soil and vegetation to building roof surfaces can lessen the adverse effects on local ecosystems and can reduce the buildings' energy consumption.

Figure 30 SUNY College of Environmental Science and Forestry green roof and PV arrays
Courtesy ©Architerra Inc., Architect

Living or *green roofs* have been shown to increase sound insulation, fire resistance, and the longevity of the roof membrane. Living roofs can reduce the energy required for maintaining comfortable interior climates because vegetation and growing plant media intercept and dissipate solar radiation. *Green roofs* can also mitigate stormwater runoff from building surfaces by collecting and retaining rainfall, thereby reducing the flow into stormwater infrastructure and urban waterways. The biophilic connection to nature with a greenspace amenity is an invaluable benefit, and as John Muir states, we receive far more than we seek. Other potential benefits include habitat for wildlife, air quality improvement, and reduction of the urban heat island effect. AHB

In every walk with nature, one receives far more than he seeks.
—John Muir

See also: **Biophilic Design • SITES Initiative • Solar Reflectance Index • Sustainable Site Design • Thermal Insulation • Urban Heat Island • Vegetated Walls**

Further sources: EBN; Green Roofs for Healthy Cities; International Green Roof Congress; US GSA; WBDG; Wikipedia

Green Star Certification

The first rule of sustainability is to align with natural forces, or at least try not to defy them. —Paul Hawken

The Green Building Council of Australia (GBCA) launched the *Green Star* building assessment in 2003 as the only national sustainable rating system. It was modeled after the existing tools of BREEAM in the U.K. and LEED in the U.S., and has been adopted by New Zealand and South Africa. Now the rating tool includes Sustainable Communities, Design and As Built, Interiors, and Performance. *Green Star* is a formal certification process during which a third-party expert panel awards a rating through a document-based assessment.

Communities are evaluated on categories of livability, economic prosperity, environment, design, governance, and innovation. *Green Star* rates building designs according to their environmental performance in nine sustainable categories: management, energy, environmental quality, water, materials, land use and ecology, emissions, transport, and innovation. The success of achieving these benchmarks increases significantly if the design of the building first "aligns with natural forces," as according to Paul Hawken as the "first rule of sustainability." Category weights are by relative importance, and the weightings are adjusted to reflect the priorities of each state, such as the many parts of Australia that suffer severe water shortages. In South Australia, which suffers from water scarcity, the water efficiency total score is 15%; while it is only 10% in the Northern Territory, which is less populated and wetter. Energy is 25% of the total points in most of Australia's states.

Green Star is flexible in allowing category credits to be added or deleted depending if relevant to the particular building project or type. Assessment ratings can be earned at all stages of the project's life-cycle, such as communities in the planning stage; for buildings in the design and construction phase; and during the ongoing operation after occupied. There are two conditional requirements, similar to LEED prerequisites: first, the project must achieve minimum performance in Australian Building Greenhouse Rating (ABGR); and second, the project location must not be on a site of high ecological or social value.

See also: **BREEAM Certification • Energy Star Certification • Green Building Certification Systems • Green Globes Certification • LEED Building Certification • Living Building Challenge**

Further sources: GBCA.org; Hawken (1993); Iyengar (2015: 238); Kibert (2016: 142)

Greenhouse Gases   **I**

Gases that pollute the air and cause the warming of the Earth's atmosphere. —Merriam-Webster Dictionary

We are perturbing our poor planet in serious and contradictory ways. Is there any danger of driving the environment of the Earth toward the planetary Hell of Venus or the global ice age of Mars? —Carl Sagan, *Cosmos*

Scientists have conclusively proven that human activities are interfering with the climate. Climate change poses significant risks for both human and ecological systems, both now and in the future. Human activities, such as burning fossil fuels and deforestation, produce *greenhouse gas* (GHG) emissions that trap solar radiation in the atmosphere and therefore affect the temperature and climate of the Earth's air, land, and oceans. The leading *greenhouse gases* include carbon dioxide (CO_2), methane, hydrofluorocarbons, and nitrous oxide. Carbon dioxide absorbs long-wave infrared radiation as it is reflected from the Earth's surface, and traps heat in the atmosphere. Life on our planet cannot exist without this greenhouse effect, but the concentrations of CO_2 and other *GHG*s have substantially increased over the last 275 years.

    The Kyoto Protocol to the UN Framework Convention on Climate Change was entered into force in 2005, and legally bound the agreeing countries to reduce human-generated greenhouse gases by at least 5% below the 1990 emission level. Later in the Doha Amendment to the Kyoto Protocol, new 2013–2020 commitments were established, again without the support of the U.S. or Canada.

    Concentrations of CO_2 have risen from nearly 280 parts per million when the Industrial Revolution began in 1750, to 401 parts per million in 2016. Nature absorbs about five billion tons of CO_2 per year in our oceans, soils, and vegetation, but nearly half of the remaining emissions stay in the atmosphere, pushing up CO_2 levels.

    According to the IPCC 2014 Fifth Assessment Report, some 9.8 billion tons of carbon were emitted from fossil fuel use, accounting for about 91% of the total human sourced CO_2 emissions. These global CO_2 emissions originate primarily from the burning of coal (42%), oil (33%), and gas (19%), and cement production (6%). Changes in land use, such as deforestation and development, are responsible for about 9% of all global emissions. In 2015, China with its tremendous growth was responsible for 28% of CO_2 emissions, followed by the U.S. with 16%, and the E.U. at 10%.

    The IPCC quantifies the maximum CO_2 the world can still emit and have a likely chance of keeping the average global temperature rise below 2°C above pre-industrial temperatures. This benchmark is critical to prevent us from becoming—as in Carl Sagan's words—like the "planetary Hell of Venus or the global ice age of Mars" with extremes in weather events, droughts, species migration, and rising sea levels, resulting in loss of many coastal cities and island nations. In the COP21 Paris Climate Agreement signed in December 2015, 196 countries agreed to reduce the risks of global temperature rise to below 2°C, even aiming for 1.4°C.

See also: **Carbon Footprint • Climate Change • Global Warming • Kyoto Protocol • Methane • Paris Climate Agreement**

Further sources: CO_2 Earth; EPA; IPCC Fifth Assessment Report

GreenScreen

The chemical war is never won. —Rachel Carson, *Silent Spring*

The most important pathological effects of pollution are extremely delayed and indirect. —Rene Dubos, American microbiologist

Toxic chemicals in our environment are increasingly linked to modern diseases and cancers. Homes, schools, and workplaces are full of products with chemicals that escape into the surrounding air, water, and soil. As we are exposed more and more to the risks of chemical exposure, our bodies are increasingly contaminated with hundreds of synthetic chemicals whose effects are "extremely delayed and indirect," according to microbiologist Rene Dubos.

In response to the demand for transparency in how to identify and use safer chemicals, the Clean Production Action group that promotes green chemistry developed *GreenScreen for Safer Chemicals*, a method of chemical hazard assessment intended to classify chemicals of high concern and identify safer replacements. *GreenScreen* structures the evaluation of a substance and assigns a risk level based on assessing eighteen human health and environmental "fate" and toxicity endpoints.

GreenScreen defines four benchmarks in promoting safer chemicals, with each increasing benchmark defining progressively safer chemicals. A reference point 1 score corresponds to "Avoid—Chemical of High Concern," and a benchmark score of 4 corresponds to "Prefer—Safer Chemical." It consolidates data on a chemical's inherent characteristics into a set of hazard endpoints ranked as high, medium, or low. This expands on the U.S. EPA's Design for the Environment (DfD) alternatives assessment method and the principles of green chemistry, which includes information on the human health effects, environmental impacts, toxicity, safety, and the hazards posed when the chemical is broken down into the environment. By ranking chemicals, *GreenScreen* is used by industry, government, and companies to support product design and development, procure materials, and meet regulatory requirements. Preferable product procurement tools—such as environmental standards, ecolabels, and scorecards—can also use the assessment.

Benchmark 1 of *GreenScreen* clearly defines the criteria for chemicals hazardous to human health and the environment as consistent with other global regulations, such as the E.U. REACH regulation. These criteria include carcinogens; reproductive, developmental and neurodevelopment toxicants; mutagens; persistent, bioaccumulative, and toxic chemicals; very persistent and very bioaccumulative chemicals; and endocrine disruptors.

The *GreenScreen* List Translator protocol, an abbreviated version of the *GreenScreen* method, allows a company to quickly check its substances online against any of the forty authorized lists of high hazard

chemicals to allow early detection of an associated risk level and substitute a safer alternative. All the comprehensive human health and
environmental data are shown in a full *GreenScreen* method assessment based on the eighteen hazard endpoints. This allows companies
to help move our society toward the use of greener and safer chemicals,
but as Rachel Carson states in *Silent Spring*, "the chemical war is never
won."

See also: **Cradle-to-Cradle • Declare Label • Design for the
Environment • Environmental Product Declaration • Formaldehyde •
Green Chemistry • Health Product Declaration**

Further sources: Carson (1962); Clean Product Action; EBN; EPA;
Healthy Building Network; WBDG

GRESB Initiative

An investment in knowledge pays the best interest. —Benjamin
Franklin

Know what you own, and know why you own it. —Peter Lynch

Cities, countries, and future building developments are preparing
for climate change adaptation and the needed resilience policies
in addressing the related risks, infrastructure requirements, and
increased demands for water, energy, and human population shifts.
To increase market competitiveness, investors, lenders, and building
owners are addressing energy efficiency, green building features, and
transparent corporate responsibility. The real estate sector in the U.S.
consumes nearly half of all energy produced, as well as a significant
role in water, waste, and transportation use. As awareness of these
environmental and economic impacts grows, there is more demand
for sustainable real estate, as reflected by Greenpeace.

An investment isn't an investment if it destroys our planet.
—Greenpeace

The *Global Real Estate Sustainability Benchmark (GRESB)* is an
investor-driven system that scores the sustainability performance
of real estate portfolios around the world. Investors and owners can
use collected data to measure and rank the performance of portfolios concerning social responsibility, the environment, and corporate governance. The information can evaluate the entire real estate
value chain, from building property managers up to financial investors
in real estate markets. *GRESB* collects annual assessments of real
estate portfolios, debt providers, and infrastructure assets to then
score the sustainability data for comparison to competitive peers in
the same region, type, or infrastructure. This is for the informed with
sustainability in mind, and who follow the financial advice of Peter
Lynch: "know why you own it."

The system provides two levels of assessment: funds assessment, which focuses on management and investment processes; and the asset assessment, which is organized around eight core aspects, such as asset level policies, ground actions, and operational performance. *GRESB* data scores are used by certified international sustainability reporting frameworks and standards to then optimize the risk management, growth, and returns on capital investments. *GRESB* works using the wise words of Benjamin Franklin that an informed "investment in knowledge pays the best interest."

See also: **Social Equity • Sustainability • Sustainable Development • Triple Bottom Line**

Further sources: EBN; GRESB; GBCI; USGBC

Greywater

Water is the driving force of all nature. —Leonardo da Vinci

Water is increasingly becoming a scarce resource, and the construction and operation of buildings can consume enormous amounts of water. Over four hundred years ago, Leonardo da Vinci perceptively valued water as "the driving force of all nature." A building's water cycle and energy use are intertwined, as massive amounts of energy are required to extract water from surfaces or ground, the pumping needed for distribution, and then the treatment of the water before use. After customer use, even larger amounts of energy are required to pump the contaminated wastewater through sewers to wastewater plants for treatment. Water treated to make it suitable for drinking is referred to as potable or "white water" and is then often wasted on irrigation and toilet flushing.

When a building's water consumption is reduced, the municipal water and energy demands are lowered, as well as energy-related pollution. Designing a building to reduce water consumption can incorporate wastewater strategies to encourage water reuse, reduction, or recovery, such as with *greywater* reuse. *Greywater* is wastewater produced from commercial office buildings or households from water processes, not including toilet water, referred to as sewage or "blackwater" with fecal contamination. Some definitions of blackwater also include dishwasher, kitchen sink, or disposal water. *Greywater* usually includes domestic water from showers, bathtubs, bathroom sinks, clothes washers, and commercial building greywater from rainwater, air conditioning condensate, cooling tower blow down, steam condensate, and industrial process water. As the degree of contamination increases, the treatment requirement increases, and options for suitable water reuse decreases.

Water is at the center of every chemical reaction, and therefore should be the Earth's most precious gift. —Janine Benyus

Treated *greywater* is used for site irrigation, toilet flushing, urinals, or cooling tower water—purposes that do not require drinking water quality—

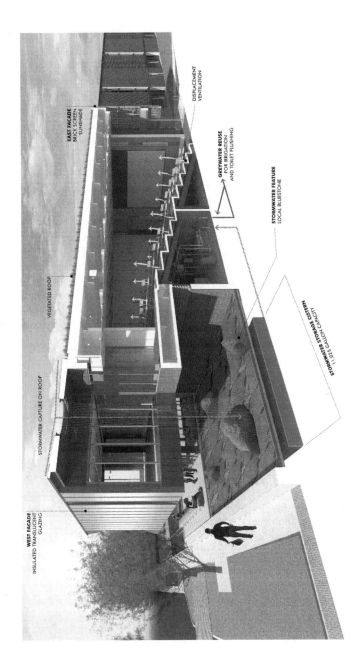

Figure 31 Center for Building Energy and Innovation greywater reuse
Courtesy ©KieranTimberlake

and then water becomes valued which, as Janine Benyus states, "should be Earth's most precious gift." Buildings with *greywater* systems need two waste piping systems: one for *greywater* and one for blackwater. *Greywater* is much easier to treat and reuse, as it has less contamination than blackwater. Captured *greywater* runs to a central tank for collection on site, and then it is filtered, drained, or pumped for irrigation or other uses. Organic material in the water will quickly decompose, and anaerobic bacteria will create unpleasant odors, so *greywater* cannot be stored for an extended time.

The KieranTimberlake Architects' design for the new Center for Building Energy and Innovation in Philadelphia captures rainwater from the roof into a storage cistern and then is processed along with *greywater* for use as toilet flushing and irrigation (Figures 31, 15, 32). Many green high-performing buildings are celebrating and showcasing rainwater harvesting and water reuse to create awareness to what Loren Eiseley called the "magic on this planet."

If there is magic on this planet, it is contained in water. —Loren Eiseley

Recycling *greywater* can significantly reduce the demanded amount of freshwater extraction, especially in urban water systems, as well as the contaminated water discharged into sewer systems requiring treatment, which can save energy, wastewater chemical treatment, and plant infrastructure costs. Other environmental benefits of *greywater* recycling include groundwater recharge, nutrient reclamation, and greater quality of ground and surface water due to natural soil purification.

See also: **Naturescaping • Rainwater Harvesting • Reclaimed Water • Water Efficiency • Water-Energy Nexus • Xeriscaping**

Further sources: Design Building Wiki; EBN; Sustainable Sources; US EPA; WBDG

▌Ground Sourced Heat Pump

Geothermal heat pumps use the constant temperature of the earth as an exchange medium for heat. Although many parts of the country experience seasonal temperature extremes—from scorching heat in the summer to sub-zero cold in the winter—the ground a few feet below the earth's surface remains at a relatively constant temperature. —Energy.gov: geothermal heat pumps

The Earth's ground temperature just five feet or more below the surface is usually a stable temperature, approximately 55°F, year round regardless of weather. Geothermal conditioning uses the Earth's thermal storage capacity for heating, cooling, and ventilation by using a series of pipes inserted into the ground in loops to deposit or extract low-intensity heat. The heat from the ground is transferred indoors to satisfy some of the heating load and can be reversed to reduce the cooling load by pumping excess heat from indoors to the outside.

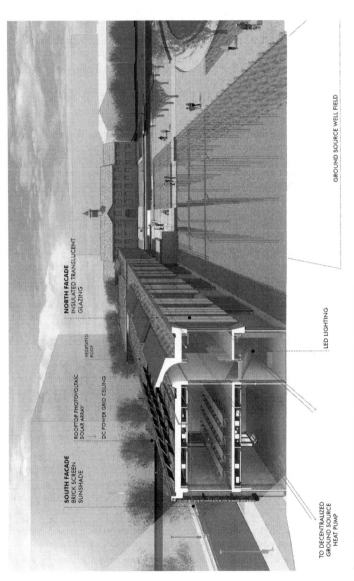

Figure 32 Center for Building Energy and Innovation ground source system
Courtesy ©KieranTimberlake

SOUTH FACADE
BRICK SCREEN
SUNSHADE

ROOFTOP PHOTOVOLTAIC
SOLAR ARRAY

DC POWER GRID CEILING

VEGETATED
ROOF

NORTH FACADE
INSULATED TRANSLUCENT
GLAZING

LED LIGHTING

GROUND SOURCE WELL FIELD

TO DECENTRALIZED
GROUND SOURCE
HEAT PUMP

A *ground sourced heat pump* system, also called a geo-exchange or geothermal heat pump, saves energy because the heating or cooling is not created, but is transported. This heat pump system is not the same as the geothermal heat located miles below the surface used to generate electricity in power plants.

The *ground sourced heat pump* works by extracting heat from one location and releasing the heat to another place. In the cooling mode, a refrigerant is used to absorb the heat indoors and then goes through a mechanical compressor, which squeezes out the heat again. This heat is released to the Earth rather than to the already hot outside air. In the heating mode of the heat pump, the process is reversed bringing the heat inside.

With a *ground source heat pump*, the connection to the ground is through pipes containing a heat transfer liquid, often glycol, either laid in loops horizontally in trenches or with vertical boreholes often drilled over two hundred feet deep. *Ground source heat pumps* can be either a closed-loop system, with no outside liquid entering the loop field or an open-loop system that pumps groundwater through the loop system. Both types have a ground heat exchanger, a heat pump, and some means to distribute the heat, usually an underfloor heating system or radiators.

The retrofit for the Center for Building Energy and Innovation in Philadelphia by KieranTimberlake Architects is a living laboratory for advanced energy retrofit technology. The design showcases many energy-saving strategies in lighting and mechanical systems and has an extensive well field for the *ground sourced heat pump* system (Figures 32, 15, 31).

See also: **Energy Efficiency • Thermal Comfort • Water Sourced Heat Pumps**

Further sources: ASES; Geothermal Energy Association; Geothermal Exchange Organization; Renewable Energy Hub; Sustainable Sources; US DOE

Hannover Principles   **I**

Our present systems of design have created a world that grows far beyond the capacity of the environment to sustain life into the future. The industrial idiom of design, failing to honor the principles of nature, can only violate them, producing waste and harm, regardless of purported intention. If we destroy more forests, burn more garbage, drift-net more fish, burn more coal, bleach more paper, destroy more topsoil, poison more insects, build over more habitats, dam more rivers, produce more toxic and radioactive waste, we are creating a vast industrial machine, not for living in, but for dying in.
—William McDonough, architect

In 1992, William McDonough created a set of sustainable design principles for the Expo 2000 in Hannover, Germany. McDonough established nine key green building principles for designers and architects that proposed rethinking the foundation of sustainability to stress the interdependent relationship with nature.

McDonough defined sustainable design as an approach, emphasizing all design is interdependent with the environmental, economic, and social systems that surround it. The framework for his principles were Earth, Air, Fire, Water and Spirit, and all sustainable design strategies were to be in the context of these elements. He expanded the solely human perspective of sustainability to embrace the idea of a global ecology by allowing all parts of nature to meet their needs now and in the future.

Known as *The Hannover Principles*, these fundamentals have had a valued and philosophical impact on all those involved in the built environment:

1. Insist on the rights of humanity and nature to coexist.
2. Recognize interdependence.
3. Respect relationships between spirit and matter.
4. Accept responsibility for the consequences of design.
5. Create safe objects of long-term value.
6. Eliminate the concept of waste.
7. Rely on natural energy flows.
8. Understand the limitations of design.
9. Seek constant improvement by the sharing of knowledge.

The Hannover Principles are to be seen as a living document to recognize humanity's interdependence with nature, and the responsibility on the part of humans to protect it, which is a philosophical foundation of green building design. The principles eloquently voice the spirit and relationship between the environment, its natural ecosystem processes, and the people who inhabit the planet.

See also: **Circular Economy • Cradle-to-Cradle • Ecological Design • Green Building • Hannover Principles (***Theoryspeak***) • Life-Cycle Assessment • Natural Step • Passive Design • Social Equity • Sustainability**

Further sources: Edwards (2005: 99–103); Kibert et al. (2012: 300); McDonough + Partners and Braungart (1992: 5, 2002, 2013)

Health Product Declaration

Materials matter and the choices architects and interior designers make have consequences for the health of building occupants, communities, and ecological systems. —Robin Guenther, FAIA, Perkins+Will

Buildings were constructed in the past from materials available from the surrounding natural environment, such as stone and wood, but now manufacturers use complex composite materials with problematic chemistry and unknown supply chains from around the world. Most people are not aware of the many chemicals they are exposed to daily or the hazards associated with these substances, but as Robin Guenther, FAIA states, "materials matter" and the choices "designers make have consequences." Consumers, manufacturers, and designers now understand the ecological, human health, and ethical issues surrounding the sourcing, production, use and disposal of building products. The U.S. Environmental Protection Agency states that the average North American spends 90% of their time indoors, and also that many indoor environments have at least two to five times higher pollutant levels than outdoor levels.

The Health Product Declaration Collaborative (HPDC) developed the ingredient-reporting standard, the *Health Product Declaration* Open Standard, as an automated formatting tool. Manufacturers use the standard to report what materials are in their products, and any potential hazards that need revealing to consumers. *Health Product Declarations (HPDs)* are standardized lists that detail the material ingredients of building products, and their potential health impacts, as identified by the International Safety Data Sheet, GreenScreen for Safer Chemicals, or other screening lists.

The *HPD* Open Standard, used primarily in North America, ensures for those specifying and selecting products for construction projects that the material information provided by product companies about their products is reported accurately, reliably, and consistently throughout product categories. The standardized and automated format allows the transparent, accurate, and consistent disclosure of product content and associated health information, which is then published in the *HPD* Open Standard for specifiers or end users to compare products. The inventory of complete product contents and all associated hazards is critical and must be disclosed down to 100 ppm (parts per million) as delivered for end use by the consumer.

Health Product Declarations can be used to supplement life-cycle assessment documentation, as well complementing Environmental Product Declarations, which assess the environmental impact of a product or system. *HPDs* are recognized by green building systems, such as in WELL Building Feature 97, and LEEDv4 Materials and Resource Credits, though an *HPD* disclosure of 1,000 ppm is required for LEED points. *Health Product Declaration* information is recognized in GreenScreen, Cradle-to-Cradle, Pharos, Portico, and Quartz, which are all resources for chemical and material product disclosures.

See also: **Cradle-to-Cradle • Declare Label • Design for the Environment • Environmental Product Declaration • Formaldehyde • Green Chemistry • GreenScreen • LEED Building Certification • REACH Regulation • WELL Building Standard**

Further sources: AIA; HPD User Guide; HPDC; US EPA Indoor Air Quality, https://www.epa.gov/indoor-air-quality-iaq/inside-story-guide-indoor-air-quality; USGBC; WELL

High-Performing Buildings   **I**

The new high-performance building is not just a technological marvel; it's also a cultural touchstone, it's a brand beacon, it's an innovation accelerator. —Peter Weingarten, Gensler architect

The physics-based field of building science has made tremendous improvements in the last few years in understanding how heat, air, and moisture function in a building relative to energy performance, as well as occupant comfort and health. Concerns about energy efficiency, indoor air quality, productivity, investment returns, and the environmental impacts of buildings have called for *high-performance building* strategies that can bring superior efficiency, durability, and occupant health and comfort, by "building the new" and "not on fighting the old" in the words of Socrates over 2,400 years ago.

The secret of change is to focus all of your energy, not on fighting the old but building the new. —Socrates

High-performing buildings are integrated whole building designs that balance both passive design features with the highly efficient equipment, glazing, and materials needed to maintain peak performance. Passive design strategies can address proper site-responsive orientation and climate responsive form to efficiently balance needed daylighting with solar heat gain, to effectively capture natural ventilation, and to maximize the use of wind or solar renewables, all to reduce the building's energy demands and maintain a healthy indoor environment. One of the key strategies of high performance in buildings is to focus early on the building envelope; the walls, roof, and foundations. New innovative materials and technologies have increased the superior performance of buildings with highly efficient mechanical systems, intelligent automated controls, super insulation, high-performing glazing, and advanced renewable energy systems.
The U.S. GSA Federal Center South Building 1202 by ZGF Architects is a net-zero *high-performing building* by integrating innovative active and passive strategies as well as innovative materials to transform a Seattle brownfield site into an award-winning example of sustainable design. Using structural piles for geothermal heating and cooling and phase change thermal storage tank, the Federal Center South used newly designed products of chilled sails, lighting, and a reclaimed wood/concrete composite floor to achieve aggressive energy targets. Rainwater is reused for toilets, rooftop cooling tower, atrium features, and for irrigation (Figure 33). This is the type of building, that in his words above Peter Weingarten of Gensler Architects, might call a "cultural touchstone" and an "innovation accelerator".
The U.S. Energy Policy Act of 2005 defined a *High-Performance Building* as a "building that integrates and optimizes all major high-performance building attributes, including energy efficiency, durability, life-cycle

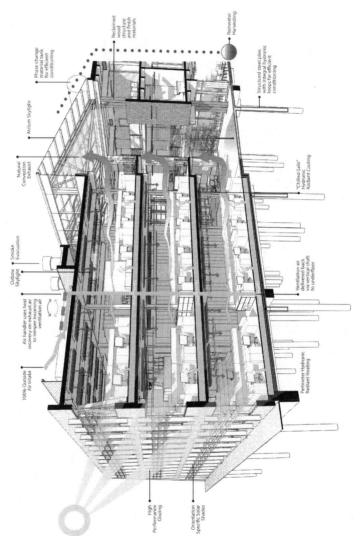

Reclaimed wood structure and finish materials

Phase change material tank for efficient conditioning

Rainwater Harvesting

Atrium Skylight

Structural steel piles with integral hydronic loops for efficient conditioning

Natural Convection Exhaust

"Chilled Sails" Hydronic Radiant Cooling

Smoke Evacuation

Oxbow Skylight

Ventilation air delivered back via vertical shaft to underfloor

Air handler uses heat recovery on exhaust air to temper incoming ventilation air

100% Outside Air Intake

Perimeter Hydronic Radiant Heating

High Performance Glazing

Orientation Specific Solar Shades

Figure 33 GSA Federal Center South Building 1202, Seattle
Courtesy ©ZGF Architects LLP

performance, and occupant productivity." With the Energy Independence and Security Act of 2007, the definition expanded to include
"energy conservation, environment, safety, security, durability, accessibility, cost-benefit, productivity, sustainability, functionality, and operational considerations."

The performance of a building looks at specific characteristics based
on quantifiable benchmarks, or points of reference, that can be evaluated and verified, such as energy consumed or generated, and water
consumed, captured, or reused. When looking the energy performance
of a building, the thermal transfer and air leakage are evaluated, while
the environmental performance looks at the environmental footprint of
the building, the acoustic transmission, and ballistic protection.

The level of safety would be the ability to protect the occupants and
resist the effects of seismic, wind, flood, and fire events, while a building's level of security would assess the protection from blasts, chemical, biological or radioactive exposures. The buildings durability looks
at the service life, migration of water vapor, and water penetration,
while the operational performance estimates the potential interruptions of building operations.

The level of sustainable characteristics would be using such strategies as renewable energy and daylighting. All of these features are
interdependent with each other, and all work together to create a completely integrated *high-performing building.*

See also: **Climate Responsive Design • Durability • Ecological
Footprint • Energy Efficiency • Green Building • Life-Cycle Cost
Analysis • Passive Design • Renewable Energy • Sustainability •
Universal and Inclusive Design • Water Efficiency**

Further sources: EBN; High-Performing Building Council; National Institute of Building Sciences; U.S. Energy Policy Act 2005; WBDG

Hydrofluorocarbons

**There's never been a clearer threat to survival, or to justice, than the
rapid rise in the planet's temperature caused by and for the profit of
a microscopic percentage of its citizens.** —Bill McKibben

In October 2016 in Kigali, Rwanda, at the 28th Meeting of the Parties
to the Montreal Protocol on Substances that Deplete the Ozone Layer,
an international agreement was reached to phase out *hydrofluorocarbons (HFCs)* in efforts to fight climate change. These *hydrofluorocarbons* are used in air conditioners and refrigerators, and are considered
the world's fastest growing climate pollutants. These pollutants are
causing in the words of Bill McKibben, a "rapid rise in the planet's
temperature."

Hydrofluorocarbons are combinations of hydrogen, fluorine and carbon atoms, and are used in manufacturing and are also emitted as
byproducts of industrial processes. *HFCs* were introduced in the 1980s
as alternatives to the ozone-depleting substances of partially halogenated hydrocarbons that were used for commercial, personal and
industrial purposes. These earlier ozone-depleting substances (ODSs),

which were eliminated in the 1987 Montreal Protocol, contained either chlorine or bromine and were also considered greenhouse gases. *HFCs* are not a threat to the ozone layer, as they do not contain chlorine, but *HFCs* have a very high global warming potential (GWP) and are listed as prohibited greenhouse gases in the Kyoto Protocol.

Hydrofluorocarbons currently emit as much pollution as 300 coal-fired power plants. —John Kerry, former Secretary of State

The ability of *HFCs* to trap the heat radiating off the Earth is hundreds or thousands of times more potent than that of carbon dioxide. The danger from *HFCs* has grown as the sale of refrigerators, air conditioners, insulating foam, and even inhalers, have rapidly increased in emerging economies, such as China and India. This danger, as alluded to by former U.S. Secretary of State John Kerry, will continue to grow as air conditioners and refrigeration are attained by millions of new households worldwide.

The UN Environmental Program predicts that reducing *HFCs* under the Kigali Amendment to the Montreal Protocol could reduce global warming by 0.5°C by the end of the century, and is—in the following words of David Doniger—essential to meeting the climate goals of the Paris Agreement.

[The Kigali Agreement] is equal to stopping the entire world's fossil-fuel CO_2 emissions for more than two years. —David Doniger, NRDC

See also: **Climate Change • Global Warming • Greenhouse Gases • Kyoto Protocol • Montreal Protocol • Paris Climate Agreement**

Further sources: EBN; NRDC; UNEP; US Department of State

▌Hydrogen Fuel Cells

Hydrogen is high in energy, yet an engine that burns pure hydrogen produces almost no pollution. NASA has used liquid hydrogen since the 1970s to propel the space shuttle and other rockets into orbit. Hydrogen fuel cells power the shuttle's electrical systems, producing a clean byproduct —pure water, which the crew drinks. —Renewable Energy World

A promising source of clean power for the planet is hydrogen, which is the simplest, most abundant element in the universe. The word hydrogen comes from the Greek word for water, "hydro," and forming, "genes." Essential for life and present in nearly all molecules in living things, hydrogen rarely occurs as a gas naturally. It is usually combined with other elements, primarily oxygen (O), and with water (H_2O) and other organic matter.

Hydrogen is produced by the separation from its source material, purification, and then pressurization. Any hydrogen-rich fuel can be processed to extract its hydrogens, such as natural gas, oil, methane, or ethanol. A "reformer" is used to reformulate non-hydrogen fuels to extract the hydrogen. Hydrogen is used in manufacturing processes, such as glass and silicon chips; reducing metallic ores, hydrogenation of fats and oils; rocket fuels and a pollution-free fuel for vehicles, which William Clay Ford, Jr. believes could end the dominance of the internal combustion engine.

I believe fuel cells could end the 100-year reign of the internal combustion engine. —William Clay Ford, Jr.

Hydrogen is a clean-burning fuel with no carbon emissions. In a *hydrogen fuel cell*, hydrogen fuel is brought in combination with oxygen to create electricity, with water as the only emission. Fuel cells consist of the fuel electrode and an oxidant electrode separated by an ion-conducting membrane, and come in different types, such as phosphoric acid, alkaline, solid oxide, molten carbonate, and proton exchange membrane (PEM) fuel cells.

However, there are challenges with hydrogen, such as the availability and costs of compressed carbon, and the production of hydrogen is not pollution free. Most hydrogen production comes from the steam methane reforming (SMR) method, causing the methane in natural gas, to react with steam, which produces not only hydrogen but also carbon monoxide (CO). The carbon monoxide then goes through more reactions with steam, creating more hydrogen as well as carbon dioxide (CO_2), the primary greenhouse gas impacting climate change.

The way hydrogen is sourced, produced, purified, and distributed all affect the total global warming emissions generated. So far, the most promising and clean way to produce hydrogen is by splitting water into hydrogen and oxygen by using the renewable energy of the sun.

See also: **Alternative Fuels • Energy Efficiency • Global Warming • Greenhouse Gases • Renewable Energy**

Further sources: Union of Concerned Scientists USA; US DOE Hydrogen Program; WBDG

Hydropower

It should be borne in mind that electrical energy obtained by harnessing a waterfall is probably fifty times more effective than fuel energy. —Nikola Tesla, inventor

The harnessing of waterfalls is the most economical method for drawing energy from the sun. —Nikola Tesla

Water is constantly moving in the hydrologic cycle, and *hydropower* uses this power of moving water to generate hydroelectric energy and is the largest source of emission-free renewable energy worldwide. Nikola Tesla, the inventor who is best known for his contributions to the design of the alternating current, was an avid proponent of hydropower as shown by his words above, and is commemorated with a statue at Niagara Falls.

A hydroelectric plant typically uses three different types of facilities: run-of-the-river, impoundment, and pumped storage. A run-of-the-river system diverts a portion of river water, rotating a turbine to create electricity. An impoundment system uses a dam creating a large reservoir, where openings in the dam drop water down through pipes to spin turbines, generating electricity. A pumped storage system uses water that has already flowed through turbines back to a storage pool to store for when energy demands are low. The advantages of this are cost-effective power for daily peak demands, while also working in conjunction with other intermittent renewable resources, such as wind and solar.

Hydropower generation does not emit global warming gases or air pollutants, but the construction and operation of *hydropower* projects can have negative environmental and social consequences. Blocking rivers with dams can damage water quality, prevent fish migration, impair river habitats, and oust local communities. Dams that flood areas with live vegetation risk organic material decomposing and emitting massive amounts of methane. Reducing flows downriver can alter water temperatures, seasonal flows, sediment flows, oxygen levels, and degrade habitats. Salmon migrating from the ocean to their upstream spawning grounds was decreased by 90% at one point in building four dams in the U.S. on the Snake River. Fish ladders and barging up fish are current attempts at remediation. In creating reservoirs, lands are flooded and often dislocate entire communities, livelihoods, and cultures of people.

China has been the global leader in hydroelectric development for over ten years, adding more new installed *hydropower* capacity each year than the rest of the world combined, though the Three Gorges Dam in China also famously dislocated 1.2 million people. China is also the world leader in total low-carbon renewable energy, adding huge capacities of wind and solar while showing a determined effort to combat its staggering urban air pollution.

Small-hydro, micro-hydro, and mini-hydro, which are all incrementally smaller, can have lower environmental impacts and ecological footprints due to scale. All *hydropower* systems can aim to maintain and protect environmental flows, water quality, upstream and downstream fish passage, watersheds, culture, and all species habitat protection.

See also: **Biodiversity • Ecological Design • Renewable Energy**

Further sources: International Hydropower Association; IRENA; UNEP; Union of Concerned Scientists USA, http://www.ucsusa.org/clean_en ergy/our-energy-choices/renewable-energy/how-hydroelectric-ener gy.html#bf-toc-2; WBDG

Indoor Environmental Quality   I

Now I see the secret of making the best person: it is to grow in the open air and to eat and sleep with the earth. —Walt Whitman

With city dwellers spending well over half their time indoors, the quality of the environment inside our buildings is vital to human health and well-being, as we are not "in the open air" and "sleep with the earth" as Walt Whitman advocates. People inhale over 33 pounds of air daily, and the quality of this indoor air depends on the control of pollutants, removing outdoor air contaminants, and supplying some fresh outdoor air. This air impacts our health, as indoor air can be 3–5 times more contaminated than outdoor air. The quality of these building conditions, including the quality of indoor air affecting the physical and psychological health of its occupants, is referred to as *indoor environmental quality (IEQ)*.

Green buildings with good *indoor environmental quality* can protect the health and comfort of the building's occupants, with the proper design of daylighting, views, thermal comfort, acoustical comfort, pollutant control, and Indoor Air Quality (IAQ), which are all responsible for the *indoor environmental quality* of a building.

The Natural Resources Defense Council Expansion in New York by Croxton Collaborative Architects achieved the highest Platinum LEED Commercial-Interiors rating ever achieved in designing the NRDC workplace into a more sustainable universal plan that increases occupant density while improving well-being. The space encourages collaboration, "democratizes" window space and views, and provides superior *indoor environmental quality* with deep daylighting and controls, healthy product selection, flexible partition arrangements, task lighting, and occupancy sensors (Figure 34).

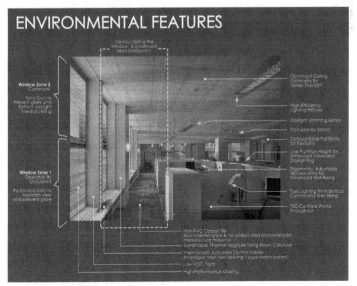

Figure 34 Natural Resources Defense Council
Courtesy ©Croxton Collaborative Architects

High-quality indoor environments can enhance occupants' well-being and working conditions while decreasing sick building syndrome, building-related illnesses, liability, complaints, and absenteeism, and can increase worker productivity and building value. Amory Lovins eloquently stated the qualities of the perfect indoor environment in his following words.

[Spaces should create] . . . delight when entered, pleasure when occupied, and regret when departed. —Amory Lovins

Strategies to improve the *indoor environmental quality* of a building are to ensure good quality design. connections to the outdoors with views. integration of natural elements. provide occupant thermal controls. intelligent ventilation design. prevent airborne bacteria and mold by managing moisture sources. use pollutant-free building products, and design for optimal acoustic performance.

Most green building assessment and certification systems—such as LEED, Green Globes, WELL, and Living Building Challenge—require a responsible relationship between the indoor environment and the health and comfort of building occupants. The USGBC LEED *Indoor Environmental Quality (IEQ)* category addresses indoor air quality with ventilation and thermal comfort requirements, while also demanding low-emitting materials, source control, lighting quality, advanced day-lighting strategies, quality views, and enhanced acoustical performance.

The many design strategies and environmental factors involved in providing high-quality indoor environments in schools, offices, or residences, all have a significant impact on the health and well-being of building occupants, and influences the way we learn, work and live.

See also: **Daylighting • Declare Label • LEED Building Certification • REACH Regulation • Sick Building Syndrome • Thermal Comfort • Volatile Organic Compounds • WELL Building Standard**

Further sources: CDC; EBN; ILFI; US EPA; USGBC; WBDG

Industrial Ecology

[Industrial Ecology] is a field of study and practice that focuses on how industry can be developed or restructured to reduce environmental burdens throughout the product life cycle. —
Dictionary of Sustainable Management

[To do] . . . more and more with less and less until eventually, you can do everything with nothing. —Buckminster Fuller

Earth's human and natural systems are in a time of rapid change. With increasing development, there are major issues with resource availability, increasing the release of toxic chemicals, climate change effects, and the destruction of our natural capital (air, water, minerals, soil, and all living things). In our oceans alone we can see these impacts: the dumping of plastics entering our food chains, warming oceans causing coral bleaching, and sea level rise, along with less salinity in our ocean waters due to ice melting.

Industrial ecology is a systems practice for rapidly industrializing countries, such as in China and India, and companies to deal with the complex problems of waste and material management, energy access, water quantity and quality, which all relate to greenhouse gas emissions. The *industrial ecology* process reduces these climate-changing emissions, along with air, land, and water pollution from fossil fuel combustion, with energy conservation, dematerialization, and reuse of material byproducts—as Buckminster Fuller states, to do "more and more with less and less." Industrial processes shift from "open-loop" systems that produce waste materials, to "closed-loop" systems where wastes become inputs or "nutrients" for new processes, either within a manufacturing plant or used by another process.

The first law of ecology is that everything is related to everything else. —Barry Commoner

Industrial ecology calls for restructuring industrial systems as living systems interdependent with natural processes where, as Barry Commoner states, "everything is related to everything else." This calls for the designed coordination of the entire life-cycle of products and processes, from extraction, production, use, and disposal. Along with life-cycle planning, critical industrial ecology practices are minimizing material and energy consumption, dematerialization and decarbonization of products, reducing ecological impacts, eco-industrial parks, producer responsibility, and eco-efficiency.

See also: **Circular Economy • Closed-Loop Supply Chain • Cradle-to-Cradle • Dematerialization • Greenhouse Gases • Life-Cycle Assessment**

Further sources: Fuller (2000); Hawken (1993: 61–67)

Integrated Design   █

When we try to pick out anything by itself, we find it hitched to everything else in the Universe. —John Muir, naturalist

The process of designing a product at Apple was integrally related to how it would be engineered and manufactured. To do so required total collaboration between the designers, the product developers, the engineers, and the manufacturing. —Steve Jobs

Throughout the test of time, the best durable, elegant and useful buildings constructed have been the consequence of superior design constancy at all levels. *Integrated design* calls for the early, active and continuing collaboration of qualified participants such as architects, engineers, contractors, specialized consultants, landscape architects, code officials, financial advisors, the owner, users, and community members, all acting as a team in the design process. Getting the right multi-disciplinary team around the table at the outset invites innovative ideas and decisions made together, based on a holistic understanding of the building project. When the insights and various skills of the vested participants, proposed systems, and business practices are integrated together into a collaborative process, the project can maximize environmental, economic, and resource efficiencies throughout all phases of the design, construction, and occupancy.

Integrated design differs from the conventional linear design process, which approaches problems independent and individually, while an integrated process tackles each issue with the varied viewpoints of all the disciplines and participants involved where, as John Muir points out in the opening quote, everything is "hitched to everything else in the universe."

Participants' efforts are distributed for collaboration from building inception to delivery, and all are trusted to focus on entire project positive outcomes rather than individual specialized goals. As Steve Jobs stated at the beginning of this chapter, great things are done by "collaboration" and a "team of people." Frank Lloyd Wright referred to this critical process as organic design, using the integral relationship between all the parts to the whole, just as it is with the participants to the team.

Great things in business are never done by one person. They're done by a team of people. —Steve Jobs

Many crucial sustainable design decisions are made early in the design process, so it is vital to set goals and get valuable input from the design team and key stakeholders early before schematic design begins. Visioning design charrettes start very early in the team process and continue to collaborate and test ideas through the final design and even construction. Key decisions and judgments are made by the project team as a whole on the merits of achieving the best environmental and resource-efficient results for the entire project.

Research and analysis are essential to reducing environmental impacts and increasing the efficiencies, especially in site, water, material and energy systems. Ideas are tested through energy modeling and analytical tools, and then tested again. The strength of *integrated design* is thinking outside of the box and letting assumptions and rules of thumb be replaced by strong up to date analytical modeling tools. Early in the process, knowing the program and site, the team can play with the major parameters in modeling such as building size, shape, and orientation. As the design progresses, comparisons in insulation levels, envelope types, window performance and other energy efficiencies can be analyzed using Building Information Modeling software.

See also: **Building Information Modeling • Charrette (***Archispeak***) • Green Building • High-Performing Buildings • Integrated Practice (***Theoryspeak***) • Sustainable Design**

Further sources: EBN; 7 Group (2009); Keeler (2009); WBDG

Intergovernmental Panel on Climate Change   I

If we take all this action, and it turns out not to be true, we have reduced pollution and have better ways to live; the downside is very small. The other way around, and we don't act, and it turns out to be true, then we have betrayed future generations, and we don't have the right to do that. —Tony Blair, former U.K. Prime Minister

The *Intergovernmental Panel on Climate Change (IPCC)* is the major international authority for the assessment of climate change. Established in 1988 by the UN Environment Programme (UNEP) and the World Meteorological Organization (WMO), the *IPCC* is responsible for providing scientific and technical reports for the UN Framework Convention on Climate Change. The *IPCC* does not handle the research or monitor climate data, but the group reviews the assessments and then reports on the most recent worldwide information concerning the human-induced effects, the impacts, and the options for the adaptation and mitigation of climate change. The Nobel Peace Prize was shared between the *IPCC* and Al Gore in 2007.

The *IPCC's* fifth assessment report (AR5) was released in 2014, and the sixth is scheduled to be released in 2022. The AR5 report confirms the evidence that the human influences on the climate system are clear, and the recent anthropogenic emissions of greenhouse gases are the highest in history. Recent climate changes have already caused widespread impacts on human and natural ecosystems. The report found the continuation of human activities causing these greenhouse gas emissions will create the continued warming and long-lasting changes that will disrupt the climate system, increasing the chance of dangerous, inescapable, and permanent impacts on people and the environment. As Tony Blair, the former U.K. Prime Minister urges in his quote opening this chapter, "we don't have the right" to betray future generations by not acting now.

This report tells us that we have two clear choices: cut emissions now and invest in adaptation—and have a world that has challenging and just barely manageable risks, or do nothing and face a world of devastating and unmanageable risks and impacts. —Samantha Smith, World Wildlife Fund

The *Intergovernmental Panel on Climate Change* highlights that we have the ability avoid the risks of climate change by limiting our temperature increase to below 2°C relative to pre-industrial levels if we act urgently. The world must make the right choice to "cut emissions now and invest in adaptation" as Samantha Smith of the World Wildlife Fund so clearly states in the preceding quote, emphasizing that if we continue with business as usual and wait to take action, the environmental, social, and economic costs and challenges will be far far greater.

We cannot despair of humanity since we ourselves are human beings. —Albert Einstein

See also: **Anthropogenic • Climate Change • Global Warming • Kyoto Protocol • Paris Climate Agreement**

Further sources: IPCC; NASA; UNEP; WMO

International Green Construction Code

International Green Construction Code is the first model code to include sustainability measures for the entire construction project and its site —from design through construction, certificate of occupancy and beyond. The new code is expected to make buildings more efficient, reduce waste, and have a positive impact on health, safety and community welfare. —IgCC Council 2012

Green building rating systems and certifications have motivated high-performance building design, but most of these systems are not mandatory, usually unless by a government mandated regulation. Unlike the LEED rating system certification, the *International Green Construction Code (IgCC)* is mandatory and designed to be integrated with existing codes and ordinances. The *IgCC* is a step toward performance-based design, leading to a positive outcome-based design. The *IgCC* is an alternative compliance system in relation to ASHRAE 189.1, which is supported by the AIA, ASTM, ASHRAE, USGBC, and the IES.

The *International Green Construction Code* covers Administration and Definitions, Jurisdictional Requirements & Life Cycle Assessment, Site Development and Land Use, Material Resource Conservation and Efficiency, Energy Conservation, Water Resource Conservation, Indoor Environmental Quality and Comfort, Commissioning, Operations and Maintenance, and Existing Buildings. A few examples of *International Green Construction Code* criteria are: site development is prohibited on floodplains; 55% of construction materials must be recycled, recyclable, bio-based or indigenous; and water conservation measures of collecting rainwater and use of greywater for lower quality purposes, such as flushing toilets.

The *International Green Construction Code* is intended to increase the efficiency of using natural resources in the built environment while paving the way for more zero-energy buildings in the future. MM

See also: **Energy Efficiency • Indoor Environmental Quality • Materials and Resources • Sustainable Site Design • Water Efficiency**

Resources: EBN; EPA; ICC; WBDG

International Organization for Standardization

Standard: A specification that establishes a common language, and contains a technical specification or other precise criteria and is designed to be used consistently, as a rule, a guideline, or a definition. —British Standards Institution

As the world's largest provider of international standards, the *International Organization for Standardization (ISO)* has over twenty-one thousand standards associated with a wide variety of industries, such as manufactured products, technology, food safety, healthcare, agriculture, and environmental management, that touch nearly all aspects of life. Founded in 1947 and headquartered in Geneva, the *ISO* is a non-governmental organization, whose members are the various standards organizations from 165 member countries.

The *International Organization for Standardization* develops common standards among nations to facilitate world trade on a fair basis by ensuring all tradable products are safe, reliable, and of high quality. These standards allow certified products to be directly compared using the minimum international standards set while safeguarding the end consumer of the services or products. *ISO* has approximately three thousand technical committees for the rigorous standards development process, and are reviewed every five years.

As a document, the *International Organization for Standardization* provides the requirements, guidance, and specifications needed to ensure the consistency of quality products and efficient services. For example, the *ISO* 26000 implements corporate social responsibility standards by applying the seven primary principles of socially responsible behavior: accountability, transparency, ethical behavior, respect for investors' interests, respect for the rule of law, respect for the international norms of behavior, and respect for human rights. The *ISO* 14000 implements environmental management standards to ensure organizations follow an ecofriendly management and policy system and comply with environmental laws and regulations. Within the 14000 standard, then *ISO* 14020 addresses environmental labels and declarations, such as Health or Environmental Product Declarations.

The *International Organization of Standardization's* standards on toy safety, road safety, food safety, and auto safety are just a few that make everyone safer. Standards that address greenhouse or ozone-depleting gases, radiation exposure, and the environmental impacts to the water, air, and soil quality contribute immensely to preserving the health of humans and the environment.

See also: **Environmental Product Declaration • Health Product Declaration**

Further sources: ANSI; BSI; EPA; ISO

JUST Program

Because equal rights, fair play, justice, are all like the air: we all have it, or none of us has it. That is the truth of it. —Maya Angelou

A society that embraces all sectors of humanity and allows the dignity of equal access and fair treatment is a civilization in the best position to make decisions that protect and restore the natural environment that sustains us all. —JUST, International Living Future Institute website

The International Living Future Institute's *JUST program* is a voluntary social justice label for organizations to improve social equity and engagement by disclosing how employees are treated and where financial and community investments are made. As a "nutritional label," the *JUST program* shows how socially just and equitable an organization is by diversity, equity, safety, worker benefit, local benefit, and stewardship. A few of the measurable voluntary engagements to increase social justice are charitable giving, community volunteer hours, healthcare, pay-scale equity, family friendly, living wage, and worker happiness, among others. These are what Maya Angelou so eloquently states are "all like the air: we all have it, or none of us has it."

The *JUST program* is an outgrowth of the International Living Future Institute's (ILFI) green building assessment system, The Living Building Challenge. The Equity Petal credit category of the Living Building Challenge promotes fostering a just and equitable community that is inclusive, regardless of background, age, class, race, gender, or sexual orientation.

Figure 35 Rene Cazenave Apartments for the disabled and formerly homeless in San Francisco, CA.
Courtesy ©Leddy Mahtum Stacy Architects

We need to defend the interests of those whom we've never met and never will. —Jeffrey Sachs

These principles of embracing all sectors of humanity are exemplified in the words of Jeffrey Sachs in the preceding quote, by protecting the interests of those who we will never meet. An inspiring project that embodies the dignity of equal access and fair treatment is the sustainable award-winning Rene Cazenave Apartments (RCA) in San Francisco designed by Leddy Mahtum Stacy Architects. The RCA provides a permanent home and services for formerly chronically homeless residents, many with physical and mental disabilities. The residents have affordable and accessible mini-studio apartments along with life-changing social, educational, and medical facilities (Figure 35).

See also: **Affordable Housing • Smart Growth • Social Equity • Sustainability • WELL Building Standard**

Further sources: EBN; ILFI; LEED; WELL

Kyoto Protocol

On climate change, we often don't fully appreciate that it is a problem. We think it is a problem waiting to happen. —Kofi Annan, former UN Secretary-General

By the time we see that climate change is really bad, your ability to fix it is extremely limited. The carbon gets up there, but the heating effect is delayed. And then the effect of that heat on the species and ecosystems is delayed. That means that even when you turn virtuous, things are actually going to get worse for quite a while. —Bill Gates, Microsoft co-founder

In Kyoto, Japan in 1997, the United Nations Framework Convention on Climate Change (UNFCCC) negotiated the *Kyoto Protocol*, an internationally binding treaty to bring countries together to reduce global warming, acknowledging worldwide that global warming does exist and that human-made carbon dioxide emissions have caused it. UN Secretary-General Kofi Annan's charge was to make countries fully appreciate "that it is a problem" and not a problem waiting to happen. In agreeing to cope with the effects of temperature increases mostly caused by 150 years of industrialization, the ratifying countries decided to reduce the six major greenhouse gases (GHG) that contribute to global warming: carbon dioxide (CO_2), methane, nitrous oxide, hydrofluorocarbons, perfluorocarbons, and sulfur hexafluoride. These countries realized that, in the words of Bill Gates, "even when you turn virtuous, things are actually going to get worse for quite a while."

The goal of the *Kyoto Protocol* was to reduce these global emissions by at least 5% below the 1990 global level between 2008–2012. Recognizing that developed countries are primarily responsible for the high levels of GHGs in the atmosphere, the Protocol placed a heavier burden on developing nations under the idea of shared but also differentiated responsibilities. These countries were allowed to use emissions trading, a market-based approach, which allowed nations that could easily meet their targets to sell credits to those countries that cannot.

Under terms of the agreement, the *Kyoto Protocol* would not take effect until at least 55 countries involved in the UNFCCC ratified it, and had to represent at least 55% of the world's total CO_2 emissions for 1990. The agreement was entered into force when Russia ratified the agreement in November 2004. Under President George W. Bush, the U.S. withdrew support for the Kyoto agreement in 2001 and Canada withdrew in December 2011, but by the end of the first commitment period, 191 countries had ratified the proposal. The detailed rules for implementation for the years 2008–2012 were adopted at the Conference of Parties (COP) in 2001 in Marrakesh, Morocco and referred to as the Marrakesh Accords.

In Qatar, the Doha Amendment to the *Kyoto Protocol* was adopted in December 2012, providing several updates to the agreement, such as a revised list of greenhouse gases, increasing the reductions to at least 18% from 1990 levels, and extended a second commitment period from 2013–2020.

The *Kyoto Protocol* was seen as the critical first step toward real worldwide emission reductions to stabilize greenhouse gas emissions and provided the structure and cooperation for the future 2015 International Paris Agreement on climate change, where in 2015 Canada and the U.S. rejoined the international climate change struggle. Later in 2017 under the administration of U.S. President Donald Trump, the U.S. has taken measures to withdraw from the Paris Climate Agreement, though many individual states and cities remain strongly committed.

See also: **Climate Change • Fossil Fuels • Global Warming • Greenhouse Gases • Hydrofluorocarbons • Methane • Paris Climate Agreement**

Further sources: EBN; IPCC; UN Framework Convention on Climate Change; World Watch

Land Ethic

We abuse land because we regard it as a commodity belonging to us. When we see land as a commodity to which we belong, we may begin to use it with love and respect. —Aldo Leopold, *A Sand County Almanac*

Like winds and sunsets, wild things were taken for granted until progress began to do away with them. Now we face the question whether a still higher "standard of living" is worth its cost in things natural, wild and free. —Aldo Leopold, *A Sand County Almanac*

Land Ethic is a philosophy and theoretical system regarding our relationship with nature. It was developed by Aldo Leopold and first appeared in his *A Sand County Almanac* (1949).

Ethics generally is concerned with definitions of human values, good behavior and living the virtuous life. Ethics addresses our relationships with other individuals and with society. It essentially entails a limitation of human freedom for the good of the whole. Ethical principles are based on the concept that an individual is a member of a community of interdependent parts. In his *land ethics*, Leopold expands this respect and concern for community to include nature.

For Leopold, our community includes the soil, water, air, plants, and animals. He believed it is ultimately best for us to live in a healthy ecosystem where nature's rights are as important as our own. *Land ethics* holds that an action is right when it promotes and preserves the integrity, stability, health, and beauty of the land and its biotic community, and that human attitudes and actions affecting the land should not be solely driven by economic, utilitarian, or libertarian motives. *Land ethics* sees nature as having intrinsic value not requiring human imposition of anthropocentric concepts for determination of worth.

All ethics so far evolved rest upon a single premise; that the individual is a member of a community of interdependent parts. The land ethic simply enlarges the boundaries of the community to include soils, waters, plants and animals, or collectively the land. —Aldo Leopold, *The Land Ethic* 1949

Leopold was not opposed to the use of natural resources for human purposes but held that use of the land should be thoughtful, modest, measured, and respectful, and that all human engagements and transactions with nature be with knowledge of the land and care for the long-term renewability and well-being of ecosystems.

Land ethics is not a list of rules but rather an attitude, disposition, and orientation toward nature. Leopold recognized that specific land use principles would evolve over time as our understanding of natural processes expanded. *Land ethics'* goal is to simply shift humanity from master and conqueror of nature to citizen and steward of the biosphere.

There is a clear kinship between land ethics and sustainability. They share many values, goals, and strategies. Any sustainability-oriented design decisions will necessarily align with and support the land ethics vision.

Natural resources conservation and renewal, simpler lifestyles, efficient transportation systems, less wasteful human processes, passive
thermal comfort, water harvesting and recycling, and creative use of
waste are examples of land ethics and sustainability common ground. EW

See also: **Biodiversity** • **Biophilic Design** • **Certified Wood** •
Ecological Design • **Forest Stewardship Council** • **Forest Sustainable
Management** • **Materials and Resources** • **Social Equity** • **Sustainable
Site Design**

Further sources: Aldo Leopold Foundation

Laudato Si': On Care for Our Common Home   ▌

**If we approach nature and the environment without this openness to
awe and wonder, if we no longer speak the language of fraternity and
beauty in our relationship with the world, our attitude will be that
of masters, consumers, ruthless exploiters, unable to set limits on
their immediate needs.** —Pope Francis

In hopes of creating a new dialogue of shaping the future of our planet,
"our common home," Pope Francis, the 266th Roman Catholic pope,
addressed his encyclical, *Laudato Si': On Care for Our Common Home*, to
"every person living on this planet." Released in June 2015, the encyclical addresses climate change, care for the environment, and sustainable development. *Laudato Si'* means "Praise be to you," which is the
first line of the 13th century *Canticle of the Creatures* by St. Francis of
Assisi, who felt called to care for all that exists.

The heart of the document, as stated by Pope Francis, is the urgent
appeal "for a new dialogue about how we are shaping the future of our
planet. We need a conversation that includes everyone, since the environment challenge we are undergoing, and its human roots, concerns
and affects us all." Pope Francis calls for an "ecological conversion"
where people's relationship with the world around them becomes evi-
dent in the protection of our Earth.

**Never have we hurt and mistreated our common home as we have in
the last 200 years.** —Pope Francis

Laudato Si' states that:

**Although the post-industrial period may well be remembered as
one of the most irresponsible in history, nonetheless there is reason to hope that humanity at the dawn of the twenty-first century
will be remembered for having generously shouldered its grave
responsibilities.**

The concern for the natural environment and its people is no longer
seen as "optional" but an integral part of social justice. Pope Francis
believes we must see the interconnected relationships between all the

"universal family" of creation, and this connection to the protection of human life and dignity.

The *Laudato Si'* encyclical has six chapters addressing what is happening to our planet today: the gospel of creation; the human roots of the ecological crisis; integral ecology; lines of approach and action; and ecological education and spirituality. Pope Francis identifies pressing current environmental challenges such as pollution, climate change, water scarcity, loss of biodiversity, declining quality of human life and society, and global inequality. The interconnected relationships in creation appear throughout the document, especially in affirming that in light of increasing climate change and the degradation of our environment, that all must commit with solidarity to the intergenerational common good and justice.

In noting the "need for common and differentiated responsibilities" among nations, Pope Francis in *Laudato Si'* quoted the bishops of Bolivia who stated, "the countries which have benefited from a high degree of industrialization, at the cost of enormous emissions of greenhouse gases, have a greater responsibility of providing a solution to the problems they have caused."

See also: **Climate Change • Global Warming • Hannover Principles • Our Common Future • Precautionary Principle • Social Equity • Sustainable Development**

Further sources: Action Institute; Catholic Climate Covenant; FOCUS: Laudatosi.com; Wikipedia

LEED Building Certification

Thanks to LEED, the core principles of green building (advanced energy efficiency, water conservation, nontoxic building materials, reduction in waste stream, and more) began to take hold at a time when "green building" was widely considered to be a relic from the "sixties and seventies." LEED pushed sustainable design from the margins to the mainstream. —Jason McLennan, ILFI

The U.S. Green Building Council (USGBC) is a non-profit organization promoting sustainability in building design, construction, and operation. In 2000, based primarily on U.K.'s BREEAM green building rating system, USGBC developed *Leadership in Energy and Environmental Design (LEED)*, which promotes environmentally responsible, profitable, and healthy places to live and work.

LEED provides a market-driven framework for implementing measurable green building solutions. There are five rating system construction types: Building Design and Construction (BD+C), Interior Design and Construction, Buildings Operations + Maintenance, Neighborhood Development, and Homes. The *LEED* BD+C system has rating tools for New Construction, Core and Shell, Schools, Retail, Data Centers, Warehouses and Distribution Centers, Hospitality, and Healthcare. Since the first *LEED 1.0*, USGBC has provided several upgrades and in 2013 launched a major revised *LEED* v4, adding a category for location/

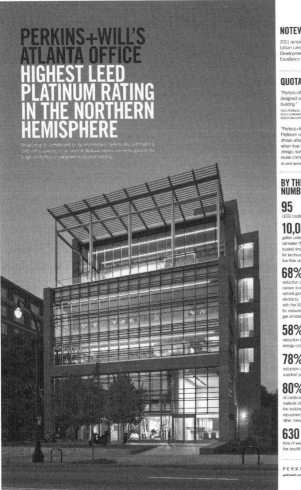

Figure 36 Perkins+Will LEED Platinum Atlanta, GA. Office
Courtesy ©Perkins+Will Architects

transportation connectivity, and greater overall credit accountability with performance measuring.

The latest global environmental concerns are addressed by *LEED v4* credit weighting in accounting for seven major environmental and social impact categories: climate change, human health, water resources, biodiversity, green economy, community, and natural resources. The *LEED v4* BD+C system has a range of categories with different weights depending on the level of impact on the environment or occupant health. The categories are: Energy and Atmosphere, Location and Transportation, Indoor Environmental Quality, Materials and Resources, Water Efficiency, Sustainable Sites, Innovation, Regional Priority Credits, and Integrative Process. Each category's points are totaled in awarding final ratings of platinum, gold, silver, and certified requiring 40–49 out of a possible 110 points.

The Perkins+Will Architects office in Atlanta received the highest LEED Platinum rating in the Northern Hemisphere. The building reuse design reduced the carbon footprint by 68% and reduced energy consumption by 58%. Located in water-stressed Atlanta, the project reduced the municipally supplied potable water 78% by capturing rainwater in 10,000-gallon cisterns to be re-circulated for irrigation and flushing low-flow urinals and toilets (Figure 36).

The USGBC's *LEED* green building rating system has been a huge success worldwide, with LEED projects in more than 164 countries, and with over 2.2 million square feet (206,300 gross square meters) being certified each day. Many incentive programs such as tax reductions, urban density bonuses, priority permitting, reduced fees, and low-interest loans have encouraged green building projects. In the words of the Living Building Challenge creator, Jason McLennan of the International Living Future Institute, *LEED* "pushed sustainable design from the margins to the mainstream." *LEED* has helped drive the global consensus toward the importance of the life-cycle design, construction, and operation of high-performing green buildings, along with their reduced impacts our health and environment.

See also: **BREEAM Certification • Energy Star Certification • Green Building Certification Systems • Green Globes Certification • High-Performing Buildings • Living Building Challenge • Sustainable Design**

Further sources: AIA; EBN; PerkinsWill.com; USGBC LEED; WBDG

▌Lifeboat Ethics

Non-violence leads to the highest ethics, which is the goal of all evolution. Until we stop harming all other living beings, we are still savages. —Thomas Edison

The ecologist and American philosopher Garrett Hardin wrote a famous article in 1974 titled "Lifeboat Ethics: The Case Against Helping the Poor." It was critical of Adlai Stevenson's speech to the United Nations in 1965, in which he popularized the metaphor of a Spaceship Earth, calling for all of humanity as crewmembers to unify together in preserving the global ecosystems that make our lives on that ship imaginable.

Stevenson's address referred to the Earth's population as "half fortunate and half miserable."

Hardin noted more accurately that it is not half the population that is poor and miserable, but a significant majority. He adopted the metaphor of a lifeboat rather than the spaceship to represent the wealthy nations. Sitting safe and secure filling the lifeboats were a small number of wealthy and fortunate residents of the world, representing the developed rich countries. The vast majority of the people, representing poor developing nations, were outside the lifeboats swimming dangerously in the open seas, wanting to get in and share the wealth.

What should the wealthy lifeboat passengers do? Welcoming all the desperately poor people into the lifeboats would have been disastrous, as the boats would have exceeded their limited carrying capacity, just as a nation's land has limited capacity to support its population and energy needs. Eventually, the boats would sink, and all the occupants would share the same disastrous fate.

This social justice metaphor of sharing resources in this situation leaves one with the ethical choice of being "our brother's keeper," which would be trying to save all the people outside the boats, or "to each according to his needs," and leave them all in the water. Hardin argues that given the limits of the physical system the end result is certain: "The boat swamps, everyone drowns. Complete justice, complete catastrophe." If meeting the needs of the disadvantaged results in environmental disaster, one can question if that is justified—so sustainability could indeed have conflicting ethical approaches, one primarily social and one primarily ecological. Though in the words of Thomas Edison earlier, we are all still savages "until we stop harming all other living beings."

A major focus of Hardin's career was the issue of human overpopulation and living within our limits. Hardin called attention to the tragedy of the commons, referring to the damage that action by innocent individuals can inflict on our environment. He argued for controversial subjects such as abortion rights, forced sterilization, limits to non-Western immigration, and the right to die with dignity by suicide, as he and his wife did together in 2003. Hardin coined his first law of human ecology—you can't do only one thing, which implies that there is at least one unwanted consequence.

See also: **Carrying Capacity • Population Growth • Social Equity • Spaceship Earth • Tragedy of the Commons**

Further sources: Hardin (1968, 1974); Kibert et al. (2012: 168)

Life-Cycle Assessment ▮

LCA addresses the environmental aspects and potential impacts (e.g. use of resources and the environmental consequences of releases) throughout a product's life cycle from raw material acquisition through production, use, end-of-life treatment, recycling, and final disposal (i.e. cradle-to-grave). —International Organization of Standardization, ISO 14040

An environmental *life-cycle assessment (LCA)* or *analysis* is a scientific method to quantify the impacts of a product or service, such as toxicity, land practices, greenhouse gases, and air or water pollution, among many others. These impact loads are assessed over the entire life-cycle of the product from its raw material extraction through its transport, manufacture, and use; to the end of its life, which is referred to as "cradle-to-grave."

Life-cycle assessments are often used for internal decision-making in product development and external reporting for regulations and selection. In early product development, *LCA* can guide manufacturer's choices of ingredients and materials based on impacts, and provide valuable benchmarks for analysis. *Life-cycle assessments or analysis* can be used to meet government regulations or third-party standards, and prove that the product is environmentally preferable to other alternatives. The International Organization of Standardization (ISO) Standards 14040 and 14044 describe the principles, frameworks, requirements, and guidelines for managing a *life-cycle assessment*.

The more direct and indirect impact factors detailed in the *life-cycle assessment*, the more complete the assessment will be. Impact factors can include mining and refining raw resources; manufacturing waste; production emissions; transportation; global warming potential; toxicity; air, water, and land pollutants, energy used during products operational life; recyclability as far as upcycling or downcycling; and the product's end of life.

The *life-cycle assessment* can have boundaries of scope in determining the life-cycle stage and what is in each stage. Some *LCAs* only consider the "gate-to-gate" impacts from only the manufacturers start to finish. The material impacts from extraction until the product exits the factory are considered "cradle-to-gate." The most extensive and beneficial *LCAs* use the "cradle-to-grave" boundaries, which include all the impacts of the material's processes between the first resource extractions to the end of life.

See also: **Athena Impact Estimator • BEES Method • Carbon Footprint • Circular Economy • Ecological Footprint• International Organization for Standardization • Life-Cycle Cost Analysis • Systems Thinking**

Further sources: Design Buildings Wiki; EBN; Glass (2002: 184); ISO; Iyengar (2015: 139); Robertson (2014: 251); WBDG; Zbicinski et al. (2006)

❚ Life-Cycle Cost Analysis

Life-cycle costing is a valuable technique that is used for predicting and assessing the cost performance of constructed assets. Life-cycle costing is one form of analysis for determining whether a project meets the client's performance requirements. —International Organization for Standardization, ISO 15686

With the shift in the construction industry toward long-term and systems thinking, the durability, life-cycle costs and paybacks and impacts of the proposed products, systems, and entire buildings are critical. The financial implications of these design decisions must be accurately accounted for to make informed decisions.

Life-cycle cost analysis (LCCA) is a method of assessing the most cost-effective options in purchasing, owning, operating, and disposing of a product, system, or building. The purpose of an *LCCA* is to estimate the overall costs of building-related alternatives, and then the data is used to select the option that ensures the lowest overall costs of ownership. This *life-cycle costing analysis* must happen early in the design processes to allow for revisions that may be needed to assure a reduction in the owner's life-cycle costs.

Life-cycle costing may look at the paybacks of incorporating sustainable building strategies such as integrated photovoltaics, shading devices, automated intelligent building systems, durable materials, daylighting and ventilation atrium benefits, green roofs, reclaimed water systems, super insulation, high-performing glazing, natural ventilation, renewable energies, and higher efficient equipment choices, among many others.

A *life-cycle cost analysis* will help the owner decide if a higher initial cost investment in a particular system or product will result in dramatically reduced operating and maintenance costs over the life of the building. Value engineering, cost estimating, and economic analyses of building-related materials or systems are other approaches to making cost-effective choices in the construction industry.

The owner's initial capital outlay cost for property acquisition is often an important factor that influences the future selection of product or system alternatives. A *life-cycle costing analysis* gives the owner the future costs of the building or product's operational costs, maintenance costs, disposal costs, and returns on investments. The *life-cycle costing* process can be simple or complex, and usually reflects the complexity of the assets being analyzed and often require computerized modeling to look at scenarios to predict the future costs or paybacks needed to make wise investment choices.

The International Organization for Standardization (ISO) 15686:2008 provides guidelines for conducting *life-cycle cost analyses* of buildings and related assets. A complete life-cycle cost projection may also include other financial and accounting costs, such as productivity increases, interest rates, the present value of money, depreciation, and discount rates.

See also: **Durability • International Organization for Standardization • Life-Cycle Assessment • Systems Thinking**

Further sources: Building Design Wiki; Glass (2002: 187); ISO; Robertson (2014: 251); WBDG

Light Pollution   I

Before we invented civilization, our ancestors lived mainly in the open out under the sky. Before we devised artificial lights and atmospheric pollution and modern forms of nocturnal entertainment we watched the stars. There were practical calendar reasons of course, but there was more to it than that. Even today the most jaded city dweller can be unexpectedly moved upon encountering a clear night sky studded with thousands of twinkling stars. When it happens to me after all these years, it still takes my breath away. —Carl Sagan, *Pale Blue Dot*, 1994

Life on Earth has existed for billions of years in a consistent pattern of light and dark from the timely changing natural brilliance of the sun, moon, and stars. Humans navigated by the stars, planted by the moon, and rested after sunset. As Carl Sagan so poetically explains in *Pale Blue Dot*, we have a deep connection with the stars and moon that moves us from within.

The increasing and widespread use of nighttime artificial lighting is not only decreasing our view of the universe and nighttime visibility, but also creating an abundance of problems with our environment, the disruption of nocturnal and diurnal rhythms of humans and wildlife, safety, health, and energy consumption. Recent studies are concerned with how deep the skyglow penetrates the ocean, disrupting aquatic life.

Light pollution is the brightening of the night sky caused by the inappropriate or excessive use of artificial light. *Light pollution* is an international concern as over 50% of the Earth's populations are now living in urban areas under brightened night skies caused by excess lighting for advertising, sports settings, interior and exterior building lighting, and streetlights. Components of *light pollution* can include light clutter, light trespass, skyglow, and glare. Light clutter is confusing, bright, and excessive groups of lights; light trespass is unwanted light where it is not needed; skyglow is brightening of the sky; and glare is an intensely bright light that causes discomfort.

As awareness of *light pollution* has increased, strategies for reduction of skyglow and light trespass have been incorporated into codes and green building rating systems, such as LEED and Green Globes, using both prescriptive and performance-based measures. The recent IES/IDA luminaire classification system, BUG Rating, classifies fixtures regarding backlight, uplight, and glare to reduce light trespass and pollution from outdoor lighting.

For reducing interior lighting's contribution to *light pollution*, the principal strategy is to reduce the amount of light produced at night inside the building, and then to automatically shield light from exiting the buildings. For outdoor lighting, strategies include lighting only where and when needed, minimizing parking and street lighting's upward light transmission by using full cut-off fixtures and low-reflecting surfaces, and using computer modeling to design efficiently and correctly for the project's needs.

See also: **Backlight-Uplight-Glare (BUG) Rating • Lighting • SITES Initiative • Solar Reflectance Index • Sustainable Site Design**

Further sources: IESNA; International Dark Sky Association; Sagan (1994); UN DESA (2014)

▌Lighting

Architecture is the learned game, correct and magnificent, of forms assembled in the light. —Le Corbusier

Even a space intended to be dark should have just enough light from some mysterious opening to tell us how dark it really is. —Louis Kahn

Designing sustainable and energy-efficient *lighting* systems for build-ings requires using natural daylighting to the greatest extent possible and supplementing with efficient and visually comfortable electrical *lighting* systems and controls. Interior *lighting* systems consume sig-nificant amounts of electrical energy and can have major heat impli-cations in a building. The quality of *lighting* can affect the well-being of occupants, both physically and emotionally, and can add drama as in the words at the beginning of this chapter of Le Corbusier and Louis Kahn, both master architect designers of light. In commercial build-ings, electric *lighting* loads are often a third to half of a building's total energy demand. Today energy-efficient *lighting* design uses innovative state-of-the-art lamps, such as LEDs (light emitting-diodes), and auto-mated controllers, sensors, and optic equipment to significantly reduce energy consumption.

Lighting selection must take into account both the performance and aesthetics of the design. The *lighting* lamp selection is usually based on the efficiency (lumens per watt), the color-rendering index, color temperature, life and maintenance, switching, dimming ability, and economics. Luminaire fixtures are usually selected for their *lighting* effectiveness, distribution, efficacy, aesthetics, construction quality, and costs. The visual comfort of *lighting* is measured by the illumination lev-els, including brightness and color, and the distribution in the space. The light spectrum distribution has a significant role in overall visibility and as well on occupants' circadian rhythms, where one's mental and phys-ical behavior follows the twenty-four-hour daily cycle of light and dark.

Bringing in usable natural daylighting can tremendously reduce the electric lighting requirement of a building and is significantly impacted by the building's orientation, form, massing, and ceiling heights. Day-lighting strategies should be integrated with early siting and mass-ing issues such as orienting the building to the south, higher ceilings, using narrower floor plates, and creating openings in the section of the building, such as with atriums or light wells. Interior surface finishes, textures, and colors can all impact *lighting* quality due to reflectivity. Exterior *lighting* is needed for nighttime visibility and security, but care must be taken to prevent glare and light trespass issues.

The programmed use of each interior space determines the quantity and quality of light needed for the tasks to be performed. Solid-state *lighting* technologies, such as LED and organic LED (OLED) products, with a broad range of capabilities and requirements are permeating the market. Solid-state *lighting* equipment influences the building's elec-trical system because it is a non-linear load and special considerations must be taken in the design of compatible systems.

Intelligent building automated systems with sensors for daylighting, occupancy, and occupant needs can also significantly reduce energy loads. Sustainable *lighting* design should first use free natural daylighting to reduce energy demands and then supplement with luminaires selected for the best task use and distribution, while specifying energy-efficient light sources with the most lumens of light per watt of power.

See also: **Building Automated Control System • Daylighting • Energy Efficiency • Light Pollution**

Further sources: Autodesk; EBN; Stein et al. (2006); US DOE; WBDG

▌Livable Streets

Perhaps the soul could remember a little of its origination when people still belong to the spirit of a place. —Martin Prechtel, *Secrets of the Talking Jaguar*

Streets and transportation corridors have historically given precedence to vehicles, often failing to create safe places where people can walk, bicycle, drive, take transit, or socialize. Creating livable streets is a movement to redesign and reinvest in streets as public places for people, as well as critical traffic arteries.

Planning and retrofitting vehicular-oriented streets to serve other functions and users, such as pedestrian and bicyclist needs, stormwater catchment and ecological services, often results in more safe and valuable streets, places with a "spirit of place" in the words of Martin Prechtel. In the United States, urban sprawl and the lack of adequate urban planning has led to vehicular-centric transportation corridors that are often highly connected via vehicular modes of transportation, but often highly isolated for pedestrian and bicyclist connectivity. This results in a lack of community connectivity, dangerous roadways, and declining property values.

In the pre-automobile era, the American tradition was to lay out cities with an orthogonal grid of streets and lots, modeled after James Oglethorpe's plan for the town of Savannah, Georgia. The Oglethorpe Plan was based on the concept of "wards," where squares and orthogonal city blocks create a hierarchical series of functionality within the city. The design maximizes lot coverage on buildable lots while minimizing the open space requirement (as open space is provided in the public realm). The system allows for adaptability, repetition, and rhythmically placed public open space. Automobile traffic is naturally limited to speeds of about 20 mph, which is the threshold for pedestrian comfort in a mixed-modal shared space environment.

With the rise of the automobile in the 1920s, the mobility and efficiency of the motorist took priority over pedestrian needs. Space for parking became an increasing demand, and the urban grid was criticized as inefficient, as small blocks create a large number of intersections. The transition from the urban grid transitioned to more auto-centric plans, as developers sought to minimize the amount of land devoted to roadway infrastructure. By the late 1970s, most subdivisions were built with loop and cul-de-sac type street systems that created no through routes and few if any blocks.

A truly green street considers small-scale components such as street shade, stormwater, and sidewalk width, as well as larger scale principles of urban planning, including hierarchy, transects, and connectivity.

See also: **Neighborhood Development • Sense of Place • SITES Initiative • Sustainable Site Design • Urban Design • Urban Heat Island • Urban Tree Canopy**

Further sources: Burns and Kahn (2005: 240); EBN; SITES; WBDG; Wikipedia

Living Building Challenge   ■

To make the world work for 100% of humanity in the shortest possible time through spontaneous cooperation without ecological offense or the disadvantage of anyone. —Buckminster Fuller

The *Living Building Challenge* is the most rigorous and demanding green building certification on the market today. The *Living Building Challenge* *(LBC)* is a building design framework and also a regenerative philosophy to create places that give back more than they take, as in Buckminster Fuller's elegant opening words to make "the world work for 100% of humanity." The International Living Future Institute's *LBC* requires certified buildings to be 100% net-positive energy with on-site renewables, 100% net-positive water with collection and treatment, and divert or recycle 100% of construction waste. All of *LBC's* principles are mandatory and performance-based, requiring twelve months of continuous building operation with an on-site audit to ensure compliance.

One of the first Living Building Challenge certified buildings is the Omega Center for Sustainable Living in Rhinebeck, New York, a multipurpose wastewater filtration facility designed by BNIM Architects. An Eco Machine or "living machine" system is used for treating wastewater, a rainwater system provides greywater for toilets, and three solar photovoltaic arrays provide renewable energy to achieve net-zero energy and net-zero water (Figure 37).

Figure 37 Omega Center for Sustainable Living, Rhinebeck, NY
Photo ©Assassi, Courtesy of BNIM

In designing for the future, the *Living Building Challenge* looks at both upstream and downstream impacts of modern buildings and materials. The *LBC* hopes to create buildings that are regenerative, in connecting occupants to light, air, food, nature, community; and self-sufficient, by remaining within the site resource limits; and have positive impacts and interactions with human and natural systems.

What if every single act of design and construction made the world a better place? —Living Building Challenge website

Imagining that a building can be as efficient as a "flower," the *Living Building Challenge* uses the "flower" as a symbol for the built environment and organizes it into seven performance areas or "Petals," including Place, Water, Energy, Health and Happiness, Materials, Equity, and Beauty. Each performance area (Petal) has twenty further detailed requirements, called Imperatives. In addition to *LBC* full certification, buildings can be "Petal Certified" by satisfying three of the seven petals, and at least one must be Energy, Water, or Materials.

Developed by Jason McLennan in 2006, the *Living Building Challenge* along with the Cascadia Green Building Council is now overseen by The International Living Future Institute (ILFI). The ILFI manages the umbrella Living Future Challenge, the Living Product Challenge, and the Living Community Challenge. The ILFI also oversees a Net-Zero Energy Building (NZEB) certification under the *Living Building Challenge*. This requires a building to meet 100% of its energy needs by on-site renewable energy on a net-annual basis, and meet four required imperatives in the *LBC* rating system: Limits to Growth, Rights to Nature, Beauty and Inspiration, and Inspiration and Education.

See also: **BREEAM Certification • Energy Efficiency • Green Building Certification Systems • Green Globes Certification • Green Star Certification • LEED Building Certification • Net-Zero Energy Building Certification • Renewable Energy • Water Efficiency • Zero Waste • Zero-Energy Building**

Further sources: EBN; ILFI; WBDG

Location and Transportation

I have an affection for a great city. I feel safe in the neighborhood of man, and enjoy the sweet security of the streets. —Henry Wadsworth Longfellow

The location of a building or residence directly corresponds to the transportation method that is used to get to and from school, work, recreation, shopping, restaurants, and home. Buildings that are integrated into a vibrant, livable community promote walking to take advantage of existing public transit, pedestrian paths, restaurants, bicycle networks, and nearby basic services and conveniences. For occupants, this physical activity encourages a healthy lifestyle, and closeness to essential amenities can also promote productivity and happiness, as Longfellow states in his quote opening this chapter.

Location and Transportation (LT) is a USGBC LEED green building credit category that encourages responsible decisions about where to locate a building by encouraging compact development, alternative transportation access, and connectivity to local amenities within the surrounding community. LEED *Location and Transportation* supports choosing transportation alternatives other than private vehicles, which strain the environment with pollution from fossil fuel combustion, pressures on road and bridge infrastructure, greenhouse gas emissions, public land lost to parking, health costs related to air pollution, and noisy traffic congestion with related productivity loss. Most privately owned vehicles sit unused 95% of the time, according to the Rocky Mountain Institute, and still account for 15% of all U.S. emissions. The U.S. EPA states that buildings and transportation together are responsible for over 60% of greenhouse gases, and 70% of U.S. energy consumption.

Coming together is a beginning; keeping together is progress; working together is success. —Henry Ford

Reusing previously developed or abandoned land, cleaning up contaminated sites with remediation, and investing in areas that have fallen into neglect can help protect sensitive greenfield sites, prevent sprawl, and reduce negative transportation impacts. A project can encourage the users of a building to take alternative transportation with fewer environmental impacts by limiting the parking that is available; by providing bicycle parking; showering facilities; available alternative fuel facilities, and provide preferred parking for low-emission or electric green vehicles. If we work together, as Henry Ford stated, the future social trends and emerging technologies of electric and autonomous vehicles and drones can successfully change how we live our lives within transit-friendly and walkable communities and cities.

See also: **Community Connectivity • LEED Building Certification • Neighborhood Development • New Urbanism • Urban Design**

Further sources: EBN; ILFI; RMI Mobility Transformation, https://www.rmi.org/our-work/transportation/mobility-transformation/; USGBC; USDOT; WBDG

Materials and Resources

We are using resources as if we had two planets, not one. There can be no "plan B" because there is no "planet B." —Ban Ki-moon, former UN Secretary-General

In the 20th century alone, the global population grew from about 1.65 billion to over 6 billion and is projected to reach 11.2 billion people by 2100. As population and economic growth increase, more resources are consumed on a per capita basis. As Ban Ki-moon states in his quote above, we are consuming as if "we had two planets." Humans have consumed more resources in the past fifty years than in all the previous history of our planet.

The extraction, use, and even after-use effects of materials can impact human health and our environment. Products are increasingly made from synthesized petrochemicals, and the advances in complex materials science have exposed us to substances not around during our human evolution. Production processes often release waste byproducts that contain bioaccumulative and toxic pollutants, harming the health of humans and environment. Currently the building industry is driven by the repetitive use of the same materials, resources, and techniques. Designers today have an ethical responsibility to promote material transparency by understanding all the life-cycle impacts of the materials we use.

The sustainable approach to selecting construction materials is using materials that do not deplete non-renewable or scarce natural resources and have no adverse environmental effects. This is almost impossible, but a goal worth striving for by: using source reduction methods; creating less waste; designing to use less material; using reclaimed, rather than new, materials; and using renewable materials.

For the Van Dusen Botanical Garden Visitor Centre in Vancouver, designed by Perkins+Will Architects, materials were chosen for their health, carbon footprint, and ability to be recycled, for selecting the most appropriate long-lasting components. Wood is the primary material; much of it salvaged, which will store carbon dioxide for the life of the building. The center oculus, made from salvaged wood, also assists with natural ventilation by operating as a solar chimney (Figures 38, 5, 23), with "the nature of materials and method and purpose" all being in unison as implied by Frank Lloyd Wright in the following quote.

Form and function thus become one in design and execution, if the nature of materials and method and purpose are all in unison. — Frank Lloyd Wright

The majority of materials used in the U.S. are non-renewable metals, minerals, and fossil fuel-based products, according to the U.S. Green Building Council. Currently, the U.S. reliance on minerals requires the extraction of more than twenty-five thousand pounds of new nonfuel minerals per person each year. Negative construction impacts can be reduced by using closed-loop thinking, lower embodied energy materials, reducing the transport distance to save fuel and emissions, preventing construction waste going to landfills, and

Figure 38 Van Dusen Botanical Garden Visitor Centre, Vancouver, British Columbia, Canada ©Nic Lehoux. Courtesy Perkins+Will Architects

designing for disassembly, deconstruction, reuse, and recycling at the end of life.

With the current challenges of limited energy and resource availability, climate change, and international security threats, new innovative construction materials are required for resiliency, durability, longevity, and security. These must address reduced energy use, and enhanced protection of the building and occupants against natural and human-made disasters, such as earthquakes, fire, weather, and blasts.

Green building assessment tools—such as LEED, Green Globes, BREEAM, and Living Building Challenge—all focus on reducing the embodied energy, and impacts from extracting, processing, transporting, maintaining, and disposing of building materials. LEED's *Material and Resources* (MR) category addresses the collection of recyclables, construction and demolition waste, reducing building life-cycle impacts, environmental product declarations, raw material sourcing, and the disclosure and optimization of material ingredients.

Databases and certifications, such as GreenScreen, Cradle-to-Cradle, and REACH, can be used in life-cycle approaches to selecting environmentally preferable products that avoid hazardous chemicals. The goal is to create a materials industry that is environmentally restorative, non-toxic, transparent, and socially equitable.

See also: **Circular Economy • Closed-Loop Supply Chain • Cradle-to-Cradle • Declare Label • Design for Disassembly • Factor 4 and Factor 10 • Green Globes Certification • GreenScreen • LEED Building Certification • Life-Cycle Assessment • Living Building Challenge • Natural Step • Off-site Prefabricated Construction • REACH Regulation • Skin (*Archispeak*) • Smart Materials (*Archispeak*) • Upcycling • Waste Reduction**

Further sources: BREEAM; EBN; ILFI; LEED; UN DESA; US EPA; USGBC

Methane

Methane: a colorless, odorless, flammable gas produced by decomposition of organic matter or from coal —Merriam-Webster Dictionary

Methane (CH$_4$), also called methyl hydride, is the primary component of natural gas and is produced by the anaerobic decay of organic matter at shallow levels. It is emitted from several natural and human-related sources. Natural sources of *methane* include wildfires, oceans, wetlands, volcanoes, permafrost, and digestive process of animals. Human-linked sources of *methane* come from burning fossil fuels such as coal, natural gas, oil, and gasoline, which is used for vehicles; the generation of electricity from coal burning power plants; and hydraulic fracking.

Methane is the second largest contributor to atmospheric concentrations of greenhouse gases, as it absorbs heat in the atmosphere and then resends the absorbed heat back to the Earth's surface, contributing to climate change. In the first two decades after its release, *methane* is about 84 times more potent than carbon dioxide as a greenhouse gas in absorbing and keeping heat in our atmosphere, according to the Environmental Defense Fund, while also a major contributor to ozone formation.

The Global Methane Initiative (GMI) is an international partnership working in a collaborative effort to reduce *methane* gas emissions, advance recovery, and use as a clean energy source. The Initiative focuses on reducing the five largest anthropometric *methane* emitters: agriculture (livestock), coal mining, municipal wastewater, municipal solid waste, and oil and gas systems.

See also: **Climate Change • Global Warming • Greenhouse Gases • Kyoto Protocol • Ozone Depletion**

Further sources: Environmental Defense Fund, https://www.edf.org/methane-other-important-greenhouse-gas; EPA; GMI; NIH Toxtown

Mitigation

Alice laughed. "There's no use trying," she said. "One can't believe impossible things."
"I daresay you haven't had much practice," said the Queen. "When I was your age I always did it for half an hour a day. Why, sometimes, I've believed as many as six impossible things before breakfast."
— Lewis Carroll, *Through the Looking Glass*, 1865

In the face of the emergencies of human-induced climate change, social exclusion and extreme poverty, we join together to declare that: Human-induced climate change is a reality, and its decisive mitigation is a moral and religious imperative for humanity. —Pope Francis, Climate Change Conference 2015

Mitigation is the reduction or prevention of heat-trapping greenhouse gases flowing into our atmosphere to prevent the future climate change impacts. These *mitigation* efforts can be reducing greenhouse gas emission sources, such as not burning fossil fuels for power, transportation, or heat, and enhancing the "sinks" that capture, store, or sequester these gases, such as with forests and oceans.

The Shanghai Natural History Museum in China designed by Perkins+Will Architects has a carbon sequestering living wall on the south side of the museum, along with an extensive green roof spiraling up from the ground, both as mitigation strategies. Composed of a metal vine-covered trellis, the living green wall brings the horizontal plane of the adjacent park onto the vertical surface of the museum representing Earth's vegetated surface (Figures 39, 8, 67).

Figure 39 Shanghai Natural History Museum, Shanghai, China
© James and Connor Steinkamp Photography. Courtesy Perkins+Will

Since the Industrial Revolution began, the oceans, soil, and forests have sequestered about half of the CO_2 emitted, but the other half is still in the atmosphere. If worldwide CO_2 emissions were immediately stopped, it would still take hundreds of years to get back to pre-industrial levels. With the accumulated CO_2 existing in our atmosphere, and with the "committed warming" due to the thermal capacity of the oceans' delay in catching up to the atmospheric temperature, future climate impacts will be increasingly more severe. Both adaptation and *mitigation*, as complementary strategies, will be needed to simultaneously diminish the long-term and short-term impact risks.

The 2014 UN *Climate Change: Mitigation of Climate Change* report called for international cooperation, carbon pricing, and various sectors of the global economy to limit or reverse greenhouse gas emissions through greater efficiency. In 2015, Pope Francis held a Climate Conference in Rome, stating "mitigation is a moral and religious imperative for humanity" and calling on all peoples to work together in the face of the emergency of climate change.

Reducing carbon emissions from electrical power plants is a very cost-effective means to limit climate change. Industry and municipalities' energy intensity could be reduced 25% by using currently available technologies. Transportation issues can be decoupled from economic growth by investing in smart growth planning, transit-oriented development, and compact urban areas to support walking and bicycling. The building sector is responsible for about 32% of global energy use, and this is expected to double by 2050.

Green building standards and retrofits of existing buildings are a cost-effective way to lower building emissions. Rapid urbanization has often resulted in low-density sprawl, damaged ecosystems, and increased traffic congestion. Responsible urban planning can locate high-density residential together with high employment densities, increasing diversity, accessibility, and integration of land uses.

Agriculture, forestry and other land uses account for about 25% of anthropogenic greenhouse gas emissions, primarily from deforestation, agriculture, and livestock. With tree-planting afforestation measures, sustainable forest management, and sustainable grazing and farming practices, the land sector could hopefully become a primary *mitigation* source of CO_2 sequestration in the future.

See also: **Adaptation • Anthropogenic • Carbon Footprint • Carbon Price • Circular Economy • Climate Change • Fossil Fuels • Global Warming • Intergovernmental Panel on Climate Change • Laudato Si': On Care for Our Common Home • Paris Climate Agreement**

Further sources: IPCC; educate-sustainability.eu; NASA; UN IEA; Designing Building Wiki; Climate Wiki; UNEP; WBDG

Montreal Protocol

The Montreal Protocol is a model of cooperation. It is a product of the recognition and international consensus that ozone depletion is a global problem, both in terms of its causes and its effects. —Ronald Reagan, former U.S. President

Enacted in 1987 in Montreal, Canada, the *Montreal Protocol on Substances that Deplete the Ozone Layer* is intended to protect the Earth's protective ozone layer by phasing out products that have been shown responsible for ozone depletion. President Reagan and other national leaders often referred to the *Protocol* as one of the most successful and cooperative international environmental agreements. It has since gone through numerous revisions with remarkable expediency in the policy making process to allow for the control of new chemicals, as well as the creation of a financial mechanism to enable developing countries to comply.

The *Montreal Protocol* is structured around a group of partially halogenated hydrocarbons that deplete stratospheric ozone, where ozone is created by the interaction between solar ultraviolet radiation and molecular oxygen (O_2). In the *Montreal Protocol*, all of the ozone-depleting substances (ODSs) contain either chlorine or bromine, and all are considered greenhouse gases. In the 1970s, several chemists realized the impacts of chlorofluorocarbons, and the resultant chlorine atoms, as well as nitric oxide (NO) on the breakdown of the Earth's stratospheric ozone layer. Researchers Paul Crutzen, Mario Molina, and F. Sherwood Rowland were awarded the 1995 Nobel Prize in Chemistry for their work on the ozone depletion problem.

The environmental consequences of this discovery were that because the stratospheric ozone absorbs most of the harmful ultraviolet-B (UV-B) radiation reaching the planet, depletion of the ozone layer by chlorofluorocarbons would lead to increased harmful UV-B radiation reaching the Earth. Ultra-violet B radiation causes damage to the fundamental building block of life, deoxyribonucleic acid (DNA). Without the ozone layer in the upper atmosphere to protect us, life as we know it would not exist. The negative impacts of UV-B are increased skin cancer, damage to human health, damage to crops, and harm to land and marine ecosystems.

The Montreal Protocol has prevented millions of cases of fatal skin cancer and tens of millions of cases of cataracts. —Multilateral Fund for Implementation of Montreal Protocol

The prime ozone-depleting substances that were controlled by the *Montreal Protocol* are chlorofluorocarbons (CFCs), hydrochlorofluorocarbons (HCFCs), halons, carbon tetrachloride, and methyl chloroform, among others. Hydrofluorocarbons (HFCs) were then produced, mostly in developed countries, to replace CFCs and HCFCs. Hydrofluorocarbons are not ozone-depleting substances as they do not contain chlorine, but are very potent greenhouse gases.

In late 2016 in Rwanda, the Parties to the *Montreal Protocol* agreed to the Kigali Amendment to phase down hydrofluorocarbons, and this is estimated to prevent up to 0.5°C in global warming above industrial levels by the end of the century. Hydrofluoroolefins are a new class of unsaturated hydrofluorocarbon refrigerants which have lower global warming potentials and shorter atmospheric lifetimes when compared to other HFCs, are not included in the Kigali Amendment.

The *Montreal Protocol* is one of the prime global contributors in the fight against climate change, with most of the prohibited ozone-depleting substances also being potent greenhouse gases. This accomplishment is an inspiring tribute to the success of global cooperation in the face of a common threat to our planet.

Perhaps the single most successful international agreement to date has been the Montreal Protocol. —Kofi Annan, Seventh UN Secretary-General

See also: **Chlorofluorocarbons • Climate Change • Global Warming • Greenhouse Gases • Hydrofluorocarbons • Kyoto Protocol • Ozone Depletion • Paris Climate Agreement**

Further sources: UNEP Kigali Amendment, www.unep.org/africa/news/kigali-amendment-montreal-protocol-another-global-commit ment-stop-climate-change; Earth Observatory; NASA; US EPA; Multilateral Fund

▌Nanotechnology

We are the very beginning of time for the human race. It is not unreasonable that we grapple with problems. But there are tens of thousands of years in the future. Our responsibility is to do what we can, learn what we can, improve the solutions, and pass them on.
—Richard P. Feynman

Nanotechnology is the branch of technology that can see and manipulate individual atoms and molecules of materials with dimensions of less than 100 nanometers. Everything on Earth is made up of atoms, and today scientists are creating new nano-enhanced materials and products. A nanometer is a billionth of a meter, or about 25.4 million nanometers to an inch. On a comparative scale, a human hair has about 80,000 nanometers of thickness. Nanoparticles can only be seen, organized, or manipulated by using powerful electron microscopes. Material properties change greatly when miniaturized, taking a "quantum leap" to below the 100-nanometer scale. As a material's particles get down to a nanoscale, the proportion of atoms on the surface increases relative to those inside, leading to unique properties. Gravity becomes unimportant and electrostatic forces take over. At this scale, scientists can take advantage of the enhanced nanostructured material properties, such as higher strength, lighter weight, better heat or electricity conduction, light spectrum control, enhanced chemical reactivity, or different magnetic properties, compared to their larger scale material counterparts. Using nanomaterial science creates new recipes for innovative material applications, such as medical advances, lighter airplanes, durable building materials, water desalination, and pollution remediation.

The *nanotechnology* concept began in 1959 with physicist Richard Feynman, who stated (www.nano.gov) his responsibility was to do, learn, "improve the solutions, and pass them on." And so *nanotechnology* didn't develop until 1981 when atoms could be "seen" with the scanning tunneling microscope. Carbon nanotubes, which are hollow tubes whose walls are latticed with carbon atoms, can have a strength-to-weight ratio three hundred times that of steel. Nanoparticles can conduct electricity a thousand times better, and heat ten times better, than copper. Graphene sheets are carbon atoms one layer thick that are bonded to each neighboring atom, making a material two hundred times stronger than steel, and a better heat and electrical conductor than any known material. Graphene has the potential to make super hard, super heat resistant, electrical conducting plastics, which can improve the efficiency and durability of products, such as solar cells and ultra-dense energy storage. The prime ingredient of both these materials is carbon, the fourth most abundant element in the universe.

Nanotechnology is manufacturing with atoms. —William Powell

Molecular *nanotechnology* has the potential to significantly improve a building's environmental performance, enhance service life, change life-cycle costs, and significantly improve the efficiency of energy storage and solar energy. In construction, this nanoscience of "manufacturing with atoms" as Powell states in the preceding quote, is radically

improving building products, such as stronger, lighter, and more durable structural materials; self-cleaning surfaces; fire protection and
insulation qualities; water repellant coatings; air pollution cleaning
surfaces; and even nano-sized sensors with safety and health monitoring abilities.

The most problematic issue of *nanotechnology* is the lack of clarifica-
tion of nanoscale materials' effects on ecosystems and human health.
Potential problems are of nanoscale materials leaching into freshwater
and saltwater resources, and the release and exposure of nanoparticles
into the air. Precautions must always be taken to ensure that materials
used in building do not conflict with the overall sustainable goal of environmental and human health, now and in the future.

See also: **Green Chemistry • Materials and Resources •
Precautionary Principle • Seventh Generation Principle**

Further sources: EBN; Naam (2013: 125); National Nanotechnology Initiative, www.nano.gov; US EPA

Natural Capital   **I**

**He who knows what sweets and virtues are in the ground, the waters,
the plants, the heavens, and how to come at these enchantments, is
the rich and royal man.** —Ralph Waldo Emerson

In the context of sustainability, we have social and human capital, built
capital and *natural capital*, as opposed to money and material goods,
which are the usual notions of capital. These "community" capitals all
need to be managed, nurtured, and improved over time to have thriving societies and flourishing economies. Earth's *natural capital* consists
of all its natural resources, the services provided by its ecosystems,
and the magnificent beauty of nature, as eloquently expressed by
Ralph Waldo Emerson in the quote an opening this chapter. Capital is
a resource that enables the production of more resources, and *natural
capital* nurtures the resources of our spirit and soul.

Natural resources, such as water, plants, animals, fossil fuels, metals, and minerals, are taken out of nature and used as part of a product
or raw material. These can end up as wastes, products, or both. Our
ecosystem services are processes of nature that we rely on in our daily
lives, such as soil for food, wetlands to filter water, rainforests for med-
icine, and plants for oxygen and carbon sequestration. The aesthetics
of nature give us flowers, parks, the rustle of leaves, birds singing, and
views of stars and mountains, which as Einstein expresses in the following quote brings understanding to our world.

Look deep into nature, then you will understand everything better.
—Albert Einstein

Investing in our *natural capital* allows for growth, progress, health,
prosperity, and often peaceful relations. When we degrade our wetlands, farmlands, aquifers, fishing grounds, and rainforests, we are
living off the principle of our capital, rather than the interest we could

be growing, and we damage the future carrying capacity of our nat-ural ecosystems. Currently, we are depleting—at an accelerating rate—our *natural capital*, faster than can be replenished by the Earth. For the financial capital of the developed world, our economies have grown, although much to the expense of our natural resources, through exploitation, degradation, and over-development, often in other poorer, developing countries.

Sustainability requires maintaining life-supporting natural capital in order for our socioeconomic goals to be met. —Warren Flint, sustain-able ecologist

The connections between business impacts and *natural capital* are needed for our socioeconomic goals to be met, according to Warren Flint. Attempts to quantify the value of these systems to measure negative or positive risks and opportunities are necessary tools. The Natural Capital Project, a partnership of the World Wildlife Fund, Nature Conservancy and others, is working to provide decision mak-ers with dependable ways to assess the true value of *natural capital* services that nature provides to protect our biodiversity and ecosys-tem services.

See also: **Carrying Capacity • Circular Economy • Closed-Loop Supply Chain • Conservation (***Theoryspeak***) • Green Economy • Greenfield (***Archispeak***) • Materials and Resources • Nature (***Theoryspeak***) • Upcycling • Waste Reduction**

Further sources: WWF; Natural Capital Coalition; Sustainable Mea-sures

Natural Step

Business is the economic engine of our Western culture, and if it could be transformed to truly serve nature as well as ourselves, it could become essential to our rescue. —Karl-Henrik Robert

Dr. Karl-Henrik Robert, a Swedish oncologist dealing with the healthi-ness or malignancy of cells, developed the *Natural Step (NS)* to provide a simple, science-based framework to encourage human health and environmental thinking in material selection and sustainable develop-ment. People's health problems can result from daily exposure to car-cinogenic and polluting materials, such as from heavy metal or fossil fuel extractions, and from non-natural chemical or synthetic products. The *Natural Step* framework looks at the root causes of our health and unsustainability and proposes we follow certain Earth system condi-tions based on the laws of gravity, the laws of thermodynamics, and studies of socio-ecological systems.

If we think systematically, we will stop asking, how much is nature worth? We will know that we are a piece of nature ourselves. —
Karl-Henrik Robert

In the *Natural Step*, Karl-Henrik Robert identifies ecological processes that have been systematically damaged by society, and recommends four system conditions for correction:

1. Concentrations of substances extracted from the Earth's crust must not systematically increase in nature. Fossil carbons, minerals, and metals that are rare in nature should be replaced with those abundant in nature, while reusing materials efficiently, and reducing reliance on fossil fuel.
2. Concentrations of substances produced by society must not systematically increase in nature. Persistent and unnatural compounds such as synthetics, oil-based plastics, and endocrine disruptors must be replaced with naturally abundant substances, and should not be produced at a faster rate than nature can break down.
3. The productivity and diversity of nature must not be systematically deteriorated. We must not harvest more than nature can reproduce, such as by land use changes, overfishing, aquifer depletion, and deforestation.
4. Societies worldwide must not be subject to the systematic undermining of meeting their needs. Just and efficient measures must enable the ability of all people to meet basic human needs, such as safe working conditions, livable wages, affordable education, and fair and efficient resource distribution.

The *Natural Step's* first three conditions challenge how people interact with the Earth and its resources, and the last confronts all people to achieve a just, sustainable, and equal society worldwide. This demands a shift from the current linear processes of production and consumption to a more resourceful cyclical system of processes. The *Natural Step* uses the "backcasting" approach of imagining the future end vision, and moves backward with the positive steps to achieve that successful outcome, much like Steward Brand's "future hindsight" in the following quote. These actions and strategies can be the efficient and fair use of resources, using abundant and environmentally friendly materials rather than rare or toxic substances, protecting valuable ecosystems, and developing new and innovative technologies in the move toward sustainability.

Hindsight is better than foresight. Make the building responsive to future hindsight—perpetual late reappraisal and adjustment.
—Steward Brand

See also: **Carrying Capacity • Cradle-to-Cradle • Declare Label • Dematerialization • Ecological Footprint • Green Chemistry • Industrial Ecology • Lifeboat Ethics • Materials and Resources • Nanotechnology • Precautionary Principle • REACH Regulation • Seventh Generation Principle**

Further sources: Brand (1994); Futureproofing; Kibert (2016: 62); The Natural Step; Wikipedia

Natural Ventilation   ▌

Basically what you learned was that, OK, the sun is here, so you should create natural ventilation here —an unbelievable amount

of really sound principles that have been completely abandoned, so now everything is air conditioned with big machines. —Rem Koolhaas, architect

Natural ventilation introduces fresh air into buildings and distributes it for the benefit of the occupants by using the natural driving forces of wind and temperature differences. Green buildings often use *natural ventilation* strategies for increased indoor air quality and cooling, by supplementing or replacing the demand for energy-intensive mechanical air conditioning.

Most early buildings were naturally ventilated, allowing for daylighting, views, fresh air, and outdoor connections. Modern air conditioning started with cheap energy in the 1960s and resulted in building design's total disregard for solar orientation, climate responsive façade design, and operable windows, as Rem Koolhaas refers to in his quote opening this chapter. Buildings became bland sealed boxes with all façades the same, regardless of climate or solar impacts, and became windowless placeless environments in which to work, live and learn.

With increased awareness of the environmental impacts of energy use, *natural ventilation* is returning as an attractive strategy to reduce energy consumption and costs, while providing comfortable healthy indoor environments where many people spend 70% of their time, while also increasing productivity and learning. In favorable climates, some building types can save over 30% of total energy consumption with *natural ventilation*.

Pressure differentials drive the flow of fresh air through a building using the natural forces of the wind and buoyancy. Both strategies use the principle that air moves from a high-pressure area to a low-pressure area. Using natural wind currents and convection forces are very effective methods to reduce the energy-cooling load of a building. The amount of ventilation depends on the size and placement of openings in the building, along with the openness of the interior spaces, to provide the supply and the exhaust needed for airflow. There are strong interrelationships between building form, orientation within the site, and the building layout.

An excellent example of this interrelationship of form and orientation is the Global Ecology Research Center at Stanford University by EHDD Architects uses operable windows with prevailing northwest breezes and stack ventilation. Chilled water for building radiant cooling uses the night sky system of spraying a thin film of water on the roof at night to be cooled by cool deep space radiation (Figure 40).

All buildings require fresh air to provide oxygen for breathing, to increase thermal comfort, and to dissipate odors. Designing a building for *natural ventilation* has three major advantages: the energy savings can be significant in feasible climates; the enhanced indoor air quality of spaces reduces occupant sick leave days and increases productivity; and the psychological satisfaction of being able to hear, feel, and connect to the outdoor dynamics of nature, such as rustling leaves and blowing wind, as Truman Capote so eloquently refers to as part of us in the following quote.

The wind is us—it gathers and remembers all our voices, then sends them talking and telling through the leaves and the fields.
—Truman Capote

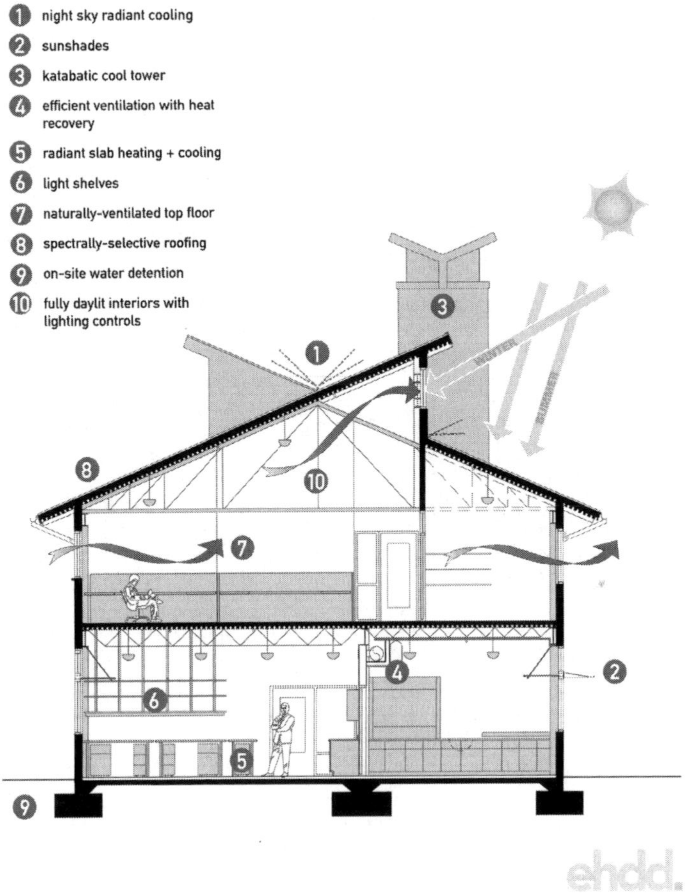

1 night sky radiant cooling
2 sunshades
3 katabatic cool tower
4 efficient ventilation with heat recovery
5 radiant slab heating + cooling
6 light shelves
7 naturally-ventilated top floor
8 spectrally-selective roofing
9 on-site water detention
10 fully daylit interiors with lighting controls

Figure 40 Global Ecology Research Center, Stanford University, California
Courtesy ©EHDD

Natural ventilation has two main strategies: cross-ventilation, which uses the differences in air pressure caused by the wind; and stack ventilation, which takes advantage of the increased buoyancy of warmed air. The specific design of the operable windows, corridors, and fans can help direct the airflow through the building. Just a slight increase in airflow velocities can reduce the occupant's perceived indoor temperatures, but *natural ventilation* is not effective in reducing the humidity of the incoming air. Mixed mode or hybrid ventilation systems are those that integrate *natural ventilation* systems with some mechanical equipment support.

See also: **Biophilic Design • Daylighting • Energy Efficiency • Indoor Environmental Quality • Passive Design • Sick Building Syndrome • Solar Chimney • Stack Ventilation • WELL Building Standard • Wind Tower**

Further sources: Autodesk Sustainability; EBN; Iyengar (2015: 47–49); Robertson (2014: 194); WBDG

▌Naturescaping

Naturescaping, or greenscaping, is an ecological design approach to creating balanced, self-sustaining ecosystems to inspire our connections with nature and place. In landscapes across America, the typical lawn is striving to emulate an 18th century landscape from England, where wealthy landowners maintained expansive pastoral views. Frederick Law Olmstead, the designer of New York City's Central Park, set the tone for suburban landscape development with his Chicago Riverside development, which mandated extensive open lawns with scattered trees and houses set far back from the sidewalk.

Today suburbs all across the country in America are planted with the same monoculture of Kentucky bluegrass, despite very different climates and soils. Lawn maintenance (noisy mowing, blowing, trimming) accounts for approximately 5% of the nation's air pollution, and watering lawns consumes, on average, 30% of municipal freshwater in the U.S., with double that in drier areas. The EPA has shown that mowing a lawn for one hour emits the same amount of smog as driving a car 650 miles. Maintaining lush lawns creates resource and environmental burdens along with fertilizer and pesticide chemicals which can end up in stormwater runoff and groundwater, which is a large source of water pollution. Extensive urban growth and suburban sprawl over the last few decades have also significantly damaged the biodiversity of native bird and wildlife habitats.

Can we not create, from a beautiful natural landscape, an environment inhabited by man, in which natural beauty is retained, man housed in community? —Ian McHarg

Reconnecting place to nature is an integrative, environmentally responsive approach by putting ecology at the forefront of design, as the ecological landscape architect Ian McHarg proposes. Using native plants, flowers, and trees can also attract and support beneficial insects, birds, and other wildlife, which also gives us a stronger positive connection with nature uplifting our spirits as expressively said by Emerson in the following quote.

The Earth laughs in flowers. —Ralph Waldo Emerson

Using the sustainable mandates of reduce, reuse and recycle in minimizing energy and water consumption, reducing pollution, fostering health and beauty, restoring ecosystems and biodiversity, and preserving habitat, this responsible approach tries to improve natural systems or reverse environmentally destructive impacts. *Naturescaping* strives to create vibrant, diverse, and self-sustaining ecosystems that exist in greater harmony with our natural environment, while quieting our souls as the architect Peter Zumthor expresses in the following quote.

My relationship to plants becomes closer and closer. They make me quiet; I like to be in their company. —Peter Zumthor

See also: **Biodiversity • Biophilic Design • Ecological Design • Place (*Archispeak*) • SITES Initiative • Sustainable Site Design • Xeriscaping**

Further sources: EPA; Designing Buildings Wiki; SITES

Neighborhood Development   ▌

The creation of a more peaceful and happier society has to begin from the level of the individual, and from there it can expand to one's family, to one's neighborhood, to one's community, and so on. —Dalai Lama

Today more than half the global population lives in cities, and this is expected to increase to over 70% by the year 2050, according to the Population Reference Bureau. By accommodating this rapid urban growth, society is turning resources into wastes faster than they can be regenerated or absorbed, while releasing toxins into the atmosphere, water, and ground. Population growth and the affluent patterns of resource extraction, usage, and discarding are depleting and polluting our finite sources of energy, water, and materials. Most of this urbanized growth is projected to be communities of 100,000–250,000 people, so the fundamental neighborhood unit, distinguished by its inhabitants or character, will be the critical place for urban transformation and sustainable innovation.

This rapid urbanization will require community planning processes at the neighborhood level to address the lack of affordable housing, climate protection, natural public space, public transit, public amenities, quality schools, and public health improvement. Community planning will also need to address issues of deteriorating existing infrastructure, food, deserts, crime, and site contamination, among many others.

A green design approach can reduce the adverse impacts of construction on human health and the environment, creating a "viable neighborhood" of community, as noted by Wendell Berry below, while restoring natural systems, community health, and well-being.

A viable neighborhood is a community: and a viable community is made up of neighbors who cherish and protect what they have in common. —Wendell Berry

The U.S. Green Building Council (USGBC), in partnership with the U.S. National Resources Council and the Congress for New Urbanism, launched the LEED rating system for *Neighborhood Development (ND)* in 2009. There are seven major global environmental and social impact categories addressed in the LEED v4 green rating system: climate change, human health, water resources, biodiversity, green economy, community, and natural resources. LEED-*ND*'s goals are to optimize restorative strategies, conserve energy and water, reduce greenhouse gas emissions, reduce the waste sent to landfills, lower operating costs and increase the asset values, and maximize healthy and productive environments for occupants. The LEED-*Neighborhood Development* rating system has three major categories: Smart Location and Linkage, Neighborhood Pattern and Design, and Green Infrastructure and Buildings, with points weighted based on the relative importance of its contributions to LEED-*ND*'s overall goals.

At the broad scale of a neighborhood, green benefits can be magnified, enabling green opportunities to be synergistic in helping the entire community of people creating a more "peaceful and happier society" in the Dalai Lama's words in his quote opening this chapter that spreads "to one's community, and so on" and can have enduring paybacks for future generations.

Don't buy the house; buy the neighborhood. —Proverb

See also: **Affordable Housing • Community Connectivity • LEED Building Certification • New Urbanism • Place (Archispeak)
• Population Growth • Scale (*Archispeak*) • Sense of Place • Smart Growth • Spirit of Place (*Theoryspeak*) • Urban Design • Urban Tree Canopy • Walkability (*Archispeak*)**

Further sources: Congress for New Urbanism; EBN; Global Footprint Network; Population Reference Bureau, http://www.prb.org/Publications/Lesson-Plans/HumanPopulation/Urbanization.aspx; UN-Habitat; USGBC

▌ Net-Zero Energy Building Certification

It's all about efficient and restorative use of resources to make the world secure, prosperous and life sustaining. —Amory Lovins

Buildings today account for nearly half of the energy produced in the United States and are responsible for nearly half the carbon dioxide emitted, according to the U.S. Energy Information Administration (EIA). In striving to achieve the utmost of high-performing buildings, many architects, build-ers, and owners are seeking to have net-zero energy performance, where the building generates as much energy as it consumes. These buildings depend on exceptional energy conservation and use on-site renewable energy to produce all of their heating, cooling, and electricity needs.

The International Living Future Institute (ILFI) Living Building Chal-lenge oversees a rigorous system for a *Net-Zero Energy Building (NZEB) certification. NZEB certification* requires a building to meet 100% of its energy needs on a net-annual basis to be met by on-site renewable energy, meaning that the building uses no more energy annually than is generated by the building's renewable energy systems. The *NZEB certification* confirms that a building has operated for twelve consecu-tive months of net-zero energy performance by using energy from the sun, wind, or Earth to exceed the building's net annual demand. Off-site renewables, such as renewable energy certificates or green tags, or any combustion cannot be used in achieving the net-zero energy per-formance certification.

The LEED Platinum-certified David and Lucile Packard Foundation, in Los Altos, CA, designed by EHDD Architects, is the largest International Living Future Institute Net-Zero Energy Certified building in the cur-rently. The net-zero energy approach is driven by passive and bioclimatic strategies of daylighting, enhanced envelope design, high-efficient HVAC systems, and a strenuous effort to halve the plug load energy. Triple glazing and insulated wood-framed walls reduced thermal bridging and the need for perimeter heating. Chilled beams and radiant cooling pan-els can reduce the electrical energy demand by almost 25% compared with a conventional system. The Packard Foundation uses the "efficient and restorative use of resources," as Amory Lovins states in the quote opening this chapter, to make "life sustaining" (Figures 41, 78).

Figure 41 David and Lucile Packard Foundation, Los Altos, CA
Photo: © Jeremy Bittermann. Courtesy EHDD Architects

The ILFI *NZEB certification* extends beyond just the energy scope of being net-zero energy certified, to also meet four of the twenty imperatives of the Living Building Challenge rating system. The Limits to Growth imperative requires projects to only be built on previously developed land, such as brownfield or greyfield sites, and not contribute to development sprawl. The Rights to Nature imperative requires buildings not shade another building or in other ways reduce the quality of sunlight, fresh air, or natural waterways. The Beauty + Inspiration imperative requires design features specifically for human delight and the celebration of culture, spirit, and place. The Inspiration + Education imperative requires that building owners must provide building design and operational educational information and open the building to the public at least one day a year to motivate others.

Energy saved is energy produced. —Proverb

See also: **Energy Efficiency • Green Building Certification Systems • High-Performing Buildings • Living Building Challenge • Renewable Energy • Renewable Energy Certificates • Sustainable Design • Zero-Energy Building (***Theoryspeak***) • Zero-Energy Building**

Further sources: Architecture 2030, http://architecture2030.org/buildings_problem_why/; EBN; EIA; ILFI; PM Engineer magazine, www.pmengineer.com/articles/89744-chilled-beams-get-a-warm-reception; WBDG

New Urbanism

I would like to use architecture to create bonds between people who live in cities and even use it to recover the communities that used to exist in every single city. —Toyo Ito, architect

New Urbanism is defined as an urban planning approach that encourages walkable communities where residential neighborhoods are located near a number of basic services including parks and public spaces. The concept of *New Urbanism* is based on urban principles created and successfully implemented for centuries throughout the world. At its core, these principles include the integration of residential neighborhoods with cultural and commercial amenities as well as a number of essential services. Architecture, as Toyo Ito explains in the quote opening this chapter, can be used "to create bonds between people" and further this sense of community. *New Urbanism* promotes the creation of meaningful and pedestrian-oriented spaces such as streets with wide sidewalks, pedestrian-only streets, plazas, and parks.

Other distinctive features associated with *New Urbanism* include a combination of dwelling types such as townhomes and single-family homes organized around a centralized public space. The majority of the dwellings are typically located within a five-minute walk from the urban center and from the walkable distance to a school and playground. Buildings are usually aligned along narrow streets shaded by trees to create an outdoor room. In addition, major streets are often terminated by iconic public buildings used by the community.

Ideas associated with *New Urbanism* started to emerge during the 1970s and 1980s in the U.S., though it was not until 1993 that they became formally articulated with the founding of the *Congress for the New Urbanism*. The *New Urbanism* movement arose as an alternative model to the current and prevalent automobile-driven urban planning model, which originated in the 1940s and is still widely applied as the norm in the U.S. today.

The overarching goal of *New Urbanism* is to foster more meaningful physical and social environments for people by improving the quality of the urban fabric and create mixed-use walkable neighborhoods (Figure 42). This urban planning approach presents a number of positive outcomes such as energy savings and pollution reduction associated with a reduced reliance on the automobile, health benefits, and an overall sense of physical well-being and of belonging to a community. OC

Figure 42 Collegetown mixed-use development, Tallahassee, FL
Courtesy ©Elliott Marshall Innes Architects, P.A.

See also: **Community Connectivity • Location and Transportation • Neighborhood Development • Place (*Archispeak*) • Sense of Place • Smart Growth • Spirit of Place (*Theoryspeak*) • Townscape (*Archispeak*) • Urban Design • Urban Tree Canopy • Urbanism (*Theoryspeak*) • Walkability (*Archispeak*)**

Further sources: Charter of the New Urbanism; Congress for New Urbanism; Barton (1985)

Ocean Energy

There is no drop of water in the ocean, not even in the deepest parts of abyss, that does not know and respond to the mysterious forces that create the tide. —Rachel Carson, *The Sea Around Us* 1950

Over 70% of the Earth's surface is covered by water and carries large amounts of energy due to the impacts of the wind, tides, and ocean currents. *Ocean energy* is free, infinite, renewable energy generating electricity from waves, tidal streams, temperature differences, or differences in salinity.

Tidal energy is power that uses the changing tidal movement of large bodies of water tugged by the gravitational pull of the moon and sun, and the rotation of the Earth, which Rachel Carson in *The Sea Around Us* eloquently calls the "mysterious forces that create the tide." Tides usually have two highs and two lows within a twenty-four-hour period, making the energy more predictable than wind or solar, but a significant ten-foot tidal range is needed to provide power economically. There are very few tidal systems, such as tidal barrage dams, tidal fences, and tidal turbines, operating globally and all are expensive, and most have negative impacts on ecosystems and marine life.

Waves are created as the wind blows over the surface of open water. Wave power devices capture energy directly from the surface motion of the waves, or from pressure variations below the surface. Ocean wave energy can have tremendous power but is variable, intermittent, and applicable in few locations, such as west coasts of U.S. and Europe, and coasts of New Zealand and Japan. Wave energy can be channeled into a reservoir or basin, where water flows through turbines at lower levels, creating power similarly to a hydroelectric dam.

Ocean thermal energy conversion uses the temperature differential between the warmer top layers of the ocean and the colder, deep ocean temperature to produce electricity. These conditions exist in tropical coastal areas, requiring a temperature difference of at least 36°F (20°C) to power a turbine, such the Hawaii Ocean Thermal Energy Conversion (OTEC) system. Power can be produced day and night, but costly infrastructure is a challenge, such as the large-diameter cold-water intake pipe submerged over a mile deep. Some believe if this technology can become cost-competitive, it can compete with wind and solar.

Another type of *ocean energy* is osmotic power, or salinity power, which converts the pressure differential between high-salinity water and water with low or no salinity into hydraulic pressure, which powers a turbine to generate electricity. This osmotic pressure can happen naturally where a river meets the sea, or from engineered industrial sources, such as a wastewater treatment or desalination plant. While still in early stages, osmotic energy could have enormous potential as an available, clean, cost-effective and reliable renewable energy source that recycles nature's resources, such as seawater and wastewater.

See also: **Ecological Design • Renewable Energy • Solar Energy • Wind Energy**

Further sources: Carson (1950); US EIA; www.altenergymag.com

Off-Site Prefabricated Construction   I

Architects are no longer limited to the fragmentary representation of physical ideas; we can now fully pre-form them. This composite understanding of architecture before it actually becomes substance offers a deep understanding of the elements of architecture that affect our daily lives. Refabricating architecture leads toward a new humanism. —Kieran and Timberlake, *Refabricating Architecture* 2004

A house is a machine for living in. —Le Corbusier

Prefabricated or shop-fabricated components are pre-engineered building components, often modular and panelized units, which are fabricated in an *off-site* factory and transported to a building site for assembly in temporary, relocatable, or permanent construction. *Prefabrication* promises many benefits in pursuit of green building, such as reduced construction waste, resilient and energy-efficient construction, and reduced transportation impacts.

The terminology in the *off-site* and *prefabricated* industry is not standardized and can be called factory-built, prefab, modular, systems-built or shop-fabricated. The process involves the designing, planning, fabricating, transporting, and on-site assembly of the building components that demands the critical integrated design of all parties. *Off-site construction* methods include a range of scales, materials and systems innovations used in the enclosure, interior partitions, structural and service systems.

Handcraft was once the tool of commodity, but today it is the machine that is the tool of commodity. —Kieran and Timberlake, *Refabricating Architecture*

The *prefabricated* industry can significantly reduce environmental impacts, such as reduced resource waste and time, stronger structural qualities, better-insulated structures and easier disassembly for reuse than site built construction. Stephen Kieran and James Timberlake's book, *Refabricating Architecture: How Manufacturing Methodologies Are Poised to Transform Building Construction*, expresses the practices used for their award-winning prefabricated Loblolly House. They present a strong argument for the transition from conventional piece-by-piece linear construction to the integrated approach of using manufacturing technology and prefabrication production methods. Rather than Le Corbusier's famous and controversial words of a "house is a machine for living in," prefabrication uses a machine to create the house.

The intelligent design of *prefabrication* achieves lower costs and less waste in cutting equipment programmed to maximize material use, tracking assembly line waste to be recycled, and storage of materials for future reuse. *Prefabrication* plants can even be zero waste by using any non-recyclable wastes in on-site power generation. The controlled factory environment allows for better quality of construction and protection of materials and equipment, and avoids the challenges of unpredictable weather, scheduling trades, and the average delays of on-site construction.

Modular *prefabrication* manufacturing occurs from the inside out using many different materials such as wood, cold-formed steel, hot-rolled steel, concrete, or a combination of materials. Frames are constructed as planes, fitted as cubicles and then completed working toward the outside allowing for efficient air sealing and insulation qualities. The *prefabrication* construction industry is focused on lean production techniques, as perfected in Japan with Toyota's streamlined auto manufacturing process to save time, materials, and money.

Quality and scope are directly proportional to cost and time. —Kieran and Timberlake, *Refabricating Architecture*

Newer *prefabrication* plants can adopt high-performing building practices with sustainable and recycled materials, super insulation, and precision-made steel buildings which minimize air leakage for improved thermal efficiency, lowering costs and reducing carbon emissions. Reducing the carbon emissions from transportation is achieved by few site deliveries and fewer construction workers traveling to and from traditional construction sites. Reusing modular buildings can repeatedly help reduce environmental construction impacts of energy, time, financial resources and material resources.

See also: **Dematerialization • Design for Disassembly • Factor 4 and Factor 10 • Materials and Resources • Modular (*Archispeak*) • Structural Insulated Panels**

Further sources: Kibert (2016); Kieran and Timberlake (2004); NIBS; Off-site Construction Council

Operations and Maintenance

Operations: Activities related to the normal performance of the functions for which a facility or item of equipment is intended to be used. —Federal Real Property Council

Maintenance: to repair unscheduled and scheduled deficiencies during the time period in which they occur. This includes preventive maintenance for buildings. —Federal Real Property Council

Once *Operations and Maintenance* personnel consisted of a janitor who knew where the fuses, keys, and brooms were. Today, *Operations and Maintenance* (O&M) has become a highly technical area of facilities management. Buildings have increasingly become sophisticated, complex, high-performance machines with thousands of moving parts, often digitally controlled with sensors. Managing the operation of these buildings now requires expertise in mechanical, electrical, and computer systems engineering. Maintenance of the building systems is paramount to sustaining a high level of performance. It is no longer a matter of keeping up with cleaning the facility. Maintenance now involves the complex task of ensuring that sophisticated electronic equipment is functioning at peak performance. That may include rooftop photovoltaic panels, greywater tanks, and pumps, filtration systems, monitors, sensors, actuators, and green roof or wall installations. As high-performance buildings become the norm, maintenance programs will be dependent on a highly trained professional maintenance staff.

There have been well-documented building failures due to inadequate maintenance. The 1987 Institut Du Arabe building by Jean Nouvel is a case in point. The innovative design of the south façade included 240 independently controlled photoelectric oculi that proved to be difficult to maintain. Unfortunately, they eventually stopped working as intended. It has been an important object lesson for the *operation and maintenance* of the high-tech buildings of the 21st century. EO

See also: **Building Automation Control Systems • Design Quality Assessment • Facilities Management • Facility Performance Evaluation • Life-cycle Assessment**

Our Common Future   **I**

Our most basic common link is that we all inhabit this planet. We all breathe the same air. We all cherish our children's future. And we are all mortal. —John F. Kennedy former U.S. President

In 1983, Norwegian Prime Minister Gro Harlem Brundtland was invited by UN Secretary-General Javier Pérez de Cuéllar to chair a World Commission on Environment and Development. Since the 1970s, public awareness had been growing on population increase pressures, along with technological and consumer demand on the planet's resources. Industries belched smoke, air pollution whiffed of prosperity, and autos spewed leaded gas emissions. In America, the first Earth Day was celebrated on April 22, 1970, which along with Rachel Carson's 1962 *Silent Spring* raised public awareness and concern for living organisms and the links between pollution and human health. In the 1980s, a new generation of environmental worries came to attention: global warming, species loss, toxic wastes, and deforestation—all caused by global development, which was not decreasing global poverty.

The 1987 Brundtland Commission Report, *Our Common Future*, provided the most often used, but broad, definition of *sustainable development* as "development that meets the needs of the present without compromising the ability of future generations to meet their own needs" (Chapter 2, p. 1). This global-change framework was an intergenerational concept to advance human economic development—in particular, the vital needs of the poor—while also limiting the long-term impacts on the environment's ability to meet present and future needs. During the time the Commission met, tragedies such as the African famines, the leak at Bhopal's pesticide factory, and the nuclear disaster at Chernobyl solidified many grave predictions for the future of the planet. We were all in this together and former President Kennedy's words at the beginning of this chapter rang true, "that we all inhabit this planet."

Recognizing that the poor were really not the ones consuming Earth's supply of fossil fuels, warming the climate with carbon emissions, poisoning water and air with chemicals, or consuming the world's resources, rather the industrialized countries were to blame, it was recommended that the links between pervasive poverty and inequality and the effects of insensitive environmental degradation needed to be understood. The commission proposed long-term environmental strategies, greater and effective cooperation and multilateralism between developed and developing countries, working across cultural and historical barriers, and shared perceptions and actions for protecting and enhancing the environment.

The Brundtland Commission Report, *Our Common Future*, declared that only with the social and economic advances of sustainable development could these needs be met. Using these sustainable development goals, the hope was to satisfy humans with a healthy and productive life, along with protecting air, water, land and all living organisms, and assuring the ability of future generations to meet their own needs in all *our common futures*.

See also: **Globalization • Green Economy • Laudato Si': Our Common Home • Sustainable Development • Sustainability**

Further sources: Bruntland Commission (1987:1); UN Our Common Future

▌Ozone Depletion

The hole in the ozone layer is a kind of skywriting. At first, it seemed to spell out our continuing complacency before a witch's brew of deadly perils. But perhaps it really tells of a newfound talent to work together to protect the global environment. —Carl Sagan

In the stratosphere, ozone is created by the interaction between solar ultraviolet radiation and molecular oxygen (O_2), which we breathe. This stratospheric ozone layer in the upper atmosphere protects us from excessive amounts of harmful ultraviolet-B (UV-B) radiation. As Werner Hertzog poignantly states in the following quote about the fragility of human civilization, life could not exist without this protective layer of ozone.

Civilization is like a thin layer of ice upon a deep ocean of chaos and darkness. —Werner Hertzog

Researchers in the 1970s first realized the damaging effects of certain chemicals on the ozone layer. Later in 1984 with British scientists discovering the ozone hole over Antarctica, the breakdown of the Earth's stratospheric ozone layer was apparent to the public. The damaging chemicals included conventional refrigerants and aerosol propellants, such as hydrocarbons, chlorofluorocarbons, and the resultant chlorine atoms, as well as nitric oxide (NO). The 1995 Nobel Prize in Chemistry was awarded to these scientists for their *ozone depletion* breakthrough research.

The significance of this environmental research showed that when the stratospheric ozone layer is depleted by chlorofluorocarbons, it is no longer able to absorb the ultraviolet-B radiation in the atmosphere, leading to that increased harmful UV-B radiation striking the surface of the Earth. UV-B radiation causes damage at the molecular level to the fundamental building block of life, DNA (deoxyribonucleic acid), as reiterated by David Suzuki below. The proven negative impacts of *ozone depletion* are significant increases in skin cancer rates, damage to crops, marine ecosystem decline, and land ecosystems deterioration.

Virtually all of the extremely important services that nature provides are completely ignored by conventional economics. The ozone layer, for example, shields all life from DNA-damaging ultraviolet radiation. —David Suzuki

The Montreal Protocol on Substances that Deplete the Ozone Layer was enacted in 1987 to protect the Earth's protective ozone layer by phasing out the chemicals shown responsible for atmospheric *ozone depletion*. All the ozone-depleting substances (ODSs) listed in the Protocol are considered greenhouse gases and all contain either chlorine or bromine. Chemical companies quickly researched substitutes that would be as efficient as conventional refrigerants without the harmful environmental side effects. In the quote opening this chapter, Carl Sagan praises this united global effort and the "newfound talent to work together to protect the global environment."

The problem though is by using less efficient refrigerants; more electrical energy is needed to accomplish the same amount of cooling. This results in more carbon dioxide emissions from power plants burning fossil fuels, which leads to more global warming potential (GWP). So the chemicals that have high ozone-depleting potential (ODP) usually have low GWP, and those chemicals with a low ozone-depleting potential usually have a high GWP.

See also: **Climate Change • Global Warming • Greenhouse Gases • Kyoto Protocol • Montreal Protocol • Paris Climate Agreement**

Further Sources: IPCC; NASA; Sagan (1997); Suzuki (2004); UN EP

▌Paris Climate Agreement

The document you have just been presented is historic. It promises to set the world on a new path to a low-emissions, climate-resilient future. —Ban Ki-moon, UN Secretary-General

The present generation is the first to feel the side effects of climate change caused by humans. This change refers to the average temperature increases in the Earth's oceans, and atmosphere, caused by human-generated greenhouse gas (GHG) emissions, and not caused by climate's natural variability. These GHG emissions, which drive economic growth and human comfort, are polluting the Earth's atmosphere through fossil fuel combustion, deforestation, and agricultural activities that are degrading the Earth's climate system, a resource shared by all species. Countries such as the U.S. and China with high economic outputs are considered "free riders" because they export much of the damage created by their greenhouse gas emissions. The Earth's atmosphere intermingles globally, thereby leading to inequity between the responsible emitters and the vulnerable countries impacted with climate change burdens. This intermingling acts as a disincentive for "free riders" to mitigate their emissions. Climate change inequity is globally pervasive and possibly will get significantly worse in the near future.

In Paris, France on December 12, 2015, 196 countries approved the *Paris Agreement: COP21*, in one of the greatest diplomatic efforts in the last thirty years, to reduce the risks of a global temperature rise to below 2° Celsius. The Intergovernmental Panel on Climate Change (IPCC) has concluded a rise of over 2°C from pre-industrial levels will have increasingly disastrous climate events, such as flooding, droughts, rising temperatures, and sea level rise. Warming is already halfway to that tipping point, and the world is already feeling extremes, with the past several years being the hottest years on record.

The COP21 *Paris Agreement*, led by UN Secretary-General Ban Ki-moon, entered into force on November 4, 2016 reaching its goal of an

"international agreement on climate that is universal, ambitious about keeping global warming below 2° Celsius, flexible by taking into account the need and capabilities of each country, balanced in terms of adaption and mitigation, and long-lasting, with ambitions revised upwards at regular intervals." —European Commission Climate Action

Five major actions were specified in the Agreement: reduction in energy-intensive industries (e.g. aluminum, glass, steel, cement); increased investment in cleaner energy systems (e.g. renewables); investments in energy efficiency (e.g. urban planning, retrofits, building standards); adjusted resource pricing (e.g. market-oriented cost of energy); and increased transparency leading to effective legal implication (e.g. releasing pollution data, new laws, enforced violations).

Our duty, as men and women, is to proceed as if limits to our ability did not exist. We are collaborators in creation. —Pierre Teilhard de Chardin

The *Paris Climate Agreement* is non-binding, with no specific required steps, but can be a solid base to structure the consensus-driven change needed for the challenges ahead. Developing countries, such as China and India, will need to reframe their models on how to prosper in the next thirty-five years, while wealthier countries will have the responsibility to clean up their already intense carbon-emitting economies. In 2017, the Trump administration announced the withdrawal of the U.S. from the *Paris Climate Agreement*, which will take a minimum three years. Meanwhile many U.S. states, cities, and corporations have stated their intention to redouble their responsibilities and duties to reduce U.S. carbon emissions, proceeding as Pierre Teilhard de Chardin proclaimed in the preceding quote, "as if limits to our ability did not exist."

See also: **Agenda 21 • Climate Change • Fossil Fuels • Global Warming • Greenhouse Gases• Intergovernmental Panel on Climate Change • Kyoto Protocol • Montreal Protocol • Seventh Generation Principle • Sustainable Development • Sustainability**

Further sources: COP 21; European Commission Climate Action, ec.eu ropa.eu/clima/policies/international/negotiations/paris_en; IPCC; UNEP

Parksmart Certification   I

Urban development patterns have created a landscape dominated by vehicles, where vehicles spend 95% of their time parked (Shoup 2011). There are over 1.2 billion cars in the world, and that number is expected to double by 2030. Low-density auto-oriented communities force more people to drive, thereby increasing sprawl, impervious surfaces, heat island effect, and increased stormwater runoff. Buildings and transportation are the two largest emitters of CO_2, and smarter solutions are needed when combining these two into parking garages. Parking is one of the largest land uses in cities. Locating parking near existing public transit or enhancing alternative modes of transportation, such as biking, can significantly reduce vehicle miles, fuel, emissions, and costs.

Parksmart, formerly known as Green Garage Certification, is a voluntary system addressing smarter parking strategies to reduce energy consumption, prioritize performance, and minimize wastes through the design and operation of garages. *Parksmart* is managed by Green Business Certification, Inc. (GBCI) and complements LEED. The system encourages careful siting, energy-efficient lighting and ventilation, charging stations, car sharing, bike parking, guidance systems for faster parking, idle-reduction strategies, and stormwater management strategies.

In Boston's Post Office Square in the Financial District, a *Parksmart-certified* parking garage was formerly a rundown, three-story, aboveground parking garage. Today it is a modern seven-story underground facility with a high-efficient ventilation system and a green roof that is a 1.7-acre park dotted with trees, fountains, and a covered café.

The *Parksmart* standard has three major categories: Management, Programs, and Technology and Structure Design. The Management category addresses materials, maintenance, commissioning, waste management, and life-cycle assessment. The Programs category stresses placemaking, access to mass transit, wayfinding, rideshare, alternative vehicles, and bicycle parking or sharing, among others. The Technology and Structure Design category addresses resiliency, grey-water reuse, VOCs, lighting, HVAC, rainwater harvesting, durability, and renewable energy generation. *Parksmart* structures can potentially reduce operational energy costs up to 25% from the national average, through efficient strategies of lighting, ventilation, controls, stringent facility management, and commissioning.

See also: **Green Building Certification Systems • Light Pollution • Location and Transportation • Place (***Archispeak***) • Sense of Place • Spirit of Place (***Theoryspeak***)**

Further sources: GBCI; Parksmart; Shoup (2011)

▌Passive Cooling

Layering and changeability: this is the key, the combination that is working into most of my buildings. Occupying one of these buildings is like sailing a yacht; you modify and manipulate its form and skin according to seasonal conditions and natural elements, and work with these to maximize the performance of the building. —Glenn Murcutt, Pritzker Prize architect 1996

Passive design strategies can be natural ventilation, solar gain or pro-tection, and natural lighting, along with efficient building practices of insulation and airtightness. Passive strategies need to be optimized in the initial design and are often used in hybrid combinations with active systems in high-performing buildings.

Passively cooled buildings reduce the demand for mechanical cooling by using natural ventilation to carry away heat, evaporative air-cooling, and shading to block unwanted heat. *Passive cooling* mea-sures use the building itself as the passive system by site orientation, shape, earth-berming or earth tubes to capture Earth's cool thermal mass, overhangs to shade openings, and ventilation control. Unoccu-pied building spaces, such as storage rooms, mechanical spaces, and garages can be used to buffer unwanted heat gain, along with higher insulation values. Higher interior ceilings and slanted roofs can provide cooling by allowing natural heat cycles to circulate air through a space, as with stack ventilation and night-purge ventilation.

The low-energy KAUST University in Thuwal, Saudi Arabia, by HOK Architects, is a contemporary, climate responsive design rooted in the local Saudi culture and the world's largest LEED Platinum project. The circulation thoroughfares are shaded and passively cooled with water for evaporative cooling as in the traditional Souk marketplaces, and a monumental roof spans the building masses, blocking the sun as a Bedouin tent and filtering the light as the traditional Mashrabiya lattice-work screens (Figures 43, 16, 58, 75). Solar wind towers naturally cool with stack ventilation to release warm air at the top and draw in cooler air at the bottom. This project by HOK also exemplifies the key strategy of Glenn Murcutt to "manipulate its form and skin according to seasonal conditions and natural elements" in order to maximize the performance of the building.

Figure 43 KAUST University, Saudi Arabia
Courtesy ©HOK

Sun angle modeling calculates where solar radiation falls on the building, and then windows, shading devices, and overhangs are designed to block heat gain with appropriate sizes, heights, and locations. The winter sun is low in the sky so that heat gain can be allowed in below overhangs to add warmth. The summer sun is high and longer in the sky, so overhangs, brise-soleil, and other shading devices need to block solar heat gain from overhead and the sides, especially west.

Designers can use specific location wind charts to determine the prevailing wind directions and speeds during the extremes of winter and summer. The building design shape and orientation can block cold winter winds and encourage cooling summer breezes to flow through the building.

A building's site can provide *passive cooling* with deciduous trees planted on the south for summer shading, and allow winter sunlight through for warmth in the winter. Planting evergreen trees to the north can block winter winds. Trees can sequester carbon and reduce air pollution, but also can cool with evapotranspiration by moving water up from the soil, and evaporating this moisture through the leaves out into the air. Fountains and water features in or around the building can also provide this evaporative air-cooling.

Sustainable and resilient design imperatives emphasize the critical need for passively designed buildings. These buildings can maintain livable conditions and temperatures, not only to reduce energy demand but also for "passive survivability," when there is no external power source to use active systems, for lighting, cooling or heating, in disaster or emergency situations.

See also: **Brise-Soleil • Daylighting • Natural Ventilation • Passive Design • Passive Solar Heating • Passive Survivability • Shading Coefficient • Solar Heat Gain Coefficient • Solar Reflectance Index • Stack Ventilation • Urban Tree Canopy**

Further sources: ASES; Autodesk; EBN; Robertson (2014: 191); WBDG

Passive Design

Nature does nothing uselessly. —Aristotle, philosopher 384-322 BC

I don't believe architecture has to speak too much. It should remain silent and let nature in the guise of sunlight and wind. —Tadao Ando, architect

In order to reduce the consumption of our planet's finite non-renewable energy resources and the associated negative consequences such as carbon dioxide emissions, the designer or architect should optimize passive solar design strategies in creating improved thermal comfort conditions in organizing the plan, the shape of the built form and the enclosure system. *Passive design* means the designer takes full advantage of the resources of nature and site to improve the environmental performance of a building by using radiation, conduction, and natural convection to distribute heat and daylight for lighting, and using nature to the fullest, as "nature does nothing uselessly" in Aristotle's words. Our life on Earth tracks the cycles of the sun as it arches across the sky and so connects us with the rhythm of nature. Passive solar design does not use mechanical, electrical or photovoltaic means to satisfy heating, lighting, or cooling loads.

Strategic awareness, understanding and precise responses to site and place, climatic conditions, landscaping, design and construction, solar orientation, placement windows and shading devices, and thermal mass are used to redistribute the sun's energy. Passive solar design (or bioclimatic design) provides thermal comfort by using natural energy sources and sinks, such as solar radiation, thermal mass, thermal chimney effect, daylighting, evaporation, and vegetation depending on the local climatic conditions.

The net-zero live/work Yin-Yang House by Brooks + Scarpa Architects, is a good example of using the passive measures of a tight building envelope, cross-ventilation, daylighting, a thermal chimney, and a large cantilevered roof overhang for shading (Figures 44, 11). This project typifies Tadao Ando's ideas at the beginning of this chapter, letting the architecture "remain silent" and lets "nature in the guise of sunlight and wind."

In a cold climate, passive measures would aim to design a built form so that solar gains are maximized—but in a hot, dry climate, the primary goal would be to reduce solar gains and maximize natural ventilation. These principles require attention to orientation and building form such as by elongating a building in the east-west orientation to provide an ideal configuration, as south-facing sunlight can be controlled as opposed to low-angle east- or west-facing sunlight. Additional computer modeling of these basic principles can often help achieve even further energy reductions.

See also: • **Building Orientation** • **Daylighting** • **Ecological Design** • **Green Building** • **Natural Ventilation** • **Passive Cooling** • **Passive Solar Heating** • **Passive Survivability** • **Sustainable Design** • **Thermal Insulation** • **Zero-Energy Building**

Further sources: Ander (2003); Hopfe and McLeod (2015); Iyengar (2015); Knowles (2006); Kwok and Grondzik (2007); Olgyay (1963); Roaf, Chrichton, and Nicol (2005)

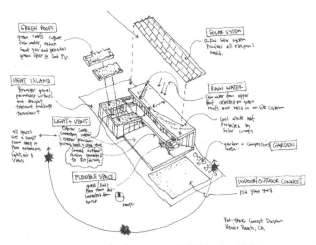

Figure 44 Yin-Yang House, Venice, CA
Appleton Photography. Sketch ©Larry Scarpa. Courtesy ©Brooks + Scarpa Architects

Passive House Building Standard

To develop and promote . . . passive building standards, practices, and certification for buildings, professional, and products to create structures that are durable, resilient, comfortable, healthy, and super energy efficient. —Passive House Institute US website

The *Passive House Building Standard* is a rigorous voluntary building standard for energy efficiency. It has very strict energy limits, requires airtight construction, and high-performing properties of the thermal envelope. *Passive House* buildings are meant to be durable, have high thermal comfort values, and superior indoor air quality. Some strategies and technologies were specifically developed for the *Passive House*, while others existed, such as super insulation and passive solar building design, which reaches back to the first shelters ever built by humans.

Rigorous strategies are required to achieve the significant heat energy reductions required by *Passive House*, such as passive solar building design and energy-efficient landscaping, super insulation to reduce heat transfer, advanced window technology with triple-pane insulated glazing, airtight building envelopes, passive natural ventilation, passive solar gain along with internal heat resources, and passive and active daylighting strategies. The cost savings from not using a conventional heating system are to then go toward upgrading the building envelope and the needed heat recovery ventilation system.

The first *Passive House*, called *Passivhaus*, was built in 1992 in Darmstadt, Germany, starting the first Passive House Institute (PHI). In North America, the Passive House Institute U.S. (PHIUS) broke with its European founders in 2011 and has since modified the original *Passivhaus* standard to adapt to the North American climate and market. When the original German *Passivhaus* standard was implemented in North America, using the very thick insulation and high-tech windows required, it was not cost-effective. The significant upgrade costs were much higher than the value of the energy to be saved by over the life of the building. The updated *PHIUS+ 2015 Passive Building Standard—North America*, released in March 2015, now uses different energy use targets for space conditioning and separate window U-factor specifications for the broad range of climate and market conditions in North American climate zones.

Buildings designed and constructed to the *PHIUS+* Standard consume 86% less energy for heating and 46% less energy for cooling when compared to conventional code-compliant buildings. *PHIUS+* is the only passive building standard using climate specific performance and comfort criteria with the goal of achieving the most durable, resilient and energy-efficient buildings possible.

See also: **Energy Efficiency • Envelope Driven Design • Green Building Certification Systems • Passive Cooling • Passive Design • Passive Solar Heating • Solar Heat Gain Coefficient • Thermal Comfort• Thermal Insulation • Windows and Glazing**

Further sources: PHI; Passive House Institute US; RMI

Passive Solar Heating

Just think that man can claim a slice of the sun. —Louis Kahn, architect

We are born of light. The seasons are felt through light. We only know the world as it is evoked by light. —Louis Kahn

Passive design uses the natural movement of heat and air to provide thermal comfort and to daylight buildings. Passive design strategies can be natural ventilation, solar gain or protection, and natural light, along with building efficiency practices of insulation and airtightness. Active design uses utility purchased energy for mechanical systems. High-performing buildings use a combination of passive and active design strategies, called hybrid systems, to keep occupants comfortable, and reduce energy needs.

Passive solar heating uses the radiant energy of the sun for thermal comfort and to reduce space heating demand, by collecting, storing, and distributing solar heat. *Passive solar heating* strategies involve access to direct solar heat, massing and orientation for heating, thermal mass, heat gain window collectors, and shading control. Solar gain is collected from south-facing glazing with high heat gain coefficients, to capture the low-angle winter sun. Heat can be stored in high thermal mass materials, such as concrete, brick, tile, or even water, which all have high heat capacities to even out temperature swings. This stored heat can then be distributed to the desired spaces using the natural heat flows of convection, conduction, and radiation. The influential architect Louis Kahn was noted for his innovative use of daylighting and passive solar heating by "claiming a slice of the sun" to "feel the seasons."

Shading, brise-soleil, roof overhangs, and correctly sized glazing can control the heat gain and glare to reduce the building cooling loads. *Passive solar heating* strategies must be incorporated during the initial design phase for evaluation in context with the building envelope, window sizing and placement, and heating and cooling equipment zoning and sizing.

The high-performing NASA Sustainability Base at the Ames Research Center in Mountainview, CA. Designed by McDonough + Partners Architects, uses brise-soleil, vegetated screens, horizontal sunscreens, louvered sunshades and an internal bottom-up fabric sun shade to control the solar heat gain, blocking summer sun and allowing low-angle winter sun in for warmth (Figures 45, 10, 16, 19, 52).

There are many benefits of properly designed *passive solar heating*, such as letting sunny daylight into a building to connect occupants with natural views and the nuances of climate and seasons. Temperature swings can be moderated by thermal mass and result in a more stable indoor environment that promotes thermal comfort and well-being.

Sustainable and resilient design imperatives call for passively designed buildings that can maintain livable conditions and temperatures. These buildings are not only important for reducing energy demand, but also for "passive survivability," when there is no external power source to use active systems, such as for disasters or emergency situations. Passive solar designs can reduce resource depletion, contribute to healthy indoor environments, and do not contribute to climate change with carbon emissions.

SUSTAINABILITY BASE: SECTION

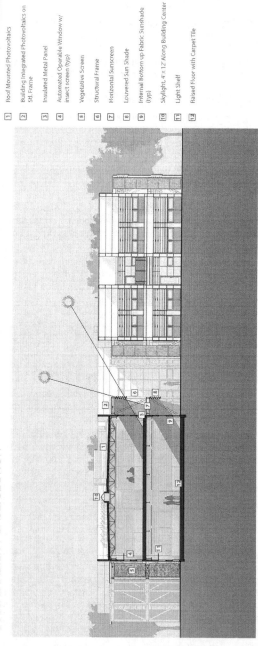

Keynotes

1. Roof Mounted Photovoltaics
2. Building Integrated Photovoltaics on Stl. Frame
3. Insulated Metal Panel
4. Automated Operable Window w/ insect screen (typ)
5. Vegetative Screen
6. Structural Frame
7. Horizontal Sunscreen
8. Louvered Sun Shade
9. Internal Bottom up Fabric Sunshade (typ)
10. Skylight, 4' x 12' Along Building Center
11. Light Shelf
12. Raised Floor with Carpet Tile

Figure 45 NASA Sustainability Base, California
Courtesy ©McDonough + Partners

See also: **Brise-soleil • Daylighting • Natural Ventilation • Passive Cooling • Passive Design • Passive Survivability • Shading Coefficient • Solar Heat Gain Coefficient • Stack Ventilation**

Further sources: ASES; Autodesk; EBN; Kahn (1957); Robertson (2014: 191); WBDG

Passive Survivability   **I**

The more we exploit nature, the more our options are reduced, until we have only one: to fight for survival. —Mo Udall, American politician

With increasingly more frequent and severe weather and temperature extremes caused by global climate change, and with the availability of energy sources threatened by terrorism or long-term supply, the need for buildings to be designed to provide comfort, refuge, water, and shelter in an emergency are vital. The Chicago heat wave of 1995 killed more than 700 people in a one-week period, the 1998 Canadian ice storm left millions without power, and Superstorm Sandy in the Northeastern U.S. are examples of extreme weather events that have left many vulnerable to life-threatening conditions even after the event.

Alex Wilson of Environmental Building News (EBN) proposed the notion of *passive survivability* and its life-saving design strategies after the casualties from Hurricane Katrina in 2005. Many debate whether the frequency and severity of these storms can be attributed to climate change due to us having "exploited nature," but as Mo Udall states opening this chapter, we will need to continue fighting for survival as our "options are reduced." *Passive survivability*, according to EBN, is a building's ability to continue acute life support conditions for the occupants if services such as power, heating, cooling, or water are lost for a prolonged period. The idea is to create buildings using passive design means that will not threaten the lives of the occupants when the grid loses power, or when the conventional solution of backup generators does not work or is not feasible.

Passive survivability incorporates strategies of energy efficiency; such as heat gain avoidance, natural ventilation, controlled passive solar gain, water storage, natural daylighting, and superefficient thermal envelopes. Using renewable energy, such as photovoltaic, in producing and storing electricity, and using rainwater harvesting to save water for flush toilets or bathing, can enhance these passive design strategies even more.

A great example of *passive survivability* is KieranTimberlake's Special No. 9 house in the New Orleans Make It Right development for Hurricane Katrina's displaced residents. The storm-resistant sustainable house uses an advantageous building orientation, raised elevation, and vegetated trellises to limit solar gain in the summer, along with a well-constructed envelope of structural insulated panels (Figure 60). A rainwater cistern provides non-potable water, large operable windows provide natural light and ventilation, and the roof provides a place for photovoltaic energy and safe refuge from flooding.

The notion of resilient design builds on *passive survivability* in the ability to adapt to changing conditions and sustain or regain building functionality by rebounding back after a disruption or stress. Design-ing buildings to be energy- and resource-efficient, climatically suitable, and ecologically responsible are critical, whether referred to as green, resilient, sustainable, or *passively survivable* buildings.

See also: **Climate Responsive Design • Natural Ventilation • Passive Cooling • Passive Design • Passive Solar Heating • Photovoltaics • Rainwater Harvesting • Renewable Energy • Resilient Design • Structural Insulated Panels**

Further sources: AIA Resilient Design; EBN; Make It Right; Resilient Design Institute; USGBC

▌PEER Certification Standard

PEER is a third-party certification program and road map for sustainable power system performance . . . designed to provide dependable, sustainable power for all, all while lowering electricity costs. —USGBC PEER website

Electricity from large power plants is transmitted to consumers through extensive and vulnerable networks with significant power losses. The U.S. Energy Information Administration (EIA) estimates electricity trans-mission and distribution losses average about 6% annually. This is sep-arate from the "heat-work-energy" cycle power plants, such as nuclear, coal-fired, or natural gas, whose electricity generation is only about 35% efficient. Power outages, usually from severe weather, have serious eco-nomic, infrastructure, and health and well-being risks as well.

PEER, *Performance Excellence in Electricity Renewal* is a third-party rating program that certifies smart grid performances for electrical utility power systems. Modeled after USGBC's LEED building program and managed by GBCI, the *PEER Certification Standard* provides energy professionals with a framework for assessing power system perfor-mances. The system evaluates the efficiency, quality, reliability, resil-iency, and environmental impacts of the power system's generation, transmission, and distribution systems, from leaving the generator to reaching the customer.

The *PEER Certification Standard* has four categories of assessment: Reliability and Resiliency, Energy Efficiency and Environment, Oper-ational Effectiveness, and Customer Contribution. The Reliability and Resiliency category addresses power supply, quality, risk mitigation, interruptions, restoration, redundancy, and microgrid capabilities. The Energy Efficiency and Environment category addresses energy efficiency of delivery, resource use, renewable energy credits, air emissions, and power delivery impacts. The Operational Effectiveness category deals with electricity costs, load shaping, asset utilization, operational expenses, indirect costs, capital investment and spending, and mainte-nance. The Customer Contribution category involves customer grid ser-vices, meter data access, tools, choice, pricing, and incentives. The *PEER Certification Standard* can be used for existing projects, or new designs and developments, with the goal of improving power quality, reliability, higher efficiencies, and achieving major reductions in carbon emissions.

See also: **Energy Efficiency • Facility Performance Evaluation • Fossil Fuels • Resilient Design**

Further sources: GBCI; ILFI; PEER; US EIA; USGBC

Permeable Pavement   ∎

Plans to protect air and water, wilderness and wildlife are in fact plans to protect man. —Stewart Udall, American politician

Environmental pollution is an incurable disease. It can only be prevented. —Barry Commoner, American ecologist and politician

Conventional site development can change the natural water flow and watersheds through impervious hardscapes, soil compaction, and loss of natural drainage patterns. High levels of impervious paved surfaces can lead to increased stormwater runoff, water degradation due to pollutants, and increased urban heat island effect.

Permeable pavement systems, also called pervious or porous paving, are specific types of low-impact pavements that mimic nature's high porosity in allowing rainwater to filter through to the soil below. Stormwater gets absorbed and filtered, and the sediments and pollutants are broken down in the soil rather than carried off to downstream water bodies. Once pollution happens, as American ecologist Barry Commoner alludes to in his earlier quote, it is "incurable" and can only be "prevented", which is what *permeable paving* achieves. The stormwater volume and velocity is reduced, keeping the water on the site to recharge underground aquifers, and eliminating retention basins and water collection infrastructure. Rainwater is treated as a valuable resource rather than a waste to discharge.

Permeable pavement systems come in four types: pervious concrete, porous asphalt, permeable interlocking concrete pavers, and reinforced turf or gravel. All systems require a paved surface layer, aggregate and base layers, a fabric filter, and sometimes an under drain. *Permeable paving* can be used in parking lots, low-volume residential streets, sidewalks, driveways, overflow parking areas, recreation facilities, maintenance drives, and places with no high volume of vehicular traffic.

Design consideration must be given to the volume and structural loads of traffic, high water tables, and the proximity to drinking water wells. Due to the porosity and open voids of the pervious concrete and asphalt, these materials are not as strong as conventional paving materials. Certain types of *permeable pavement* require regular maintenance of vacuuming and flushing to prevent particles and solids from clogging the pavement pores. *Permeable paving* should not be used in areas used for vehicle maintenance and fueling, or where there is possible contamination potential to underlying soils and water.

Green building certification systems encourage the use of *permeable pavement* systems. LEED v4's Sustainable Sites: Rainwater Management credit addresses reducing the peak rate and flow of discharge and also filtering pollutants and total suspended solids from the stormwater runoff.

The use of *permeable pavement* systems protects and conserves water by using low-impact development strategies to reduce the stormwater runoff and pollutant discharge off-site. It enables efforts to "maintain or restore the predevelopment hydrology of the site with regard to temperature, rate, volume, and duration of flow using site planning, design, construction, and maintenance strategies," according to the U.S. Energy Independence and Security Act (EISA), Section 438.

See also: **Ecological Design • Green Building • Rainwater Harvesting • SITES Initiative • Stormwater Management • SITES Initiative • Sustainable Site Design • Urban Heat Island**

Further sources: EBN; EISA; Green Building Alliance; Lake Superior Streams; Water Environment Federation; WBDG

▌Photovoltaics

The mission of the Center for Innovation is to teach students sustainability, resilience, and wholeness through the spheres of Sustainable Earth, Sustainable Design, and Sustainable Community.
—Center for Innovation

Energy moves the modern world, but using fossil fuel energy is unsustainable, threatens economic and national security, and has severe environmental impacts. Nuclear energy poses threats to the environment, humanity, and is cost-prohibitive. Wood-sourced fuel causes desertification and millions of deaths from indoor air pollution in the developing world.

Renewable energy generation has the environmental benefits of reducing carbon emissions and local air pollution. Each hour of the day, enough sunlight reaches the Earth to power the world's energy needs for almost a full year. Solar *photovoltaic (PV)* cells convert sunlight directly into electricity, using semiconductor materials with no moving parts. The *photovoltaic* term is derived from converting sunlight (photons) into electricity (voltage).

Rigid silicon-based *photovoltaic* cells combine in a series to make a photovoltaic panel that connects to other panels forming a *PV* array. Thin-film solar cells use micro-thin layers of semiconductor materials to form a semi-flexible *PV* that can be building-integrated, but currently have low efficiencies, and require almost twice the area.

Solar *photovoltaics* can power buildings entirely independent from the grid, as in rural areas, or can be grid-connected to the local utility. Using a grid-connection allows excess renewable power produced to be sent to the electric utility with net-metering, and provides backup power when *photovoltaic* generation is insufficient, such as nights, cloudy days, and even during high-level air pollution.

The South Kent School's Center for Innovation project in Connecticut, designed by Centerbrook Architects is built to LEED Platinum, Living Building Challenge and Net-Zero Energy certification standards and seeks to teach students how to actually live their educational mission stated above, in a carbon-free world with *photovoltaics*, wind turbines, and hydro-turbines. The environmental campus would be totally heated and powered by the sun, grow all their annual food needs, as well as being zero-water and zero-pollution (Figure 46).

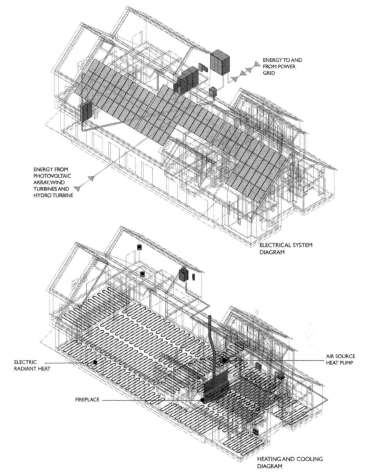

ENERGY TO AND
FROM POWER
GRID

ENERGY FROM
PHOTOVOLTAIC
ARRAY, WIND
TURBINES AND
HYDRO TURBINE

ELECTRICAL SYSTEM
DIAGRAM

ELECTRIC
RADIANT HEAT

AIR SOURCE
HEAT PUMP

FIREPLACE

HEATING AND COOLING
DIAGRAM

Figure 46 Center for Innovation, South Kent School, Connecticut
Courtesy ©Centerbrook Architects

Grid-connected systems send the direct current (DC) produced by the *photovoltaic* modules to an inverter that converts the DC to alternating current (AC) for the building needs and connecting to the local electrical utility, and do not need batteries. In off-grid systems, the DC power is sent to a charge controller before being stored, possibly in a lead acid battery.

Solar *photovoltaic* arrays can be roof-mounted, ground-mounted or building-integrated. A rule of thumb for mounting *photovoltaic* panels is to use the same angle as the latitude in degrees—and to maximize winter energy generation, add 15 degrees; and to maximize summer generation, subtract 15 degrees. Roof-mounted modules are usually mounted on south-facing aluminum racks with an air space under the arrays, which lowers the *PV* module temperatures as cooler modules produce more electricity than hotter modules. Ground-mounted *PV* arrays avoid removal for roof replacement and are easier to keep clean and snow-free than roof-mounted arrays. *PV* arrays can be at a fixed angle or can track the sun automatically as the sun moves across the sky, increasing the efficiency, but also adding significant cost and maintenance. Building-integrated *photovoltaic* arrays can be combined with façades, glazing, and roofing.

Renewable solar *photovoltaic* energy is a significant investment in reducing the carbon footprint of a building. Energy conservation and renewable energy efficiency must go hand in hand. Building the envelope with the best materials, installing superefficient windows, proper insulation, maximizing passive strategies, energy-efficient equipment and lighting investments, and intelligent automated building controls can all further the efficiency of on-site renewables. Renewable energy generation, especially *photovoltaics*, can significantly reduce the carbon footprint of buildings to meet the climate targets of holding global temperature rise to below 2°C.

See also: **Building-Integrated Photovoltaics • Energy Efficiency • Green Building • High-Performing Buildings • Life-Cycle Cost Analysis • Net-Zero Energy Building Certification • Renewable Energy • Solar Energy • Zero-Energy Building**

Further sources: ASES; Autodesk; EBN; RMI; SEIA; US DOE; US EPA; WBDG

▌Population Growth

Remember that impact is the product of two factors: population multiplied times impact per person. —Jared Diamond, *Collapse*

Fifty years ago, it did not seem critical to understand the relationship between growth and a healthy environment because our natural resources seemed unlimited and we did not understand the damage we were doing to our climate, land, air, water and sea. Now well into the new millennium, we know we have damaged most all of our ancient forests, farmers and ranchers are withdrawing billions more gallons of water than is replaced by rainfall, and fertile topsoil is being lost at

10–40 times the rate it can be naturally replenished, some say to be gone in sixty years.

These critical losses are occurring while the world population is now seven billion plus, and increasing at the rate of eighty million people per year (1.13%), and is estimated by mid-2030s to reach 8.4 billion, and by mid-2050 to 9.6 billion, according to the UN DESA report, *World Population Prospects: The 2015 Revision*. Ever since 1798, when Thomas Malthus wrote his *Essay on Population*, we have pondered when humankind would exceed the capacity of our planet to feed us.

In the last few thousand years, life expectancy has tripled, but the birth rate has recently declined, enabling societies to focus on children's well-being and quality of life. But every additional person born increases the total impact on the planet by requiring food, water, and energy, which all then produce more polluting waste. In the developing countries of the world, where the population is growing the fastest, only a tiny proportion of global resources are used, compared with the comfortable and abundant lifestyles of Western countries.

Society's structure created a conflict between the short-term interests of those in power, and the long-term interests of the society as a whole. —Jared Diamond, *Collapse*

In *Guns, Germs, and Steel* and *Collapse* Jared Diamond points out the real problem is that people in the U.S. consume 30–40 times more resources than do the poor in developing nations, who will be the ones hit the hardest by severe climate change, deforestation, and resource degradation. The toll we are paying for this consumptive lifestyle is the planet itself, as the land, water, air, and sea have become not abundant life-supporting systems, but degraded repositories for our waste.

See also: **Carrying Capacity • Ecological Footprint • Lifeboat Ethics • Social Equity • Tragedy of the Commons • Urban Design**

Further sources: Diamond (1999, 2005); Hawken (1993: 204); Population Reference Bureau

Precautionary Principle   **I**

Technology causes problems as well as solves problems. Nobody has figured out a way to ensure that, as of tomorrow, technology won't create problems. —Jared Diamond, ecologist and author

Advances in science and technology have diminished many threatening risks from nature and have eliminated numerous hardships of life, but these advances have also contributed to negative environmental effects threatening the quality and existence of human life. With continuing environmental impacts from increasing industrialization and populations, the compensation notion of the "polluters pay principle" has not been enough to repair or deter the damages caused.

With new scientific developments, such as bioaccumulative and toxic compounds, emerging with unpredictable and possible catastrophic risks to health and environment, the *precautionary principle* has evolved as a strategy of extreme caution when making any decisions or implementing new products that may negatively affect humans, nature, and global ecosystems. This *precautionary* approach suggests that we should prevent potentially harmful acts, products, risks or policies even if we are not scientifically certain of the potential harm, much like saying "better safe than sorry" and "precaution is better than the cure." As Jared Diamond the ecologist warns in his above quote, we haven't figured out a way yet to ensure that today or tomorrow, "technology won't create problems."

Industry and manufacturers can carry the burden of proof to assess and quantify effects before releasing new chemicals into the environment. Examples of such potential risks are new estrogen-mimicking chemicals, global warming reduction strategies, oil and gas exploitation, genetically modified organisms (GMOs), and powerful new technologies such as nanotechnology. In the past, chemicals and materials have been assumed "innocent until proven guilty"—for example, asbestos, bisphenol A, polyvinyl chloride, and formaldehyde—but the *precautionary principle* turns the tables to call for materials and chemicals to be "guilty until proven innocent."

The Rio Declaration from the UN Earth Summit of 1992 states:

In order to protect the environment, the *precautionary* approach shall be widely applied by States according to their capabilities. Where there are threats of serious or irreversible damage, lack of full scientific certainty shall not be used as a reason for postponing cost-effective measures to prevent environmental degradation.

The burden of proof is at the heart of the issue, and many see it as a threat to progress.

The Wingspread Conference of 1998 developed a formal definition stating:

When an activity raises threats of harm to human health or the environment, precautionary measures should be taken even if some cause and effect relationships are not fully established scientifically. In this context, the proponent of an activity, rather than the public, should bear the burden of proof.

The *precautionary principle* builds on ethical notions of equity and sustainability for both current and future generations in safeguarding against serious and potentially irreversible harm to our natural resources while preparing for any unseen challenges ahead. Similar to the 1142 AD Iroquois Seven Generation Principle which states the decisions that we make today should result in a sustainable world for those seven generations into the future, the *precautionary principle* is about drawing moral lessons from the millions of years our natural systems have evolved and endured. The challenge is achieving long-term sustainability on a finite planet where never before has nature had to deal with so many new industrial chemicals and human-made impacts.

See also: **Carrying Capacity • Ecological Footprint • Green Chemistry • Lifeboat Ethics • Life-cycle Assessment • Seventh Generation Principle**

Further sources: Diamond (1999, 2005); EBN; UNEP (1992); Wingspread Statement on the Precautionary Principle, http://sehn.org/wingspread-conference-on-the-precautionary-principle/; World UNESCO

Prescriptive Versus Performance-Based Design

It takes far less energy to move from first-rate performance to excellence than it does to move from incompetence to mediocrity. — Peter Drucker, management consultant

A *prescriptive-based design* uses a traditional energy efficiency approach with using building codes to meet specific energy standards, while *performance-based design* uses the final energy results of the building to meet the standards without a prescribed method. *Performance-based design* relies in part on regulations and ordinances, so it is not yet at its full potential. For example, to design for energy codes, one can follow a prescriptive method list, or design consciously based on energy concepts, and then evaluate with the performance method. The components of *performance-based design* are codes, standards, and evaluation and design tools.

The codes are the minimum performance objectives to meet the health, safety and welfare measures of the built environment. Standards reflect documents based on references to apply codes as objectives. For example, egress standards provide architects with methods to comply with requirements (human safety), such as building measurements and the number of occupants based on the building type. Evaluation and design tools guide designers through the review and verification process to meet the standards.

Performance-based design investigates beyond the codes and rules of thumb by evaluating the actual performance of a building. These evaluation tools help move from "first-rate to excellent" in building performance, in Drucker's explanation, as usually these projects being measured are seeking to be excellent in the first place. Building energy modeling is an example of applying performance-based design, which meets Leadership in Energy and Environmental Design (LEED) criteria as a standard. Outcome-based design, as indicated by the AIA, is the future *of performance-based* procedure to design more efficient buildings by targeting the post-occupancy evaluations.

If you can't measure it, you can't improve it. —William Thomson, Lord Kelvin

Moving from *prescriptive-based* to a *performance-based design* is becoming more prevalent in the field, requiring energy modeling, because as Lord Kelvin states "if you can't measure it, you can't improve" the performance. As such, green building rating systems are encouraging designers to comply with green building standards, while the next step will mandate the evaluation of outcomes. MM

See also: **ASHRAE Standards • Energy Efficiency • Evidence Based Design (***Theoryspeak***) • Facility Performance Evaluation • Operations and Maintenance • Performance-based Design (***Theoryspeak***) • Vital Signs (***Archispeak***)**

Further sources: EBN; Meacham (1997); WBDG

Rainwater Harvesting   █

All the water that will ever be is, right now. —Proverb

Water is critical for sustainable development, including environmental integrity and the alleviation of poverty and hunger, and is indispensable for human health and well-being. —United Nations

Over the past century, the world's population has doubled in size while global water consumption increased by six times. By 2025, the United Nations has predicted that two-thirds of all countries will be water-stressed. The demand for fresh water is growing at a critical rate world-wide, primarily from agriculture, as rivers and aquifers are being drained and polluted from nitrogen, pesticides, and toxic chemicals. Biofuels and food crops are increasingly competing for the same scarce water sources, causing continuing rising prices and escalating tensions worldwide.

We know the worth of water when the well is dry. —Chinese proverb

Rainwater harvesting has been a critical source of survival for thousands of years, especially in arid parts of the world. Rainwater is an excellent source of water, especially for developing areas with no utility-provided water or to supplement water from existing utilities to reduce building water demands. Rain is collected from roofs or other catchment surfaces and stored in a cistern or tank, until needed on-site for irrigation or domestic use. *Rainwater harvesting* systems usually have the following components: a catchment area or roof for collection; a roof wash system to eliminate dust and contaminants; a delivery system of gutters; a pre-storage filtration for leaves and debris; an aboveground or belowground storage cistern; a water delivery system, usually pump- or gravity-fed; and a water treatment system to protect plumbing and irrigation lines from sediment and algae.
    Water capture and reuse can improve water quality with filtration, reduce stress on municipal water infrastructure, recharge groundwater, reduce erosion, and reduce stormwater runoff. Captured water reduces the need for utility provided water and can be used for irrigation, livestock, domestic consumption, and with proper treatment for drinking, cooking, and toilet flushing. An excellent example is the rainwater harvesting system in the Marin County Day School in Corte Madera, CA., designed by EHDD Architects, which harvests and filters rainwater in underground cisterns for reuse in cooling towers and toilet flushing, while the cistern tanks also double as thermal energy storage (Figure 47).
    Rainwater harvesting systems, since using a natural resource, score high in green building rating systems, such as the Living Building Challenge, LEED, and BREEAM. The rigorous Living Building Challenge certification standard demands that buildings must achieve net-zero water use by reducing their reliance on municipal water systems and capture 100% of their water from the rain through *rainwater harvesting* systems, cisterns, and closed-loop systems.

See also: **Green Roofs • Greywater • Passive Survivability • Resilient Design • Stormwater Management • Water Efficiency • Water-Energy Nexus**

Further sources: EBN; Design Building Wiki; HPB; UNEP; WBDG

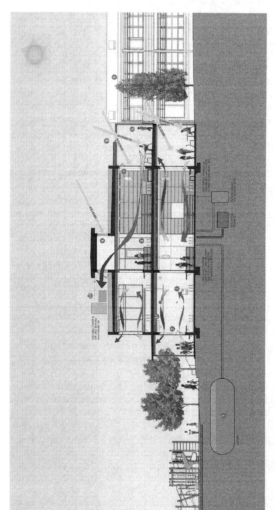

SUSTAINABILE STRATEGIES

1 sunshades
2 high-performance glazing
3 natural ventilation
4 fully daylit interiors with
  lighting controls
5 exterior circulation;
  less conditioned space
6 trees for shading

7 on-site cistern; stormwater retention
8 radiant slab heating + cooling
9 deep overhangs for shading
10 100% outside air unit
11 future cooling panels

Figure 47 Marin Country Day School, Corte Madera, CA
Courtesy ©EHDD

REACH Regulation   I

For the first time in the history of the world, every human being is now subjected to contact with dangerous chemicals, from the moment of conception until death. —Rachel Carson

For years, large numbers of chemical substances have been manufactured and marketed, often in high amounts, without sufficient information on the potential hazards to human health and the environment, and as Rachel Carson points out above, we are "subjected to contact with dangerous chemicals" all our lives. In 2001, the European Commission proposed a "future chemical strategy'" that would require chemicals manufactured in certain amounts to be registered, evaluated, or authorized depending on the numbers. Those that were carcinogenic, mutagenic, or toxic to reproduction (CMR) would require prior approval before use.

The *Registration, Evaluation, Authorisation and Restriction of Chemicals (REACH)* regulation came into force in June 2007 as a European Union regulation addressing the production and use of chemical substances, and their potential impacts on both human health and the environment. It is estimated by the Competitive Enterprise Institute that in the European Market alone, there were over thirty thousand chemical substances with over a ton used per year without sufficient potential hazardous information. With the *REACH regulation*, manufacturers and importers are required to obtain information on the properties of their chemical substances to allow safe handling, and to then register the information in the European Chemicals Agency (ECHA) in Helsinki. The Agency manages the central databases, coordinates the evaluations of suspicious chemicals, and builds the database of hazardous substances for public information. The amount of data required is usually proportional to the amounts of the manufactured substance. If the material data is not registered, then the manufacturer can no longer legally supply the materials.

Health is the greatest of human blessings. —Hippocrates

As a European Union legislative action, the *REACH regulation* took seven years to pass, and though complicated and strict, it is thought to be the most relevant legislation in over two decades. The regulation will affect industries around the world in the production and use of chemical substances, and their potential impacts on people's health and the environment.

See also: **Athena Impact Estimator • Declare Label • Design for the Environment • Environmental Product Declaration • Green Chemistry • GreenScreen • Health Product Declaration • Natural Step • WELL Building Standard**

Further sources: Carson (1962); Competitive Enterprise Institute (CEI), www.cei.org/pdf/4951.pdf; EBN; ECHA; European Commission; HSE UK; REACH; Wikipedia

Reclaimed Water

No water, no life. No blue, no green. —Sylvia Earle, American marine biologist

All water has a perfect memory and is forever trying to get back to where it was. —Toni Morrison, speech "The Site of Memory"

According to the World Wildlife Fund, with the global population growth and increasing climate change, over half the world's population will face water shortages by 2030. These droughts will cause significant health risks and promote the spread of waterborne diseases due to drinking unsanitary water, and widespread food shortages due to threatened agricultural production. And as Sylvia Earle, the renowned marine biologist and advocate for preserving our waterways and oceans, expresses: "no water, no life." With increasing water needs, recycling the available water is imperative to meet demands. *Reclaimed water* is previous sewage or wastewater that has been treated for reuse as landscape irrigation, industrial or commercial applications, and drinking water.

Greywater is the wastewater reused from showers, bathroom sinks, and washing machines. Blackwater is sewage wastewater from toilets and kitchen sinks containing feces and food and is hazardous to humans and the soil. Greywater is often recycled, usually distributed in lavender piping for irrigation or power generation, while blackwater is sent to sewage treatment plants for disposal. Though the treatment of blackwater for reuse is more intensive and costly, it can be thoroughly reclaimed, cleaned and returned as potable water.

Southern California, parts of the U.K., and other countries have been using wastewater treatment facilities for years to recycle sewage and return the water to the drinking supply. The process usually works by re-routing the millions of gallons of daily wastewater to a three-step process. Microfiltration first removes solids, oils, and bacteria, and then the liquid goes through reverse osmosis, using a fine membrane to filter out pharmaceuticals and viruses. Lastly, treatment with ultraviolet light removes any residual organic compounds to meet strict quality control standards, before combining with groundwater supply in indirect reuse or distributed with direct potable reuse to consumers. Our water is the same water that has been around for millions of years, and as Toni Morrison so eloquently has stated, it "is forever trying to get back to where it was," whether nature cleans it or we do.

As a water insecure country, Singapore was previously reliant on imported water and now provides 30% of its water needs through the NEWater reclamation facility, according to the World Wildlife Fund. The output exceeds standards for potable use and is so clean it's used for industrial processes requiring ultra clean water. Over half the inhabitants of sub-Saharan Africa face water insecurity and often-fatal diarrhea risks, but a Namibia wastewater treatment plant has been alleviating water shortages and waterborne diseases for over forty years. In Orange County, California their innovative wastewater treatment facility recycles wastewater for over 850,000 people a day. Many *reclaimed water* systems can produce clean water for less than desalination efforts.

As the world population requires more clean water, and waste disposal burden increases, the need for water reclamation will increase, especially as technology and membranes efficiencies increase and costs drop.

See also: **Climate Change • Constructed Wetland • Greywater • Population Growth • Water Efficiency • Water-Energy Nexus**

Further sources: Climate Tech Wiki; Earle (2010); Designing Buildings Wiki; EBN; Green Age Company; US EPA; WBDG; World Wildlife Fund: Water Scarcity, www.worldwildlife.org/threats/water-scarcity

Regenerative Design   **I**

Regenerative design is a process-oriented systems theory based approach to design. The term "regenerative" describes processes that restore, renew or revitalize their own sources of energy and materials, creating sustainable systems that integrate the needs of society with the integrity of nature. —Wikipedia

Regenerative Architecture is the evolution of Green Architecture. — REGENARCH

Having its roots in agriculture, regeneration has become a popular water cooler topic since the release of the 1993 movie Jurassic Park and more recent efforts to regenerate the mastodon from retrieved DNA. These developments have excited the imagination of children, science fiction enthusiasts, ethicists, and designers. Plants have always regenerated on their own—can the man-made or artificial eventually do the same? It would require design.

Regenerative design is a more complex challenge than planting a seed or giving birth. We already have regenerated human limbs with the aid of three-dimensional printing. We have also started to grow organs in the laboratory. Designer babies are a technical possibility, only held off by ethical concerns. The design of regenerative biological organisms seems to be a natural extension of humanity's fascination with the growth mechanisms of the biological world. One day we may even have self-generative design as artificial intelligent equipped robots repair, replace, or replicate themselves.

To design large regenerative man-made artifacts, including buildings, will require materials and methods that are only now emerging. Nascent 4D printing technology promises to create materials that are generative, self-directed, and self-healing. At a nanoscale, 4D printed objects are programmed to behave in specific ways in response to external stimuli. Typically, that stimulus is heat or moisture, the same stimuli that act on the skin of buildings. Soon those skins will be able to shape and regenerate entirely independently, unfettered by electronic or mechanical controls.

Until then, *regenerative design* will consist of the design of objects that can be regenerated with external assistance. An early example is Archigram's "Walking Cities" (1965) proposal in which Megastructure

BUILDING LIKE A TREE™: DESIGN POSITIVE

ENERGY POSITIVE
Living things thrive on the energy of current solar income. Similarly, human constructs can utilize renewable energy in many forms—such as solar, wind, geothermal and gravitational energy—thereby capitalizing on these abundant resources while supporting human and environmental health.

ECONOMY POSITIVE
Construction practices can facilitate easy building disassembly and material reuse. Develop long-term relationships with product manufacturers, such as product leasing arrangements, to ensure companies take responsibility for materials in the short and long term, and that they return nutrients to the biosphere or technosphere as appropriate.

WATER POSITIVE
The interplay between industrial and natural systems creates a new model for the regeneration of air, water, soil, and habitat. An integrated system of green roofs, vegetated swales and pervious paving capures, cleanses and releases clean water.

PEOPLE POSITIVE
Promote individual human dignity with safe working conditions. Promote fairness, so groups of laborers or suppliers aren't exploited with dangerously low wages or prices along the entire value chain.

MATERIAL POSITIVE
Prefer products which can be characterized as "biological nutrients" (those that can safely biodegrade and improve soil health) or "technical nutrients" (those that can be fully recycled, safely returning to high-valued uses in new products).

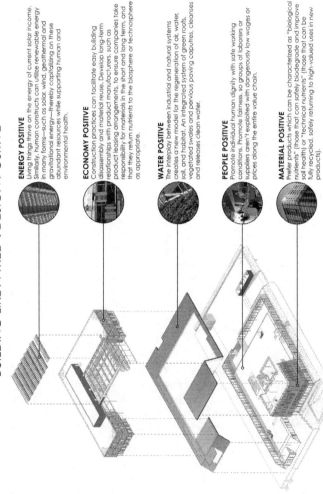

Figure 48 Bosch Siemens Centre, Netherlands
Courtesy ©McDonough + Partners

cities would be built to be relocatable by walking to the next "pasture" to allow a stressed ecosystem to regenerate. Another example of designed regeneration is the pneumatic structure that can be regenerated with the addition of air pressure. A similar type of regenerative design is illustrated by the basketball venue at the 2012 London Olympics. The design was conceived as a fully reusable, fully recyclable venue. It was designed to be subdivided and reconfigured if necessary, but being built almost entirely of PVC and steel, it is almost wholly recyclable when its lifespan is done. Designed to be regenerated in a different location after serving as a basketball facility, it was reconstituted as a community center in northern England.

The architect William McDonough + Partners design for the Bosch Siemens Experience Centre in the Netherlands applies the idea of 'buildings like trees' and 'cities like forests' to regenerate the environment. Ideally the design becomes photosynthetic and biologically active, accruing solar energy, cycling nutrients, releasing oxygen, fixing nitrogen, purifying water, providing diverse habitats, and changing with the seasons. Photovoltaic arrays and green roofs become the system's leaves and roots, harvesting renewable energy, absorbing and filtering water, and producing food and habitat for other living things (Figures 48, 12, 69).

As virtual reality technology supplants more and more reality, a new class of virtually regenerated designs will appear. As they have no material substance, they will be relatively Earth-friendly. No materials will be consumed in the making of the virtual artifact. The environmental costs will be in the energy consumed to manufacture the virtual reality equipment and to run it.

As an aspect of the current interest in green architecture and biomimicry, *regenerative design* is poised to become a major aspect of the second decade of 21st century design. It will contribute to the ongoing evolution away from our lingering machine zeitgeist design traditions. EO

See also: **Adaptation • Building Automated Control Systems • Building Science • Climate Responsive Design • Ecotechnology • Green Chemistry • Mitigation • Nanotechnology • Precautionary Principle**

Further sources: Thompson (1917); www.regarch.org; Herron and Crompton (1980)

Renewable Energy   **I**

Fire made us human, fossil fuels made us modern, but now we need a new fire that makes us safe, secure, healthy and durable. —Amory Lovins, environmental scientist

There is an urgent need to stop subsidizing the fossil fuel industry, dramatically reduce wasted energy, and significantly shift our power supplies from oil, coal, and natural gas to wind, solar, geothermal, and other renewable energy sources. —Bill McKibben, environmental activist

Since the Industrial Revolution, fossil fuel combustion has been the engine of development and the primary contributor to climate change.

Fossil fuels are non-renewable, carbon-based sources formed hundreds of millions of years ago and when burned release CO_2, creating the greenhouse effect of warming. As Amory Lovins states in the quote above, we need a new type of "fire" that creates a better future.

Renewable energy is clean and healthier, and generated from replenishing natural sources such as sunlight, wind, rain, tides, waves, and the Earth's heat. Increasingly efficient technologies and automated controls are being used for photovoltaics (PV), solar thermal, wind turbines, water-powered microturbines, and biomass. Hydrogen fuel cells are considered renewable if the hydrogen has been renewably generated, but nuclear energy is not.

Once you've identified a problem, and that you're part of the problem, you need to be a part of the solution. —Jim Rogers, Duke Energy Chairman

As the fastest growing source of global electricity generation, *renewable energy* provides energy in rural off-grid services, transportation, air and water heating, and cooling. As Bill McKibben argues in his earlier quote for shifting to renewables, the International Panel on Climate Change (IPCC) also believes renewables can meet 80% of the world's energy needs by 2050. Solar PV and wind turbines generate electricity at zero-cost, and therefore have a high return on investment. Other benefits are energy security, foreign oil independence, decentralized collection and generation, and local energy to rural off-grid areas, particularly in developing countries. Duke Energy Chairman Jim Rogers acknowledges that as a primarily fossil fuel company, they were "part of the problem," so they are now investing in renewables and efficiency.

Meeting the ambitious Paris Climate Agreement goals of 2°C will require dramatic changes in government policies, drastic consumer energy reductions, and rapid acceleration in ultra-efficient low-carbon renewable technologies to become carbon-neutral by 2100. Implementing the current Paris pledges only will just slow rising global temperatures, and not enough to limit the average global temperature 2.7°C target by 2100. For example, in 2016 there were only 1.3 million electric vehicles, and the IEA World Outlook 2016 states the number needs to exceed seven hundred million by 2040 to avoid the worst climate change impacts.

In 2016 in the E.U., according to the IPCC, *renewable energy* made up 86% of newly installed capacity, coming from wind, solar, biomass, and hydropower and Germany alone lead globally in 2016 with wind energy installations. China, the world's largest carbon emitter, has the most installed wind energy capacity and the second highest installed solar PV capacity. The U.S. is fifth in solar photovoltaics and second in installed wind capacity, but U.S. energy demand far outpaces their renewable capacity.

The AIA Committee on the Environment (COTE) award-winning Arizona State University Health Services Building by Lake|Flato Architects used as many as possible passive design strategies to minimize any energy loads before any active design strategies were even considered. Massing, orientation, and super insulation are used, along with a 69-kilowatt photovoltaic array and *renewable energy* certificates in achieving the LEED Platinum certification (Figures 49, 18, 64).

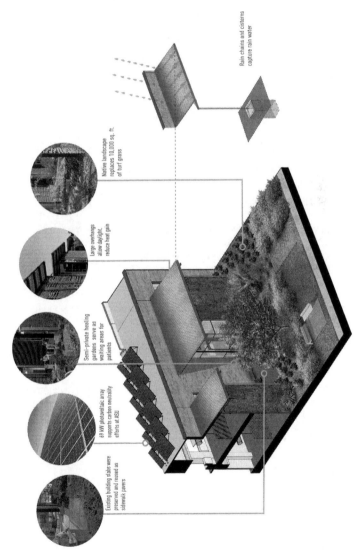

Rain chairs and cisterns capture rain water

Native landscape replaces 10,000 sq. ft. of turf grass

Large overhangs allow daylight, reduce heat gain

Semi-private healing gardens serve as waiting areas for patients

69 kW photovoltaic array supports carbon neutrality efforts at ASU

Existing building slabs were preserved and reused as sidewalk pavers

Figure 49 Arizona State University Health Sciences Building, Tempe, AZ
Courtesy ©Lake|Flato

Major global investments, policy, research, and incentives are needed to achieve critical climate goals. Increasing government-forced coal plant closures, such as United Kingdom's 2025 commitment, should provide prospects for future *renewable energy* developments. The International Renewable Energy Agency estimates that doubling global renewables by 2030 would save $4.2 trillion dollars annually in avoiding air pollution and climate change expenditures.

See also: **Biomass Power • Fossil Fuels • Geothermal Energy • Ocean Energy • Paris Climate Agreement • Renewable Energy Certificates • Solar Energy • Wind Energy**

Further sources: Hawken, A. Lovins, and L. Lovins (1999); IPCC, https://www.ipcc.ch/news_and_events/docs/ipcc33/PRESS%20RELEASE%20 Updated%20version%20-%20Potential%20of%20Renewable%20Ener gy%20Outline.pdf, p. 1; IRENA; Nature; Statistic.com; WBDG; IEA World Outlook 2016; IPCC

▌Renewable Energy Certificates

Doing all we can to combat climate change comes with numerous benefits, from reducing pollution and associated health care costs to strengthening and diversifying the economy by shifting to renewable energy, among other measures. —David Suzuki, Canadian environmental activist

Renewable Energy Certificates (RECs) are a tradable currency, also known as green certificates, renewable energy credits, or green tags, which represent proof that a unit of electricity was generated from a renewable energy source. *RECs* were created to encourage renewable power development and sources, while supporting those who may not have access to the possibility of renewable energy production. Certificates are sold separately from the electricity itself, and allow users to purchase green power whether or not they use conventionally generated electricity. As David Suzuki urges in his quote above for "shifting to renewable energy", *Renewable Energy Certificates* can be used to comply with renewable energy policy requirements and to meet voluntary renewable energy targets.

A *Renewable Energy Certificate* indicates the generation of one megawatt-hour (MWh) of electricity is from an eligible renewable power source. Each *REC* is a claim to the environmental benefits of that energy source and must show the generation source, location, and year. Markets are created by energy policies requiring utilities to incorporate a minimum level of renewables in their electricity supply. The Renewable Portfolio Standards (RPS) and the Renewable Electricity Standards (RES) are both policies that designate eligible energy resources and how electricity utilities must comply.

Purchasing *Renewable Energy Certificates* is can be complicated, and usually requires using an independent third-party certification to meet the environmental and consumer protection standards required. The Center for Resource Solutions administers the most common standard, Green-e, which ensures the electricity and *RECs* are from authentic sources, in the correct amounts, and not claimed by other parties. The

Green-e standard certifies the electricity is generated from solar electric, wind, biomass, low-impact hydro, fuel cells using renewable fuels, or geothermal.

Green building rating systems, such as LEED and BREEAM, accept *Renewable Energy Certificates* allowing project owners to receive points by purchasing credits or carbon offsets. The Living Building Challenge, though, requires that 105% of the building's energy on a net-annual basis must be supplied by on-site renewable energy to meet its rigorous net-positive energy standard.

The use of *Renewable Energy Certificates* can allow companies to achieve their renewable energy goals, support renewable power projects, and show a commitment to clean renewable generation.

See also: **BREEAM Certification • Embodied Energy • Energy Efficiency • High-Performing Buildings • LEED Building Certification • Renewable Energy**

Further sources: EBN; EERE; World Resources Institute; US DOE

Resilient Design   **I**

Notice that the stiffest tree is most easily cracked, while the bamboo or willow survives by bending with the wind. —Bruce Lee, martial artist, philosopher

Resilience is all about being able to overcome the unexpected. Sustainability is about survival. The goal of resilience is to thrive. — Jamais Cascio, futurist

Our natural world is full of beauty and inspiration but can be very unpredictable. Globally, we have been having weather extremes such as coastal and valley flooding and warmer temperatures in many parts of the world, attributed to climate change. Disasters such as the 2012 Superstorm Sandy in New Jersey, the 2005 Hurricane Katrina in New Orleans, the 2004 Indian Ocean tsunami, the U.S. Midwest extreme tornadoes, and the Haiti 2010 earthquake are but a few of the recent devastating worldwide natural occurrences.

Housing, food, medical facilities, sanitation, and power were in most cases non-existent. Resiliency is the ability to bounce back with a speedy recovery from these problems, an analogy being Bruce Lee's words of the "willow survives by bending with the wind." Our working built environment provides the life-safety benefits of shelter, protection, security and comfort so as not to be at risk of vulnerability, hazard, and exposure. Many of those who died after these disasters were the elderly and the young as they were more susceptible to disease, predators, temperature extremes, and food shortages. Many were trapped inside with no exits to escape the rising waters, extreme heat with no means of natural ventilation, or access to fresh water. Resiliency is "being able to overcome the unexpected" and then to "thrive" as stated by futurist Jamais Cascio.

Resilient design, which encompasses the notion of passive survivability, emphasizes how to minimize the initial damage to buildings, landscapes, and communities while providing for short-term survival for the occupants when future disasters strike. As well as designing for extreme weather events such as intense storms and wildfires, *resilient design* must address the gradual and longer-term changes occurring. These changes can be sea level rise, increased flooding, severe droughts, global warming, landslides, extended power outages, interruptions in fuel supplies, and terrorism or other direct human actions. These must be addressed at the scale of place with effective planning for the resident communities. There is no area, region or country immune to the effects of climate change.

Resilient designs that combine the responsiveness to climate change's severe weather, along with incorporating smart growth principles, emergency planning, and hazard mitigation, are some of the strategies needed to achieve a more durable and thriving future civilization.

See also: **Adaptation • Climate Change • Global Warming • Mitigation • Passive Survivability • Smart Growth • Universal and Inclusive Design**

Further sources: AIA Resilient Design; EBN; Resilient Design Institute; ResilientCity

Reveal Label

The Reveal Label provides a clear, third-party verified program for validating reaching the 2030 Challenge targets or achieving a Zero Net Carbon building. —Edward Mazria, Architecture 2030

Building owners, designers, and engineers are currently producing some of the most efficient projects around the world, often reducing their energy consumption by up to 90% from the average by using renewables and energy conserving strategies. Many of these buildings are not being celebrated for their climate solution efforts of reducing the carbon emissions and environmental impacts of their projects. The International Living Future Institute (ILFI) developed a third-party tool for measuring building energy performance, the *Reveal label*, to highlight the outstanding energy efficiency, sustainability profiles, and leadership visibility of these projects.

The *Reveal label* tries to make commercial building energy consumption and savings more transparent by marking their energy use. There is no minimum threshold, and projects are not required to use renewables. *Reveal* is a verification of post-occupancy energy performance for other sustainability initiatives, such as the AIA 2030 Commitment and the Architecture 2030 Challenge, by using their Zero tool. The Architecture 2030 Zero tool uses the original 2030 Challenge energy use data for one fixed baseline to have a consistent energy performance description over time. The *Reveal label* also works with the New Buildings Institute to include the Zero Energy Performance Index used by the International Green Construction Code.

The *Reveal label* shows a building's energy use intensity, zero energy performance index score, the reduction in energy use from the baseline, and the on-site and off-site renewable energy generation if used.

Projects must have twelve months of valid energy consumption data and if applicable, the renewable generation data to be verified with a *Reveal label.*

See also: **Architecture 2030 • Energy Efficiency • Energy Use Intensity • Facility Performance • Evaluation High-Performing Buildings • Net-Zero Energy Building Certification • Operations and Maintenance • Renewable Energy • Zero-Energy Building**

Further sources: AIA 2030 Commitment; Architecture 2030; EBN; ILFI

SBTool Assessment

The SBTool framework was developed . . . to actively facilitate and promote the adoption of policies, methods, and tools to accelerate the movement towards a global sustainable built environment.
—Sustainable Building Alliance website

The *SBTool* is a generic assessment framework for rating the sustainable performance of sites and building projects and was developed by the International Initiative for a Sustainable Built Environment (iiSBE) in the late 1990s to further worldwide sustainability in the built environment. Third parties can use the framework of the *SBTool*, formerly called GBTool, in developing rating systems relevant for a variety of regions and building types, such as have been adopted for the differing national contexts of Italy, Spain, Portugal, and the Czech Republic.

The iiSBE *SBTool* is based on the philosophy that for a rating system to be meaningful, it must be suited to the local conditions and the particular building type to be assessed. As a generic framework or toolkit, the *SBTool* requires the insertion of these regionally meaningful benchmarks. Local research-based organizations describe the typical performance characteristics and local context conditions, and define weights and performance criteria that are regionally significant to the building being assessed.

There are seven different assessment categories for scoring and weighing in the *SBTool*. The overall categories are Site Regeneration and Development, Urban Design and Infrastructure; Energy and Resource Consumption; Environmental Loading; Indoor Environmental Quality; Service Quality; Social, Cultural, and Perceptual Aspects; and Costs and Economic Issues.

The *SBTool* recognizes the most important design decisions are made early in the process, and once these are made, it becomes increasingly difficult to make improvements in performance as the process develops. Therefore, there is an Integrated Design Process (IDP) management tool included to support early and effective design teamwork. Rather than the marketing benefits of a label, the iiSBE *SBTool* can provide meaningful performance results about certain building types within their local building contexts, while promoting a practical framework toward the overall goal of a global sustainable built environment.

See also: **Climate Responsive Design • Energy Efficiency • Green Building Certification Systems • Integrated Design**

Further sources: iiSBE; Sustainable Building Alliance; WBDG

Sense of Place

The responsibility of an architect is to create a sense of order, a sense of place, a sense of relationship. —Richard Meier

Place is security, space is freedom. —Yi-Fu Tuan

The *sense of place* refers to the perceptions, experiences, feelings, thoughts, meanings, beliefs, and expectations that we have about a location. It is a particular kind of relationship between people and environments.

A place may be natural or human-made. Its scale can be large (country, region, town, park) or small (room, trail, gate). Objects, people, events, processes, and situations may be sensed as places. A painting, companion, concert, game, and lawsuit are examples. Mental and emotional environments such as worry or joy can be places we inhabit. These are kinds of environments that can evoke a *sense of place*. In architecture, we are interested in constructed places such as cities, neighborhoods, streets, plazas, buildings and rooms. Richard Meier, the architect, states in his quote opening this chapter that one of the responsibilities of architecture is "to create a sense of place."

Sense of place is the sixth sense, an internal compass and map made by memory and spatial perception together. —Rebecca Solnit

A *sense of place* may be positive or negative, abiding or fleeting, singular or recurring, strong or subtle. It can be personal and idiosyncratic or public and shared. The sense of a place is always a relationship between what the locale offers and presents to us, and what we bring to it. It is a conversation between place attributes and personal interpretation, in what author Rebecca Solnit expresses in her preceding quote as a "sixth sense, an internal compass." A location's history, reputation or myths often contribute to our sense of the place, and our sense of a place can have more to do with our personal experience and unique history there than with the place's attributes. Repeated visits, sustained habitation, strong place qualities or vivid experiences tend to promote a strong sense of place, such as happens in Daley Plaza in Chicago (Figure 50). As Yi-Fu Tuan expresses, "place is security" while space becomes freedom.

Figure 50 Daley Plaza, Chicago
Courtesy Elizabeth Lewis

A built environment dedicated to and shaped by sustainability goals offers attributes and experiences that foster a sustainability-flavored *sense of place*. Our actions, thoughts, perceptions, feelings, and memories there respond to environmental elements, ensembles, and qualities that have been configured to create sustainability processes and aesthetics, a green genius loci. Overall building form, roof shape, the relation of building to ground, materials, landscaping, building plan, and parking treatment offer clues as to the facility's sustainability orientation. Passive heating and cooling, water recycling, solar power, and other elements contribute as well.

Our sense of a sustainability shaped place is also often holistic. It is an awareness and appreciation of the fact that we inhabit a structure that strives to promote responsible living and mindful respect for the natural environment. EW

See also: **Community Connectivity • Ecological Design • Livable Streets • Locus (*Archispeak*) • Personal Space (*Archispeak*) • Place (*Archispeak*) • Spirit of Place (*Theoryspeak*) • Thereness (*Archispeak*)**

▌Seventh Generation Principle

We do not inherit the earth from our ancestors; we borrow it from our children. —Native American proverb

We cannot simply think of our survival; each new generation is responsible to ensure the survival of the seventh generation. —International Institute for Sustainable Development, 1992

Indigenous people have always had an interdependent relationship with the Earth based on a delicate balance among all living things. Native teachings passed down over thousands of years believe people are placed on the Earth (Mother) to be the caretakers of life on the planet— the plants, animals, minerals, human beings, and all life, as if they were part of it themselves. The *Seventh Generation Principle* is based on an ancient philosophy of the Iroquois that the decisions made today should result in a sustainable world seven generations into the future. The first recorded concept dates from approximately 600–700 years ago, in the writing of The Great Law of Iroquois Confederacy. This Great Law formed the ceremonial, political, and social structure of the original Five Nation Confederacy, and also influenced the writing of the U.S. Constitution due to Benjamin Franklin's respect for the Iroquois system of government.

Mitakuye oyasin (Lakota); Nogomaq (Algonquian); Gakina-awiiya (Anishinaabe); Ea Nigada Qusdi Idadadvhn (Cherokee); We are all related to, and respect, everything in life (English). —Native American Indian wisdom

The *Seventh Generation Principle* is used today in regard to the state of our environment, and decisions made today about energy, water, air, and natural resources that will ensure a sustainable future for seven generations ahead and beyond. Understanding that the current path of development is not sustainable, and the survival of humanity is at stake, these ancient voices strike a resounding wisdom in the responsibility of environmental stewardship as stated above by the International Institute for Sustainable Development.

Indigenous people, though dominated and conquered, still have a sense of obligation and connection to the Earth that comes from The Great Law, and believe each generation has a responsibility to ensure the survival of the seventh generation.

See also: **Natural Step • Precautionary Principle • Sustainability • Sustainable Development**

Further sources: IISD

Shading Coefficient   ▌

A room is not a room without natural light. —Louis Kahn, architect

Solar transmittance is important to describe the amount of solar heat gain into a contained space. The total solar heat transmittance is the solar heat transmitted directly through the glazing or material in addition to the solar heat that is absorbed by the material and then re-emitted into the contained space. In the winter, the warmth of solar heat gain can be helpful in reducing the energy needed to supplement with heat. In the summer, solar heat gain should be prevented to avoid overheating and the supplemental energy required for cooling. A design should be able to enhance or reduce the heat gain depending on the seasons, while getting the most natural light, to which the architect Louis Kahn states is required to make a "room."

The *shading coefficient (SC)* is the amount of solar heat that passes through a piece of transparent or translucent material, such as glazing. This is relative to the amount of solar heat that passes through a sheet of 1/8 inch (3.1 mm) clear float glass with a *SC* of 1.0 or a total solar heat gain coefficient of 0.87. This ratio of radiant heat gain can range from 0–1 and is an index of the effective performance of solar heat rejection of a given type of glass. A lower *shading coefficient* number indicates there is less heat gain.

The *shading coefficient* is based solely on the glass portion of a glazing assembly and does not consider the frame, but it does take into consideration the entire fenestration, such as a combination of glass, any interior solar controls such as blinds or drapes, and possible exterior shading devices. An excellent example of using the shading coefficient for solar heat gain control are the proposed shading devices for 1640 Baltimore, the BNIM Architects office design proposal for Kansas City (Figure 51).

The *shading coefficient* has largely been replaced in the manufacturing industry by the solar heat gain coefficient (SHGC) and window solar factors (g-values). But, the *shading coefficient* is still useful in practice for comparing glass types and for showing the benefits of external or internal solar controls. A glass with outdoor adjustable louvers may rate with a shading coefficient as low as 0.15.

Figure 51 BNIM Kansas City Office Proposal: 1640 Baltimore
Courtesy ©BNIM Architects

See also: **Brise-Soliel • Climate Responsive Design • Daylighting • Energy Efficiency • Envelope Driven Design • Passive Design • Solar Heat Gain Coefficient • Thermal Comfort**

Further sources: EBN; Efficient Windows Collaborative; Pilkington Glass; WBDG

▌Sick Building Syndrome

We're on the threshold of just horrific health problems. We are looking at an asthma epidemic. There are schools now where a third of the kids have inhalers. —Dr. Richard Jackson, environmental health scientist

In developed countries, we spend almost 90% of our time indoors, according to the Environmental Protection Agency, often in building environments that are making us sick. The EPA estimates the chemical and pollutant concentrations, such as volatile organic compounds, may be 2–5 times higher inside a building than outside. The impacts of bad indoor air quality (IAQ) on human health created by pollutants in built environments are divided into three conditions: *sick building syndrome* (SBS), multiple chemical sensitivity (MCS), and building-related illness (BRI).

Sick building syndrome is used to describe when occupants experience irritations of eye, nose, and throat; headaches; sensitivity; rashes; fatigue; or nausea—among others—which are linked to time spent in a building. These symptoms usually dissipate when the occupant is no longer in the building and yet no particular cause can be determined, but symptoms may be associated with modern mass-produced construction materials that can off-gas irritating volatile organic compounds (VOCs).

Building-related illness is when permanent identifiable health impacts can be diagnosed and can be directly linked to exposure to airborne chemicals and contaminants in the indoor environment. Indoor air pollution is a leading cause of cancer responsible for 4,000–6,000 deaths a year, according to the EPA. Multiple chemical sensitivity, also called environmental illness is debatable, thought to be psychological, and yet some propose is the cause of multiple sensitivities, arthritis, and colitis. It is believed to be caused by various chemicals that are emitted from building materials, pesticides, chemical cleaners, tobacco smoke, VOCs, and petroleum products, such as office equipment, solvents, and cosmetics.

An ounce of prevention is worth a pound of cure. —Proverb

The symptoms of *sick building syndrome* are likely the result of a mixture of factors and possibly the VOCs that are present may act in combination, especially at low levels where they are individually thought to be safe. In most cases of *sick building syndrome*, the causes are poor building design, maintenance issues, and errors in operating the building's ventilation system. Poor ventilation can be the source of irritants and can result in a build-up of pollutants within the building. Conditions conducive to biological contamination, such as water damage and dampness, have been related to upper and lower respiratory problems from mold, yeast, fungi, and bacteria. And as the environmental health scientist Dr. Richard Jackson states above, some schools have almost one-third of the students using inhalers.

Remediation measures can be taken in the building to replace or renovate ventilation equipment, prevent leaks and dampness, review chemicals used, review cleaning practices, and possibly mold removal to prevent the continued and future symptoms of *sick building syndrome* illnesses.

See also: **Indoor Environmental Quality • Natural Ventilation • REACH Label • Volatile Organic Compounds • WELL Building Standard**

Further sources: EPA Report on the Environment 2017, https://cfpub. epa.gov/roe/; Environmental Illness Resource; Bonda and Sosowchik (2014: 50); Kibert (2016: 63)

Site Analysis   ▌

When I concentrate on a specific site or place for which I am going to design a building, I try to plumb its depths, its form, its history, and its sensuous qualities. —Peter Zumthor

I never design a building before I've seen the site and met the people who will be using it. —Frank Lloyd Wright

Site analysis is a component of the building design process where information about the project property is researched for its possible influence on the planning of the new facility. The purpose of *site analysis* is to understand the existing conditions on and around the building's future location so that the new facility is appropriately responsive to those conditions and relates in positive ways to its context.

Examples of *site analysis* information needed are location of the property; neighborhood context surrounding the site; legal and jurisdictional aspects; covenants and restrictions; site dimensions; zoning

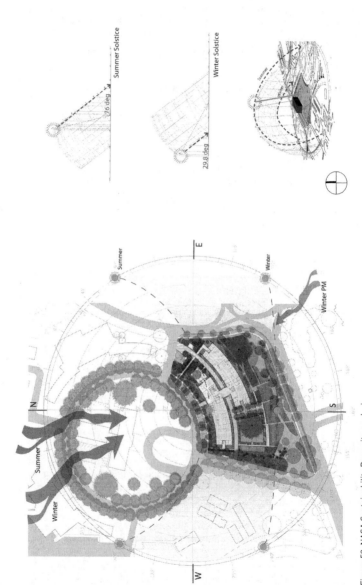

Figure 52 NASA Sustainability Base site analysis
Courtesy ©William McDonough + Partners

regulations; pedestrian and vehicular circulation on and around the location; existing on-site structures; natural site elements and features; views, noise, and odors; utilities; and climate data.

There will be many interactive relationships between the site conditions and the newly built facility. Site conditions affect the building, and the building affects site conditions. For example, the building's utility bills are impacted by the sun's path changing over the seasons. And the new building's functions and siting will affect the site drainage and traffic patterns in the surrounding street system.

In studying a site, the architect is especially interested in conditions that are restrictive or challenging and also in those that present unique opportunities to contribute to the neighborhood, enhance the quality of life for the future building's occupants, and improve the health and beauty of the project property.

The kinds of design decisions that site research can affect include location of the building on the site, position and layout of parking and exterior functions on the property, building footprint configuration, building massing and form, interior building layout, on-site pedestrian and vehicular circulation, land contour shaping, landscaping; building foundation and structure systems, and positions of exterior entries and exits.

If a project has a sustainability focus, site data is tailored to property conditions that may affect that domain of design decisions, such as shown in the site diagram of the NASA Sustainability Base of the Ames Research Center in Mountainview, CA. designed by William McDonough + Partners Architects (Figures 52, 10, 19, 45, 61).

Some examples:

- Type, condition, and age of existing trees are studied for possible use in building fenestration shading.
- Microclimates of various site areas are analyzed to determine best positions for exterior functions.
- Sun path and solar availability are investigated to refine passive heating strategies.
- Rainfall patterns and land contours are addressed to investigate stormwater retention for landscape irrigation.
- Code influences on building massing and façade orientation are studied in relation to reducing summer solar heat gain.
- Ambient seasonal and diurnal climate conditions are researched in relation to building occupancy schedule to determine the limits of passive heating/cooling strategies. EW

See also: **Naturescaping** • **Passive Design** • **Site Appraisal** (*Archispeak*) • **SITES Initiative** • **Sustainable Site Design** • **Topography** (*Archispeak*) • **Urban Heat Island** • **Urban Tree Canopy**

Site Remediation

We abuse land as we regard it as a commodity belonging to us. When we see land as a community to which we belong, we may begin to use it with love and respect. —Aldo Leopold, *A Sand County Almanac* 1949

Green building site and landscape practices call for protecting prime agricultural land, woodlands, and open space against the influences of sprawl to preferably build within existing urban areas and on previously disturbed sites. Building construction can change the health, biodiversity, and water flows of a site, often leaving it abused and damaged, as Aldo Leopold warns in his quote opening this chapter.

Green building practices encourage the reuse and restoration of contaminated land, minimizing automobile use, and increasing building density to reduce the need for development on undeveloped land. Sustainable land practices include not building on environmentally sensitive property, in flood-prone areas, on agricultural land, or on greenfields, which are undisturbed forests, fields, ranchland and farmland. Responsible design protects greenfield sites by "land recycling," which is reusing land impacted by human development, such as brownfields, greyfields, and blackfields. Proper site selection provides the opportunity to move beyond just greening the building to the potential of preserving valuable resources by choosing a distressed site to achieve *site remediation*, which is the restoration of existing or contaminated land.

The U.S. EPA considers brownfields to be "abandoned, idled, or under-used industrial and commercial facilities where expansion or redevelopment is complicated by real or perceived environmental contamination." Greyfields are urban properties that are economically blighted and underused, but not contaminated, such as abandoned big box stores, old strip malls, or boarded-up housing. These sites, which are often in prime location, offer the opportunity for carefully planned mixed-use development to restore the density of the urban fabric, such as surrounding the High Line in New York City. Blackfields, a type of brownfields, are abandoned strip and subsurface coalmines whose land and water are contaminated with sulfates, aluminum, iron, and manganese.

The most alarming of all man's assaults upon the environment is the contamination of air, earth, rivers, and sea with dangerous and even lethal materials. —Rachel Carson

Many such sites were contaminated by heavy use when environmental regulations were not in place or ignored, so the soil and groundwater are usually contaminated with toxic chemicals and heavy metals. Many sites are located in old urban industrial areas, and the cleanup was often complicated by the degree of contamination, liability, and the financial burden.

One such industrial brownfield site in Philadelphia was a haven for the homeless and drug dealers, and bordered by a noisy elevated transit line. SMP Architects remediated the site, designing the award-winning Kensington High School by creating noise buffering zones, community agricultural spaces, and green roofs, and achieved community revitalization (Figure 53).

Grants and technical assistance are now offered for contamination assessment, *site remediation* job training, and safe cleanup for the reuse of contaminated properties. Environmental remediation of contaminated land in New Orleans became a standard construction practice after the 2005 Hurricane Katrina.

Figure 53 Kensington High School, Philadelphia
Photo: Halkin Mason Photography. Courtesy ©SMP Architects

Green building certifications, such as LEED, Green Globes, and SITES, encourage using project sites requiring site remediation. Reinvesting in cleaning up brownfields and blackfields, while giving new life to greyfields, improves and protects the environment and human health, increases local tax bases, facilitates job growth, reduces blight, utilizes existing infrastructure, and allows for the protection of green spaces.

See also: **Green Building Certification Systems • Regenerative Design • Site Analysis • SITES Initiative • Sustainable Site Design • WELL Building Standard**

Further sources: Carson (1962); EBN; Leopold (1949); US EPA, www.epa. gov/grants/united-states-environmental-protection-agency-grants-and-fellowship-information; Waste Management

SITES Initiative   ▌

The environment is in us, not outside us. The trees are our lungs, the rivers our bloodstream. We are all interconnected, and what you do to the environment ultimately you do to yourself. —Ian Somerhalder, actor director

Earth's systems depend on water, land, wetlands, and other regenerative services to flourish, and these are all interconnected as eloquently expressed in the quote opening this chapter. These ecosystem services, or "natural capital," have been degraded with deforestation, soil erosion, lower water table levels, and species extinction. Recent development and suburban sprawl have encroached on the few remaining natural habitats, and have replaced them with hardscapes and non-native vegetation. The U.S. Forest Service says between 1982–2001, the U.S. lost thirty-four million acres of open space to development. These paved and roof hard surfaces increase the heat island effect and reduce natural water infiltration, and increased rainwater runoff carries pollutants, fertilizers, and petroleum to rivers.

The *Sustainable SITES Initiative (SITES)* is an ecosystem-based sustainable site rating system administered by the Green Building Certification Inc. (GBCI). The *SITES* rating system was developed as a result of USGBC's LEED green building rating system, which provided a limited measure of the sustainability and value of sites and landscapes. *SITES* certified projects address environmental and social issues of stormwater runoff, wildlife habitat, energy and water consumption, air quality, carbon storage, outdoor recreation, and human health and well-being. As of 2016, individual *SITES* and LEED credits can be used reciprocally.

The *SITES* rating system has a series of performance measures that focus on understanding natural ecosystem processes, ecological restoration, and human health and happiness. The system includes eighteen prerequisites and forty-eight credits totaling two hundred potential points to measure the sustainability of a project. Certification levels of performance are awarded starting with the minimum of seventy points to be Certified, then increasing to Silver, Gold, or Platinum.

The *Sustainable SITES Initiative* credit categories are Context, Pre-Design, Water, Soil + Vegetation, Materials, Human Health + Well-Being, Construction, Operations + Maintenance, Education + Performance Monitoring, and Innovation or Exemplary Performance. Each credit value is based on its potential effectiveness toward the goals of fostering resiliency and regenerative ecosystems, mitigating climate change, protecting natural resources, enhancing well-being and strengthening community, and elevating the property value.

See also: **Conservation (*Theoryspeak*) • Green Roofs • Greenfield (*Archispeak*) • LEED Building Certification • Naturescaping • Permeable Pavement • Sustainable Site Design • Urban Heat Island • Urban Tree Canopy • Vegetated Walls**

Further sources: SITES; GBCI; WBDG; Architecture Record

Smart Growth

When strangers start acting like neighbors . . . communities are reinvigorated. —Ralph Nader, consumer protection activist

We have all known the long loneliness, and we have found that the answer is community. —Dorothy Day, American journalist

Development decisions as to where, what, and how communities are built affects many aspects of people's lives, such as their daily commutes, health, taxes, schools, natural environments, recreation opportunities, and investment growth. *Smart growth* is the development and conservation strategies that support the economic growth of active and socially diverse communities while protecting environmental health.

Community developments are using creative measures to preserve natural and environmentally fragile land areas, protect air and water quality, and reuse previously developed land. Rehabilitating and reinvesting in existing infrastructure and historic buildings conserve valuable material and energy resources. Neighborhoods with amenities nearby, such as parks, schools, libraries, shops, houses of worship, and access to public transit, give residents the options of walking, biking, and not driving a car, which reduces commuting times and greenhouse gas emissions. A range of housing types allows the elderly to age in their homes, the young to be able to afford to buy, and many options in between, creating a socially diverse and vibrant place to live, work and play, which Ralph Nadar and Dorothy Day both stress as the importance of "community."

The *Smart Growth* Network has established ten principles to direct smart growth strategies:

1. Mix land uses.
2. Take advantage of compact building design.
3. Create a range of housing opportunities and choices.
4. Create walkable neighborhoods.
5. Foster attractive communities with a strong sense of place.
6. Preserve open space, natural beauty, and critical environments.
7. Strengthen and direct development towards existing communities.
8. Provide a variety of transportation choices.
9. Make development decisions predictable.
10. Encourage community collaborations in development decisions.

It must be awfully frustrating to get a small raise at work and then have it all eaten by a higher cost of commuting. —Ben Bernanke

Many residents are frustrated by the long drives between work and home and are proponents of using existing infrastructure of communities, roads, sewers, and services rather than building out on the fringe, and having to spend money on polluting fuel, as stressed by former U.S. Federal Reserve chairman Ben Bernanke. *Smart growth* strategies give more opportunities to make smart personal choices in where to live, how to physically move around, and how to socially interact with those around them.

See also: **Community Connectivity • Neighborhood Development • Location and Transportation • New Urbanism • Urban Design**

Further sources: smartgrowth.org; Sustainable Management Dictionary; WBDG

Social Equity

The good we secure for ourselves is precarious and uncertain until it is secured for all of us and incorporated into our common life. —Jane Addams, activist 1860–1935

Inequality is the planet's main "environmental" problem. —
Brundtland Commission

Successful sustainable construction involves having a positive impact on the environment, long-term return on investment, and creating a place in society that benefits all who use, work, or live there. The three-legged stool of sustainability is made up of the economy, the environment, and equity. Of these, *social equity*, or social justice, is the degree of fairness with which people and communities are given equal access to resources, decision-making, and opportunities. The achievement of *social equity* is often related to poverty relief; employment and income; ethnic, gender and age inclusiveness; intergenerational education opportunities; and the availability of natural, health, and financial resources, which Jane Addams, the 19th century activist, stressed in her quote opening this chapter should be "secured for all of us."

An excellent example of *social equity* in the built environment is the Bud Clark Commons, a centerpiece of Portland, Oregon's Ten Year Plan to End Homelessness (Figures 54, 66). Designed by Holst Architecture, the LEED Platinum project combines 130 furnished supportive housing studios, a ninety-bed temporary homeless shelter, and a community resource center with a walk-in day center providing meals, public courtyard, and health services.

Figure 54 Bud Clark Commons for the homeless, Portland, OR
Courtesy ©Holst Architecture

More than machinery, we need humanity. More than cleverness, we need kindness and gentleness. Without these qualities, life will be violent, and all will be lost. —Charlie Chaplin, English silent film actor

Urban neighborhoods with low social and economic status can feel powerless facing pervasive and systemic problems of poor health, illiteracy, lack of livelihoods, and civil insecurity, often linked to violence and corruption, as Charlie Chaplin stresses in our need for humanity, kindness and gentleness. In concentrated rural poor areas, marginal land and limited resources can lead to over-exploitation and degradation of the land, such as deforestation.

Buildings are an integral part of the community and where they are located should contribute to enhancing the quality of life, social well-being, and the public good of the community. Buildings can provide clean air and water, affordable housing, fair wages, job opportunities, accessibility, quality schools, and shared public space. In the community master planning process, community engagement and design charrettes can result in the socially-conscious weaving of a building into the community fabric, for example with front porches for socializing, walkable neighborhoods, access to fresh food and transportation, and public outdoor spaces with shade trees and seating. Integrating mixed-income housing, mixed-use, retail, commercial, and essential services can also enhance a social community. Typical green building strategies, such as improved indoor air quality, healthy building materials, better daylighting, views, providing public space, locating near public transit, and encouraging public and shared access have all improved the lives of the people that work, use, and live in buildings.

The green building industry has developed several guiding tools and programs to promote *social equity* practices. The International WELL Building Institute's WELL Building Standard connects occupant health and well-being with the building impacts of air, water, nourishment, light, fitness, comfort and mind. The International Living Future Institute's (ILFI) Living Building Challenge Equity Petal category promotes a just and equitable community that is inclusive, regardless of background, age, class, race, gender, or sexual orientation. The US Green Building Council's LEED v4 certification system fosters *social equity* with three pilot credits: Social Equity within the Project, the Community, and the Supply Chain. The International Living Future Institute's JUST program is a voluntary social justice label for organizations to improve *social equity* and community engagement.

Social equity in the built environment can enhance the quality of life by promoting a strong sense of place; providing affordable, equitable, and resilient communities; improving resource access for neighborhood completeness; and promoting human rights and environmental justice.

See also: **Affordable Housing • JUST Program • LEED Building Certification • Living Building Challenge • Our Common Future • Smart Growth • Sustainable Development • Sustainability • Urban Design • WELL Building Standard**

Further sources: Brundtland Commission; EBN; IWBI; ILFI; JUST; LEED; WELL

Solar Chimney   I

Convection: the movement in a gas or liquid in which the warmer parts move up and the cooler parts move down. —Merriam-Webster Dictionary

Passive design maximizes the natural ambient flows of heat and air movement to create comfortable conditions inside buildings, without using mechanical or electrical systems. Passive strategies harness environmental conditions such as solar heat radiation, cool night air, and air pressure differentials to heat and cool the interior environment of buildings. Active systems use mechanical and electrical systems to create comfortable conditions. Most high-performing buildings use both systems to maximize both comfort and energy efficiency.

Solar chimneys, or thermal chimneys, are a passive building design strategy constructed to promote the ventilation of unwanted heated or stale air to the outside by using air pressure differentials due to height. *Solar chimneys* are usually tall, wide structures constructed to face the sun with dark surfaces to absorb solar radiation. As the air inside the chimney heats up and now has a lower air pressure, it rises with the buoyancy of natural convection, as with stack ventilation or a Trombe wall. The building is cooled by this movement of rising warm inside the solar chimney drawing hot air up and venting out of the building, which in turn draws in fresh cooler air from windows or vents at a lower level.

The Conrad N. Hilton Foundation Headquarters, by ZGF Architects is an excellent example of using passive solar *chimney* design. Certified as LEED Platinum and designed for net-zero energy consumption, the building uses the green strategies of a solar thermal-heating system, water-cooled chilling, green roof, and a passive-downdraft HVAC system with seventeen solar chimneys around the building's exterior perimeter (Figure 55).

Figure 55 Conrad N. Hilton Foundation Headquarters, Agoura Hills, CA
Nick Merrick/Hedrich Blessing Photographers Courtesy @ZGF Architects LLP

In the winter, *solar chimney* vents to the outside can be closed and the heated air inside the chimney is directed inside the building for heating demands. *Solar chimneys* can be used to encourage passive ventilation in buildings where cross-ventilation or stack ventilation may not be adequate to complement conventional climate control systems. *Solar chimneys* are most useful in hot, humid climates that have a very high cooling demand and must vent above the roof level with proper ventilation hoods to prevent interference from prevailing winds.

See also: **Building Orientation • Natural Ventilation • Passive Cooling • Passive Design • Stack Ventilation • Thermal Comfort • Trombe Wall • Wind Tower**

Further sources: Autodesk; Designing Buildings Wiki; WBDG

Solar Energy   **▌**

I'd put my money on the sun and solar energy. What a source of power! I hope we don't have to wait til oil and coal run out before we tackle that. —Thomas A. Edison, 1930, America's great inventor

Sunlight is known as the most abundant of all carbon-neutral energy sources, with 160,000 terawatts (TW) of *solar energy* reaching the surface of the Earth. This *solar energy* input is about ten thousand times the amount of energy, at about seventeen terawatts, that humans consume globally, including all the coal, oil, gas, wind, solar, hydro, nuclear and others combined.

The harvesting of *solar energy* has three approaches: solar electricity, solar fuels, and solar thermal. Solar electricity is photovoltaic electricity produced by semiconductor solar cells. Solar fuels are dominated by biomass, which is non-fossilized solid or liquid organic material derived from the photosynthesis process of plants such as switchgrass. Solar thermal can include both passive systems, such as solar warming of buildings; and active systems, which can use blowers, pumps, optical concentrators, and tracking devices, such as for thermally generated electricity.

It is projected the world needs between 15–20 TW of energy a year, and the only renewable resources potentially able to meet those demands are solar, wind, geothermal and ocean waves (Naam 2013). Taking the extractable energy available and the challenges of all, only sunlight—as about 30% of the sun strikes land—is actually capable of meeting our needs with renewables, which almost a hundred years ago Thomas Edison proclaimed "what a source of power!" Of that, we only need less than 0.6% of the land area on Earth to meet our current demands. Wind would be second, as it has the geographic challenge of most extractable power residing over the deep oceans.

Solar thermal provides heat using the sun, and then either directly uses that heat (solar thermal), or transforms the heat into either chemical fuels (solar thermal fuels) or electricity (solar thermal electricity) to be transported and consumed elsewhere. Solar thermal heat, both passive and active, must be used at the location where it is harvested. Passive solar thermal always dominates active solar thermal with efficiency, though it is hard to measure the Earth's passive use of the sun's energy to warm building spaces. Active solar thermal includes additional energy-consuming components to thermally generate electricity or achieve low-temperature space and water heating.

Costs and storage have been the primary challenges to increased solar use, but that is rapidly changing with efficiency gains, and price drops, and in some sunny places solar is competitive with grid electricity. Renewables were only projected to be only 28% of the electricity produced worldwide by 2021 (Naam 2013).

Continuing opportunities for innovative research, investment, and development of renewable energy resources remains a significant and urgent challenge in replacing reliance on fossil fuels if we are to stay below the 2°C climate targets set to prevent disastrous impacts for the future of the planet.

See also: **Passive Cooling • Passive Design • Passive Solar Heating • Photovoltaics • Renewable Energy**

Further sources: ASES; Naam (2013: 158); Science.gov; WBDG

▌Solar Heat Gain Coefficient

My studio cube is an experiment in solar heating and design. The south wall is covered with glass planks that collect and distribute heat naturally to my work studio on the second level. —Steven Holl, architect

The solar transmittance of a wall or window assembly is important to understanding the solar heat gain into an enclosed space under sunny conditions. Solar heat can be helpful in the winter for passively warming spaces, and reducing the energy needed to heat, but in the summer, solar heat gain can cause the discomfort of overheating, and more energy is required to mechanically cool the space.

The *solar heat gain coefficient (SHGC)* represents the heat from solar radiation transmitted through the glass or material, along with the heat energy absorbed and emitted inward from the glass and the frame. The *SHGC* demonstrates the ability of the window assembly, including the glass and frame, to resist heat gain from solar radiation. The SHGC is a dimensionless number, with 0 representing the total resistance of solar heat and 1 representing no resistance. Lower SHGCs are better for hot sunny climates where cooling demands are high, and higher SHGCs are better in cold climates to enhance passive solar heating and reduce heating needs. Most window assemblies usually range from 0.2–0.9.

The AIA Committee on the Environment award winning, LEED Platinum and Living Building Challenge certified Chesapeake Bay Brock Environmental Center, designed by SmithGroupJJR Architects, has a low heat gain coefficient for the south clerestory glazing to block heat gain. The north clerestory allows in natural daylighting without the negative associated heat gain or glare (Figures 56, 7, 71).

The previous industry standard used the shading coefficient (SC) to describe the amount of solar heat transmitted through a material compared to the solar heat transmitted through a sheet of 1/8 inch (3.1 mm) clear glass with an *SC* of 1 or a total solar heat gain coefficient of 0.87. Manufacturers in the U.S. are now using primarily the *SHGC*, while in

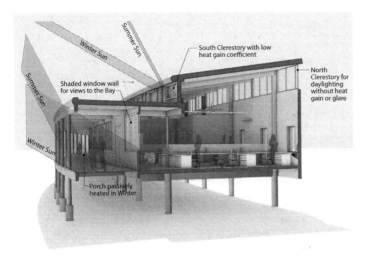

Figure 56 Chesapeake Bay Brock Environmental Center solar diagram
Courtesy ©SmithGroupJJR

Europe the window solar factors and g-values are used. The g-value is equal to the total solar heat gain divided by the incident solar radiation. Even though the U.S. and European systems use differing values for the air mass, they all represent the incident solar radiation transmitted by a window or material where 1 accounts for the maximum possible solar gain and 0 accounts for no solar heat gain. The U.S. DOE and the EPA have developed an Energy Star tool for selecting the desired energy performances and *solar heat gain coefficients* recommended for windows, doors, and skylights based on four climate zones.

See also: **Climate Responsive Design • Daylighting • Energy Efficiency • Envelope Driven Design • Passive Design • Shading Coefficient • Thermal Comfort**

Further sources: Design Buildings Wiki; Energy Star; Iyengar (2015: 158) Hootman (2012); US DOE

Solar Reflectance Index

When there is a huge solar energy spill, it is just called a "nice day."
—votesolar.org

In designing high-performing building enclosures to reduce the thermal heat load on the building, all sides of the enclosure, especially the roof, must be modeled to achieve the maximum reduction in heat gain. Because heat transmission is a function of temperature differences, where hotter temperatures move to cooler temperatures, keeping the exterior building surfaces cool is important not only for reducing building heat gain but also to reduce heat island effect. Heat island effect is the absorption of heat by hardscapes, such as dark non-reflective pavements and buildings, causing thermal radiation to be emitted to surrounding areas and therefore raising the overall urban temperature.

The *Solar Reflectance Index (SRI)* of materials is a measure of a surface's capacity to stay cool in the sun by reflecting solar radiation and emitting infrared thermal radiation back into the environment. Solar reflectance, or albedo, is the ability to reflect sunlight, and thermal emittance is the capacity to emit or shed absorbed heat back into the environment. An good example using the solar reflective index is the first building in Florida to achieve the USGBC LEED Gold certification, the University of Florida's Rinker Hall in Gainesville. The building designed by Croxton Collaborative Architects, uses *solar reflective* light shelves to bounce light up to the reflective sloped ceilings to get light deep into the classrooms (Figure 57).

The *Solar Reflectance Index* is defined such as a standard black surface (initial solar reflectance 0.05, initial thermal emittance 0.90) has a 90°F (50°C) temperature rise in full sun, with an initial *SRI* of 0. A standard white surface (initial solar reflectance 0.80, initial thermal emittance 0.90) would have only a temperature rise of 14.6°F (8.1°C), with an initial *SRI* of 100. A perfect *SRI* value is approximately 122, similar to a mirror, in which no sunlight is absorbed, and the emissivity is very low.

The Cool Roof Rating Council Standard can be used to obtain the solar reflectance and thermal emittance of a particular material to calculate the *SRI*. The *Solar Reflectance Index* is calculated according to American Standard Testing Method (ASTM). Green building certification systems—such as LEED, BREEAM, Green Globes, Living Building Challenge, and Sustainable Sites Initiative, among others—offer credits for the reduction of heat island effect and provide *SRI* levels for site design, paving materials, and roofs of different types and slopes.

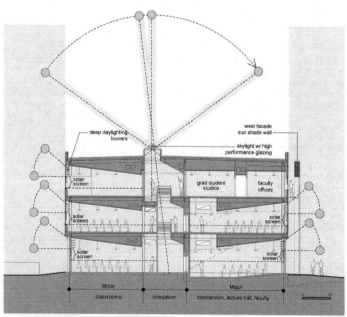

Figure 57 Rinker Hall at University of Florida
Courtesy ©Croxton Collaborative Architects

See also: **Cool Roofs • Green Roofs • Sustainable Site Design • Urban Heat Island • Urban Tree Canopy**

Further sources: Cool Roof Rating Council; Sustainable SITES; US DOE; USGBC

Spaceship Earth   ▮

The only true and effective "operator's manual for spaceship earth" is not a book that any human will ever write; it is hundreds of thousands of local cultures. —Wendell Berry, *What are People For?*

The planet is a resilient system, but humanity's impact on Earth has set about significant changes. The call for steering our future on this planet to avert global crisis and ensure our long-term success of humanity and our ecosystems calls for a world-view. The term *Spaceship Earth* encourages all occupants to act as a harmonious crew working toward our greater good, and as Wendell Berry states, it will take "hundreds of thousands of local cultures."

Henry George in 1879 referred to a "well-provisioned ship, this on which we sail through space" in *Progress and Poverty*, and George Orwell in 1937, paraphrases George as "the world is a raft sailing through space with, potentially, plenty of provisions for everybody" in *The Road to Wigan Pier*.

In a speech to the United Nations in 1964, Adlai Stevenson popularized the metaphor of a *Spaceship Earth* to call for all of humanity as crewmembers to unify together in preserving the global ecosystems that make our lives on that ship imaginable.

We travel together, passengers on a little spaceship, dependent upon its vulnerable reserves of air and soil, all committed for our safety to its security and peace; preserved from annihilation only by the care, the work, and, I will say, the love we give our fragile craft. We cannot maintain it half fortunate, half miserable, half confident, half despairing, half slave to the ancient enemies of man, half free in a liberation of resources undreamed of until this day. No craft, no crew can travel safely with such vast contradictions. On their resolution depends the survival of us all. —Adlai Stevenson, 1964

R. Buckminster Fuller also popularized the term publishing *Operating Manual for Spaceship Earth* in 1968. The book portrayed his vision for widespread planetary planning and strategies to enable all of humanity to live freely with dignity and comfort, without negatively affecting Earth's ecosystems or regenerative capacity. *Spaceship Earth* is also the name given to his geodesic sphere design, popularized in the U.S. by Buckminster Fuller, at Walt Disney World's Epcot theme park.

Among Fuller's many designs was the Dymaxion map, or Fuller Projection, which is the only map of the entire Earth which presents our planet as flat and one island in one ocean, without any visual distortions of the relative sizes and shapes of the land areas, and without separating continents. Fuller's idea was if we were able to visualize the entire planet as one interdependent system of relationships, we would be better able to address the challenges in our common future on *Spaceship Earth.*

See also: **Carrying Capacity • Lifeboat Ethics • Population Growth • Tragedy of the Commons**

Further sources: Buckminster Fuller Institute

▌Stack Ventilation

When skyscrapers were first developed at the turn of the century, people had to invent revolving doors because you couldn't open the front door due to the stack effect pressure. —Building Green Advisor

The stack effect is a type of passive ventilation that uses air pressure differentials to move air through a building. Air density decreases as the temperature of the air increases, so the lower pressure hot air rises with buoyancy pulling air higher in the building. This stack effect is often referred to as *stack ventilation* or buoyancy ventilation, and after wind ventilation, *stack ventilation* is the most often used form of passive ventilation. The stack effect is very efficient and inexpensive to implement, especially when optimizing with a solar chimney and at night when wind speeds are lower.

In *stack ventilation*, cooler outside air is drawn into the building through lower openings, is then warmed in the building, possibly with solar gain, equipment, or people, and this warmed air rises to be exhausted out at a higher opening. Designing for openings at the top and bottom of an open space will encourage natural *stack ventilation.* The effective ventilation rate is proportional to the area of the openings and should be similar in size to promote even airflow through the vertical space. The lower intake openings should be adjustable to regulate the amount of cooling and fresh air, such as with operable windows or ventilation louvers, and can be optimized with automatic thermostat controls.

A critical consideration is to have a significant height difference between the lower intake openings and the higher exhaust openings in the stack. Chimneys and towers can increase this height difference and be useful in carrying air up and out. Solar radiation can be used to increase the *stack ventilation* by heating up the interior surface temperatures to increase the flow of air between the top and bottom openings. For the stack effect to effectively work, the internal temperature must be higher than the outdoor temperature, and the airflow must be able to rise between the different levels of the building, so atriums, airshafts, and operable skylights can significantly increase the airflow up and out.

The largest LEED Platinum project in the world is the HOK Architects design for the extensive King Abdullah University of Science and Technology (KAUST) campus, in high temperature Saudi Arabia. The project uses stack ventilation in wind towers to exhaust heat from the building interiors and screened courtyards (Figures 58, 16, 43, 75). Computer analysis is often needed in larger buildings to design for the complex interactions between building geometries, cross-ventilation, *stack ventilation*, and openings distributed for the intake and exhaust needed.

SUSTAINABILITY DIAGRAM
LABORATORIES AND PEDESTRIAN SPINE

1 High performance roof
2 Solar tower
3 Passive ventilation
4 High performance glazing
5 Integrated shading
6 Local evaporation
7 Passively cooled courtyards
8 Filtered daylight

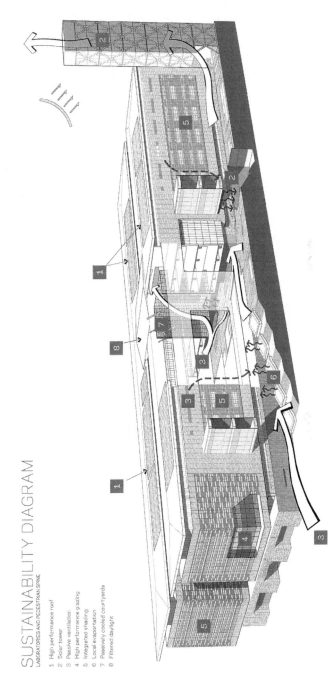

Figure 58 KAUST University ventilation diagram, Saudi Arabia
Courtesy ©HOK

See also: **Energy Efficiency • Indoor Environmental Quality • Natural Ventilation • Passive Cooling • Passive Design • Passive Solar Heating • Solar Heat Gain Coefficient**

Further sources: A Better City; Iyengar (2015: 52); Glass (2002: 282); Green Building Advisor; Szokolay (2004: 16); WBDG

Stormwater Management   ▌

Water pollution happens when toxic substances enter water bodies such as lakes, rivers, oceans and so on, getting dissolved in them, lying suspended in the water or depositing on the bed. This degrades the quality of water. —World Wildlife Fund

To reduce the impacts of runoffs on urban stream, EPA expanded the Clean Water Act in 1987 to require municipalities to obtain permits for discharges of stormwater runoff. —Center for Watershed Protection

A site's natural hydrological systems and watersheds are disrupted when conventional site development compacts the soil, builds impervious surfaces, removes vegetation, and loses natural drainage patterns. Typical rainwater management is to pipe the runoff as quickly as possible into large structures at the base of the drainage area. This practice increases the peak flow, volume, temperature, and duration of runoff that can erode streams.

Stormwater is considered a heavy amount of water that falls to the surface of the Earth. This water becomes polluted as it gathers and carries pollutants, such as oil, trash, pesticides, chemicals, and metals along roads, drains, channels, and storm sewer systems. Most of this fast-flowing polluted water is discharged into nearby water bodies and streams, damaging wildlife habitats, property, and infrastructure. When rain falls on natural, undeveloped land, the soil and plants absorb and filter the water, and the natural water aquifer is recharged.

Low-Impact Development (LID) is a *stormwater management* measure to manage runoff by using micro-scale controls distributed around the site to mimic a site's water flow patterns from before development. Aligning with LID is the cost-effective, resilient approach of Green Infrastructure which restores the natural water management cycle by using plants, soils, and microbes to capture, clean, and reduce rainwater runoff. Strategies would include rain gardens, rainwater harvesting, bioswales, green roofs, permeable pavement, and preserving or increasing the urban tree canopy.

These *stormwater management* strategies are clearly shown in the Wade Science Center at the Germantown Friends School in Philadelphia, designed by SMP Architects. The stormwater from the upper roof is collected in two aboveground cisterns that then supply the building with non-potable water for flushing toilets. Green roofs enhance the *stormwater management* while the courtyard rain gardens direct the stormwater through natively planted recharge swales to a final overflow bed in the courtyard (Figures 59, 24).

Stormwater

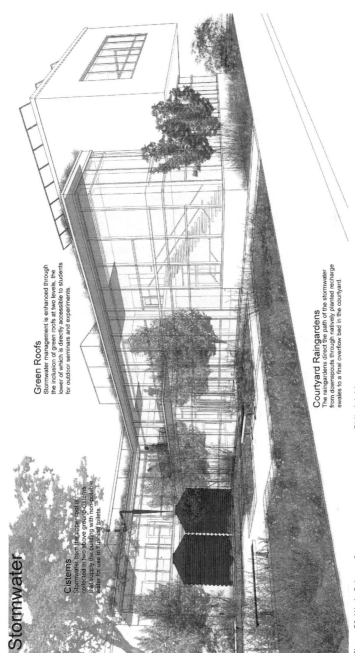

Cisterns
Stormwater from the upper roof is collected in two above ground cisterns that supply the building with non-potable water for use in flushing toilets.

Green Roofs
Stormwater management is enhanced through the inclusion of green roofs at two levels, the lower of which is directly accessible to students for outdoor seminars and experiments.

Courtyard Raingardens
The raingardens direct the path of the stormwater from downspouts through natively planted recharge swales to a final overflow bed in the courtyard.

Figure 59 Wade Science Center stormwater management, Philadelphia
Courtesy ©SMP Architects

Environmental Site Design (ESD), also called Better Site Design (BSD), also mimics natural, low-maintenance systems along the stormwater flow pattern on the development site. The stormwater flow is reduced gradually on its way to the downstream water body, which reduces the amount of conventional stormwater structure needed. Effective *stormwater management* practices might include minimizing impervious surfaces, preserving natural areas, reducing land disturbance, using conservation zones and vegetative channels, and strategies to reduce parking ratios required.

We believe clean water and healthy natural resources are essential to life on Earth. —Center for Watershed Protection

See also: **Ecological Design • Green Roofs • Naturescaping • Permeable Pavement • Rainwater Harvesting • Sustainable Site Design**

Further sources: American Rivers; ASLA; Center for Watershed Protection; US EPA; WWF

Structural Insulated Panels

Structural insulated panels (SIPs) are a high performance building system for residential and light commercial construction. SIPs are manufactured under factory-controlled conditions and can be fabricated to fit nearly any building design. —Structural Insulated Panel Association website

A *structural insulated panel (SIP)* is a composite building system that consists of a layer of rigid insulation glued between two layers of structural sheathing. The most commonly used sheathing material is oriented strand board (OSB), but plywood, fiber cement board, metal panels, and magnesium oxide boards are also available. The rigid insulation component can be expanded polystyrene (EPS), extruded polystyrene (XPS), Polyisocyanurate, or polyurethane foam. *Structural insulated panels* typically use conventional building materials such as wood studs, rigid insulation, and oriented strand board sheathing though the system provides increased structural integrity and energy efficiency when compared to conventional wood framing construction. The continuous lamination of structural boards to rigid insulation creates a very rigid system with high shear resistance and increased compressive strength when compared to a conventional stud wall. The continuity of the insulation material within each panel significantly increases the R-value of the overall building envelope as it minimizes thermal bridging.

The sheathing materials and rigid insulation are usually glued using a formaldehyde-free adhesive. *Structural insulated panels* are available for a variety of building components such as walls, roofs, and floors. In residential application *SIP*, roof components can be supported by *SIP* wall panels, conventional wood stud partitions, wood beams, or roof trusses. In commercial applications, *structural insulated panels* may be applied to a primary structural system. Panel-to-panel connections are achieved using screws 8–12 inches long.

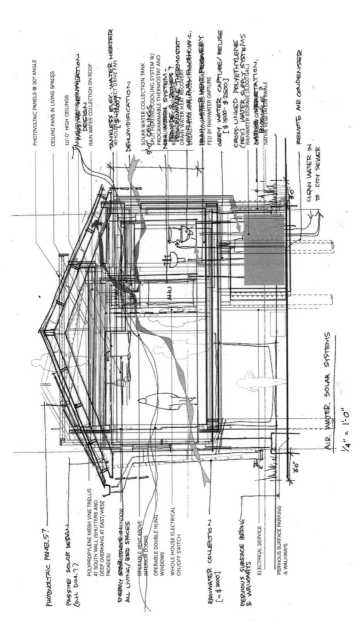

PHOTOVOLTAIC PANELS?

PASSIVE SOLAR DESIGN
(o.h. DIM. ?)

POLYPROPYLENE MESH VINE TRELLIS
AT SOUTH WALL (SHUTTERS AND
DEEP OVERHANG AT EAST/WEST
FACADES)

ENERGY STAR ENERGY STAR/WINDOW
ALL LIVING / BED SPACES

OPERABLE VENT ABOVE
INTERIOR DOORS

OPERABLE DOUBLE HUNG
WINDOWS

WHOLE HOUSE ELECTRICAL
ON/OFF SWITCH

RAINWATER COLLECTION
[~ $ 3000]

PERVIOUS SURFACE PARKING
& WALKWAYS

ELECTRICAL SERVICE

PERVIOUS SURFACE PARKING
& WALKWAYS

PHOTOVOLTAIC PANELS @ 30° ANGLE

CEILING FANS IN LIVING SPACES

10'-0" HIGH CEILINGS

MINIMUM VENTILATION
DESIGN
RAIN WATER COLLECTION ON ROOF

TANKLESS ELEC. WATER HEATER
W/ HOLDING TANK PRODUCT DRIVE FAN

DEHUMIDIFICATION

SOLAR WATER COLLECTION TANK

SPLIT CEILINGS COOLING SYSTEM W/
PROGRAMMABLE THERMOSTAT AND
MINIMUM ENERGY SYSTEM -
PROVIDE (4) ZONES ?
PROGRAMMABLE THERMOSTAT
DRAIN WATER HEAT RECOVERY
EACH FLOOR AIR PLENUMS SHOWN I.C.

BRAIN WATER HEAT RECOVERY
FED BY RAINWATER CAPTURE

GREY WATER CAPTURE / REUSE
[~ $1500 - $ 2500]

CROSS-LINKED POLYETHYLENE
(PEX) WATER SUPPLY SYSTEMS
RAINWATER STORAGE (3,000 GAL.)

NATIVE VEGETATION.
BIOSWALE

REMOTE AIR CONDENSER

CLEAN WATER IN
TO CITY SEWER

AIR. WATER. SOLAR SYSTEMS

¼" = 1'-0"

Figure 60 Special No. 9 House: Make It Right uses structural insulated panels, New Orleans
Courtesy ©KieranTimberlake

Though *Structural Insulated Panels* gained traction in the 1970s, the Forest Product Laboratory in Madison, Wisconsin, which was leading the research at that time, initially developed the concept in the 1930s. The interest for panelized construction originated from an attempt to use wood resources more efficiently. Such systems gained renewed interest in the 1970s due to rising energy costs during that period.

Though it has enjoyed increased attention in the past twenty years with sustainable programs such as the USGBC LEED certification system, *SIP* technology represents a very small portion of the overall construction market despite some obvious benefits. *Structural insulated panels* do provide advantages regarding both design and construction by increasing construction speed and allowing for more spacious conditioned spaces.

Building envelopes built with *structural insulated panels* display improved qualities with regards to structural integrity, air infiltration, soundproofing, and insulation. Because prefabrication is involved, projects using *SIPs* also generate less waste. As a consequence of providing a better building envelope, *SIP* buildings have made significant energy savings and overall life-cycle savings. Therefore, when compared to mainstream residential wood framing, the initial construction cost of a *structural insulated panel* system is offset by long-term operating costs savings. In addition to being used in residential applications, *Structural Insulated Panels* have proven attractive for large commercial and public projects such as schools, churches, warehouses, and both roofing and re-roofing projects.

The KieranTimberlake Architect's Make It Right Foundation Special No. 9 House was designed as a prototype to rebuild the Ninth Ward neighborhood of New Orleans that was wiped clean by Hurricane Katrina. The house uses structural insulated panels for ease of construction, mass production, thermal insulation, airtightness, speed of construction, and resilience to wind forces. The design features passive survivability strategies with a raised first floor for potential flooding, natural daylighting and ventilation, solar PV, rainwater harvesting, and roof access for safe refuge (Figures 18, 60). OC

See also: **Materials and Resources • Off-site Prefabricated Construction • Passive Survivability • Waste Reduction**

Further sources: Structural Insulated Panel Association

▎Sustainability

But the care of the Earth is our most ancient and most worthy and, after all, our most pleasing responsibility. To cherish what remains of it, and to foster its renewal, is our only hope.
—Wendell Berry, *The Art of the Commonplace*

Sustainability is a sweeping, far-ranging philosophy or a way of thinking to address the ability of humans and other life to endure and flourish on this planet forever. As a civilization, we cannot continue down our current destructive path with our negative environmental impacts on our planet Earth and all its species. Wendell Berry urges us to "cherish what remains of it, and to foster its renewal" as our only hope.

With our increasing use and disposal of limited resources, such as water, energy, and materials, we are seeing the resultant land, air and water pollution, insurmountable waste build-up, increasing severity of climate change events, and resource scarcity. The emission of greenhouse gases from fossil fuel combustion; deforestation for grazing or timber; overfishing; desertification; limitless water consumption; contamination of land, air, and water with toxic chemicals; and explosive land sprawl are just a few of the many damaging actions that threaten the future of generations to come. The question of *sustainability* asks of each of us what kind of world we will leave to future generations. What is our responsible role? Edmund Burke expresses it in the following quote as a partnership among the past, living, and future societies.

Society is a partnership, not only between those who are living, but between those who are living, those who are dead, and those who are to be born. —Edmund Burke

The UN 1987 Brundtland Commission Report, *Our Common Future*, resulted in the most widely quoted definition stating "sustainable development is development that meets the needs of the present without compromising the ability of future generations to meet their own needs" (Brundtland Commission 1987). *Sustainability* requires understanding the three mutually reinforcing pillars of sustainability: environmental, social, and economic needs. *Sustainability* is often defined as maintaining and enduring, but we must also work collectively to restore our natural world. As the world's population has increased to over 7.5 billion, our natural living systems have weakened.

Many believe that sustainability is such a powerful philosophy that it will soon change the course of all aspects of our life on this planet. —Jason McLennan, The Philosophy of Sustainable Design

Jason McLennan, the founder of the International Living Future Institute and the Living Building Challenge, proposes that sustainability as a philosophy will "soon change the course of all aspects of our life on this planet" (McLennan 2004: 36). To live sustainably will require that society reach for a balance among environmental protection, social improvement, and economic development, while working in harmony with Earth's natural ecosystems. Ways of living more sustainably will demand we reduce our dependence on fossil fuels, underground metals, and minerals, to reduce our dependence on synthetic chemicals, to reduce our consumption of limited resources such as water, to reduce our encroachment on nature, and to meet human needs fairly and efficiently.

The LEED Platinum certified NASA Sustainability Base in California by William McDonough + Partners is a superb example of using high-performing strategies toward the goal of *sustainability*. Designed as a space-age facility, the intent is to blend NASA's space exploration expertise with sustainable design for the built environment. The NASA building reduces many environmental impacts by using extensive passive and active design strategies, such as on-site renewable energy generation, solid oxide fuel cells, smart building systems, geothermal systems, daylighting, views, natural ventilation, and uses Cradle-to-Cradle products (Figures 61, 10, 19, 45, 52).

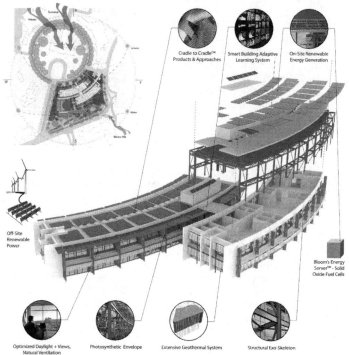

Figure 61 NASA Sustainability Base high-performing strategies
Courtesy ©William McDonough + Partners

See also: **Ecological Design • Green Building • Green Design
(*Archispeak*) • Hannover Principles • High-Performing Buildings •
Net-Zero Energy Building Certification • Our Common Future • Paris
Climate Agreement • Regenerative Design • Seventh Generation
Principle • Sustainability (*Archispeak*) • Sustainable Design •
Sustainable Development • Zero Energy Building (*Theoryspeak*)**

Further sources: Brown (2011); Brundtland Commission (1987); Carson (1962); Diamond (2005); Dresner (2002); Edwards (2005); Flannery
(2009); Hertsgaard (2011); Klein (2014); Kolbert (2006); Leopold (1949);
McLennan (2004: 36); Naam (2013); Wilson (2016)

Sustainable Design

**Sustainability, ensuring the future of life on Earth, is an infinite game,
the endless expression of generosity on behalf of all.** —Paul Hawken

Sustainability as a term has many different meanings, but the most
widely accepted concept is embracing the critical environmental preservation of our planet by the efficient use of vital resources, continuing

social development and progress, steady economic growth, and the elimination of poverty worldwide. The responsible design and construction of our built environment has enormous potential to provide a more sustainable future for our planet. If successful, it would be an "endless expression of generosity on behalf of all," as Paul Hawken has so eloquently expressed.

Half of the world's population is now living in cities, according to Architecture 2030, and buildings in developed countries account for over 40% of energy consumed, so *sustainable design* is essential to the long-term environmental, social, and economic success of our future.

The American Institute of Architects (AIA) uses the word "sustainable" as a standard industry term to describe projects that incorporate construction and design practices that intend to offer environmental benefits, enhance building occupant's health and well-being, or increase energy efficiency. *Sustainable design*, sustainable development, and sustainable practices are often usually used synonymously with sustainable construction, environmentally responsible design, green design, green building practices, and high-performance building, which usually is more about efficiencies of energy, water, and resources.

Sustainable buildings are not about fashion or style; they are about performance, resilience and adaptability. —Sue Roaf, *Closing the Loop*

Similar to the most commonly used definition of sustainability from the *Our Common Future* Brundtland Report, *sustainable design* aims to meet the current needs of working, learning, and housing environments, along with the related infrastructures needed, without compromising the ability of future generations to meet their own needs. *Sustainable design* incorporates the triple bottom line elements of economic efficiency, environmental performance, and social responsibility. As Sue Roaf, the British architect and scholar asserts, sustainable buildings are primarily about "performance, resilience and adaptability."

Sustainable design strategies typically used are: building energy and resource efficiency; long-term operations and maintenance monitoring; creating ethical standards and socially viable environments; enhancing occupant health, safety, and well-being; improving the existing site and context with remediation and regenerative practices; designing flexible and durable projects; increasing material performance; and linking together the architecture, landscape, and urban contextual fabric.

Strategies for achieving increased energy efficiency and reducing the building's carbon footprint are using on-site carbon-free renewable energy resources, passive design measures, climatically responsible design, energy conservation measures, automatic controls and building intelligence, and right-sizing equipment components.

Resource efficiency measures are using previously developed sites and existing infrastructure; using less material; recycling and using recycled materials; water conservation, efficiency, and reuse; avoiding toxins; and selecting construction materials that reduce the embodied energy and resources.

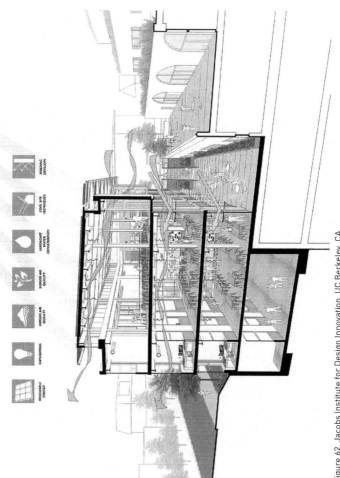

Figure 62 Jacobs Institute for Design Innovation, UC Berkeley, CA
Courtesy ©Leddy Mahtum Stacy Architects

Building strategies for enhancing the sustainability over the lifetime of the building are designing for durability, resiliency, and adaptation; recyclability with deconstruction, reuse, or disassembly; ease of repair and maintenance; and adhering to ethical and socially responsible practices for materials, construction, operations, work environments, and community empowerment.

Every project is an opportunity to think beyond the property lines.
—William Leddy, FAIA

The Jacobs Institute for Design Innovation at UC Berkeley in California designed by Leddy Mahtum Stacy Architects is an innovative example of *sustainable design* that "thinks beyond the property lines," in the words of the architect, William Leddy. This high-performing building uses strategies of cantilevering a photovoltaic renewable energy array, maximizing daylighting with light shelves, enhancing indoor air quality with natural ventilation, conserving landscape water with bioswales and rain gardens, cool site techniques to reduce the urban heat island effect, and a climate responsive building envelope (Figures 62, 26).

See also: **Climate Responsive Design • Design for Disassembly • Durability • Ecological Footprint • Embodied Energy • Energy Efficiency • Indoor Environmental Quality • Location and Transportation • Materials and Resources • Our Common Future • Renewable Energy • Sustainable Site Design • Water Efficiency**

Further sources: AASHE; AIA; Architecture 2030; Design Buildings Wiki; EBN; ILFI; Roaf, Crichton, and Nicol (2005: 15); USGBC; WBDG

Sustainable Development   **❚**

Saving our planet, lifting people out of poverty, advancing economic growth . . . these are one and the same fight. We must connect the dots between climate change, water scarcity, energy shortages, global health, food security and women's empowerment. Solutions to one problem must be solutions for all. —Ban Ki-moon, UN Secretary-General 2011

The 1987 UN Commission on Environment and Development, known as the Brundtland Commission, published *Our Common Future*, a "global agenda for change" attempting to connect issues of environmental stability and human economic development. This report provided the most often used, but broad, definition of *sustainable development* as "development that meets the needs of the present without compromising the ability of future generations to meet their own needs." This initial framework was an intergenerational concept to advance human development, in particular, the essential needs of the poor, while also limiting the long-term impacts on the environment's ability to meet present and future needs.

The 1992 Earth Summit created Agenda 21 for the future 21st century, establishing a voluntary global environmental agenda for the following twenty years. In 2002, with the UN World Summit on Sustainable Development in Johannesburg, the definition evolved to a more practical all-inclusive approach linking economic development, social inclusion and environmental sustainability, as being mutually reinforcing and interdependent.

The 2012 Earth Summit, UN Conference on Sustainable Development (Rio+20), was aimed at renewing earlier global economic and environmental goals into a focused political commitment to shaping global environmental policy. The conference centered on Agenda 21 from Earth Summit 1992, suggesting ways local, state, and national governments could combat poverty, pollution, and conserve natural resources, trying to implement what former UN Secretary-General Ban Ki-moon stresses that "solutions to one problem must be solutions for all."

The United Nations wanted a green economy "road map" with twenty-year environmental goals, while developing countries endorsed new *sustainable development* goals to protect the environment, guarantee well-being for the poor, and alleviate poverty. In some areas of U.S. public discussion, Agenda 21 is controversial, with theories of adverse effects on private property rights and national sovereignty. Nevertheless, debate arises as to finding the right balance between protecting the individual and the collective.

The overall goal of *sustainable development* remains the long-term stability of the economy and the environment, and this requires the acknowledgment and integration of all economic, environmental, and social concerns and objectives across cultures, countries, and generations.

See also: **Green Economy • Laudato Si': On Care for Our Common Home • Our Common Future • Paris Climate Agreement • Social Equity • Sustainable Design**

Further sources: Brundtland Commission: *Our Common Future*; Sachs (2015)

Sustainable Preservation

Preservation is simply having the good sense to hold on to things that are well designed, that link us with our past in a meaningful way, and have plenty of good use left in them. —Richard Moe, National Trust for Historic Preservation

Reinvesting in historic buildings and older traditional communities can have a significant role in confronting the challenges of environmental degradation, decreasing resources, and climate change. The conservation and improvement of our current existing buildings and communities, especially sustainably upgrading historic buildings, offers significant savings in construction resources, minimizing environmental impacts, and the preservation of established historic character and social values.

Sustainable preservation is based not only on the ecological benefit of the aphorism that "the most sustainable building is one that is already built," but also other advantages over new construction. The benefits of building reuse can be significant when analyzed with life-cycle assessment modeling. Knowing the environmental and financial pay-backs to reusing and upgrading can help face the many challenges to *sustainable preservation*, such as the issues of energy efficiency, historic windows, adequate lighting, indoor environmental quality, HVAC issues, and national, state, and local codes and regulations.

One of the immediate and long-lasting advantages of historic building reuse and preservation is the significant embodied energy and embodied carbon of the existing building due to the durable, resource-intensive, and quality materials that were typically used in historic construction practices before the early 20th century. Unfortunately, much of the construction later in the postwar building boom was not designed or built to last, and much of this will need to be demolished in the next twenty years.

A building is not something you finish. A building is something you start. —Stewart Brand

Many early historic buildings built before the wars were constructed to last over a hundred years, with durable materials and parts that could be easily repaired or replaced. This echoes Steward Brand's statement that a "building is something you start" as a quality building is able to evolve, be repaired and adaptable. Early historic buildings used passive design strategies learned from centuries of tested building practices. They responded to the site and climate by using natural ventilation, stack effect, courtyards, cisterns, thermal mass, shading with vegetation, and natural daylighting.

Historic buildings, often built before our lives centered on the automobile, are often centrally located in established communities within walking distance of existing amenities, such as natural open spaces, parks, markets, schools, public transit, and cultural and recreation opportunities. Richard Moe of the National Trust for Historic Preservation has been an adamant advocate for preserving not only historic buildings, but the "values" of older established communities that "link us with our past in a meaningful way." Historic buildings were built with natural plant materials, old growth wood, local brick or stone, and were detailed with unique craftsmanship that defined the culture and legacy of place.

The LEED Platinum sustainable renovation of the historic 1906 King Street Station by ZGF Architects consumes 68% less energy than the previous building by digging geothermal wells for ground sourced heat pumps for heating and cooling, restoring operable windows, incorporating photovoltaics on a restored trackside canopy, and harvesting rainwater for toilet flushing, according to the firm. The red-brick Italianate station with the 242-foot-tall campanile, modeled after Venice's Piazza San Marco, also needed major seismic upgrading which consumed over 40% of the budget (Figure 63).

Preservation is in the business of saving communities and the values they embody. —Richard Moe

See also: **Adaptive Reuse • Community Connectivity • Embodied Carbon • Embodied Energy • Life-Cycle Assessment • Materials and Resources**

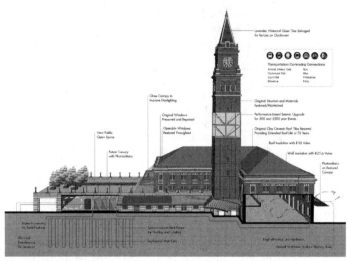

Figure 63　King Street Station, Seattle
Courtesy ©ZGF Architects LLP

Further sources: Brand (1994: 188); Carroon (2010); EarthCraft Sustainable Preservation; National Trust for Historic Preservation; Preservation Technology International; ZGF, www.zgf.com/project/city-of-seattle-department-of-transportation-king-street-station-renovation/

Sustainable Site Design

The good building is not one that hurts the landscape, but one which makes the landscape more beautiful than it was before the building was built. —Frank Lloyd Wright, American architect

Life on Earth depends on the regenerative and "natural capital" services of our forests, coral reefs, wetlands, and other natural ecosystems. The World Resources Institute (2005) states that about 60% of global ecosystems assessed are being damaged, resulting in deforestation, coral bleaching, species extinction, soil erosion, and a drop in water table levels. Farmlands and natural landscapes are being lost to rapid economic growth and sprawling developments, resulting in heat island hardscapes and water-intensive non-native landscaping. The rainwater runoff from these roofs, roads, and parking lots can carry pollutants of oil, chemicals and lawn fertilizers, which when reaching rivers contributes to eutrophication, and damage to aquatic species.

Architecture is bound to situation. And I feel like the site is a metaphysical link, a poetic link, to what a building can be. —Steven Holl, American architect

The *sustainable site design* approach to site design understands the critical inter-relationship, or as Steven Holl would call it, "the poetic link" between the project itself, surrounding buildings, and local eco-system services by protecting water bodies, restoring natural habitat biodiversity, integrating with existing ecosystems, and preserving open space. As Frank Lloyd Wright stresses, a building should make "the landscape more beautiful than it was before the building was built." Planning should minimize development of greenfield spaces by select-ing disturbed land, remediating brownfield sites, or reusing existing buildings. Site selection should ensure available clean air and water, good soil conditions, solar access, security, accessibility, and use the smart growth principles of proximity to public transportation and com-munity amenities.

The building placement and orientation on the site can take advan-tage of passive and active solar strategies of natural ventilation using prevailing wind patterns, maximize daylighting and views, and use trees for shading. Low-impact development strategies can capture and filter stormwater runoff on site with underground cisterns, vegetative swales, rain gardens, constructed wetlands, and pervious paving materials.

Planting vegetation and trees can reduce urban heat island effects, and photovoltaic arrays can shade paved sidewalks and parking. Highly reflective cool roofs, green roofs, and photovoltaic arrays can reduce energy loads and extend the life of the roof. Restoring native plantings can improve the habitat for native indigenous species, allow undis-turbed wildlife movements, and irrigating with potable water can be eliminated. Responsible lighting can provide site security with clear views, and perimeter and sidewalk lighting, without inherent light pollution.

Sustainable building certifications, such as LEED, Green Globes, and the Living Building Challenge, all require responsible site selection, site regeneration and local ecosystems integration, and preserving natural system biodiversity. The Sustainable Sites category the LEED certifica-tion system addresses construction activity pollution, site assessment, protection and restoration of habitat, open space, rainwater manage-ment, heat island reduction, and light pollution reduction.

Increasingly severe storm and drought events, often due to climate change, call for sites to be selected and ecosystems protected from flooding, erosion, wind damage, and extreme temperature threats. Land development should adhere to naturalist Aldo Leopold's "land ethic" philosophy that there is no truly "vacant" land, as there are already many species of animals and plants living there already, and they have as many rights and protections to exist on the land as we do.

The Arizona State University Health Services Building in Tempe, Ari-zona is a LEED Platinum adaptive reuse project designed by Lake|Flato Architects. The design preserved five thousand square feet of open green space, linked the entry to the historic pedestrian Palm Walk, and replaced turf grass with native landscaping irrigated by rainwater harvested from the facility's roof and stored in belowgrade cisterns (Figures 64, 18, 39).

See also: **Green Roofs • Land Ethic • Passive Design • Site Analysis • SITES Initiative • Smart Growth • Urban Heat Island • Urban Tree Canopy • Vegetated Walls**

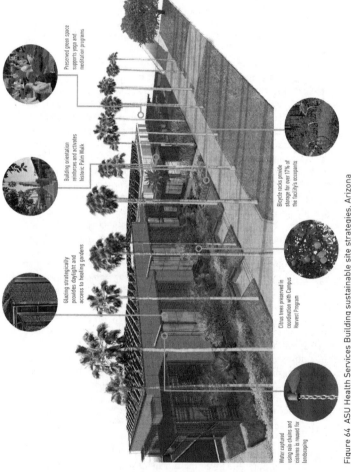

Preserved green space supports yoga and meditation programs

Building orientation reinforces and activates historic Palm Walk

Glazing strategically provides daylight and access to healing gardens

Water captured using rain chains and cisterns is reused for landscaping

Bicycle racks provide storage for over 17% of the facility's occupants

Citrus trees preserved in coordination with Campus Harvest Program

Figure 64 ASU Health Services Building sustainable site strategies, Arizona
Courtesy ©Lake|Flato Architects

Further sources: EBN; LBC; LEED; SITES; UNEP Millennium Ecosystem Assessment; USGBC; WBDG; World Resources Institute (2005)

▌Systems Thinking

**Learn how to see. Realize that everything connects to everything
else.** —Leonardo da Vinci 1452–1519, Renaissance polymath

**Its core premise is that, like the web of life, everything is connected
and the study of those connections and interactions can offer new
and different conclusions.** —Dictionary of Sustainable Management

Buildings, vehicles, machines, and processes are sets of dynamic, interactive systems using functionally interconnected elements that form a
unified whole. If designers reduce problems into individual components
to optimize the parts without thinking of the overall interactions, the
whole system may be less efficient. Nature can teach us many lessons
of the durable and efficient interconnected whole. *Systems thinking* is a
discipline of seeing whole, understanding the interconnected synergy
and dynamics of relationships, and allowing for the optimization of not
only the parts but also the entire system to achieve a higher-performing
product. *Systems thinking* is rooted in system dynamics, focusing on the
whole rather than individual parts, and realizing as Leonardo da Vinci
wrote, that "everything connects to everything else."

Using *systems thinking* in sustainable design, a team of professional
experts in energy, water, air quality, and materials—along with the
architects, engineers, owners, and occupants—all collaborate in considering the building and systems as an entire whole. *Systems thinking*
can save energy and reduce environmental impacts by reinforcing the
collaborative, integrative design process to optimize sustainable design
efficiencies and priorities such as site, energy, water, resources, construction methods, daylighting, acoustics, lighting, and mechanical
design, as well as occupant safety and comfort. Exploring these relationships with the different design team disciplines, *systems thinking*
allows even further linked connections to be revealed to still larger
scaled networks, such economies, industries, communities, and ecosystems, which also all react with each other.

See also: **Circular Economy • Integrated Design • High-Performing
Buildings • Natural Step • Sustainable Design • Whole Building
Design**

Further sources: EBN; Hawken, A. Lovins, and L. Lovins (1999); RMI;
WBDG; Wikipedia

Thermal Comfort

Thermal comfort: that condition of mind that expresses satisfaction with the thermal environment and is assessed by subjective evaluation. —ASHRAE 55

Thermal comfort is a combination of environmental factors that can provide a psychological and physiological perception of whether someone is feeling too warm or too cold, and is essential for health, well-being, and productivity. Thermal discomfort in a building can result in occupant stress, sick building syndrome symptoms, and one's loss of ability to function effectively—if people are too warm, they feel tired; and if too cold, they are restless.

A number of environmental factors and personal factors combine to result in *thermal comfort*. Thermal environmental conditions are measured in a space occupied by people, called the occupied zone. The environmental factors include air temperature, air velocity, radiant temperature, and relative humidity. The temperature of the air surrounding the occupant is measured with the dry bulb temperature. Air velocity is the movement of air over a distance in time. The faster the air moves, the greater the heat exchange between the air and people. The mean radiant temperature is weighted temperature average of the surfaces surrounding the occupant that the body exchanges heat with, such as heat-generating equipment, and exposure to the sky or the sun. The relative humidity is a percentage ratio between the actual amount of water vapor in the air and the maximum amount of water vapor the air can hold at that particular temperature. The higher the level of humidity in the air, the harder it is to lose heat by evaporating perspiration to cool the body.

The personal factors combining with environmental factors to result in *thermal comfort* include the occupant's clothing, metabolic heat, and health. A person's clothing can be controlled to insulate or promote a person's heat exchange with the surrounding air and surfaces. A person's metabolic rate produces heat through physical activity, and an active person will feel much warmer than a person sitting still, while the health or well-being of an individual may also affect maintaining a healthy body temperature.

The ASHRAE Standard 55 (Thermal Environmental Conditions for Human Occupancy) establishes the ranges of indoor environmental conditions that are acceptable to achieve occupant *thermal comfort*. The Center for Built Environment (CBE) has a *thermal comfort* online tool that allows users to input six comfort criteria. The results are displayed in a Psychrometric chart to determine if the input conditions comply with ASHRAE 55. These analyses are used as a design tool for decision-making in designing for the occupants first and the spaces later.

See also: **ASHRAE Standards • Daylighting • Indoor Environmental Quality • Natural Ventilation • Sick Building Syndrome • WELL Building Standard**

Further sources: ASHRAE; Bonda and Sosowchik (2014: 216); CBE; EBN; Kibert (2016: 438); WBDG

Thermal Insulation   ∎

You feel a certain way in a glass or concrete or limestone building. It has an effect on your skin —the same with plywood or veneer, or solid timber. Wood doesn't steal energy from your body; the glass and concrete steal heat. —Peter Zumthor, Swiss architect

In green building design, *thermal insulation* is critical to blocking or slowing the transfer of heat through the building envelope. This allows interior spaces to retain what heat they have in cool weather or to avoid gaining excessive heat from the outside in warmer weather. Heat always moves from hot to cold and is transferred by conduction, convection, and radiation. Peter Zumthor alludes to this when he states that "concrete steals heat." The human body is usually warmer than cold concrete, so your body transfers heat to the concrete.

Thermal insulation is primarily designed to prevent heat transfer by conduction and radiation. Conduction is the main factor when building materials are in contact with each other, and radiative heat transfer becomes a problem when there is an air gap between these materials. A material's resistance to the conduction of heat is measured by R-values, where a high thermal resistance equates to a high R-value. A one-inch thick vacuum insulated panel will have a high R-value of R-30 to R-50, while a one-inch thickness of poured concrete will have a lower R-value of R-0.08. A material's resistance to radiative heat transfer is measured by emissivity, where a high resistance equals low emissivity and high reflectance.

Some types of *thermal insulation* act as air barriers, while others only act as air filters and need an adjacent air barrier material. Spray and rigid foam insulations are better at stopping airflow than blown-in or batts of fiberglass. Another benefit of preventing airflow is that air can also transport moisture into the walls and roof. Insulating materials usually are in two categories: fibrous or cellular products, which resist conduction; or metallic or metalized reflective membranes, which must face an air space to be effective.

Air is an excellent thermal insulator provided the air is kept still, usually in small pockets. Fibrous or cellular materials prevent the conduction of heat by keeping the air still. Closed cell foam insulation has less convection of air within the foam so is a better thermal insulator than batt insulation. Radiant barriers are needed where the skin of the building, such as roof areas, are exposed to excessive heat. These radiative barriers are usually shiny reflective or white materials needing a low emissivity of 0.1 or less and a high reflectance of 0.9 or more. Radiant barriers only resist radiative heat transfer and do not resist heat transfer by conduction or convection. Convection is why hot air rises in a space, and then conduction transfers that heat into the materials above, so radiant barriers are better at resisting heat flowing downward through spaces than upward. Using movable insulation, such as insulated shutters, shades, or thick curtains can prevent heat loss at night, while properly placed windows can let in useful heat gain during the day.

The sun never knew how great it was until it hit the side of a building.
—Louis Kahn

The King Abdullah Petroleum Studies & Research Center (KAPSARC) in Riyadh, Saudi Arabia, designed by HOK Architects is dedicated to studying all types of energy, including solar and wind power. The KAPSARC housing community is the first project outside North America to achieve LEED for Homes certification. Designed to reflect local cultural traditions along with sustainable solutions for living in the desert climate, they are constructed of stucco and concrete with enhanced *thermal insulation*. They are arranged close together for cluster shading to keep the sun from hitting the sides of the buildings, preventing what the architect Louis Kahn refers to above (Figures 65, 68).

Figure 65 KAPSARC Housing, enhanced thermal insulation and cluster shading, Riyadh, Saudi Arabia
Photo ©Alan Karchmer. Courtesy ©HOK

See also: **Albedo • Energy Efficiency • Passive Cooling • Passive House Building Standard • Passive Solar Heating • Structural Insulated Panels • Solar Reflectance Index**

Further sources: Autodesk Sustainability Workshop; EBN; WBDG

Tragedy of the Commons

Ruin is the destination toward which all men rush, each pursuing his own best interest in a society that believes in the freedom of the commons. Freedom in a commons brings ruin to all. —Garrett Hardin, American ecologist, philosopher

The *tragedy of the commons* is a term used to demonstrate the conflict between the individual's interests and the common good. The assumption is that when people use a public asset, they do not consider the impact of their use on the asset itself, so common or public resources can become overexploited.

William Lloyd coined the *tragedy of the commons* term in 1833, according to the *Concise Encyclopedia of Economics*, referring to the unregulated sheep grazing on British common land. In 1968, American ecologist Garrett Hardin later popularized the term in *Science*. Hardin used Lloyd's article as a metaphor for the welfare state's support of the impoverished, the abuse of natural resources, and rampant human population growth. Hardin applied the *tragedy of the commons* concept to mean that any public natural resource—such as rivers, lands, oceans, and atmosphere—is open to exploitation when there are no ruling authorities to regulate individual use. In an overpopulated world, with no control over exploitation, Hardin stated that our shared resources would be depleted to extinction, and all will fail. He pressed for strengthening our ecological and economic frameworks, but at the expense of moral and social justice concerns.

Only when the last tree is cut, only when the last river is polluted, only when the last fish is caught, will they realize that you can't eat money. —Native American proverb

The *tragedy of the commons* theory is related to the environmental issues of sustainability and development and the ecological services provided by nature. Current concerns are the overuse of finite resources, such as oil, coal, minerals, water, and forests, together with fish and other impacted species. Present *tragedy of the commons* examples are the salmon run destructions on dammed rivers, clearcutting rainforests for agriculture or cattle, Russian and U.S. sturgeon overfishing, and limited water available in populated arid regions such as Los Angeles and Las Vegas. The short-term selfish wants of society can be at odds with the sustainable long-term intergenerational needs and interests.

Government regulations, interventions, and permit systems can limit the amount of common good that is available for individual use, although ideally, progressive people themselves would collaborate in the name of shared societal benefits in conserving resources for the common interest.

See also: **Ecological Footprint • Lifeboat Ethics • Population Growth • Spaceship Earth • Sustainable Development**

Further sources: Concise Encyclopedia of Economics, www.econlib.org/library/CEE.html; Kibert et al. (2012: 168); Hardin (1968: 1243–1248)

Triple Bottom Line   **I**

Measure what is measurable, and make measurable what is not so.
—Galileo Galilei, 1564–1642, Italian polymath

Traditionally corporations, businesses, and governments measured their success based on the bottom line of profits and investment returns. As consumer awareness grew on the hidden social and environmental costs of transferring manufacturing services to low-cost developing countries, public demands were made for corporate accountability. Increasing public knowledge of indiscriminate rainforest logging, pollution, greenhouses gas emissions, and cheap labor exploitation all called for corporate responsibility, fair trade, and environmental accountability.

John Elkington introduced the term the *triple bottom line* in the 1998 book, *Cannibals With Forks: The Triple Bottom Line of 21st Century Business.* He proposed broadening a business's financial bottom line to include both social and environmental responsibilities as measures of success. A *triple bottom line* report captures the spectrum of social, environmental, and economic values a business must embrace, which are often referred to as the 3Ps: "people, planet, and profit" (Elkington 1998).

The "people" bottom line element of social responsibility measures a business with regard to individuals and community capital. The social bottom line addresses fair wages for on-site and off-site labor, employee benefits, and active community involvement. Labor interest and corporate interests are seen as interdependent in fostering long-term sustainability, as a positive workplace will always be able to operate efficiently, and usually thrive.

The "planet" bottom line view relative to environmental responsibility is implementing sustainable practices of consuming fewer natural resources and reducing environmental impacts. This involves managing, monitoring, and the reporting of resource consumption, wastes, and emissions. Sustainable business practices might be promoting green initiatives; recycling programs; or even manufacturing products with sustainable, salvaged or recycled materials; or using industrial wastes instead of conventional materials.

The financial bottom line part of economic sustainability goes beyond just the traditional corporate profit but is measured regarding how great of an impact your business has had on the economic environment. Corporate sustainability measures a company's strength to endure, grow, and profit, based on its relationship with employees and the community, with their impact on the environment, and their contribution to building the economy.

See also: **Circular Economy • Green Economy • JUST Program • Sustainable Development**

Further sources: Elkington (1998); Investopedia; Sustainable Management

▌Trombe Wall

The Trombe wall is named after a French engineer Félix Trombe, who popularized this heating system in the early 1960s. The idea actually goes back a lot further. A thermal-mass wall was patented in 1881 by Edward Morse. —Alex Wilson, *BuildingGreen*

A *Trombe wall* is a south-facing exterior building wall used in cold climates to capture solar heat and conduct it to interior occupied spaces. *Trombe walls* passively heat rooms, reducing the need for mechanical heating systems.

The *Trombe wall* faces south to maximize sunlight falling on the wall. *Trombe wall* strategies have been used since ancient times, but this particular wall configuration was developed by inventor Felix Trombe in the 1960s.

The Trombe design is composed of two wall planes separated by 1–2 inches to form an air cavity between them. The wall facing the building's exterior is transparent to allow solar light through the glass, into the air cavity, and onto the surface of the second wall. The second wall has one solar heat collecting surface facing the air cavity and a second surface facing the building interior. This second wall is masonry to collect, store and transmit captured solar heat.

The masonry wall is 12–18 inches thick and made of concrete, brick, adobe, or filled concrete blocks to provide heat-storing thermal mass.

Heat is transmitted to interior occupied space in two ways. Heat works its way through the masonry wall and then radiates that heat directly into the room the wall faces. This is particularly useful when the heat arrives in the room in colder evening hours. During the day, heat from the masonry wall collected in the air cavity rises and enters the room through vents in the top of the masonry. This air movement is facilitated by cooler air on the room floor entering the air cavity through vents in the bottom of the masonry wall to be reheated and re-circulated. This loop of air provides continuous heat flow into the room.

Trombe wall glazing is typically double pane to reduce heat loss from the air cavity to the outside during the day. At night, the glazing may be covered with operable insulated shutters to inhibit heat loss through the glass to the outside air. Vents in the masonry wall can be closed at night to prevent warmed room air from being lost to the air cavity.

Masonry wall footings are insulated to reduce wall heat loss to the soil below. In the summer, there can be operable vents at the top of the air cavity to the outside so that the wall can convert to a thermal chimney, facilitating the exhaust of warm air from the interior inhabited space. Roof overhangs prevent higher summer sun from reaching the *Trombe wall* when a heated masonry wall would be counterproductive. Carefully designed roof overhangs allow low winter sun to reach the masonry wall and activate its heat capturing/circulating processes.

On the building interior, there should be nothing placed against the masonry wall that would inhibit the wall's radiant heat transmission to the room.

A *Trombe wall* variation enlarges the air cavity width to create an air cavity floor. The thermal mass floor joins the masonry wall in solar heat collection, storage, and transmission. The *Trombe wall* issue of reduced natural daylight and diminished exterior views can be addressed with windows along the top and sides of the wall. EW

See also: **Albedo • Energy Efficiency • Passive Design • Passive Heating and Cooling • Solar Reflectance Index**

Underfloor Air Distribution

UFAD systems have several potential advantages over traditional overhead systems, including improved thermal comfort, improved indoor air quality, and reduced energy use. —Center for the Built Environment

An *underfloor air distribution system (UFAD)* is a method of delivering conditioned air to the occupied space in an underfloor plenum, with some small outlets on the floor. The concept of *UFAD* started in the 1950s for buildings with high heating and cooling loads, and then further developed for office buildings in the 1970s. An *underfloor air distribution system* has the following benefits over a conventional overhead system:

- Improved occupant control based on thermal comfort.
- Natural floor-to-ceiling airflow pattern.
- Reduced energy use through thermal stratification and higher supply air temperatures.
- Reduced building floor-to-floor heights (5–10%).

An *underfloor air distribution system* must incorporate building system considerations for determining cooling and heating loads, zoning, ventilation air requirements, zone supply air temperature and flow rate, return air, calculating cooling coil load, plenum configuration, locating diffusers, and developing a control strategy. Developing *UFAD* as a new system faces difficulties such as limited compatibility to retrofit construction, and lack of standard methods. The Center for the Built Environment (CBE) at the University of California, Berkeley has developed lessons and technical information, learned from case studies, to advance *UFAD* technology.

An *underfloor air distribution system* supplies air from the air-handling unit through underfloor ducts, whereas standard ceiling distribution uses an extensive network of ducts in the ceiling. Using pressurized or zero-pressure for the underfloor plenums can be used to deliver air to the space. As for return air, *UFAD* returns are at the ceiling to work with the natural upward convection of airflow in the space. Return air is constructed as an un-ducted ceiling plenum to have mix-type air.

Since conventional systems assume a well-mixed temperature in the space, the main difference between the two occurs in cooling air supply calculations. To clarify the advantages of *UFAD*, the Berkeley CBE is monitoring and evaluating the system based on simulation, the technical aspects, cost-effectiveness and analysis, and the standard revisions to ASHRAE. MM

See also: **Building Automated Control Systems • Indoor Environmental Quality • Sick Building Syndrome • Thermal Comfort**

Further sources: ASHRAE; CBE; EBN; WBDG

Universal and Inclusive Design ▌

We need to make every single thing accessible to every single person with a disability. —Stevie Wonder

In daily life, the built environment can be a challenging place to move around in, especially for those disabled, elderly, and families with infants, or even if not disabled. Ease of access is a source of opportunity and a civil right in business, education, and society, as alluded to by Stevie Wonder.

Universal design is designing for all people, for all their life spans or abilities, without the need for adaptation or specialized design. *Universal design*, similar to *inclusive design*, is broader than just accessible design, as it emphasizes wider issues of social inclusion to make life easier, healthier, and user-friendly, and encourages social participation for all. *Inclusive design* can be thought of as design that accommodates the wide range of human diversity with respect to one's ability, language, gender, age, and culture.

Worldwide, there are many accessibility laws and codes used that establish the minimum requirements needed to protect disabled people from discrimination in the built environment, such as the American Disabilities Act and the British Equality Act. *Universal and inclusive design* goes well beyond just the minimum requirements of the law, to ensuring the usability and accessibility benefits all people with functional limitations and society as a whole. An example of *inclusive design* is the front entry to a business, museum, or hotel that accommodates everyone; whereas, in accessible design, a ramp entrance might be to the side and out of the way for all visitors but is accessible by code. The difference is that the focus of both *universal and inclusive design* is about designing for all people, and not about designing to the minimum requirements for disabled people. The U.S. Center for Universal Design at North Carolina State University stresses the following principles of universal design:

1. Equitable use.
2. Flexibility in use.
3. Simple and intuitive.
4. Perceptible information.
5. Tolerance for error.
6. Low physical effort.
7. Size and space for approach and use.

The British Standards Institute defines inclusive design as "the design of mainstream products and/or services that are accessible to, and usable by, as many people as reasonably possible." The European Commission supports the design philosophy of Design for All (DfA), which aims for the design of products, service, and systems to be used by as many people as possible without any need for adaptation.

Design for All is design for human diversity, social inclusion, and equality. —European Institute for Design and Disability

To the greatest extent possible, *universal and inclusive design* think-ing should be a constant process of supporting the self-reliance and social engagement of all people. In the whole building design process, sustainability and accessibility are interdependently linked; for exam-ple, with building site orientation, the passive design calls for optimizing solar orientation, while attention should also be given to an inclusive, accessible entry. Designing a building for lifetime equitable use by the largest diverse group of people is a big step toward sustainable design.

In Portland, Oregon the Bud Clark Commons, designed by Holst Architecture, is a socially inclusive and accessible facility serving the homeless with a diverse range of mental and physical abilities. The LEED Platinum project combines welcoming furnished housing studios, a tem-porary homeless shelter, and a walk-in community resource center pro-viding meals, a public courtyard, and health services (Figures 66, 54).

Figure 66 Bud Clark Commons universal design for homeless, Portland
Courtesy ©Holst Architecture

See also: **Integrated Design • Social Equity • Universal Design (*Theoryspeak*) • Whole Building Design**

Further sources: AIA; BSI; Center for Universal Design; Design Build-ings Wiki: Inclusive Design, www.designingbuildings.co.uk/wiki/Inclu sive_design; IDeA; WBDG; Wikipedia

▌Upcycling

We don't have an energy problem. We have a materials-in-the-wrong-place problem. —McDonough and Braungart, authors Cradle to Cradle, The Upcycle

We achieved our mission to the moon. Let's look home from that lofty perch and reimagine our mission on Earth —that is what we need to do here. Together, we can upcycle everything. The world will

be better for our positive visions and actions. —William McDonough, architect

Upcycling or creative reuse is the process of making higher quality products than the original. *Upcycling* traces back to 1994 with German automation manufacturer Reiner Pilz's use of the term *upcycling* referring to the potential of old products being given more value, not less (Yglesias 2012). The idea is later addressed in William McDonough and Michael Braungart's 2002 book, *Cradle to Cradle: Remaking the Way We Make Things* and is the primary focus of their 2013 book, *The Upcycle: Beyond sustainability—Designing for Abundance*. McDonough observes that if people design more intelligently, there will be no need for waste management and recycling because a good design provides a reuse cycle with no toxic process. The idea of *upcycling* calls for increasing positive footsteps by designing more efficiently, instead of decreasing the bad ones. The authors, McDonough and Braungart, explain the concept of a positive recycle, much like a tree, which absorbs carbon dioxide for its growth and in turn releases oxygen back to the environment for our growth.

The examples of *upcycling* remind us how natural energy such as wind power could be used in agriculture. McDonough and Braungart advocate maintaining soil health by using crop rotation to replenish soil nutrients, instead of planting one type of crop every year. While non-toxic is certainly better than toxic, the goal should be to go beyond non-toxic and identify and use sustainable, renewable materials. With this vocabulary, *upcycling* defines an efficient design, starting with a sustainable reuse cycle, and asking, "what's next?"

Cradle-to-Cradle is closely related to the idea of a "circular economy," which calls for production processes that include the useful and active reusable, sustainable life-cycle from the beginning to the end. MM

See also: **Circular Economy • Cradle-to-Cradle • Downcycling • Ecological Footprint • Ecological Rucksack • Materials and Resources • Zero Waste**

Further sources: Cradle-to-Cradle Products Innovation Institute; EBN; McDonough + Partners and Braungart (2002, 2013: 211); WBDG; Yglesias (2012)

Urban Design

Cities can be the engine of social equity and economic opportunity. They can help us reduce our carbon footprint and protect the global environment. That is why it is so important that we work together to build the capacity of mayors and all those concerned in planning and running sustainable cities. —Ban Ki-Moon, former UN Secretary-General

Urban design is defined as the process of designing cities, towns, and villages—or in other words, of organizing groups of buildings, neighborhoods, districts, streets, and public spaces—to make urban areas functional, attractive, and sustainable. Successful *urban design* requires an interdisciplinary approach involving such professionals as urban planners, architects, and civil and municipal engineers, as well as landscape architects to address functional problems and also social, economic and identity issues.

As urban centers continue to grow and urban density continues to increase, *urban design* poses itself as a discipline needed to solve technical and functional problems but also to create sustainable environments conducive to social interaction and to which people can positively identify. Notions of placemaking, environmental stewardship, social equity and economic viability are all part of a successful *urban design* process.

A superb example of great urban design is the Shanghai Natural Science Museum designed by Perkins+Will Architects, which uses the nautilus shell as a biomimetic inspiration of environmental stewardship. The museum creates special places promoting social interaction

Figure 67 Shanghai Natural Science Museum, China
Photo: ©James and Connor Steinkamp Photography. Courtesy Perkins+Will

that relate to the movement of Earth, water, and plants, while inviting urban dwellers to visit with linked urban connections to existing city pedestrian and vehicular circulation patterns as seen in the aerial view. (Figures 67, 8, 39).

Principles of modern *urban design* in Europe are associated with the Renaissance and the Age of Enlightenment and followed by the Garden City Movement initiated by Ebenezer Howard in England. The concept of garden cities came as one of the responses to the degradation of the urban environment following the economic development of the Industrial Revolution.

The widespread use and ownership of automobile contributed to the development of a different model of *urban design* in the 20th century and certainly created a rift from previous historical models. As opposed to the long tradition of mixed-use urban centers, the 20th century saw the emergence of new zoning laws assigning separate spaces for dwellings, services, commerce, and cultural and outdoor activities. This planning trend led to suburban developments requiring vast amounts of land and extensive infrastructure systems, which have raised critical sustainability issues as well as social and health concerns.

Following several decades of zoning laws based on a clear separation of human activities within a city, current movements of *urban design* are aiming at creating mixed-use models to physically and socially engage citizens within their cities. From Aldo Rossi's concept of Historicism and Collective Memory to Peter Calthorpe's manifesto for sustainable urban living and the *Charter for New Urbanism*, the past thirty years have seen a renewed interest in *urban design* as a means to create more livable and sustainable cities. OC

See also: **Community Connectivity • Compact City (*Archispeak*)
• Context (*Archispeak*) • Dense (*Archispeak*) • Livable Streets •
Location and Transportation • New Urbanism • Porosity (*Archispeak*)
• Smart Growth • Urbanism (*Theoryspeak*)**

Further sources: Boyer (1994); Charter of the New Urbanism; Rossi (1982); Venturi, Brown, and Izenour (1972); Howard (1965); Calthorpe (1993)

Urban Heat Island
The soil under the grass is dreaming of a young forest, and under the pavement, the soil is dreaming of grass. —Wendell Berry, *Given*

Large cities in the U.S. (tend) to be warming at more than twice the rate of the planet as a whole as a result of the loss of naturally vegetated land cover. —Brian Stone, *The City and the Coming Climate*

As urban and suburban areas are developed, the construction of buildings, roads, and other hardscapes replace the former natural open or vegetated land. These once permeable areas then become impermeable, with dense concentrations of hard surfaces that absorb and retain thermal heat, whereas Wendell Berry so poetically expresses, "under the pavement, the soil is dreaming of grass." These massive hard surfaces contribute to *urban heat island (UHI)* effect, where the developed areas experience warmer temperatures than their outlying rural surroundings due to the loss of vegetated land cover. These warmer temperatures increase air conditioning energy costs, air pollution, and heat-related illnesses. With increasing climate change, this will lead to more frequent, extreme, and longer heat waves in summer months, which often affect the most vulnerable populations first.

Two different aspects of *urban heat island* effect, both the surface and the atmospheric, are considered. Surfaces heated by the sun in summer, such as roofs and pavements, can be 50–90°F (27–50°C) hotter than the air, while rural surroundings, usually moist or shaded, stay close to air temperature. Atmospheric *urban heat islands* refer to air that is warmer in urban areas compared to the cooler air of rural surroundings. Atmospheric *urban heat islands* are hotter after sunset than throughout the day, due to the slow release of heat from the built infrastructure. The hotter surface temperatures of densely built-up areas, as well as the cooler surfaces of parks and green spaces, both contribute to urban atmospheric temperatures.

Most *urban heat island* effect is due to the pervasiveness of dark roofs, dark-colored pavement, and the decreasing existence of vegetation. Another is the sensible heat from tailpipes and chimneys. Several factors can be addressed with current technologies, such as using vegetative cover and materials with reflective surface properties. Tree canopies, green roofs, and using natural vegetative surfaces deflect radiation from the sun and with evotranspiration, release cooling moisture into the air which dissipates the surrounding heat. Cool roofs, surfaces with high albedo, and shading devices such as fabric architecture can help by shading building and site surfaces, as shown in the Riyadh, Saudi Arabia KAPSARC Housing's shading canopies designed by HOK (Figures 68, 65).

Figure 68 KAPSARC Housing fabric shading canopies, Saudi Arabia
Photo: ©Alan Karchmer, Courtesy ©HOK

Green roofs are a great *heat island* reduction strategy as they provide both direct and ambient cooling, improve air quality, and absorb
pollutants. Cool roofs use white reflective coatings or surfaces, such as
vinyl, to reflect at least 75% of the sun's rays, while light-colored concrete can be used for pavement, reflecting up to 50% more light than
asphalt. These *UHI* strategies can result in benefits in reducing surface
and air temperatures, air pollution, greenhouse gas emissions, and
energy costs to cool buildings, while also providing scale and beauty
with vegetation.

See also: **Albedo • Cool Roofs • Green Roofs • Solar Reflectance
Index • Urban Tree Canopy • Vegetated Walls**

Further sources: Stone (2012: 93–95); US EPA Urban Heat Island Program

Urban Tree Canopy

**The Urban Tree Canopy is the layer of leaves, branches, and stems
of trees that cover the ground when viewed from above.** —Center for
Watershed Protection

**Harmony with land is like harmony with a friend; you cannot cherish
his right hand and chop off his left.** —Aldo Leopold, *Round River*

The loss of *urban tree canopies* in the major cities has been one of the
contributing factors to the summer urban heat island effect, where city
temperatures according to the U.S. Environmental Protection Agency
can be 1.8–5.4°F hotter than out in the green suburban areas surrounding the city. The urban heat island effect is caused by the solar heat
absorption of paved surfaces and dark roofs, industrial and vehicle heat
production, and the lack of permeable surfaces and vegetation for cooling and shade in urban areas.

Creating "cooling micro-climates" for urban cooling to combat
urban heat islands within a city can be achieved with planting vegetative materials, especially shade trees, to form *urban tree canopies
(UTC)*. Shade trees along streets, roads, sidewalks, and within parking
lots can be an effective strategy to combat urban heat islands. Vegetation provides many mitigation benefits against the environmental
impacts felt in cities. Trees provide cooling shade, the cooling and
moisture of evapotranspiration, carbon sequestration, stormwater
management, pollution filtering, soil retention, water retention, species habitat, edible fruit and nuts, flowers, and the delightful filtered
dappled light.

Vegetation can help absorb unwanted sounds in the city, soften hard
urban spaces, and give a biophilic connection to nature. Green roofs,
vegetated walls, fountains, and pools can also provide cooling and connections to nature, but require much more maintenance and are not as
cost-effective. Some climates are not able to maintain living trees and
use fabric shading devices used much like a tree canopy to shade the
ground or building surfaces (Figure 68).

Carefully sited shade trees and vegetation can block solar radiation,
not only to roads and sidewalks, but also minimize heat gain to building

interiors and reducing air conditioning demands. Trees should typically shade the east, and most importantly the west walls to increase cooling energy savings. Deciduous trees work well in balancing the energy requirements throughout the year, with summer foliage blocking solar radiation, and in winter the leafless trees let solar rays pass through to warm the building.

Many major cities, such as Melbourne, Australia, and Atlanta and Seattle in the U.S. have lost a significant part of their *urban tree canopy* and like many cities worldwide have adopted aggressive tree plantings to achieve tree canopy goals. Planting urban trees is part of a global reforestation effort, not only for carbon sequestration but also to deal with increasing city temperatures due to urbanization and climate change.

See also: **Biophilic Design • Ecological Design • Green Roofs • Stormwater Management • Urban Heat Island • Vegetated Walls**

Further sources: Center for Watershed Protection; Global Cool Cities; Leopold (1993: 145–146); US EPA Urban Heat Island Effect, www.epa.gov/heat-islands

Value Engineering   ▮

**Value engineering is used to solve problems and identify and
eliminate any unwanted costs, while improving function and quality.**
—Design Buildings Wiki

Broadly speaking, *value engineering* refers to an examination process
which seeks to create value by assessing how a certain function can
still be fulfilled but at a lower cost. In the realm of architecture and
construction, a *value engineering* process looks at how the primary
functions of a project can be preserved while costs saving strategies
are being pursued. *Value engineering* focuses primarily on alternative
solutions to existing functions to lower overall cost. During the design
phase of an architectural project, *value engineering* usually provides
alternative design solutions and material options to reduce mostly
construction costs while attempting to maintain project scope and
quality.

In the field of architecture, unlike other sectors such as product
design where *value engineering* is systematically part of the design process, such a cost-driven process is usually triggered by preliminary
cost estimates. Whether the delivery method of a project is Design-Bid-
Build or Construction Management, *value engineering* is typically considered when projected costs do not align with planned budgets.

Value engineering has been widely embraced by the building industry
on both the design and construction side as architects and construction companies need to deliver buildings in construction markets, which
can widely fluctuate. *Value engineering* is especially relevant in circum-
stances when costs are rising while clients' needs and expectations
remain unchanged.

The basic premise of *value engineering* is to apply creative thinking
and design ideas to achieve cost savings without negatively impacting
the overall quality of a project. In situations where the expected cost
savings are substantial, this does affect the ability of value engineering to remain true to its original definition. It is typically unrealistic
to expect to achieve significant savings without impacting a project's
scope and quality. Though in theory *value engineering* was conceived as
a creative exercise which generates value, significant cost savings also
can have an impact on the quantity and quality of material and environmental resources.

Though it may be challenging in many situations when important
savings need to be achieved, *value engineering* remains a valuable process to improve cost-to-value ratio and overall efficiency. Some of the
positive outcomes of *value engineering* include a critical analysis of both
design and construction processes with regards to both building and
life-cycle costs, and the tendency to lead to better overall projects. OC

See also: **Building Information Modeling • Dematerialization • Design
Quality Assessment • Integrated Design • Life-Cycle Cost Analysis**

Further sources: Cooper (1997); Design Buildings Wiki; Mukhopayaya
(2009)

Vegetated Walls

A simple wall can become something poetic. —Patrick Blanc,
Botanist and green wall pioneer

**The gardens are the climatic lung of the building, the breathing
apparatus.** —Stefan Behnisch, architect

A *vegetated wall*, also known as a living wall or green wall, incorporates plants into the building design by covering the outside façades or
inside building walls with vegetation. *Vegetated walls*, as with all plants,
can improve both outside and indoor air quality by filtering out airborne
chemical pollutants and taking in volatile organic compounds and par-
ticulate matter. The *vegetated walls* that move from inside to outside in
the Bosch Siemens Centre, by William McDonough + Partners, Architects, (Figures 69, 12), as well as the vegetated wall on the Shanghai
Natural History Museum, by Perkins+Will Architects, (Figure 39), provide the benefits of cleaning the air, sequestering carbon dioxide and
providing a biophilic connection to nature. Stefan Behnisch refers to
these plants and gardens as the "climatic lungs of the building" in the
design for the Genzyme Center, by Behnisch Architekten (Figure 20).
Green walls are increasingly getting credit for their ecological, physiological, and societal benefits with evolving new building mandates
encouraging green vegetated surfaces for the health and well-being of
humans, species habitats, and the environment.

Figure 69 Vegetated walls outside and inside Bosch Siemens Centre, Netherlands
Photo: Van der Torren Fotografie. Courtesy ©William McDonough + Partners

The mainstreaming of green roofs and the increasing growth of interior *vegetated walls* has created greater confidence in designing exterior
planted façades. Façades are a building's most visible feature, and by
adding vegetation, new aspects of nature, texture, color, and seasonal
symbolism can be added, while creating poetry from a simple wall as

expressed by the green wall pioneer Patrick Blanc. Careful choice of orientation and plant species on buildings can provide breeding and nesting habitats, along with food sources for invertebrates, on which other insects and birds can feed, increasing biodiversity.

Depending on the type and density of the vegetated façade, the living plants can have a cooling effect on the outside temperature of the building by shading the building skin and can also cool through the transpiration of water vapor, therefore reducing the urban heat island effect. Vegetated façades can shield a building's cladding materials from the damaging effects of acid rain, ultraviolet rays, heavy driving rain, and hail, much like a green roof protects the roofing membrane. The plants and soil in a green wall system can provide sound insulation by absorbing and deflecting unwanted sound, both outside as a sound barrier, and inside by separating work areas. Continuous green walls can make a building an extension of the surrounding habitat if properly maintained, fertilized and irrigated.

Vegetated walls are thought to have a positive social and psychological impact on human well-being and productivity by reducing stress with the biophilic connection with nature. These positive human effects, however, can be difficult to separate from the pleasant conditions conducive to plant growth, such as daylighting, moderate temperatures, and humidity.

See also: **Biodiversity • Biophilic Design • Ecological Design • Green Roofs • Indoor Environmental Quality • Stormwater Management • Thermal Insulation • Urban Heat Island**

Further sources: Architecture Record; Building.Co.UK; EBN; WBDG

Figure 70 Vernacular-inspired Southwood Country Club, Tallahassee, FL
Courtesy ©Elliot Marshall Innes, P.A.

Vernacular Architecture

You could say that my aim is "to recover the place." The place is a result of nature and time; this is the most important aspect. I think my architecture is some kind of frame of nature. With it, we can experience nature more deeply and more intimately. —Kengo Kuma

[To mediate with] elements derived indirectly from the peculiarities of a particular place. —Kenneth Frampton, *Towards a Critical Regionalism* 1983

Vernacular architecture comes from the need to provide practical shelter against the weather, animals, and enemies. Closely tied to environmental design, *vernacular architecture* uses the practical adaptation of the ecology of a particular place, the unique aspects of the community culture, and the generations-honored building traditions, all surmised as the "peculiarities of a particular place" as quoted by Kenneth Frampton. The *vernacular architecture* around us defines the soothing and comforting spatial experience of most of our lives. Simple, durable, practical, the ability to repair, and reliance on available local resources are typical characteristics.

The act of building begins with the basic need for durable shelter, but then architectural design arises from a higher, elegant urge of reflecting and honoring one's place and heritage. Based on using natural materials in time-honored building techniques, as well as the importance of location and orientation, *vernacular* building traditions are based primarily on function. These functional needs are a response to a particular way of life, often passed from generation to generation, such as traditions of farming, nomadic herding, and fishing.

I think of architecture as a piece of clothing to wrap around human beings. —Toyo Ito, architect

The greatest sheltering factor in *vernacular architecture* was in building for the extremes of climate, which Toyo Ito poetically calls a "piece of clothing to wrap around human beings," while also protecting the all-important hearth fire. Construction was determined by the closeness, availability, and adaptability of materials. Roofs needed to respond to solar radiation, temperature swings, the wind, snow and rainfall. In wet temperate and cooler areas, steep slopes are used, with long sloping overhangs keeping rainwater off the walls. In hot, dry areas, flat roofs captured the occasional rainfall, and thick walls were needed for thermal lag insulation depth to absorb solar heat gain before the heat can reach the dwelling area inside. The thicker the wall, the greater the thermal lag to retain the heat from the fire, as well as to keep the buildings cool in the summer.

In the hot and humid American South, the *vernacular* design of the raised "dog trot" house allowed for ventilation underneath and through the open center, allowing for heat to be ventilated away. The wealthy homeowners in the American Antebellum South had raised, deep porches all around, tall operable windows for ventilation, shutters for shading, and operable cupolas allowing heat to escape at the top using stack ventilation. Mediterranean-style farmhouses were designed to cope with the scorching weather with massively thick walls and roofs, while building for site drainage and availability of water.

Vernacular architecture has its expressions today in many of the passive design strategies incorporated into sustainable design. Kengo Kuma, the Japanese architect and prolific writer, expresses that his aim is to experience nature more intimately by designing to "recover the place," a "result of nature and time." Glenn Murcutt, the Australian Pritzker Prize-winning architect, has designed many innovative, *vernacular*-inspired, and environmentally sensitive buildings having an enormous influence worldwide. As quoted by Kenneth Frampton, Murcutt said he is interested in buildings that "adapt to changes in climate conditions according to the seasons, buildings capable of responding to our physical and psychological needs in the way that clothing does." His approach of "touch the earth lightly" is seen as a way to nurture well-balanced, adjustable buildings that work with and complement the surrounding landscape.

See also: **Climate Responsive Design • Context (*Archispeak*) • Daylighting • Natural Ventilation • Passive Design • Precedent (*Archispeak*) • Stack Ventilation • Vernacular (*Archispeak*)**

Further sources: Frampton (2002: 1); Ryan (2011: 9)

Volatile Organic Compounds   **I**

Any organic (carbon-containing) compound that evaporates readily into the atmosphere at room temperature. —GreenFacts.org

Organic compounds are chemicals containing carbon and hydrogen atoms and are found in all living things. *Volatile organic compounds (VOCs)* are organic chemical compounds that can evaporate into the indoor air under normal temperature conditions from materials such as plant-based, natural, engineered, or from animals. Along with carbon, they contain elements such as hydrogen, oxygen, fluorine, chlorine, bromine, sulfur, or nitrogen. Long-term exposure to high concentrations of some *VOCs* has been linked to chronic health problems, such as asthma, pulmonary disease, liver and kidney damage, and cancer. Reactions such as irritation of the eyes, nose, and throat and headaches can be caused by even short-term exposure or inhalation.

Some *volatile organic compounds* occur naturally in our environment, but higher concentrations are often found indoors due to inadequate ventilation, and *VOC* emissions from building materials and furnishings. Buildings are constructed almost entirely of materials that are synthetic, chemically processed or treated. The EPA estimates we spend 90% of our time indoors, potentially breathing these hazardous chemical emissions from the wall, floor, and ceiling interior finishes, as well as thermal and acoustic insulation and furniture.

Volatile organic compounds can often be hazardous air pollutants, and when evaporating in outdoor air and combine with nitrogen oxide (NO_2), the reaction forms ground-level ozone, or smog, which contributes to climate change. Nitrogen oxide is in agricultural fertilizers and can result from fossil fuel combustion in vehicles and coal-fired power plants. Examples of *VOCs* are gasoline, benzene, air fresheners, aerosols and dry cleaning solvents, and formaldehyde, which is a strong toxic respiratory irritant and carcinogen found in many built environment products.

Semi-volatile organic compounds (SVOCs) are a subgroup of *VOCs* that have a higher molecular weight such as plasticizers, flame retardants, and pesticides. The concentration of *VOCs* in the air is measured in parts per million, so if the concentration is 1 ppm then for every million molecules of air, there is one molecule of the *VOC*. The term *total volatile organic compound (TVOC)* is used in reporting the total concentration of multiple airborne *VOCs* present in the air. In a building with high levels of heat and moisture, the conditions and nutrients can cause the growth of molds and bacteria, which produce *microbial volatile organic compounds (MVOCs)*.

Source control is the best means of managing indoor air pollution from products such as flooring, furniture, paints, sealants, and adhesives, cleaning products, wall coverings, office equipment, wood products and insulation. On-site wet-applied paints, adhesives, and sealants can directly impact the health of installers through skin and inhalation exposure. Wet-applied materials in a factory-controlled setting are usually used with worker and environmental protections.

Building-related organizations have produced standards for material health transparency of products, such as Greenguard, FloorScore, GreenScreen, Cradle-to-Cradle, Green Label for carpets and Green Seal for paints, among others. Specifying low-emitting and non-emitting materials, while also maintaining quality indoor air conditions to prevent *MVOC* growth, can significantly reduce exposure to these contaminants, especially to the young who are the most vulnerable.

See also: **Environment Product Declaration • Green Building Certification Systems • GreenScreen • Health Product Declaration • Indoor Environmental Quality • Natural Ventilation • Sick Building Syndrome • WELL Building Standard**

Further sources: EBN; EiR; EPA; Iyengar (2015: 222); Kibert (2016: 425); NIH; Robertson (2104: 140); Tox Town; US EPA; WBDG

Waste Reduction   ▮

The Earth, our home, is beginning to look more and more like an immense pile of filth. In many parts of the planet, the elderly lament that once beautiful landscapes are now covered with rubbish. —Pope Francis, *Laudato Si'*

Material use around the world is the foundation of the economy, and its use influences energy consumption, growth, and climate change. Growing populations, economies, and technologies also convert directly into increased energy, water, and material consumption. Waste materials that are no longer needed have for centuries been discarded to the world's landfills, which are now filled with billions of tons of waste and recyclable resources, such as glass, aluminum, scrap metals, and rare Earth materials. In a blunt passage of his *Laudato Si': On Care for Our Common Home*, Pope Francis strongly voiced that "our Earth, our home," is becoming "an immense pile of filth." Each year people dump at least 1.6 billion tons of material waste that must go "somewhere" as Annie Leonard explains in her book *The Story of Stuff*. Recycling efforts have increased, but with a post-consumer process, most products are downcycled into lesser quality items.

There is no such thing as "away", when we throw anything away it must go somewhere. —Annie Leonard, The Story of Stuff

Worldwide, countries are adopting *waste reduction* regulations, such as the U.S. Waste Avoidance and Resource Recovery Act, and the E.U. Circular Economy Package. By 2030, the Package targets recycling 65% of municipal waste and 75% of packaging waste, by promoting product reuse and industrial symbiosis, where one industry's byproduct becomes another industry's raw material or "industrial nutrient." The International Business Center of Sustainable Development (IBCSD) promotes Industrial Upcycling (IU) by using the "6R" principles of Recognize, Reconsider, Realize, Reduce, Reuse, and Recycle.

Other waste management hierarchies also use priorities for the efficient use of resources by preventing or reducing waste generated by households, industry, and governments; resource recovery by reusing, recycling, reprocessing, and energy recovery; and disposal using environmentally responsible methods. The "3Rs" mantra of Reduce, Reuse, and Recycle is expanded in the U.S. EPA's waste hierarchy, listed from the most favorable to least favorable:

1. Prevention.
2. Minimization.
3. Reuse.
4. Recycling.
5. Energy recovery.
6. Disposal.

Preventing or avoiding waste can be achieved by just not producing a product in the first place, as with plastic trash bags, or to make a product more efficient and durable. Minimizing waste can be achieved by increasing efficiency of the manufacturing process, especially industrial and chemical practices. Reusing products prevents the extraction of virgin resources to produce new products. Reusing part of a product to re-purpose at a higher or equal value is referred to as "upcycling." Recycling is breaking down a product into its raw materials before making into different products, usually downcycled with a lower value. Energy recovery captures the energy of waste materials by burning to generate electricity or heat. Offsetting the use of fossil fuels, energy recovery also avoids landfill methane emissions, but care must be taken to prevent other pollutant emissions, such as dioxins and sulfur-containing products. As Eric Lombardi voices from Eco-Cycle, disposal is the last resort, as discarded materials become lost resource opportunities, emit greenhouse gases, and often can take thousands of years to break down.

Landfills are like black holes, where resources go in and never come out. —Eric Lombardi, Eco-Cycle International

See also: **Circular Economy • Construction Waste Management • Cradle-to-Cradle • Downcycling • Energy Recovery • Upcycling • Zero Waste**

Further sources: IBCSD; Leonard (2010); Naam (2013: 152); US EPA; WARR

▌Water Efficiency

When you put your hand in a flowing stream, you touch the last that has gone before and the first of what is still to come. —Leonardo da Vinci

It takes 1,000 tons of water to produce 1 ton of grain. As water becomes scarce and countries are forced to divert irrigation water to cities and industry, they will import more grain. As they do so, water scarcity will be transmitted across national borders via the grain trade. Aquifer depletion is a largely invisible threat, but that does not make it any less real. —Lester Brown, *Vital Signs* 1999

Water is our most precious resource, the "soul" of the Earth. The same water has been around for millions of years as alluded to by Leonardo da Vinci in touching the past and the future. Water is needed for human life, our health, agriculture, industry, and energy production. The conservation, efficiency and reuse of water are critical as only 3% of the planet's water is freshwater, and over two-thirds of this is frozen in glaciers. Over the last fifty years, freshwater withdrawals have tripled, and estimates are that by 2030 global demand will be even 40% higher than today and consumed faster than it can be replenished.

With major shifts in precipitation patterns and frequency due to climate change, and with urbanization, massive pollution, lack of adequate wastewater treatment, and the increasing demand for clean water, by 2030 most of the world will face water stress and scarcity. According to the World Health Organization's World Water Day Report, more than one billion people worldwide currently lack access to safe drinking water, and over two million die each year from waterborne illnesses. At the same time, in the developed world, water is taken for granted with energy-intensive municipal systems that allow ready access to precious clean water with the turn of a tap or flushing toilets. Increases in water use have resulted in significant biodiversity loss, and negatively affected rivers and aquifers, with over half of the world's wetlands disappearing over the last century.

About 70% of water costs are tied to the energy-intensive cleaning and transporting of water. The average American household uses over three hundred gallons of water per day, which is about 110,000 gallons of water a year. In the U.S., almost half of the water extracted is used for thermoelectric power generation, agricultural irrigation uses about another third, and buildings account for about 12% of water consumption. As Lester Brown informs us in *Vital Signs*, the water intensity of grain is enormous. Foreign countries are already exporting huge amounts of water in the form of grain from the U.S. and this will only escalate as water scarcity increases.

The core sustainable design strategies to reduce clean water requirements are through reduction, reclamation, recycling, and reuse. When water consumption is reduced, the entire water infrastructure impacts are minimized by less groundwater pumping, reduced wastewater chemical treatment, and distribution. Efficient design can easily reduce water consumption by over 50% by incorporating irrigation-less native landscapes, water-efficient fixtures, waterless urinals and toilets, rainwater harvesting, and reusing greywater for non-potable water needs, such as for cooling tower use, toilet flushing, or irrigation.

The exemplar design for the LEED Platinum Chesapeake Bay Brock Environmental Center by SmithGroupJJR Architects achieved the rigorous Living Building Challenge certification by being net-positive water, waste, and energy. The Brock Environmental Center received one of the first federal commercial permits for drinking filtered and treated rainwater. Composting toilets reduce the demand for water, and greywater from sinks and showers and excess roof runoff is piped to an above sea level greywater rain garden that naturally filters and allows infiltration (Figures 71, 7, 56).

Green building certifications, such as LEED, Green Globes, and Living Building Challenge (net-zero water use), require water conservation, water quality protection, and the protection of local and regional natural hydrological cycles. The LEED *Water Efficiency (WE)* category addresses indoor water consumption in fixtures and equipment; outdoor irrigation water; and water metering. EPA's WaterSense labeling helps consumers select water-conserving fixtures. In designing for *water efficiency* in green buildings, the goal should be to get the most efficient use from the least amount of water and with the smallest environmental impact.

See also: **Green Globes Certification • Greywater • LEED Building Certification • Living Building Challenge • Rainwater Harvesting • Reclaimed Water • WaterSense**

Further sources: Brown, Renner, and Halweil (1999: 19); Brown (2011); EBN; USGBC; Wikipedia; WHO World Water Day Report, www.who.int/ water_sanitation_health/takingcharge.html; WWC; WBDG

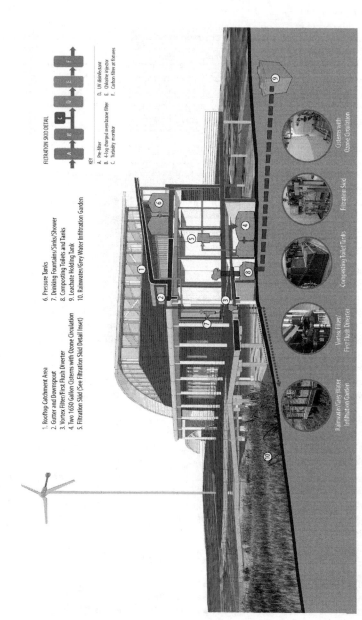

FILTRATION SKID DETAIL

KEY

A. Pre-filter
B. 4-log charged membrane filter
C. Turbidity monitor

D. UV disinfectant
E. Chlorine injector
F. Carbon filter at fixtures

1. Rooftop Catchment Area
2. Gutter and Downspout
3. Vortex Filter/First Flush Diverter
4. Two 1650 Gallon Cisterns with Ozone Circulation
5. Filtration Skid (See Filtration Skid Detail Inset)

6. Pressure Tanks
7. Drinking Fountains/Sinks/Shower
8. Composting Toilets and Tanks
9. Leachate Holding Tank
10. Rainwater/Grey Water Infiltration Garden

Rainwater/Grey Water
Infiltration Garden

Vortex Filter/
First Flush Diverter

Composting Toilet Tanks

Filtration Skid

Cisterns with
Ozone Circulation

Figure 71 Chesapeake Bay Brock Environmental Center water diagram
Courtesy ©SmithGroupJJR

Water Sourced Heat Pumps   ▮

**Water sourced heat pumps use the constant temperature of the
water as a medium for exchange instead of extracting the heat from
the outside air.** —Renewable Energy Hub

Water sourced heat pumps take advantage of the relatively consistent
geothermal temperatures found in a body of water below the surface.
These heat pumps work on the same principle as ground sourced or air
sourced heat pumps, by using the thermal storage capacity of water to
heat or cool by using a series of flexible pipes submerged into a lake,
river, or stream to deposit or extract low-intensity heat. A heat pump
pushes the refrigerant working fluid through the series of pipes, and
the fluid absorbs or releases the heat into the surrounding water as it
moves. The system has a water-sourced heat exchanger, a heat pump,
and some means to distribute the heat or cool.

Water sourced heat pumps work by extracting heat from one place
and releasing the heat into another location. In the cooling mode, a
refrigerant is used to absorb the heat from indoors, either from radiant
flooring, radiant ceiling tubing or radiators, and then moves through a
mechanical compressor that squeezes the heat out of the refrigerant
again. This heat is released to the water body rather than to the already
hot outside air. When the heat pump is in the heating mode, the process
is reversed. The heat can also be plumbed to supplement the hot water
system. Once the heat exchanger removes the heat from the refrigerant, the fluid is once again pumped back through the tubing to continue
the cycle again.

A *water sourced heat pump* system is more efficient than a ground
sourced heat pump system as the heat transfer rate is higher with
water than with earth. If the water source is a moving body of water,
then the heat or cool is always being replaced as new water moves
along to replace the water that has already exchanged heat with the
system's working fluid.

See also: **Energy Efficiency • Ground Sourced Heat Pumps**

Further sources: Geothermal Energy Association; Geothermal Exchange
Organization; Renewable Energy Hub; Sustainable Sources; US DOE

Water-Energy Nexus   ▮

**Anything else you're interested in is not going to happen if you
can't breathe the air and drink the water. Don't sit this one out. Do
something. You are by accident of fate alive at an absolutely critical
moment in the history of our planet.** —Carl Sagan

Water and energy systems are tightly interconnected, primarily due to
the energy needed to treat and distribute water, and the properties of
water that are used in producing energy. This *water-energy nexus* or
interconnection is also referred to as "watergy" in describing the strong
link between energy and water in municipal water systems. Energy is

needed to extract, convey and distribute good quality water for many of people's needs, and then again to treat the discarded wastewater before returning to the environment.

The energy sector uses enormous amounts of freshwater withdrawals for thermoelectric cooling, energy mineral mining and extraction, emissions control, and fuel processing. Most power plants generate their power by boiling water to produce steam that then spins turbines to produce electricity. Significant amounts of water are then needed to cool that steam. Fuel production also requires extensive water amounts for mining coal, natural gas extraction, or growing biofuel crops. Natural gas may need as little as three gallons of water to produce one million BTUs, while agriculturally based ethanol fuel might require as much as twenty-nine thousand gallons of water for the same energy. The quality and temperature of water can be affected by fracking, hydroelectric power, or drainage from coal and uranium mining operations.

The growing renewable energy technologies, such as wind and solar photovoltaics, require very little water. Rainfall patterns are already variable due to climate change, and dry areas are expected to become even drier in the future. When available water supplies shrink in the future, energy production's water needs will conflict with human drinking water needs and agriculture demands. China, which is coal rich and water poor in some areas, is currently working to reduce the water intensity of its coal-fired power plants.

Water has two unique qualities that make it very energy intensive. One, water has a high heat capacity, so it requires a lot of energy to raise its temperature, not only for domestic or industrial hot water heating but also to produce steam for electricity generation. Second, water is heavy and requires significant energy to pump long distances, especially to higher elevations and over mountains. This is especially true in places where water is scarce, and populations are spread out, as in the U.S. Southwest and California.

The Josey Pavilion of the Dixon Water Foundation in Texas is an education/meeting center that promotes healthy watersheds through sustainable land management and showcases the bioclimatic and environmental strategies related to water and energy use. Rainwater harvested from the roof is used for sewage conveyance and a constructed wetland cleans and returns all water used in the pavilion to the aquifer (Figure 72).

According to the World Energy Outlook, the global energy consumption needed for water supply is projected to double by 2040, with the largest increase coming for desalination. Qatar, which is fossil fuel rich and water poor, is relying more and more on desalinated water for drinking, and increasingly using renewable energy sources for water.

We are "at an absolutely critical moment in the history of our planet," as Carl Sagan so passionately states, "Don't sit this one out. Do something." For a sustainable water future, we must first acknowledge this vital intrinsic *water-energy nexus*, and then we must save water to save energy, and save energy to save water.

See also: **Climate Change • Energy Efficiency • Synergy (*Archispeak*) • Water Efficiency**

Further sources: EBN; EPA; DOE; WEO

BIOCLIMATIC & ECOLOGICAL STRATEGIES

STRATEGIES INCLUDE:

1. Slotted wood doors can be opened to allow maximum ventilation through the central gathering space and along the porches, which are oriented to capture the cooling summer breezes from the southeast.

2. Glass pivot doors on the east and west of the pavilion can be adjusted to allow for the southeast corner to be entirely open and maximize the impact of cooling breezes in the space.

3. The cupola perched on top of the roof not only provides daylight for the space, but also utilizes the negative pressure resulting from the breezes gliding over the roof, which helps draw the hot air out of the pavilion and increases the velocity of the air moving through the space.

4. The building fully supports a deeper understanding of rangeland conservation and the important collateral benefits, including carbon sequestration and water, energy, and ecosystems balance.

5. The large ceiling fans in the space supplement the natural ventilation and help keep occupants cool when the breeze is not sufficient.

6. The photovoltaic panels are mounted on the south facing roof and produce more energy than is needed to operate the building, making this a net positive project.

7. As part of the building's water treatment and purification system, the rainwater collected in a 13,000 gallon storage tank provides for 100% of non-potable uses.

Figure 72 Josey Pavilion of Dixon Water Foundation, Decatur, TX
Photo: Casey Dunn. Courtesy ©Lake|Flato Architects

WaterSense

Water is life's matter and matrix, mother and medium. There is no life without water. —Albert Szent-Gyorgyi, MD, Nobel Prize winner

Managing water is a global concern as many communities face increasing demands on water supply and infrastructure. In 60% of European cities with more than a hundred thousand people, according to the European Environmental Agency, groundwater is being used faster than it can be replenished. Buildings in the U.S. account for 13.6% of potable water consumption.

In 2006, the U.S. Environmental Protection Agency (EPA) created *WaterSense*, seeking to preserve the future of water and protect the environment. *WaterSense* helps customers use less water by promoting water-efficient labeled products to conserve water. After a manufacturer's product meets the EPA specifications and third-party water efficiency testing, the product is awarded the *WaterSense* label. Americans use an average of a hundred gallons of water a day at home and can reduce their water consumption by 30% by installing water-efficient fixtures and appliances.

WaterSense labeled products must show water efficiency by achieving at least 20% less water than EPA's water use baseline, achieve national water savings, provide measurable results, and perform as well or better than similar products. The *WaterSense* label can be on many types of equipment, such as toilets, faucets, showerheads, flushing urinals, pre-rinse spray valves, cooling towers, chilled water systems, and landscape irrigation systems. *WaterSense* can label new water-efficient homes, provide facility water management guidance, and professional certification programs. The *WaterSense Water Budget Tool* and website has regional climate data for irrigation and efficient water strategies. The *WaterSense* tools are used in green rating systems, such as USGBC's LEED, in measuring indoor and outdoor water use in the Sustainable Sites and Water Efficiency categories.

Water and energy are interdependent in the water-energy nexus. In the U.S., 4% of energy is used to extract, convey, and deliver water, and then treat wastewater before its return to the environment. The U.S. energy sector uses 27% of non-agricultural water. Reducing water use in commercial and institutional facilities is cost-effective, as it also reduces the energy and operating costs of storage, heating and water movement throughout the building. Water reductions at the consumer-end relieve the burdens on the associated water supply and wastewater utility infrastructure. As the Nobel Prize winner—and discoverer of Vitamin C—Dr. Szent-Gyorgyi poignantly expresses our precious water is "mother and medium," and "there is no life without water," so we must ensure a clean and sustainable water supply for future generations.

See also: **Water Efficiency • Water-Energy Nexus**

Further sources: Alliance for Water Efficiency; Climate Protection Partnership 2008; DOE; EBN; US EPA WaterSense; WEO; European Environmental Agency, The Problems of Water Stress 2016, www.eea.europa.eu/publications/92-9167-025-1/page003.html

WELL Building Standard   ▋

It is a curious thing to observe how almost all patients lie with their faces turned to the light, exactly as plants always make their way towards the light. —Florence Nightingale, 1860, Victorian nurse, social reformer

The way people learn, work, and live in the built environment can be influenced by design strategies and environmental factors, such as air quality, lighting quality, acoustic design, and control over one's surroundings. Studies have shown that buildings with good indoor environmental quality protect the health and comfort of building occupants, while also enhancing productivity, decreasing absenteeism, building value improvement, and reducing liability.

The *WELL Building Standard* is the world's first building standard directed exclusively on human health and wellness. *WELL* is a performance-based system that measures and monitors features of the built environment that impact the wellness of the occupants in the buildings, such as the importance of daylighting which in noted by the social activist and founder of modern nursing Florence Nightingale.

WELL focuses on seven categories of health and well-being in building performance: air, water, nourishment, light, fitness, comfort, and mind. Taking a holistic view, the *WELL Standard* incorporates alternative health concepts with promoting psychological and emotional well-being, along with physical health. In optimizing the environment, the science of wellness addresses the issues of sleep quality, respiratory health, cardiovascular health, and healthy weight and metabolism.

The sustainable building design and operations of *WELL* focus on responsible efficiencies in mechanical systems, air filtration, cleaning practices, lighting design, acoustics, and electromagnetic fields (EMF). The potential toxicity of building materials, particularly interior finishes and furnishings are addressed while also linking with Health Product Declarations and the Living Building Challenge's Red List of ingredients.

The *WELL Building Standard* is administered by the International WELL Building Institute (IWBI), alongside the Green Business Certification Inc. (GBCI), and is aligned with the BREEAM and LEED building rating systems.

See also: **Biophilic Design • Daylighting • Green Building Certification Systems • Indoor Environmental Quality • Natural Ventilation • Volatile Organic Compounds**

Further sources: BREEAM; EBN; IWBI; Kibert (2016: 462); USGBC

Whole Building Design   ▋

Synergy is the only word in our language that means behavior of whole systems, unpredicted by the separately observed behaviors of the system's parts. —Buckminster Fuller, architect, inventor

Architecture to me is whole. I cannot say I only care about this 25% and the other 75%. I let go . . . it's just I want to work the way I want to work. —Peter Zumthor, Swiss architect

Buildings today provide many more roles than just shelter. Buildings' roles are constantly changing in communication, productivity, culture, life support, community, health, and many other parts of life. The goal of high-performing buildings today is to integrate and optimize the energy and resource efficiency, durability, life-cycle performance, and occupant health and productivity. To do this, *whole building design*, often referred to as integrated design, is a process that sees the building as a system, not a collection of parts, much as architect Peter Zumthor sees the "whole."

The *whole building* approach involves interaction between the issues of site, materials, energy, air quality, and natural resources, as well as between the design team participants, owner, contractor, and community groups. The "synergy" of these issues, as Buckminster Fuller notes, as well as the strategies and life-cycle requirements, should be addressed early in the planning process, and throughout the entire building development.

An example of *whole building design* is the Chandler City Hall in Arizona, which is a community-government complex located in a historic downtown area that was in major disrepair with no public activity. Designed by SmithGroupJJR to revitalize the Chandler downtown area, the new city hall center brings identity to the community by gathering all departments together to promote future city-center development (Figure 73).

Figure 73 Chandler City Hall, Arizona
Photo: ©Bill Timmerman. Courtesy SmithGroupJJR

This interdisciplinary approach and decision-making allows for creative solutions, cost control, and better performance, and often creates opportunities for combining functions and benefits from a single design strategy. Planning workshops, or charrettes, occur early in the project with all involved disciplines and stakeholders. Life-cycle cost analysis—along with modeling, testing and evaluation of many building solutions—takes place to compare and analyze different proposed strategies. Simulation of issues such as water and energy efficiency, daylighting, and mechanical airflows can be modeled and analyzed to decide which is appropriate to achieve the desired performance levels.

Overall, some of the *whole building design* objectives that should be addressed by all disciplines are cost-effectiveness, functional operation, occupant productivity and health, security and safety, aesthetics, and the sustainable goals of energy efficiency, resource responsibility, and environmental friendliness.

See also: **Charrette • High-Performing Buildings • Integrated Design • Systems Thinking**

Further sources: EBN; Kibert (2016: 11); WBDG

Wind Energy   **I**

As yet, the wind is an untamed, and unharnessed force; and quite possibly one of the greatest discoveries hereafter to be made, will be the taming, and the harnessing of it. —Abraham Lincoln 1860, US President

The sun strikes our planet with about 160,000 terawatts of energy, and roughly 1–2% of that energy is transformed into wind. *Wind energy* has been harnessed for years to pump water, grind grains, and later supply electricity. Wind turbines work when the blades capture wind energy and rotate into mechanical energy, turning a gearbox increasing the rotating speed, and then spinning a generator to produce electricity.

Wind turbines are mounted on tall towers, usually over a hundred feet tall, to capture the faster and less turbulent winds. Computer simulation can graphically show the wind speed and direction with a "wind rose," providing insight into siting, orientation, and blade angle. A typical wind turbine starts generating power at speeds of 6–9 mph (3–4 mps), and shuts off to prevent equipment damage around 45 mph (20 mps).

Currently two main types of wind turbines are used, named for their orientation: horizontal axis and vertical axis. Horizontal axis turbines are more efficient and can range from 100W–5MW, and are used for offshore wind, onshore wind, electric utilities, and small wind applications. Vertical axis turbines are less efficient, and the central rotating shaft requires anchoring or guy wires to remain rigid, limiting the size and location. The innovative LEED Platinum design for the Method Manufacturing Facility by William McDonough + Partners, located on a Chicago brownfield has a refurbished 230-foot 600kW on-site wind turbine capturing *wind* energy that provides 30% of the factory's energy. Three solar trees over the parking rotate to track the sun and provide over 45.9 kW of energy each (Figure 74).

The UNEP 2016 Global Wind Energy Outlook report predicts that wind could supply 20% of global electricity by 2030, creating 2.4 million

Figure 74 Method Manufacturing Facility: South Side Soap Box, Chicago
Photo: Patsy McEnroe Photography. Courtesy ©William McDonough + Partners

new jobs, and reduce CO_2 emissions by 3.3 billion tons per year. To meet the Paris Agreement climate targets, the global electricity supply would need to be completely de-carbonized well before 2050, by using wind, solar, hydro, geothermal, and biomass.

Onshore *wind energy* is now one of the most competitive electricity sources available, delivering electricity as low as 4 U.S. cents per kWh. The International Renewable Energy Agency (IRENA) estimates that doubling current global renewable energies by 2030 would save up to $4.2 trillion dollars annually in avoiding air pollution and climate change expenditures.

In 2016, more than half of the E.U.'s installed capacity was in wind farms, surpassing coal as the E.U.'s second largest source of electricity generation. Germany led the 2016 wind installations, with France, the Netherlands, Finland, and Ireland all setting records for wind installations.

Worldwide, over a million people are employed by wind industries, and according to the U.S. Department of Labor, the fastest growing job in America is "wind turbine technician." Over $7.3 billion a year in public health benefits are saved by wind energy in eliminating harmful pollutant emissions. If renewables were doubled, up to four million lives could be saved by 2030.

A typical new wind turbine will avoid enough CO_2 emissions annually to equal the carbon emissions of nearly 900 cars, helping curtail the energy sector's two-thirds share of global greenhouse emissions. Coupled with efficient energy measures, the renewable energy industry can deliver half the emission reductions needed to keep temperature rise to below 2°C, using what President Lincoln presciently referred to over 150 years ago in his quote at the beginning of this chapter as one of the "greatest discoveries hereafter to be made."

See also: **Greenhouse Gases • Kyoto Protocol • Paris Climate Agreement • Renewable Energy**

Further sources: Danish Wind Industry Agency; IPCC; IRENA; UNEP

Wind Towers   ∎

A wind tower (wind catcher) is a traditional Persian architectural element to create natural ventilation in buildings. —Wikipedia

Wind towers are hollow masonry towers atop buildings that capture breezes and direct the collected air down into interior spaces. The towers are passive ventilation and cooling devices used in hot, arid climates. They are particularly applicable in dense urban settlements where ground-level wind cannot easily reach exterior windows to enter buildings.

Wind towers employ fluid dynamics principles to shape and guide airflow to enhance human comfort in built structures. *Wind towers*, or wind catchers, vary in design and complexity. Simple configurations have one air scoop opening at the top of the tower. This aperture is essentially a window aimed at the prevailing summer breeze direction. All tower designs are capped at the top to force air down the tower shaft. Airflow into the inhabited space below is promoted by exterior windows in the room that allows the incoming tower air to move through the space and escape to the outside. This air movement establishes ventilation in the room.

Where breeze direction varies, air scoop openings at the top of the tower may be multiple and oriented to capture air from all wind movements. The air-capturing windows in multi- scoop designs are operable to close apertures not facing the breeze.

In situations where rooms below *wind towers* have no exterior windows, the towers may have two air chambers. One shaft chamber guides breezes down into the space while the second chamber allows air to escape from the space and back to the outside. The exiting air escapes through an aperture at the top of the tower that faces away from the wind. This air entry-exit pattern establishes ventilation in the space.

In seasons with little breeze, *wind towers* may serve as solar chimneys to evacuate warm air from the space. Narrow horizontal slits in the space's exterior wall admit the lower, cooler outside air to replace the evacuated warmer air. For winter months, the tower's wind scoops are closed to prevent heated air in the building's rooms to be lost up the shaft.

Wind towers can passively cool a building by incorporating water features that reduce the circulating air temperature by evaporation. Cooling by evaporation is especially effective in dry, hot climates. The interior surfaces of the tower shaft wall may be kept damp using sumps, pumps, and nozzles at the top of the shaft. Porous mats that are kept moist can be placed over air scoop openings to evaporatively cool incoming air passing through the mats. In cases where there is a water reservoir below the floor of the occupied space, air brought down through the tower is guided over the reservoir to be cooled before entering the room through floor openings.

In larger buildings, several *wind towers* can be placed on the roof to meet the expanded ventilation/cooling needs. Modern wind catchers employ rotating weather vanes to orient scoop openings toward any breeze direction.

The King Abdullah University of Science and Technology (KAUST) in Thuwal, Saudi Arabia is a research university established to drive innovation in science and technology, and is the world's largest LEED Platinum project. It was designed by HOK to be a contemporary low-energy sustainable project while also rooted in local Saudi culture and traditions. The passive ventilation strategies of traditional Arabic houses influenced the designs of the two large solar-powered wind towers that harness energy from the sun and Red Sea winds to passively create airflow in the pedestrian walkways (Figures 75, 16, 43, 58). EW

Figure 75 Wind Tower at KAUST University, Saudi Arabia
Courtesy ©HOK

See also: **Natural Ventilation • Passive Design • Solar Chimney • Stack Ventilation**

Windows and Glazing   ∎

We no longer have an outside and an inside as two separate things. Now the outside may come inside, and the inside may and does go outside. They are of each other. —Frank Lloyd Wright, American architect

For thousands of years, glass has been used for daylighting and weather protection in buildings since the Romans first used glass windows in Alexandria in 100 CE. *Glazing* is when a transparent or translucent material, such as glass, covers an opening in a building's envelope. *Glazing* systems are essential to high-performing buildings by integrating daylighting, natural ventilation, and passive solar design.

Windows and glazing are an important connection between the controlled interior environment and the outdoor environment's dynamically changing daylight and weather patterns. Energy-efficient *window and glazing* systems have made recent technological advances in significant energy and pollution reductions with lower heat transfer and less air infiltration with surfaces that minimize condensation and improve thermal comfort. Building automation control systems can intelligently regulate natural ventilation and solar heat gain with operable windows, shading devices, and reflectivity.

The beautifully designed Genzyme Center, a LEED Platinum biotechnology headquarters by Behnisch Architekten, maximizes daylighting and views with eighteen indoor gardens and an integrated management system controlling thirty thousand automation points. On the outside glass walls, horizontal, reflective motorized blinds reflect light up to reflective ceiling panels to reflect the light through the inner glass deep into the spaces. One-third of the façade is a double façade with a

Figure 76 Genzyme Center, Cambridge, MA
Photo: Anton Grassl. ©Behnisch Architekten

four-foot externally ventilated void (Figure 76). Operable blinds in the void block and vent solar gain in summer, and in the winter the void is not ventilated with the blinds open creating a warm building buffer. The Genzyme Center, especially in the central atrium, seems to not have "an outside and an inside" and is truly what Frank Lloyd Wright referred to when he said, "Now the outside may come inside, and the inside may and does go outside. They are of each other" (Figure 20).

High-performing *windows* can feature double or triple glazing, transparent specialized coatings, panes sandwiching insulating gas, and building-integrated photovoltaics. Most architectural *glazing* is insulated glazing (ig) units whose characteristics usually specify the window U-value, the solar heat gain coefficient or shading coefficient, and the visible transmittance and the selection which must be integrated with the building's heating and cooling systems.

The thermal efficiency of *glazing* is measured by the air-to-air heat transmission due to thermal conductance between the indoor and outdoor temperatures. This conductance is measured in U-values, where lower U-values indicate less transfer of heat through the *glazing*. Computer thermal modeling for glazed assemblies, such as with THERM, can estimate total U-values to help predict thermal performances.

Glass can be tinted, fritted, and coated to regulate the light and heat. Low-emissivity (low-E) reflective coatings reduce the interior solar heat gain through the *glazing* by reflecting solar heat energy. The solar heat gain coefficient measures how much of the incoming sunlight's heat as long-wave radiation gets transmitted into the building versus how much is reflected.

Glazing, designed to let light in and views out, is measured by the percentage of visible light that passes through, called visible light transmittance (VT, T vis, or VLT). Zero is a measure of no light, and an empty opening would measure 100%. More daylight is not always better, as it can result in glare and solar heat gain.

Monolithic expanses of building glass can be deadly to bird populations. In the U.S. alone, it is estimated by the American Bird Conservancy that over a billion birds die by colliding with glass each year. Birds mistake the reflections of the sky in the glass as a continuation of the sky. Major cities are now developing bird-friendly design guidelines, such as strategies for reducing *glazing*, shading devices, screens, and changes in materials and texture.

See also: **Building Automated Control Systems • Building-Integrated Photovoltaics • Energy Efficiency • High-Performing Buildings • Passive Design • Passive Solar Heating • Shading Coefficient • Solar Heat Gain Coefficient**

Further sources: Autodesk; EBN; American Bird Conservancy: Glass Collisions, www.abcbirds.org/program/glass-collisions; Bergman (2012: 55); Hootman (2012: 209); Robertson (2014: 188)

Xeriscaping I

**A landscaping method developed especially for arid and semiarid
climates that utilizes water-conserving techniques.** —Merriam-
Webster

Water conservation is an important part of the ecological efficiency
of preserving our ecosystems, as pollutants, periodic droughts, and
increasing urbanization place greater demands on our limited water
resources. Past conventional landscaping, with extensive turf grass and
non-native plant species, is no longer practical when minimizing water
waste and consumption.

Xeriscaping is a landscaping strategy that requires minimal to no
water maintenance, and uses native or adapted drought-tolerant plant
species, such as sedums or succulents. The word *xeriscaping* is derived
from the Greek "xeros" and "scape," meaning dry and scene.

While both natural climatic happenings and also global climate
instability results in increasing severity and durations of water shortages, the Earth experiences intense droughts. Over fifty countries
experience moderate to severe droughts yearly, while many countries
are importing more than half their water needed to produce goods,
such as cotton or wheat, including the U.K., Norway, Austria, and the
Netherlands. In America, landscape irrigation is estimated by the Environmental Protection Agency to be nearly one-third of all residential
water use, totaling about 9 billion gallons a day. In 60% of European
cities with more than a hundred thousand people, groundwater is being
extracted at a faster rate than it can be replaced, resulting in rising
costs. Droughts can be exacerbated by wasteful water infrastructure
and a lack of appropriate management of water demands.

The adoption of natural or ecological landscaping practices using
local plants and little to no irrigation, such as *xeriscaping*, can save
massive amounts of water in both urban and suburban areas, resulting
in lower water bills and reduced maintenance. Plant selection should
be based on microclimate, topography, solar exposure, light intensity, water quality, and soil characteristics, such as soil pH, aeration,
mineral analysis, and drainage. Site development can alter many of
the natural characteristics of a site with infrastructure, parking lots,
retention ponds, and artificially shaded areas from buildings. Increasing the use of mulches, selecting drought-tolerant plants, and using
berms and windbreaks can reduce both water requirements and loss
from evaporation.

The Pacific Center Campus Development design in San Diego, California by BNIM Architects transformed an existing vehicle-oriented
development into a pedestrian-oriented campus that weaves together
native canyon and desert landscape ecosystems, along with stormwater management strategies (Figure 77).

The UN estimates a population growth of an additional 2.2 billion
people by 2050, mostly in developing countries that already suffer
water stress. Water demand will increase, become more costly, and
likely result in available water conflicts, so more ways must be found
to conserve and recycle this irreplaceable resource. As only 3% of the
world's water is fresh, and 2.5% of this is frozen, humanity must rely on

Figure 77 Pacific Center Campus Development, San Diego
Photo: ©Emily Hagopian Photography. Courtesy BNIM Architects

only 0.5% of the world's water for all of humanity's and Earth's ecosystems freshwater needs.

See also: **Biophilic Design • Naturescaping • Rainwater Harvesting • SITES Initiative • Stormwater Management • Sustainable Site Design • Water Efficiency • Water-Energy Nexus**

Further sources: EBN; EPA: Outdoor Water Use, www.epa.gov/sites/production/files/2017-03/documents/ws-factsheet-outdoor-water-use-in-the-us.pdf; Millennium Assessment; UN Water; UN Sustainable Development Goals: World Population, www.un.org/sustainabledevelopment/blog/2017/06/world-population-projected-to-reach-9-8-billion-in-2050-and-11-2-billion-in-2100-says-un/

Zero Waste   ∎

I only feel angry when I see waste. When I see people throwing away things we could use. —Mother Teresa, Nobel Peace Prize winning missionary nun

We're not talking here about eliminating waste. We're talking about eliminating the entire concept of waste. —William McDonough, *Cradle to Cradle*

Every day vast quantities of waste are created and disposed of in our progressively throwaway societies. Communities that have more end up wasting more, and then unjustly dispose their pollution in communities that have less, as Mother Teresa laments, seeing people throw away as waste what others could be using. As population grows, our natural resources become scarcer and waste pollution increases. The Earth is increasingly unable to absorb these growing wastes, chemicals, and toxins.

Waste paper is thought to be the U.S.'s largest export to China by volume. Huge cargo ships that bring products from China to the U.S. return with bales of waste paper, which are used for packaging products made in China. There is really "no away" when discarding wastes. Burying wastes generates toxic liquids that leach from landfills (leachate), and also produce methane gas, a more potent greenhouse gas than carbon dioxide. Incinerating or burning garbage destroys potential resources and pollutes the air.

The *Zero Waste* concept builds on the 3Rs of "Reduce, Reuse, and Recycle" in creating innovative strategies to: rebuild the soil with compost, protect public health by not burying or burning, turning wastes into biogas, and recovering recyclables for manufacturing new products. Bottle bills are a fundamental tenet of *Zero Waste*, where producers take on the extended recycling responsibility. *Zero Waste* is a resource management approach, where the stuff we send off to disposal gets reduced, and then eventually eliminated.

The U.S. Zero Waste Business Council (USZWBC) and the Green Building Certification Institute (GBCI) created a certification program to recognize businesses, cities, and counties that divert 90% of their discarded materials from landfills and incinerators. The Zero Waste International Alliance (ZWIA) website defines *Zero Waste* as a

goal that is ethical, efficient and visionary, to guide people in changing their lifestyles and practices to emulate sustainable natural cycles, where all discarded materials are designed to become resources for others to use. Zero Waste means designing and managing products and processes to systematically avoid and eliminate the volume and toxicity of waste and materials, conserve and recover all resources, and not burn or bury them. Implementing Zero Waste will eliminate all discharges to land, water or air that are a threat to planetary, human, animal, or plant health.

This means implementing what William McDonough, co-author of *Cradle to Cradle*, calls for in, "eliminating the entire concept of waste."

Cities and regions worldwide have adopted *Zero Waste* goals, especially in the E.U., and in the U.S., where San Francisco and New York are among those cities setting goals to create *Zero Waste* by 2020. This follows the "waste not, want not" proverb, and demands: reducing consumption, not using disposables, reusing discards, comprehensive recycling and composting, banning waste incineration, and redesigning products for durability, longevity, and lack of toxins. *Zero Waste* can be a change in how we live on the planet in order to support community health, environmental justice, and sustainability.

Willful waste makes woeful want. —Proverb (1576)

See also: **Circular Economy • Closed-Loop Supply Chain • Cradle-to-Cradle • Ecological Rucksack • Materials and Resources • Waste Reduction**

Further sources: GBCI; Leonard (2010: 234); PIERS Global Intelligence Solutions; USGBC; USZWBC; ZWIA

Zero-Energy Building

Designing and constructing energy efficient buildings, combined with a massive harnessing of renewable energy, makes it not only possible but also profitable for buildings to operate without fossil fuels. —Ed Mazria, Architecture 2030

The building industry is accountable for a large share of the world's electricity consumption and raw material use. In the U.S., commercial and residential buildings together account for over 72% of electricity use and over 38% of carbon dioxide emissions. Building construction worldwide is responsible for over 40% of material use. Buildings often last for 50–100 years, so we are facing a looming obsolesce of our non-green current building stock. An energy retrofit of an existing building can cut energy use and bills by over 50%, but we need to design our buildings to use less energy at the outset.

Dramatically increasing the efficiency of our buildings is critical if we hope to slow the Earth's climate change. Ed Mazria launched the 2030 Challenge to encourage architects to design all buildings to use no fossil fuels by 2030. The goal is to transform architectural design from reliance on fossil fuels to an architecture intimately linked to the natural world in which we live. The design strategies and construction technologies available today easily enable architects to create new buildings with half the energy requirements of existing ones. Design strategies used to reduce the energy loads are natural lighting, natural ventilation, solar thermal, solar photovoltaic cells, super insulation, ground source heating and cooling, high-efficient lighting, high-performing glazing, and building intelligent automated controls and systems, among many other features.

The David and Lucile Packard Foundation in Los Altos, California is the largest International Living Future Institute Net-Zero Energy

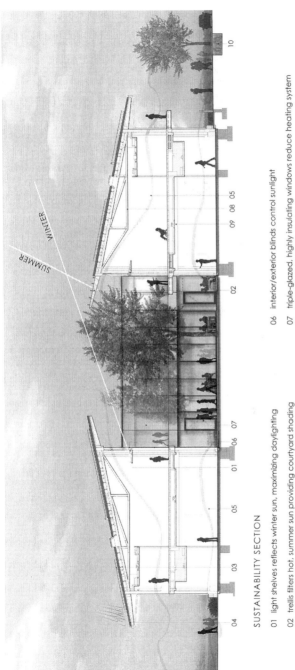

SUSTAINABILITY SECTION

01 light shelves reflects winter sun, maximizing daylighting
02 trellis filters hot, summer sun providing courtyard shading
03 PV array results in net positive energy balance
04 captured rainwater for toilet flushing and irrigation
05 40' width maximizes daylighting and natural ventilation
06 interior/exterior blinds control sunlight
07 triple-glazed, highly insulating windows reduce heating system
08 exposed FSC certified wood structure
09 chilled beams with 100% fresh air
10 "green street" strategies increase site perviousness

Figure 78 David and Lucile Packard Foundation zero-energy sustainable strategies, Los Altos, CA
Courtesy ©EHDD

Certified building in the world. Designed by EHDD Architects, the award-winning LEED Platinum project is driven primarily by the passive and bioclimatic strategies of daylighting, enhanced envelope design, reduced plug loads, and high-efficient HVAC systems. Radiant panels and chilled beams provide cooling, with an energy reduction of 90% from a conventional system (Figures 78, 41).

Recognized leaders in the green building arena are designing *zero-energy buildings* by driving innovative sustainable technologies and initiatives to provide the performance, comfort, health, and economic results expected with the fewest negative impacts on our natural resources and systems. The term *zero-energy building (ZEB)* can be confusing, but the idea is that buildings can meet all their energy requirements from locally available, nonpolluting, and renewable sources.

A net-zero energy building meets even stricter requirements that the building generates enough renewable energy on-site to meet or exceed its annual energy use. Four commonly used definitions are net-zero site energy, net-zero source energy, net-zero energy costs, and net-zero energy emissions. Renewable energy technologies, energy modeling, material science, green chemistry, and building intelligence systems are continuing to improve the innovations needed to further the goal of a fossil fuel free world.

It is the architects that hold the key to turning down the global thermostat. —Ed Mazria

See also: **Climate Change • Energy Efficiency • High-Performing Buildings • Living Building Challenge • Net-Zero Energy Building Certification • Photovoltaics • Renewable Energy • Sustainability**

Further sources: Architecture 2030; EBN; ILFI; RMI; US DOE; USGBC: Buildings and Climate Change; WBDG

Further Reading

7 Group, and Bill Reed. 2009. *The Integrative Design Guide to Green Building: Redefining the Practice of Sustainability*. Hoboken, NJ: Wiley.

Agenda 21. 1992. United Nations Conference on Environment & Development Rio de Janeiro, Brazil, 3–14 June 1992. https://sustainabledevelopment.un.org/content/documents/Agenda21.pdf.

AIA Energy Modeling Working Group. 2016. *An Architect's Guide to Integrating Energy Modeling in the Design Process*. Washington, DC: AIA.

Alexander, Christopher. 1977. *A Pattern Language: Towns, Buildings, Construction*. New York: Oxford University Press.

——. 1979. *The Timeless Way of Building*. New York: Oxford University Press.

Ander, Gregg D. 2003. *Daylighting Performance and Design*. Hoboken, NJ: Wiley.

Anderson, Ray C. 1998. *Mid-Course Correction*. White River Junction, VT: Chelsea Green.

Anderson, Ray C., and Robin White. 2009. *Confessions of a Radical Industrialist: Profits, People, Purpose—Doing Business by Respecting the Earth*. New York: St. Martin's.

ASHRAE. 2006. *ASHRAE Greenguide: The Design, Construction, and Operation of Sustainable Buildings*. Burlington, MA: Elsevier.

Atkinson, Carol, Alan Yates, and Martin Wyatt. 2009. *Sustainability in the Environment: An Introduction to Its Definition and Measurement*. Watford, WD: BRE Press.

Attman, Osman. 2010. *Green Architecture: Advanced Technologies and Materials*. New York: McGraw-Hill.

Bachman, Leonard R. 2003. *Integrated Buildings: The Systems Basis of Architecture*. Hoboken, NJ: Wiley.

Banham, Reyner. 1969. *The Architecture of the Well-Tempered Environment*. London: Architectural Press.

Barton, Reid. 1985. *The New Urbanism as a Way of Life: The Relationship Between Inner City Revitalization in Canada and the Rise of the New Middle Class*. Winnipeg, Manitoba, Canada: University of Manitoba Press.

Bennett, Jane. 2010. *Vibrant Matter: A Political Ecology of Things*. Durham, NC: Duke University Press.

Benyus, Janine. 1997. *Biomimicry: Innovation Inspired by Nature*. London: William Morrow.

Bergman, David. 2012. *Sustainable Design: A Critical Guide*. New York: Princeton Architectural Press.

Berry, Wendell. 2015. *Our Only World: Ten Essays*. Berkeley, CA: Counterpoint.

Biello, David. 2009. *How Much Is Too Much? Estimating Greenhouse Gas Emissions*. Scientific American, April 29, 2009. https://www.scientificamerican.com/article/limits-on-greenhouse-gas-emissions/.

Birkeland, Janis. 2002. *Design for Sustainability: A Sourcebook of Integrated Eco-Logical Solutions*. London: Earthscan.

Blackburn, Simon. 1994. *Oxford Dictionary of Philosophy*. Oxford: Oxford University Press.

Blair, Tony. 2004. "The Environment and Urgent Issue of Climate Change." *The Guardian*. September 15. Accessed June 28, 2017. www.theguardian.com/politics/2004/sep/15/greenpolitics.uk.

Blakemore, Erin. 2017. "The Essential I.M. Pei." *Smithsonian*. April 27. Accessed July 7, 2017. www.smithsonianmag.com/smart-news/essential-im-pei-180963063/.

Bonda, Penny, and Katie Sosowchik. 2014. *Sustainable Commercial Interiors*, 2nd Edition. Hoboken, NJ: Wiley.

Boyer, Christine. 1994. *The City of Collective Memory: It's Historical Memory and Architectural Entertainments*. Cambridge, MA: MIT Press.

Brand, Steward. 1994. *How Buildings Learn: What Happens After They Are Built*. New York: Viking Press.

Brown, Lester R. 2009. *Plan B 4.0: Mobilizing to Save Civilization*. New York: Norton.

——. 2011. *World on the Edge: Earth Policy Institute*. New York: Norton.

Brown, Lester R., Michael Renner, and Brian Halweil. 1999. *Vital Signs: Worldwatch Institute*. New York: Norton.

Brundtland Commission. 1987. *Our Common Future*. Oxford: Oxford University Press.

Buchanan, Peter. 2005. *Ten Shades of Green: Architecture and the Natural World*. New York: Architectural League of New York.

Burns, Carol J., and Andrea Kahn, eds. 2005. *Site Matters: Design Concepts, Histories and Strategies*. New York: Taylor & Francis.

Calkins, Meg. 2009. *Materials for Sustainable Sites: A Complete Guide to the Evaluation, Selection, and Use of Sustainable Construction Materials*. Hoboken, NJ: Wiley.

Calthorpe, Peter. 1993. *The Next American Metropolis: Ecology, Community, and the American Dream*. New York: Princeton Architectural Press.

Carroon, Jean. 2010. *Sustainable Preservation: Greening Existing Buildings*. Hoboken, NJ: Wiley.

Carson, Rachel L. 1950. *The Sea Around Us*. New York: Oxford University Press.

——. 1955. *The Edge of the Sea*. New York: Houghton Mifflin.

——. 1962. *Silent Spring*. New York: Houghton Mifflin.

Ching, Francis D. K., and Ian M. Shapiro. *Green Building Illustrated*. Hoboken, NJ: Wiley.

Contal, Marie-Hélène, and Jana Revedin. 2009. *Sustainable Design: Toward a New Ethic in Architecture and Town Planning*. Boston, MA: Birkhäuser.

Cooper, Slagmulder. 1997. *Target Costing & Value Engineering*. New York: Productivity Press.

Cottrell, Michelle. 2011. *Guidebook to the LEED Certification Process: For LEED for New Construction, LEED for Core & Shell, and LEED for Commercial Interiors*. Hoboken, NJ: Wiley.

Cowan, Henry J., and Peter R. Smith. 2004. *Dictionary of Architectural and Building Technology*, 4th Edition. London: Spon Press.

Daniels, Klaus. 2003. *Advanced Building Systems: A Technical Guide for Architects and Engineers*. Boston, MA: Birkhäuser.

Davey, Peter. 2009. *Engineering for a Finite Planet*. Boston, MA: Birkhäuser.

Diamond, Jared. 1999. *Guns, Germs and Steel*. New York: Norton.

———. 2005. *Collapse: How Societies Choose to Fail or Succeed*. New York: Viking Press.

———. 2008. "What's Your Consumption Factor?" *New York Times*. January 2. Accessed June 15, 2017.

Dresner, Simon. 2002. *The Principles of Sustainability*. London: Earthscan.

Drygiel, Eddy, and Bradley Nies. 2005. *Green BIM: Successful Sustainable Design With Building Information Modeling*. Indianapolis, IN: Wiley.

Duany, Andres, Elizabeth Plater-Zyberk, and Jeff Speck. 2000. *Suburban Nation: The Rise of Sprawl and the Decline of the American Dream*. New York: North Point Press.

Earle, Sylvia. 2010. *The World Is Blue: How Our Fate and the Oceans Are One*. Washington, D.C.: National Geographic Society.

Earth Pledge Foundation. 2000. *Sustainable Architecture White Papers*. New York: Earth Pledge.

Edwards, Andres S. 2005. *The Sustainability Revolution: Portrait of a Paradigm Shift*. Gabriola Island, BC, Canada: New Society Publishers.

Ehrlich, Paul. 1969. *The Population Bomb*. New York: Sierra Club.

Elizabeth, Lynn, and Cassandra Adams. 2005. *Alternative Construction: Contemporary Natural Building Methods*. Hoboken, NJ: Wiley.

Elkington, John.1998. *Cannibals With Forks: The Triple Bottom Line of 21st Century Business*. Gabriola Island, BC, Canada: New Society Publishers.

Ellen MacArthur Foundation. 2013. *Towards The Circular Economy: Economic and Business Rationale For An Accelerated Transition. Vol. 1*.

Emerson, Ralph Waldo. 1993. *Self-Reliance and Other Essays*. New York: Dover.

———. 2003. *Nature and Selected Essays*. New York: Penguin.

Energy and Climate Intelligence Unit. *How is the UK Tackling Climate Change?* http://eciu.net/briefings/uk-energy-policies-and-prices/how-is-the-uk-tackling-climate-change.

Environmental Protection Agency. 2016. *Climate Change Indicators: Atmospheric Concentrations of Greenhouse Gases. https://www.epa.gov/climate-indicators/climate-change-indicators-atmospheric-concentrations-greenhouse-gases*.

Evans, Marni. 2016. "Steps to Climate Responsive Architecture." *The Balance*. November 7, 2016. Accessed July 7, 2017. www.thebalance.com/designing-climate-responsive-architecture-3157812.

Fathy, Hassan. 1986. *Natural Energy and Vernacular Architecture*. Chicago: University of Chicago Press.

Flannery, Tim. 2005. *The Weather Makers: How Man Is Changing the Climate and What It Means for Life on Earth*. New York: Grove Press.

———. 2009. *Now or Never: Why We Must Act Now to End Climate Change and Create a Sustainable Future*. New York: Atlantic Monthly.

Floyd, Anthony, and Allan Bilka. 2012. *Green Building: A Professional's Guide to Concepts, Codes, and Innovation*. Washington, DC: International Code Council.

Forty, Adrian. 2000. *Words and Buildings: A Vocabulary of Modern Architecture*. London: Thames & Hudson.

Frampton, Kenneth. 2002. *Glenn Murcutt: 2002 Laureate. The Pritzker Architecture Prize*. Chicago: The Hyatt Foundation.

Franta, Greg. 2010. *Cooling the Warming: The Connection Between Climate Change and the Built Environment*. Snowmass, Colorado: Rocky Mountain Institute.

Friedman, Thomas. 2006. *The World Is Flat: A Brief History of the Twenty-First Century*. New York: Farrar, Straus and Giroux.

——. 2009. *Hot, Flat, and Crowded: Why We Need a Green Revolution—and How It Can Renew America*. New York: Picador.

Fuller, R. Buckminster. 1981. *Critical Path*. New York: St. Martin's Press.

——. 2000. *Nine Chains to the Moon*. New York: Doubleday.

Giedeon, Sigfried. 1950. *Mechanization Takes Command: A Contribution to Anonymous History*. London: Oxford University Press.

Gissen, David, ed. 2003. *Big & Green: Toward Sustainable Architecture in the 21st Century*. New York: Princeton Architectural Press.

Glass, Jacqueline. 2002. *Encyclopedia of Architectural Technology*. West Sussex, Great Britain: Wiley.

Gore, Al. 1992. *Earth in the Balance: Ecology and the Human Spirit*. Boston, MA: Houghton Mifflin.

——. 2009. *Our Choice: A Plan to Solve the Climate Crisis*. Emmaus, PA: Rodale.

Gropius, Walter. 1956. *The Scope of Total Architecture*. New York: Harper & Brothers.

Guy, Bradley. 2008. *Designing for Disassembly in the Built Environment: A Guide to Closed-Loop Design and Building*. University Park, PA: Hamer Center.

Guzowski, Mary. 2010. *Towards Zero Energy Architecture: New Solar Design*. London: Laurence King Publishing.

Hardin, Garrett. 1968. "The Tragedy of the Commons." *Science*. AAAS 162: 1243–1248.

——. 1974. "Lifeboat Ethics: the Case Against Helping the Poor." *Psychology Today*, September 1974. http://www.garretthardinsociety.org/articles/art_lifeboat_ethics_case_against_helping_poor.html.

Harman, Jay. 2013. *The Shark's Paintbrush: Biomimicry and How Nature Is Inspiring Innovation*. Ashland, OR: White Cloud Press.

Hawken, Paul. 1993. *Ecology of Commerce: A Declaration of Sustainability*. New York: HarperCollins.

Hawken, Paul, Amory Lovins, and L. Hunter Lovins. 1999. *Natural Capitalism: Creating the Next Industrial Revolution*. New York: Little, Brown & Co.

Heidegger, Martin. 1971. *Poetry, Language, Thought*. Translated by Albert Hofstadter. New York: Harper & Row.

Hemenway, Toby. 2015. *The Permaculture City: Regenerative Design for Urban, Suburban, and Town Resilience*. White River Junction, VT: Chelsea Green Publishing.

Herron, Ron, and Dennis Crompton. 1980. *Archigram: Architecture Now*. New York: Rizzoli.

Hertsgaard, Mark. 2011. *Hot: Living Through the Next Fifty Years on Earth*. New York: Houghton Mifflin Harcourt.

Heywood, Huw. 2012. *101 Rules of Thumb for Low Energy Architecture*. London: RIBA.

Hootman, Tom. 2012. *Net Zero Energy Design: A Guide for Commercial Architecture*. Hoboken, NJ: Wiley.

Hopfe, Christina J., and Robert S. McLeod, eds. 2015. *The Passivhaus Designer's Manual: A Technical Guide to Low and Zero Energy Buildings*. New York: Routledge.

Howard, Ebenezer. 1965. *Garden Cities of Tomorrow*. Cambridge, MA: MIT Press.

Hyde, Richard. 2000. *Climate Responsive Design*. New York: Spon Press.

Institute for Health Metrics and Evaluation (IHME). 2016. Michael Brauer.

Poor Air Quality Kills 5.5 Million Worldwide Annually. http://www.health data.org/news-release/poor-air-quality-kills-55-million-worldwide-annually.

Intergovernmental Panel on Climate Change. 2014. "Climate Change 2014: Synthesis Report. Contribution of Working Groups I, II and III to the Fifth Assessment Report of the Intergovernmental Panel on Climate Change [Core Writing Team, R.K. Pachauri and L.A. Meyer (Eds.)]. Geneva, Switzerland.

Iwamoto, Lisa. 2009. *Digital Fabrications: Architectural and Material Techniques*. New York: Princeton Architectural Press.

Iyengar, Kuppaswamy. 2015. *Sustainable Architectural Design: An Overview*. New York: Routledge.

Jackson, Richard. March 2004. "Curing Our Ills." *EnvironDesign Journal*. Interiors & Resources.

Jacobs, Jane. 1961. *The Death and Life of Great American Cities*. New York: Vintage Books.

Jencks, Charles, and Karl Kropt, eds. 1997. *Theories and Manifestos of Contemporary Architecture*. West Sussex: Wiley.

Johnston, David, and Scott Gibson. 2010. *Toward a Zero Energy Home*. Newton, CT: Taunton Press.

Kahn, Louis. 1957. "Order in Architecture." *Perspecta* 4. Yale University Press.

Katz, Peter. 1994. *The New Urbanism: Toward an Architecture of Community*. Portland, OR: Print Vision.

Keeler, Marian, and Bill Burke. 2009. *Fundamentals of Integrated Design for Sustainable Building*. Hoboken, NJ: Wiley.

Kellert, Stephen, Judith Heerwagen, and Martin Mador. 2008. *Biophilic Design: The Theory, Science, and Practice of Bringing Buildings to Life*. Hoboken, NJ: Wiley.

Kibert, Charles. 1999. *Reshaping the Built Environment: Ecology, Ethics, and Economics*. Washington, DC: Island Press.

——. 2016. *Sustainable Construction: Green Building Design and Delivery*, 4th Edition. Hoboken, NJ: Wiley.

Kibert, Charles J., Martha C. Monroe, Anna L. Peterson, Richard R. Plate, and Leslie Paul Thiele. 2012. *Working Toward Sustainability: Ethical Decision Making in a Technological World*. Hoboken, NJ: Wiley.

Kieran, Stephen, and James Timberlake. 2004. *Refabricating Architecture: How Manufacturing Methodologies Are Poised to Transform Building Construction*. New York: McGraw-Hill.

Kirby, Alex and United Nations Environmental Programme. 2008. *Kick the Habit: A U.N. Guide to Climate Neutrality*. Malta: Progress Press LTD.

Klee, Paul. 1961. *The Thinking Eye*. London: Lund Humphrey.

Klein, Naomi. 2014. *This Changes Everything: Capitalism Vs. the Climate*. New York: Simon & Schuster.

Knowles, Ralph L. 2006. *Ritual House: Drawing on Nature's Rhythms for Architecture and Urban Design*. Washington, DC: Island Press.

Kolbert, Elizabeth. 2006. *Field Notes From a Catastrophe: Man, Nature and Climate Change*. New York: Bloomsbury.

——. 2009. *The Best American Science and Nature Writing 2009*. New York: Houghton Mifflin Harcourt.

Koones, Sheri. 2010. *Prefabulous and Sustainable: Building and Customizing an Affordable, Energy-Efficient Home*. New York: Abrams.

Krygiel, Eddy, and Bradley Nies. 2008. *Green BIM: Successful Sustainable Design With Building Information Modeling*. Indianapolis, IN: Wiley.

Kwok, Alison G., and Walter T. Grondzik. 2007. *The Green Studio Companion: Environmental Strategies for Schematic Design*. Oxford: Elsevier.

Lally, Sean. 2014. *The Air From Other Planets: A Brief History of Architecture to Come*. Zurich: Lars Muller.

Le Corbusier. 1933. *The Athens Charter*. New York: Grossman Press.

——. 1953. *Le Poeme de L'Angle Droit*

——. 1923. *Towards a New Architecture*. Translated John Goodman. 2007. Los Angeles, CA: Getty Research.

Lechner, Norbert. 2009. *Heating, Cooling and Lighting: Sustainable Design Methods for Architects*, 3rd Edition. Hoboken, NJ: Wiley.

Leonard, Annie. 2010. *The Story of Stuff: How Our Obsession With Stuff Is Trashing the Planet, Our Communities, and Our Health—and a Vision for Change*. New York: Free Press.

Leopold, Aldo. 1949. *A Sand County Almanac*. New York: Oxford University Press.

——. 1993. *Round River*. New York: Oxford University Press.

Leslie, Russ P., Leora C. Radestsky, and A. M. Smith. 2011. "Conceptual Design Metrics for Daylighting." *Lighting Residential Technology* 44: 277–290.

Levy, John M. 2013. *Contemporary Urban Planning*. Upper Saddle River, NJ: Pearson Education.

Lovell, Jenny 2010. *Building Envelopes: An Integrated Approach*. New York: Princeton Architectural Press.

Massoleni, Ilaria. 2013. *Architecture Follows Nature: Biomimetic Principles for Innovative Design*. Boca Raton, FL: CRC Press.

McDonough, William + Partners. 1992. *The Hannover Principles: Design for Sustainability*. Charlottesville, VA: William McDonough + Partners.

McDonough, William + Partners, and Michael Braungart. 2002. *Cradle to Cradle: Remaking the Way We Make Things*. New York: North Point Press.

——. 2013. *The Upcycle: Beyond Sustainability—Designing for Abundance*. New York: North Point Press.

McHarg, Ian. 1969. *Design With Nature*. New York: John Wiley.

McLennan, Jason F. 2004. *The Philosophy of Sustainable Design*. Kansas City, MO: Ecotone.

Meacham. Brian J. 1997. "Concepts of a Performance-Based Building Regulatory System for the United States" in Yuji Hasemi Dr. Eng (ed.), *Fire Safety Science: Proceedings of the Fifth International Symposium*, 3–7 March, Melbourne, Australia, pp 701–712.

Mendler, Sandra, William Odell, and Mary Ann Lazarus. *The HOK Guidebook to Sustainable Design*. Hoboken, NJ: Wiley.

Milton, John. 1898. *Paradise Lost*. (Book 3, Line 11) New York: Harper & Brothers Publishing.

Montoya, Michael. *Green Building Fundamentals*, 2nd Edition. Upper Saddle River, NJ: Prentice Hall.

Mukhopayaya, Amil Kumar. 2009. *Value Engineering Mastermind: From Concept to Value Engineering Certification*. London: Sage.

Murray, Scott. 2013. *Translucent Building Skins: Material Innovations in Modern and Contemporary Architecture*. London: Routledge.

Naam, Ramez. 2013. *The Infinite Resource: The Power of Ideas on a Finite Planet*. Lebanon, NH: University Press of New England.

Newman, Oscar. 1972. *Defensible Space: Crime Prevention Through Urban Design*. New York: Macmillan.

Norberg-Schultz, Christian. 1979. *Genius Loci: Towards a Phenomenology of Architecture*. New York: Rizzoli.

O'Loughlin, Toni. 2009. "Number of Earth's species known to scientists rises to 1.9 million." *The Guardian*. Sept. 29. https://www.theguardian.com/environment/2009/sep/29/number-of-living-species.

Olgyay, Victor. 1963. *Design With Climate*, 2nd Edition. New York: Princeton Architectural Press.

Orr, David W. 1992. *Ecological Literacy: Education and the Transition to a Postmodern World*. New York: State University of New York.

———. 2008. *Design on the Edge: The Making of a High Performance Building*. Cambridge, MA: MIT Press.

Orwell, George. 1945. *Animal Farm*. Orlando, FL: Harcourt Brace.

Ots, Enn. 2011. *Decoding Theoryspeak: An Illustrated Guide to Architectural Theory*. New York: Routledge.

Palladio, Andrea. 1738. *The Four Books of Architecture*. New York: Dover Publications (1965)

Peña, William M., and Steven A. Parshall. 2001. *Problem Seeking: An Architectural Programming Primer*, 4th Edition. New York: Wiley.

Peterson, Kent, and Hugh Crowther. 2010. "Building Energy Use Intensity." *High Performing Buildings*: ASHRAE 12033.

Pirsig, Robert M. 1974. *Zen and the Art of Motorcycle Maintenance*. New York: Bantam.

Pollan, Michael. 2007. *The Omnivore's Dilemma: A Natural History of Four Meals*. New York: Norton.

Porter, Tom. 2004. *Archispeak: An Illustrated Guide to Architectural Terms*. London: Spon Press.

Queensland Affordable Housing Consortium. 2012. *Definition Affordable Housing*. Queensland, Australia.

Raven, Peter. 2002. "Science, Sustainability, and the Human Prospect." *Science Washington* 297, no. 5583: 954–958.

Rifkin, Jeremy. 2011. *The Third Industrial Revolution: How Lateral Power Is Transforming Energy, the Economy, and the World*. New York: Palgrave McMillan.

Roaf, Sue, David Crichton, and Fergus Nicol. 2005. *Adapting Buildings and Cities for Climate Change: A 21st Century Survival Guide*. Burlington, MA: Architectural Press.

Robertson, Margaret. 2014. *Sustainability Principles and Practice*. New York: Routledge.

Rogers, Jim. 2015. *Lighting Our World: Transforming Our Energy Future by Bringing Electricity to Everyone*. New York: St. Martin's Press.

Rose, Jonathan F. P. 2016. *The Well Tempered City: What Modern Science, Ancient Civilizations, and Human Nature Teach Us About the Future of Urban Life*. New York: HarperCollins.

Rossi, Aldo. 1982. *The Architecture of the City*. Cambridge. Massachusetts: MIT Press.

Rudofsky, Bernard. 1964. *Architecture Without Architects, a Short Introduction to Non-Pedigreed Architecture*. Albuquerque: University of New Mexico Press.

Ryan, Carole. 2011. *Traditional Construction for a Sustainable Future*. New York: Spon Press.

Sachs, Jeffery D. 2015. *The Age of Sustainable Development*. New York: Columbia University Press.

Sagan, Carl. 1980. *Cosmos*. New York: Random House Publishing.

——. 1994. *Pale Blue Dot: A Vision of the Human Future in Space*. New York: Random House Publishing.

——. 1997. *Billions & Billions: Thoughts on Life and Death at the Brink of the Millennium*. New York: Random House.

Sakamoto, Tomoko, and Albert Ferre´, eds. 2008. *From Control to Design: Parametric/Algorithmic Architecture*. New York: Actar-D USA.

Sanderson, Eric W. 2013. *Terra Nova; the New World After Oil, Cars, and Suburbs*. New York: Abrams.

Santos, Eddy. 2017. *Five Ways to Achieve High-Performance Buildings Using Energy-Modeling*. Washington, DC: AIA.

Saunders, William S. 2008. *Nature, Landscape and Building for Sustainability*. Minneapolis, MN: University of Minnesota Press.

Shoup, Donald. 2011. *The High Cost of Free Parking*. Chicago, IL: American Planning Association.

Smith, Peter F. 2006. *Sustainable Architecture*. London: Routledge.

Smith, Peter R. 1989. *Thermal Performance in Building Design and Human Performance*. New York: Van Nostrand Reinhold.

Snell, Clarke, and Tim Callahan. 2005. *Building Green: A Complete How to Guide to Alternative Building Methods*. Toronto: Lark Books.

Speth, James Gustave. 2004. *Red Sky at Morning: America and the Crisis of the Global Environment*. London: Yale University.

Stang, Alanna, and Christopher Hawthorne. 2005. *The Green House: New Directions in Sustainable Architecture*. New York: Princeton Architectural Press.

Stein, Benjamin, John S. Reynolds, Walter T. Grondzik, and Alison G. Kwok. 2006. *Mechanical and Electrical Equipment for Buildings*. Hoboken, NJ: Wiley.

Stibbe, Arran, ed. 2009. *The Handbook of Sustainable Literacy: Skills for a Changing World*. Cambridge: Green Books.

Stone, Brian Jr. 2012. *The City and the Coming Climate: Climate Change in the Places We Live*. New York: Cambridge University Press.

Suzuki, David. 2004. *From Naked Ape to Superspecies: Humanity and the Global Eco-Crisis*. Vancouver, BC, Canada: Greystone Books.

Suzuki, David, and Ian Hanington. 2012. *Everything Under the Sun: Toward a Brighter Future on a Small Blue Planet*. Vancouver, BC, Canada: Greystone Books.

Szokolay, Steven. 2004. *Introduction to Architectural Science: The Basis of Sustainable Design*. Burlington, MA: Elsevier.

Thompson, D'Arcy Wentworth. 1917. *On Growth and Form*. London: Cambridge Press.

Thoreau, Henry David. 1999. *Walden and Civil Disobedience*. New York: Penguin.

Tzu, Lao. 1961. *Tao Te Ching*. Translated by John C. H. Wu. Boston, MA: Shambhala.

United Nations. 2014. "World's Population Increasingly Urban With More Than Half Living in Urban Areas." July 10, New York. http://www.un.org/en/development/desa/news/population/world-urbanization-prospects-2014.html.

United Nations Environmental Programme. 2011. "Towards a Green Economy: Pathways to Sustainable Development and Poverty Eradication." www.unep.org/greeneconomy ISBN: 978-92-807-3143-9.

United Nations Department of Economic and Social Affairs. 2014. *World Urbanization Prospects*. New York: United Nations.

——. 2017. *The World Population Prospects: The 2017 Revision*. New York: United Nations.

United Nations Food and Agriculture Organization. 2016. *Global Forest Resources Assessment 2015: How are the World's Forests Changing?* Rome

U.S. Department of Energy. 2011. *Re-Assessing Green Building Performance: A Post Occupancy Evaluation of 22 Buildings*. Richland, Washington: Pacific Northwest National Laboratory.

U.S. Forest Service. 2016. "New Aerial Survey Identifies More Than 100 Million Dead Trees in California." November 18. https://www.fs.fed.us/news/releases/new-aerial-survey-identifies-more-100-million-dead-trees-california.

U.S. Green Building Council. 2011. *Green Building and LEED Core Concepts*. Washington, DC: U.S. Green Building Council.

——. 2011. *Roadmap to Green Government Buildings*. Washington, DC: U.S. Green Building Council.

——. 2013. *LEED Reference Guide for Building Design and Construction*. Washington, DC: U.S. Green Building Council.

Unwin, Simon. 2003. *Analyzing Architecture*. London: Routledge.

Van Der Ryn, Sim, and Stuart Cowan. 1996. *Ecological Design*. Washington, DC: Island Press.

Venturi, Robert, Denise Scott Brown, and Steven Izenour. 1972. *Learning From Las Vegas*. Cambridge, MA: MIT Press.

Vitruvius. 1960. *The Ten Books on Architecture*. New York: Dover Publications.

Von Weizsäcker, Ernst, Amory Lovins, and Hunter Lovins. 1998. *Factor 4: Doubling Wealth—Halving Resource Use*. New York: Earthscan.

Wackernagel, Mathis, and William Rees. 1996. *Our Ecological Footprint: Reducing Human Impact on the Earth*. Gabriola Island, B.C. Canada: New Society Publishers.

Wells, Malcolm. 1981. *Gentle Architecture*. New York: McGraw Hill.

White, Edward T. 1983. *Site Analysis: Diagramming Information for Architectural Design*. Tallahassee, FL: Architectural Media.

Whitman, Walt. 2007. *Leaves of Grass*. Mineola, NY: Dover.

Williams, Daniel E. 2007. *Sustainable Design: Ecology, Architecture, and Planning*. Hoboken, NJ: Wiley.

Wilson, Edward O. 1986. *Biophilia*. Cambridge, MA: Harvard University Press.

——. 2002. *The Future of Life*. New York: Vintage.

——. 2016. *Half Earth: Our Planets Fight for Life*. New York: Norton.

Wines, James. 2000. *Green Architecture*. New York: Rizzoli.

The Wingspread Statement on the Precautionary Principle. 1998. *The 1998 Wingspread*. Racine, WI. January 20. *Declaration (Science and Environmental Health Network 1998)*

World Commission on Environment and Development. 1987. *Our Common Future*. Oxford: Oxford University Press.

World Resources Institute. 2005. Millennium Ecosystem Assessment: *Ecosystems and Human Well-Being*. Washington, DC: Island Press.

World Watch Institute. 2008. *State of the World 2008: Innovations for a Sustainable Economy*. Washington, DC: World Watch Institute.

——. 2015. *Confronting Hidden Threats to Sustainability: State of the World 2015*. Washington, DC: World Watch Institute.

World Wildlife Fund. 2014. "Living Planet Report 2014, Species and Spaces, People and Places." WWF International: Gland, Switzerland.

World Wildlife Fund. 2016. "Living Planet Report 2016. Risk and resilience in a new era." WWF International: Gland, Switzerland.

Wright, Frank Lloyd. 1941. *Frank Lloyd Wright on Architecture: Selected Writings (1894–1940)*. New York: Grosset & Dunlap.

Yates, Judith and Maryann Wulff. 1999. "Housing Markets and Household Income Polarisation: A Metropolitan and Regional Analysis," National Housing Conference, Reform and Renewal in Social Housing, Sydney, Nov 29–30.

Yeang, Ken. 2006. *Ecodesign: A Manual for Ecological Design*. London: Wiley.

Yglesias, Ana. 2012. "The Positive Impacts of Upcycling." Pachamama Alliance. www.pachamama.org/blog/the-positive-impacts-of-upcycling.

Yu, Mayine L. 2014. *Skins, Envelopes, and Enclosures: Concepts for Designing Building Exteriors*. London: Routledge.

Yudelson, Jerry. 2007. *Green Building A-Z: Understanding the Language of Green Building*. Gabriola Island, BC, Canada: New Society Publishers.

——. 2009. *Green Building Through Integrated Design*. New York: McGraw Hill.

Yudelson, Jerry, and Ulf Meyer. 2013. *The World's Greenest Buildings: Promise Versus Performance in Sustainable Design*. New York: Routledge.

Zbicinski, Irenneuz, John Stavenuiter, Barbara Kozlowska, and Hennie van de Coevering. 2006. *Product Design and Life Cycle Assessment*. Uppsala: Baltic Press.

Index

Page numbers in italic indicate figures on the corresponding pages.